THE TAMING OF THE TRUE

THE TAMING OF THE TRUE

NEIL TENNANT

CLARENDON PRESS · OXFORD

1997

Oxford University Press, Great Clarendon Street, Oxford OX2 6DP
Oxford New York
Athens Auckland Bangkok Bogota Bombay
Buenos Aires Calcutta Cape Town Dar es Salaam
Delhi Florence Hong Kong Istanbul Karachi
Kuala Lumpur Madras Madrid Melbourne
Mexico City Nairobi Paris Singapore
Taipei Tokyo Toronto
and associated companies in
Berlin Ibadan

Oxford is a trademark of Oxford University Press

Published in the United States
by Oxford University Press Inc., New York

© Neil Tennant 1997

British Library Cataloguing in Publication Data
Data available

Library of Congress Cataloguing in Publication Data
Data available

ISBN 0-19-823717-0

Typeset by Neil Tennant
Printed in Great Britain
on acid-free paper by
Biddles Ltd, Guildford and King's Lynn

In memory of my father
Henry Tennant
and for my mother
Joan Rosalind Tennant
for all she gave and
for all she has gone through

Preface

My original interest in the realism debate was provoked by the writings of Michael Dummett in the 1970s. I had the good fortune, as a graduate student, of being in the audience for his address 'The Philosophical Basis of Intuitionistic Logic' to the European Summer Meeting of the Association for Symbolic Logic in Bristol in 1973. Dummett's route to intuitionistic logic through a properly constrained theory of meaning was both a revelation and an inspiration. It will be evident also just how important I have found Crispin Wright's writings. Much of what I say can be seen as an effort to get clear about the overall state of the realism debate by contrasting my thoughts with Wright's on certain key points.

Ancestral parts of the critique of Kripkean meaning scepticism have been presented to the Philosophy Department Seminars of the Research School of Social Sciences at the Australian National University, Monash University, and La Trobe University; the Philosophy Society of the University of Adelaide; the Annual Conference of the Australasian Association of Philosophy and the Australasian Association of Logic in Perth, 1988; the Symposium on Rule-Following, at the Annual Meeting of the Society for Philosophy and Psychology in Maryland, 1990; the Philosophy Colloquium at the University of Cincinnati in 1993; and the Chapel Hill Philosophy Colloquium in 1995. I am grateful to members of those audiences for useful comments, and to Norbert Hornstein as commentator at the SPP meeting.

The material on manifestionism had its beginnings—barely recognizably—in a paper presented to the Workshop on Verificationism and the Theory of Meaning in Leiden, Holland, in 1992, and later that year as one of the series of valedictory lectures to the Ockham Society in the University of Oxford, in honour of Michael Dummett on the occasion of his retirement from the Wykeham Chair of Logic. I am grateful to members of both audiences for helpful comments.

Material from a distant ancestor of the chapter on cognitive significance was given in 1989 to the Philosophy Seminar of the Research School of Social Sciences at the Australian National University, and to the Conference on Logic and Metaphysics in honour of Crispin Wright at the University of Queensland, Brisbane. I am grateful to Graham Priest as commentator on the latter occasion. A Visiting Fellowship at the Center for Philosophy of Science in Pittsburgh in 1990 helped me to develop the ideas further. John Earman deserves particular mention for helpful suggestions. Less distant ancestors were subsequently given to the Annual Popper Conference, held at the London School of Economics, in 1991; the Logic and Language Colloquium at The Ohio State University in 1993; the Department of History and Philosophy of Science at the University of Cambridge in 1994; the Workshop on Philosophy and Physics at the University of St Andrews in 1994; and the Colloquium on Significance in Semantics held at the University of Cincinnati in 1994. I am indebted to my colleagues in the OSU Logicians' Group, and Stewart Shapiro in particular, for helpful comments on an earlier version, which helped me to simplify the presentation. Shapiro also persuaded me to present the ideas within a straightforwardly classical framework, so as to make the theory more widely accessible. I am grateful to Professor Hempel for his gracious encouragement for my pursuit of a criterion of cognitive significance, in private discussion at the Carnap–Reichenbach Centennial Conference in Konstanz in May 1991.

My OSU Philosophy colleagues Diana Raffman, Stewart Shapiro, Robert Kraut, Kathleen Schmidt, and Charles Kielkopf gave helpful comments on earlier drafts of portions of the book. Robert Kraut has been a constant source of challenges and stimulation on the topic of content and objectivity. Stewart Shapiro has consistently provided intellectual stimulus and careful criticism. Harvey Friedman, of the Department of Mathematics, was also generous with his time in explaining some of his results to me.

My graduate students at The Ohio State University have provided much of the stimulus for Chapter 2, in which I take stock of the realism debate before the detailed investigations carried out in subsequent chapters. Chapters 6 and 7 have also been transformed in response to their continuing probings. I wish in particular to thank Pierluigi Miraglia, Jon Cogburn, Joe Salerno and Roy Cook for helpful discussions that have made me think more clearly about the status of content and about manifestationism, bivalence and undecidability.

During the academic year 1993-4 I benefited from discussions groups at the University of Cambridge in the Philosophy of Language and the Philosophy of Mathematics. From the former I thank Tom Baldwin, Jane

Heal and Paul Noordhof; from the latter, Timothy Smiley, Alex Oliver and Michael Potter.

Acknowledgements

I owe a special debt of gratitude to Jack Smart, who started encouraging me soon after the publication of *Anti-Realism and Logic*[1] to produce this volume, in order to see what an anti-realist treatment of empirical discourse might look like. I can only hope that the long wait will have provided him with something more focused for his realist dissent.

The Ohio State University granted me research leave overseas for the academic year 1993-4 in order that I might work on this book.

I am grateful to the Master and Fellows of Churchill College, Cambridge, for the privilege of an Overseas Fellowship for that year, which enabled me to make progress on the final version.

There are no acknowledgements of publishers' permissions to be made, since no part of the material presented here has appeared in print before.

Two anonymous referees for the Press made extremely helpful suggestions about the overall structure of the work, and criticisms of various points in the argumentation. Lee Franklin rendered valuable assistance in the task of compiling the index. Peter Momtchiloff and Robert Ritter, of the Press, were unfailingly helpful during the editorial and production process.

I would like to thank my wife Janel Hall for her loving companionship and support during the final phases of this project. She also gave me the title.

---

[1]Clarendon Press, Oxford, 1987.

Contents

Chapter 1

Introduction

1.1   The problem defined

What is in the world, and can it all be talked about? Does our taking it to be thus-and-so make it thus-and-so? How might one come to know whether what is said is true?

The realist—our adversary in these investigations—has some simple answers to these questions:

> The world could outstrip what we do or can talk about. The world is the way it is quite independently of our talking about it, or taking it to be thus-and-so. We can succeed in saying things about it, or framing thoughts about it, whose truth or falsity we might never be able to come to know. *Yet those sentences, or the thoughts they expressed, would be true, or false, for all that.*

This work is a sustained attempt to undermine this last claim of the realist. We intend to arrive at a definitive understanding of what the anti-realist thinks is telling about truth, and how, accordingly, he sees the logical lie of the land. The 'realism debate' is the debate over the tenability of a realist view of language, thought and the world. As Russell put it:[1]

> On what may be called the realist view of truth, there are 'facts', and there are sentences related to these facts in ways which make the sentences true or false, quite independently of any way of deciding the alternative. The difficulty is to define the relation which constitutes truth if this view is adopted.

---

[1] *An Inquiry into Meaning and Truth*, Allen & Unwin, London, 1940, at p. 245.

This book is devoted to showing that the difficulty to which Russell refers is insuperable. We show that, by refusing to strive officiously to overcome it, the anti-realist does not incur any other insuperable difficulties in making sense of language and thought, of the way they are rooted in our experience, and of the way they represent the world.

Ours too is an inquiry into meaning and truth. But it is squarely opposed to realism in Russell's sense, the sense that has since been made better known by Dummett under the more specific label 'semantic realism'. For our inquiry stresses that grasp of meaning must be able to be made manifest; and, correlatively, that truth is in principle knowable.

We conceive of declarative meanings as truth conditions. Neo-Quineanism is best characterized by a combination of views: that truth *values* are determinate, but that truth *conditions* are not. This gives one bivalence and classical logic, plus the indeterminacy of meaning. We shall be trying to effect for the neo-Quinean a *volte face*: we shall be arguing that it is truth *conditions* that are determinate, but that truth *values* are not. This gives one a non-classical, constructive logic, plus the determinacy of meaning.

This sea-change brings heavy weather. One has to avert scepticism about meaning, and in particular non-factualism about content. One has to rehabilitate an epistemic notion of analyticity. One has to provide a positive account of empirical meaningfulness, or cognitive significance. One has to explain how acceptance of legitimate theoretical constraints on determinate meanings leads one to refuse to accept the classical principle of bivalence. And one has to show that the resulting logical reforms leave us with a logic that is up to all the demands that we place on it in the interests of mathematics, science and—not least—philosophy. Having nailed our flag to this mast, we have to caution the reader that we shall be needing all hands on deck.

Opponents of realism fall into two broad camps: anti-realist and irrealist. The terms 'anti-realism' and 'irrealism' answer to different concerns. The former has been in philosophical currency longer than the latter, whose first appearance, to the best of my knowledge, is in Wright;[2] although Boghossian[3] uses the term 'irrealism' without sourcing it or attributing it, as though it was already widely understood. As a term of art, 'irrealism' of course covers the earlier expressed views of various writers. It took some time, however,

---

[2]'Realism, Antirealism, Irrealism, Quasi-Realism', *Midwest Studies in Philosophy, Vol. XII: Realism and Antirealism*, 1988, pp. 25–49.

[3]'The Status of Content', *Philosophical Review*, 1990, pp. 159–84.

for non-realists to mark the different ways in which extant irrealisms and the widely discussed anti-realism of Dummett were at odds with realism. In this connection, however, it is worth noting that Wright[4] has expressed the view that the only irrealisms worth considering should be construable as brands of Dummettian anti-realism. We shall in due course see how irrealism and anti-realism differ. In the meantime, one may use the term 'non-realism' wherever possible to cover both anti-realism and irrealism.

1.2   The current state of the debate

The realism debate has explored new niches in the last ten years. The terrain has become complicated. More and more criterial tenets, key theses, litmus tests, and marks of 'realist truth' have been proposed. It is difficult to keep track of all the arguments, and to be mindful of all the possible combinations of variations of themes. We have reached a stage where some might understandably think that we need less subtlety and more conviction. Instead of complicating the map, we should clear the ground. Misplaced subtlety oftens falls flat, because it covers up lurking incoherences. As the subtlety increases, so too does the variety of prima-facie possible semantic and metaphysical stances. People write as though it is more worthwhile to taxonomize possible positions than to develop convincing arguments for any one of them. They muse about the general form that a theory of meaning should take, or they list key propositions that are bones of contention among realists, anti-realists and irrealists. But they seem to have lost the art of, or their heart for, the contending itself. These metaphilosophical taxonomists also fail to raise the sorts of questions that will be raised only by someone who does contend in favour of one of the positions surveyed, especially when it is not an orthodox one. Adversarial conflict, in philosophy as in the law, produces deeper insights and more incisive argumentation than do the accommodating moves of the catholic surveyor-of-positions. It is not enough to survey the positions, if one wants to know what it is really like to view the world from one of them.

Despite the introductory characterization above, there is no widely shared understanding of 'realism'. At best, individual writers succeed (in varying degrees) in making clear what they themselves mean by 'realism'. Then they conduct the realism debate in their own clearer, but still idiosyncratic,

---

[4]'Realism: The Contemporary Debate—W(h)ither Now?', in J. Haldane and C. Wright (eds.), *Reality, Representation and Projection*, Oxford University Press, 1993, pp. 63–84.

terms. This is the case even though, in the hard and soft sciences, and in mathematics, where objectivity is at such a premium, there are well-developed and reasonably widely agreed upon methodologies and canons of inference. For all these disciplines, one is genuinely concerned to learn from philosophers—could they but speak with one voice—what there is to talk about, what we can succeed in saying when we do talk about it, and whether and how one might come to know whether what is said is true.

When one leaves the hard and soft sciences, and mathematics, and turns to the disciplines in the humanities, the realism debate takes on a different shape and significance. Here one is concerned to cultivate interpretive sensibilities, nurture the creative imagination, and reflect upon—perhaps improve, but at least transmit—our culture's norms and values. In the *Geisteswissensschaften* the realism debate focuses on the nature of human judgement on matters of meaning and of moral and aesthetic worth. Realism is conceived of as a form of cognitivism, broadly opposed to forms of non-cognitivism such as expressivism or projectivism. The debate is more concerned with what it is we take ourselves to be doing when we 'make those judgements': are we actually succeeding in saying anything (in the sense of asserting it, and thereby aiming at the truth) or are we doing something different? Are we gilding and staining the world with the colours of internal sentiment? Or are we rendering the world as we find it?

There is not, of course, a total cleavage between these two areas of the realism debate, as they occur concerning the natural sciences and the more hermeneutic disciplines in the humanities. Naturally there are common themes and common concerns. But there is also an interesting and systematic set of differences, which it is partly our concern here to elucidate. In so doing, we may perhaps come to appreciate more clearly the philosophical utility of the notions that can be deployed within both areas of the realism debate.

There are other problems of communication in addition to those that can be put down to the fields of interest and expertise of parties to the realism debate. These problems arise from the fact that, on different sides of the Atlantic, different authors, for professional and institutional reasons, serve as the focus for participants in the debate.

Many North American philosophers are steeped in the post-positivist Quinean tradition. In this tradition, philosophy is thought of as continuous with science; and one's logic is theorem-fixated. Underdetermination, indeterminacy, inscrutability and inextricability are inextricably overdetermined. Semantic and epistemological holism hold sway. Meaning is held to be illusory. Classical logic is entrenched like some Sphinx of the collective mind, while yet the analytic-synthetic distinction is rejected. In this tradition, one is invited to adopt the stance of an *alien interpreter* or translator. One is then encouraged to think of oneself as but an individual alien in the midst of fellow-speakers of the same language.

British philosophers, by contrast, are steeped in the analytic empiricism of Hume and Russell, and in the Wittgensteinian and Strawsonian tradition. Here, language is the key to all thought, and Frege the fount of the most valuable insights into the workings of language. The philosophy of language is the true home of the metaphysician. One's philosophizing is conditioned by the implicit assumption that there really is only one form of life we are all embedded in, and only one language worth knowing. (Admittedly, it was the Dutch who hit on just the right logic, but, being foreigners—so one can imagine a condescending English person complaining—they did so for entirely the wrong reasons.) In this tradition, the predicament of the philosopher trying to achieve a considered view on the realism issue is that of the *reflective participant* in the area of discourse in question.

There are also different degrees of willingness, and of intellectual preparedness, to enter into the technicalities involved in properly understanding and furthering the realism debate. Relatively few North American philosophers have received their logical training in the European tradition of proof theory, especially in the style of natural deduction, which is such a rich source of material for anti-realist writers in the British tradition. Instead, North American philosophers and logicians display a marked proclivity for model theory, or algebraic semantics. By the same token, hardly any British participant in the realism debate seems to know, or be willing to expound and draw upon, the technicalities of quantum mechanics, whose mastery has led North American figures such as van Fraassen and Putnam to many of their philosophical conclusions. The result is, to borrow a metaphor from quantum mechanics, that we do not know exactly where we all are or exactly where we are all going, in the current realism debate. The claim is not, of course, that there is no cross-fertilization, that there is an absolute chasm between the British and North American traditions, and that they therefore speak right past each other and fail to engage on common, and mutually understood, concerns. Rather, it is that there are pronounced differences in background, interests, perspectives and intellectual tendencies between the two sides of the Atlantic.

These differences tend to produce a different 'take' on the issues involved in the realism debate. Different sets of intellectual reflexes and associations are engaged. Different terminology is employed, and, where it is the same terminology, subtly different senses might be involved. Different outlooks are in fact involved among the 'realists' in the two philosophical communities. Likewise, different outlooks are involved among the 'non-realists'. These remarks should be taken as an appeal for some sort of gold standard in metaphysics and the theory of meaning. We need some common intellectual coin. We would do well, therefore, to survey as many as we can of the salient notions that have played a role in the writings of various participants in the realism debate. Only then will the desired conceptual arbitraging be possible.

1.3   The structure of this work

The next two chapters are devoted, in the main, to these expository concerns.

Chapter 2, 'The Realism Debate', provides a comprehensive survey of concepts and issues that ought both to help orientate the beginner and to foreshadow for the expert what our stand will be on these issues, and what needs to be undertaken in defence of that stand.

Chapter 3, 'Irrealism', gives a brief survey of varieties of irrealism and neutralizes that brand of irrealism—namely, irrealism about meanings or content—that would undermine the semantic anti-realist's account of meaning. For the semantic anti-realist, meaning is determinate, and facts about meaning provide the ultimate justification for one's choice of logic. We argue that although we can defuse transcendental arguments for the incoherence of irrealism about semantic discourse, nevertheless the global anti-realist need not (indeed: should not) advocate an irrealist view of semantic discourse. Rather, semantic discourse is a perfectly respectable part of our theory of nature and human interaction. It is as 'factual' as any other branch of science that aims to make sense of natural (including human) phenomena and that is based on reports on which different observers can, in principle, agree.

Chapter 4 continues the defence of meaning objectivity against the most celebrated sceptical attack of late, namely the rule-following considerations of that abstract hybrid known as Kripkenstein. We have to find a sustainable view of the status of semantic discourse itself, if our semantic theory is to be able to serve as a foundation for those anti-realist views and accompanying reforms that are to be pressed for other discourses. We seek, that is, a certain sort of reflexive stability for the whole enterprise. Semantic anti-realists presuppose a substantial and objective conception of the meanings of sentences and of their constituents. Hence they are under a pressing obligation to provide some prophylactic to the corrosive doubts about the objectivity of meaning raised by Kripkenstein. We try to discharge this obligation in the chapter on meaning scepticism. The conclusion reached is that we can allay Kripkean scepticism about the factuality of semantic discourse.

With the issues focused, and scepticism about meaning allayed, we turn next to the major task of defending the central tenets of global semantic anti-realism. These are that grasp of meaning is manifestable, and that truth is in principle knowable. The latter principle comes under attack from two sides. From within the anti-realist camp, on the one hand, the strict finitist complains that there is no principled way of distinguishing between the knowable in principle and the feasibly knowable. Therefore the manifestation argument used by the anti-realist—according to which all aspects of a speaker's linguistic understanding should be able to be manifested in his observable behaviour—will, it is alleged, precipitate a slide all the way to strict finitism. This complaint from the strict finitist will be shown to be baseless. From the realist's camp, on the other hand, comes the complaint that the principle of knowability has the paradoxical consequence that every truth is (or will be) *actually* known. This complaint, likewise, will be shown to be baseless.

Chapter 5, 'Avoiding Strict Finitism', shows how to find an acceptable reading of knowability-in-principle, so as to avoid visiting upon oneself and one's opposition the overly restrictive consequence that only the 'feasibly' or 'practically' knowable can feature in the anti-realist's manifestation requirement on grasp of meaning.

Chapter 6, 'The Manifestation Argument is Dead', explores the foundational relationships between manifestationism, bivalence and undecidability. It canvasses all the possible positions one might take on the relationships among the decidable, the knowable and the true. These positions are Orthodox Realism, M-Realism, Gödelian Optimism and Moderate Anti-Realism. For the Moderate Anti-Realist, all truth is knowable but truth need not be bivalent. We set ourselves the task of eliminating the first three of the positions just listed, leaving Moderate Anti-Realism as the only viable one. Most interestingly, perhaps, is that we find, after painstaking scrutiny, that Dummett's so-called 'manifestation argument' against the principle of bivalence is entirely unconvincing. This puts the anti-realist dialectic against the realist into a completely new light.

Chapter 7, 'Long Live the Manifestation Argument', seeks to remedy the deficiencies exposed in Dummett's 'manifestation argument' as directed against the principle of bivalence. We apply the manifestation requirement in a new way in order to argue against the principle of bivalence for undecidable discourses. The argumentative route to favouring anti-realism over other positions — most notably that of the so-called Gödelian Optimist— is new. By the end of this investigation it emerges that the Manifestation Requirement is tantamount to the principle that all truth is knowable.

Chapter 8, 'Truth as Knowable', defends the principle of knowability against the major realist attack on it, based on a classic result of Frederick Fitch, that claims that there could be truths that are in principle unknowable. The moderate anti-realist tenet that every truth is knowable in principle will be carefully reformulated in a form that will ensure that it survives unscathed, as a touchstone of one's metaphysical outlook.

This defensive groundwork for semantic anti-realism mobilizes what we believe are new and interesting resources. Having shorn up the defences of anti-realism against the main hordes at the gate, it is then time to cultivate the civilizing influences within. The remaining chapters offer what is constructively original in this work.

Chapter 9, 'Analyticity and Syntheticity', examines afresh the much maligned notion of analyticity, and rehabilitates it. We suggest that a major reason why various philosophers have had trouble applying the analytic-synthetic distinction is that they have been affected by an unarticulated dogma, to the effect that no analytic truth could possibly carry existential commitment, even if only to necessary existents (such as the natural numbers). This dogma has been like a black hole in the intellectual firmament, distorting the curvature of conceptual space, and causing the momentum of analytic empiricism to dissipate disastrously into pragmatic empiricism. Once the dogma is challenged, and its contradictory asserted, light can be shed once again, and the equilibrium of analytic empiricism restored.

Chapter 10, 'Finding the Right Logic', does what its title implies, in the light of our newly confirmed determination to justify logic as a body of *analytic* truths and inferential principles. These depend for their justification on the meanings of the logical words. What is new about our choice of logic from the standpoint of semantic anti-realism is that we insist not only on the usual *constructivism*, but provide also new grounds for insisting on *relevance* between the premisses and conclusion of a logically correct argument. Just as epistemic constraints on truth lead to a constructive logic, so too do certain epistemic constraints on consequence or deducibility lead to a relevant logic. At the confluence of both waves of reform lies our preferred logical system: intuitionistic relevant logic (*IR*), which receives its definitive statement here. *IR* is both epistemically constrained and epistemologically adequate; an attractive combination for the anti-realist.

The remaining outstanding issue for the anti-realist is how one accounts for empirical discourse—and more generally for the cognitive credentials of natural scientific discourse. Our inquiry culminates in a canon of constructive inference, and in an account of cognitive significance that shows how good scientific sense is rooted in the sensible.

Chapter 11, 'Cognitive Significance Regained', arrests the slide to pragmatic empiricism with its holistic pessimism over the prospect of ever being able to demarcate the empirically meaningful from the metaphysically meaningless. We propose a criterion of cognitive significance that will distinguish between, on the one hand, those sentences that depend, for their truth or falsity, on our understanding and experience; and, on the other hand, those sentences that would not so depend (even on the assumption that they had truth values at all).

We would argue that this criterion is itself of considerable significance even if it were to be criticized as presupposing too extreme an idealization of the logical shape of actual scientific endeavours. Even if the 'regimentation' that we offer of theory-accretion and the concomitant process of scientific concept-formation enjoys only an imperfect fit with actual scientific practice and the structure of actual theorizing, this is no fatal objection; for the project is difficult enough to accomplish as it is, even with the most austere simplifying assumptions. Once such a criterion is in hand for the austere case, however, there is the prospect of developing, extending and adapting it to the 'messier' and 'noisier' phenomena of actual scientific theory-building. The logical skeleton that we reveal could then be fleshed out even further with considerations of Bayesian probabilistic reasoning, relations of confirmation, abductive heuristics, etc. These further aspects of scientific reasoning would only hold out the prospect of enrichment, not falsification, of the austere model. Moreover, our austere account can serve as an 'ideal type'. It can be understood as a normative standard to which an ideal empirical reasoner could aspire. Such a reasoner would be trying to make sense of the hidden mechanisms in the world on the basis of his observations and experience, and helping himself only to the hypothetico-deductive method in so doing. Our criterion shows that these are materials enough to demarcate good scientific sense from metaphysical nonsense. As it turns out, this ideal reasoner could (indeed: should) also be a moderate anti-realist, the central figure in the narrative to follow; and he could (indeed: should) be helping himself to no more than intuitionistic relevant logic, which we shall be arguing is the correct canon of deductive inference by the moderate anti-realist's lights.

Chapter 12, 'Defeasibility and Constructive Falsifiability' shows how to reconcile defeasibility with hypothetico-deductivism, and furnishes a constructive account of falsifiable empirical theorizing that saves all the logico-linguistic and methodological appearances. It also accounts for how the logic of proof-based assertion in mathematics coincides with (that is, employs the same logical operators as) the logic of refutation-based scientific testing. Thus one and the same canon of constructive and relevant inference suffices both for intuitionistic mathematics and for empirical science.

1.4   Historical reflections

If a slogan is needed to catch the attention of the casual reader, let it be:

Logical Empiricism was almost right!

Logical empiricists just lost heart, and lost faith. They had the right vision, but lacked the right arguments at crucial junctures. The problem of a criterion of cognitive significance struck them, by a certain stage, as too difficult to solve. So they gave up and moved on. They gave up on the analytic-synthetic distinction, and on the distinction between the cognitively meaningful and the cognitively meaningless. Their heirs moved on to more fashionable (and less rigorous and demanding) views of logic, language and science. They opted for graduation, fuzzification, vagueness, indeterminacy, holism and theory-ladenness. All this was a regrettable mistake. The Logical Empiricists had been on the right track, and should have stuck to it.

How was Logical Empiricism almost *right*? It held to the analytic-synthetic distinction, and believed firmly in the yet-to-be-explicated distinction between the cognitively meaningful and the cognitively meaningless. It accorded a certain primacy to reports of observation; and held that there was one correct logic (though it misidentified it).

How was Logical Empiricism *almost* but not quite right? It held that the one correct logic was classical logic. It drew the analytic-synthetic distinction in the wrong place. It failed to provide a criterion of cognitive significance that would do justice to pre-theoretic intuitions—but that failure was not because such a criterion is impossible. It also failed to take seriously the power of the falsificationist or refutation-based account of natural science, which is the dual, and appropriate complement, to the verificationist or proof-based account one should give for mathematical discourse. Logical Empiricism concerned itself more with confirmation and probabilification, and lost sight of the austere deductive logic that is involved in the testing of scientific hypotheses.

The Logical Empiricists themselves are not wholly responsible, however, for not having worked out their programme successfully. The materials they needed in order to do so were, in important cases, developed only long after the heyday of Logical Empiricism. Most important, in this regard, is the proof-theoretic treatment of logic that we owe to the writings of Gentzen and Prawitz. Developments in proof theory have improved our understanding of the tighter logical relations that are needed in order to provide an account of cognitive significance. Now that we have these materials, it is time to address once again the Logical Empiricists' sometimes misconducted, but still unfinished business. We shall be as sparing as possible with logical technicalities; but we shall not be able to avoid them altogether in showing how supposedly defunct views can be revived.

Shades of Carnap and Popper will be with us throughout. As already noted, a new theory of the analytic-synthetic distinction is on offer, as well as a new criterion of cognitive significance. These two very fraught distinctions are to be rehabilitated here.

First, it is vital, for a constructive logicist account of numbers as logical objects, to have a conception of the analytic according to which it may be part of the very meaning of certain statements that they carry certain existential commitments. The conception of analyticity advocated here therefore runs against the tide of tradition, according to which no analytic statement could entail the existence of anything. Once that central dogma is dropped, and the analytic-synthetic distinction accordingly redrawn, the new distinction can be put to work in the service of a rejuvenated Logical Empiricism.

Secondly, it is vital, for an anti-realist and molecularist theory of meaning for scientific discourse about theoretical entities, to employ a conception of the cognitively significant according to which the meanings of theoretical statements are constrained and constituted by the suitably tight logical relations that they bear to the more basic statements of everyday observation. A successful theory of cognitive significance, providing a criterion for such cognitive credentials, would be of independent significance and interest, even if it were excised from its present context. That context is the development of an over-arching semantic anti-realism for both mathematical and empirical discourse. The theory of cognitive significance on offer here plays a crucial role in the wider project; but it may be commended as interesting in its own right even to the reader who is unpersuaded by the overall case made here for global semantic anti-realism. Old theories of cognitive significance had a common failing. They used the blunt instrument of classical logic in an attempt to analyse the delicate logical relations that cognitively significant sentences have to bear to observation sentences in order to be cognitively significant. Classical logical consequence, however, is not exigent enough. The new theory of cognitive significance set forth here is based on a more demanding notion of logical consequence, one which requires every aspect of sentential structure in an argument's premises and conclusion to be contributing to the argument's validity. The source of these ideas was recent work[5] on computationally efficient proof-search, which had engaged my energies immediately after the writing of *Anti-Realism and Logic* (hereafter: *AR&L*).

So much for the ghost of Carnap. What of the ghost of Popper? As already noted, an account of constructive falsification is developed, appropriately complementary to the account that we already have of constructive verification. This enables one to extend the semantic anti-realist's account from the non-defeasible discourse of mathematics to the defeasible discourse of empirical science. The project is accomplished within the insistent scope of globally anti-realist assumptions concerning the nature of meaning: its public character, and its compositionality. (Here we are visited still by the ghosts of Wittgenstein and Frege.) We shall sketch two extreme views of science and scientific method: a robust realism, and an opposing 'social constructivist' relativism. Between these two views lies the moderate anti-realist's view, which avoids the naïveté of robust realism and the overly sophisticated cynicism of the social constructivists. Moderate anti-realism stresses the accessibility of scientific 'truth', but only by courtesy of the possibility of falsification, not of outright proof, on the basis of corroborated experience. By giving an account of constructive falsification, we attain a deeper understanding of defeasibility itself, and of the uniquely self-intimating features of the correct logic: the logic that we should use both for mathematics and for testing our scientific theories. The theory of constructive falsification draws on considerations concerning harmony of rules for the logical operators, normal forms of proofs and of disproofs, and computationally efficient proof-search.

---

[5] The results of these investigations are set out in *Autologic*, Edinburgh University Press, 1992.

1.5   Relationship to *AR&L*

This volume builds on the work in *AR&L* that developed an anti-realist account of non-defeasible, logico-mathematical discourse. *AR&L* provided a pure and positive statement of the Dummettian doctrine of semantic anti-realism, and its implications for logical reform. This was no mere negative doctrine, denying central claims that realists hold dear. Rather, it was a doctrine based on a conception of meaning as essentially public. Thus it shared an important starting-point with behaviourist realists such as Quine. The behaviourism, however, was to win the day over the realism implicit in the adoption of a classical logic. Language was an instrument of communication. Grasp of meaning could only be displayed by the public exercise of suitable recognitional capacities. Meaning was (*pace* Quine) reasonably determinate, and compositional. This conception of meaning, when prosecuted to the full, leads one to advocate far-reaching reform of our deductive practices. It was proposed that classical logic be replaced by intuitionistic relevant logic. The main concern here is to extend that anti-realist account in *AR&L* to defeasible, empirical discourse. This volume therefore completes the development and defence of a global anti-realist position. Its thesis will be contentious, and its recommendations remain reformist. It takes the metaphysical and semantic realists to task, as well as those of former anti-realist persuasion who have strayed from the truth.

AR&L was written with a sequel in mind. The sequel would extend the anti-realist treatment to empirical discourse, and would take up some foundational issues, such as rule-following, deferred from *AR&L*. The sequel was also intended to be less technical than *AR&L*. But that is not quite how it has worked out. As the realism debate progressed it became clear that one would, in many ways, have to go over the same ground again. For it has been churned up, and there are ditches and earthworks where there should not be. We are faced with a ground-clearing operation. This book, then, is both the intended sequel to *AR&L* and not a sequel to it. Although complementary to *AR&L*, it can be read independently. Naturally it would not do to repeat here material and arguments developed in sufficient detail in *AR&L*. One can take the liberty, at certain junctures, of referring the reader to *AR&L* for those details as the need may arise. This book is intended to be accessible and intelligible to readers not acquainted with *AR&L*. Nothing from *AR&L* is presupposed as necessary background for one's understanding of the theses and arguments laid out here. It would nevertheless be prudent to caution the reader that some of the details of a fully comprehensive case for global anti-realism are to be found in *AR&L*, and are not being repeated here. So the full case rests on both volumes taken together, and not on either one of them in isolation.

1.6   A note on style and substance

With this much said, the table of contents should now speak for itself. Chapter 2 takes brief stock of the realism debate in the wake of seminal work by both Dummett and Wright, and foreshadows the detailed investigations carried out subsequently. The discussion in Chapter 2 is briefer, its argumentative texture is less dense, and it should prove technically less demanding, than the detailed discussions of individual topics that follow.

It is only after Chapter 2 that the reader will encounter the original arguments on offer concerning the status of content, rule-following, knowability and truth, manifestationism, bivalence and undecidability, the analytic-synthetic distinction, reformist choice of logic, and the theories of cognitive significance and constructive falsifiability. In the order of exposition, the more technical work of the last three chapters belongs at the end; in the order of importance, however, it does not.

In the course of carrying out our project, we shall endeavour to make historical and conceptual issues more accessible by means of introductory discussions in certain chapters; we shall even, at times, resort to using diagrams to make various conceptual containments or possible positions clear. We shall also be concerned to be meticulous about logical moves in crucial passages of philosophical argumentation. In order to be both rigorous and perspicuous we shall not hesitate to regiment the arguments being advanced or appraised. We shall often set them out as natural deductions using clearly stated rules of inference.[6] Philosophers enjoy a virtual monopoly of teaching logic; so they might as well enjoy its benefits. The reader can rest assured, however, that in taming the true, logic is kept on quite a tight leash. It is to be hoped, also, that by the end we shall not have logic's labours lost.

---

[6]The reader unacquainted with this method of giving proofs will find it explained in my book *Natural Logic*, Edinburgh University Press, 1978; 2nd edn. revised 1990. The final section of ch. 2 is devoted to explaining enough of the basics to enable the reader to follow the proofs set out subsequently.

Chapter 2

The Realism Debate

2.1   The central role of truth

Realism comes in two basic varieties: realism about things, and realism about truth. We may call these ontological realism, and semantic realism respectively.

Our major concern is with truth. Truth comes in different kinds. Only one of these—should it be philosophically coherent—suffices for semantic realism. The other kinds of truth form a sort of crescendo leading up to it. It starts *pianissimo*, in complete philosophical neutrality, with a deflationary conception of truth, and ends with a bang, with full-blown realist truth. At one end there is, as it were, little or no message about truth; at the other end, we are deafened as to its true nature. As always, the truth—in this case, about truth itself—lies somewhere in the middle, where it can register; or so it can be maintained. That middle range is a notion of truth that is substantial, objective, and epistemically constrained: the kind of truth that is, in principle, knowable.[1] For the semantic anti-realist, this is the only licit notion of truth. It is not just one salient option among many alternatives lying on the imaginary continuum that has just been explained. The concession of the continuum is a mere expository device. It is entertained only to humour those who want some metaphilosophical perspective on the alternatives, before being forced, by cogent argument, to commit themselves to the anti-realist position, from which the others will fade from view as inadequate or incoherent.

---

[1] For a full discussion of what is (or should be) understood by 'knowable' in this context, see below.

To continue our expository fiction then: truth comes in different kinds. The least committal, philosophically neutral kind we shall call *minimal truth*.[2] As the name suggests, we make only minimal demands on minimal truth. We do not demand any account of truth-makers for minimal truths. Nor do we demand any account of how we might come to know them. The demands on minimal truth are platitudinous, or requirements of bare material adequacy. Let us now set them out, as they have been identified by Wright.

That assertions aim for truth is one of the *Platitudes of Normativity*. Another is that truth 'supplies a parameter of appraisal'. That is, we value true assertions.

There are also the *Platitudes of Representation*: true sentences correspond to the world, fit the facts, give a correct picture, show how things are, tell it like it is.

There is the *Platitude of Negation*: every declarative sentence has a significant negation.

Finally, there is the *Central Platitude*. This is the claim that the truth-value of any declarative sentence is determined, if it is determined at all, by the meaning of the sentence and the way the world is. It will be assumed that the Central Platitude is not to be read in such a way as to commit one to a correspondence theory of truth, except in the anodyne way already provided for in the Platitudes of Representation. In the shadow of these Platitudes, we appreciate more clearly what it is that we value about true assertions. We do not necessarily value the states of affairs that make them true. Nor do we value the sentences that report these states of affairs. Rather, we value the fit between them.

Besides the platitudes of normativity, representation and negation, there is another ingredient in what one may call the philosophically neutral core of truths about truth. Truth-apt sentences must conform to the

DISQUOTATIONAL SCHEMA

'ϕ' is true if and only if ϕ,

---

[2]Minimal truth is also sometimes called deflationary truth. Advocacy of what is here called minimal truth is not to be confused with Wright's 'minimalism', in ch. 2 of *Truth and Objectivity*, Harvard University Press, 1992 (henceforth: *T&O*). Advocacy of what is here called minimal truth is more like the deflationism that Wright takes to be an inherently unstable notion inviting non-trivial 'inflation' to the position that he calls minimalism. But there is no reason to 'inflate' deflationism because of any alleged 'inherent instability' in the latter. Wright's argument that such inflation is called for is seriously flawed, as I have argued in 'On negation, truth and warranted assertibility', *Analysis*, 55, 1995, pp. 98–104.

which links object language to metalanguage; and to that schema's sibling, the

REDUNDANCY SCHEMA

It is true that ϕ if and only if ϕ

which specifies the logical power of any intralinguistic truth-attributing operator. Of course, if the object language lacks such an operator, only the Disquotational Schema will be in play. But if the object language does have such an operator, the Redundancy Schema will also be in play. Obedience to this schema is a minimal requirement, a requirement of material adequacy on any notion of truth. The notion of truth characterized by obedience to the Platitudes and the Disquotational Schema, and to them alone, is that of minimal truth.

The language-wide satisfaction of the Disquotational Schema and/or the Redundancy Schema is no guarantee that the truth predicate captures a realist notion of truth.[3] Nor, indeed, does a merely materially adequate and formally correct theory of truth, as constrained by the platitudes, by itself offer any guarantee that the notion of truth will be substantial: that is, that it will give rise to an objectivist epistemology, with appropriate discipline on assertoric practice.[4] Absent further specification of the pedigrees of truths, and of conditions for their objective appraisal, (merely) minimal truth is a non-substantial notion of truth. What more is required, then, in order for an appropriately substantial notion of truth to emerge, besides the obvious Central Platitude, Platitudes of Normativity, Platitudes of Representation and the Disquotational and Redundancy Schemata, to which, and to which alone, the notion of minimal truth conforms?

The more 'substantial' or objective kinds of truths involve truth-makers and epistemic controls. The extra substance in any substantial notion of truth consists in an account of how these truths square with the world and

---

[3]For a detailed demonstration that all instances of the Disquotational Schema can be derived within a truth theory obeying only intuitionistic relevant logic, see *AR&L*. This metalogical fact shows that a materially adequate and formally correct theory of truth (sustaining the Disquotational Schema), as constrained by the platitudes, by itself offers no justification for bivalence (or for knowledge-transcendence).

[4]This puts us in disagreement with Wright's claim (*T&O*, pp. 88–9) that 'we ought to expect that *any* class of statements which possess determinate assertoric content will thereby be associated with standards of proper assertibility which their users will acknowledge and about whose satisfaction they will, in suitables circumstances, agree.' The requirements of objectivist epistemology go strictly beyond what is required by the philosophically neutral core of truths about truth.

are encompassed by minds.[5] Examples of proposals as to what would count as more substantial kinds of truth are: warranted assertibility (based on constructive proof, say, in mathematics); Peirce's notion of truth as what we would be able to assert in the ideal limit of rational enquiry; Putnam's notion of truth as 'an idealization of rational acceptability', as what would be justified under epistemically ideal conditions;[6] and Wright's notion of superassertibility.[7] These are only proposals since, at least for some of these supposedly more substantial kinds of truth, it is controversial whether they can be coherently fleshed out. One might wish to challenge the idea that there could be any such thing as an ideal limit of rational enquiry, and wonder what the 'metric' is by which we are supposed to judge approximations to it. One might doubt whether we would be able to recognize the fact that we had attained epistemically ideal conditions. Moreover, we shall see in due course that Wright's notion of superassertibility is unacceptable to a properly reflective anti-realist.

Not only are the items on the list above of supposedly more substantial kinds of truth merely proposals; but the list itself is in no way complete. For example, if the last three items (from Peirce, Putnam and Wright) prove to be impossible to flesh out, we shall be left with warranted assertibility in mathematics as the only extant notion of non-realist but purportedly substantial truth. We shall have as yet no acceptable analogue of this for the case of empirical enquiry. Indeed, it will be a major concern here to make good this lack: to account for the peculiarities of defeasible discourse. We need an account of the latter that makes it subject to the same deductive logic as the non-defeasible discourse of (intuitionistic) mathematics, but in such a way that we appreciate that truth (or falsity) is a substantial matter, despite (indeed: by virtue of) defeasibility.

We are entertaining the fiction that truth comes in different kinds. We

---

[5] Note that the terminology adopted here may diverge from that of Wright. He introduces 'the phrase "substantial truth" ... to register the presence of realism-relevant features within a discourse' (*T&O*, p. 90, fn. 12). Provided these realism-relevant features are only necessary, but not (even jointly) sufficient for realism, that is fine by me. For me, substantiality has to do with the existence of truth-makers and our ability to appraise them. No features of substantial truth *per se* will suffice for realism. Indeed, as we shall see below, at least two of Wright's supposedly 'realism-relevant features' of substantial truth (namely, Convergence of Opinion, and Cognitive Command) are decidedly at odds with a realistic construal of the notion of truth involved.

[6] Cf. *Reason, Truth and History*, at p. 55. Wright alleges that Putnam's notion is incoherent. We shall examine and reject Wright's criticism of Putnam below.

[7] Cf. *T&O*, pp. 44–70.

have looked at minimal truth, and at more substantial notions. Now we consider briefly the kind of truth called realist truth. From the anti-realist's point of view, the notion of realist truth is ultimately illusory or incoherent. Realist truth involves the possibility of evidence-, verification-, knowledge- or investigation-transcendence. Realist truth also obeys the principle of bivalence: that every declarative sentence is determinately true, or false; and that a sentence may possess its truth-value independently of our knowledge and independently of our means of coming to know what its truth-value is. It is the appeal to bivalence that is supposed to ground the laws of classical, 'two-valued' logic. We shall take up the characterization of realist truth in greater detail below, by formulating and assessing certain key theses concerning it.

2.2   Five important contentions

Before we state and discuss the key theses that might be used to characterize a realist notion of truth, we pause to consider five contentions in the realism debate, and to register some of the key points comprehensively argued for in *AR&L*.

> *Contention No. 1.* Realism about certain classes of entities is to be distinguished from realism about certain classes of statements.

That is, ontological realism is a different matter from semantic realism. Chapter 2 of *AR&L* sought to make this clear. There it was argued that any scientific realist (someone, that is, who is an ontological realist about the theoretical entities of science) should be committed to semantic anti-realism. But even if scientific realism does not entail semantic anti-realism, nevertheless the two are consistent with each other. Realism *v.* non-realism about entities is orthogonal to realism *v.* anti-realism about statements concerning them. All four positions are possible, and have adherents. Although a proper definition of 'semantic realism' has yet to be offered, one can venture at this stage that:

(i) the nominalistically-minded classical mathematician is ontologically non-realist about the entities of mathematics, but could nevertheless be semantically realist about mathematical statements concerning 'them';

(ii) the constructive logicist is ontologically realist about the natural numbers but semantically anti-realist about arithmetical statements;

(iii) the Gödelian Platonist is ontologically realist about sets in the cumulative hierarchy, and semantically realist about set-theoretical statements; and

(iv) the nominalist finitist is ontologically non-realist about natural numbers, and semantically anti-realist about arithmetical statements.

'Kreisel's dictum' is that it is not so much the existence of mathematical objects that matters, as the objectivity of mathematical statements. But even objectivity is not enough to secure realism. For the mathematical intuitionist (who is the prime example of an anti-realist) can maintain that there are wholly objective assertibility conditions for mathematical statements, but that these assertibility conditions (thought of as truth conditions) do not sustain all the essential realist dicta about truth. The constructive logicist is the kind of mathematical intuitionist who stresses not only the objectivity of mathematical statements but also the necessary existence of the mathematical objects they talk about.

Constructive logicism was developed in *AR&L*. The constructive logicist succeeds in deriving all of the Peano–Dedekind axioms (including the schema of mathematical induction) in a modest fragment of second-order logic, from extremely parsimonious, constructive, and analytical principles governing the notion 'number of'.

> *Contention No. 2.* Realism is not necessarily *tout court*, or across-the-board. Rather, one can be a realist, or a non-realist, on different areas of discourse. Example areas are: set theory, number theory, space-time theory, theoretical physics, talk about medium-sized objects, the future, the past, inaccessible regions of space-time, other minds, secondary qualities, causation, meanings, morals, aesthetic value, the comic, and modals (possible worlds).

It is thought to be a relatively simple matter how to identify an 'area of discourse'. Sometimes, though, an anti-realist attitude might be adopted towards a class of statements with a certain sort of logical structure—such as subjunctive conditionals—which would crop up across several, if not all, of these various other 'areas of discourse'. The working consensus, though, seems to be that one can mix and match—a little realism here, a little non-realism there—and still attain a coherent world view. We shall enquire below whether this is either possible or desirable.

AR&L showed how all the basic philosophical demands on the notion of truth, and all the appropriate content-forming epistemic constraints, were met by the anti-realist's notion of constructive truth, or warranted assertibility. There was no justification, however, for thinking of the notion of truth involved as evidence-transcendent or as bivalent. From the global anti-realist's point of view, knowledge-transcendence is incoherent. It is to be rejected for all discourses. We shall see below how to defend the anti-realist's principle of knowability against the attempted *reductio* argument offered by the realist.

While realism (or non-realism) should be with respect to specific areas of discourse, anti-realists have not yet produced anything like as compelling a treatment of empirical discourse as they had (in the form of mathematical intuitionism) for pure mathematical discourse. Under 'empirical discourse' can be reckoned all genuinely assertoric discourse apart from logic and pure mathematics. (A genuinely assertoric discourse is one for which an irrealist viewpoint of the non-factualist variety is not justified; see below.) Thus one may include under this heading, most importantly, at least parts of our theories in the biological, social and physical sciences. The claim, then, is:

> there is an anti-realistically acceptable account of at least parts
> of our theories in the biological, social and physical sciences.

The claim ventures only 'at least parts' rather than 'all of', since an irrealist view of our discourse concerning theoretical entities in science would have to be considered and dismissed. The evidential statements of these theories, one may assume, escape the strictures of any proposed irrealism. For, if 'theory ladenness' were to be pushed so far as to make evidential statements subject to the same irrealism as theoretical statements are, we should have reached the extraordinarily counterintuitive conclusion that all of science had nothing to do with reality. In making a case against irrealism about theoretical statements, appeal can be made to the new theory of cognitive significance offered below—itself a major challenge, in response to a problem of considerable independent and self-contained interest in logical-empiricist philosophy of science. A proper understanding of how theoretical discourse acquires its cognitive significance will justify one in rejecting irrealism about theoretical entities, and in strengthening the claim above so as to concern all of the natural sciences, including even the most interpretive branches of the social sciences (especially semantics and psychology, both regarded as even more vulnerable to irrealist construals). The stronger claim will therefore be:

> there is an anti-realistically acceptable account of all of our theories in the biological, social and physical sciences.

The anti-realist can approach all these areas of discourse with a radically new tack. The trick is to eschew the usual approach by other theorists to these areas: namely, the pursuit of some truth-seeking analogue (such as 'defeasibly warranted' assertibility) of the non-defeasible kind of assertibility that we enjoy in mathematics. Instead, one can adopt, as we shall see below, a brand of constructive Popperianism, or hypothetico-deductivism. The mark of empirical discourse is that the key semantic notion in terms of which the theory of meaning should proceed is that of falsification, not verification. $AR\&L$ showed how in mathematics, the emphasis on proofs of apodeictic conclusions (theorems) leads the anti-realist to give a semantics in terms of conditions for warranted assertion, with a concomitant emphasis on the introduction rules for the logical operators as sense-determining. This is because it is the introduction rules that enjoy priority in recursive definitions of canonical proofs of conclusions with dominant occurrences of the logical operator concerned. One then appeals to the Principle of Harmony[8] to justify the elimination rules as sense-explicating. This principle is as follows:

> The introduction rule for a logical operator λ is so framed that its conclusion (with λ dominant) is the strongest conclusion that can be so inferred under the conditions stated. The elimination rule for λ is so framed that its major premiss (with λ dominant) is the weakest premiss that can so feature.

The suggestion now is that harmony is playing a much deeper role. In natural science, the proposed emphasis on disproofs (refutations) of defeasible assumptions (scientific hypotheses) leads the anti-realist to give a semantics in terms of conditions for warranted denial, with a concomitant emphasis on the elimination rules for the logical operators as sense-determining. This is because it is the elimination rules that enjoy priority in recursive definitions of canonical disproofs of premisses with dominant occurrences of the logical operator concerned. One then appeals to harmony to justify the introduction rules as sense-explicating. Thus it emerges that harmony is playing a

---

[8]This statement of the Principle of Harmony is from *Natural Logic, op. cit.*

much more important role; for it is harmony that ensures that the logical operators as they appear in the discourse of mathematics are precisely the same logical operators as they appear in the discourse of empirical science. We therefore attain an account of how one and the same logic is applicable to our thought both about the abstract and the necessary (mathematics) and about the concrete and the contingent (empirical science).

> *Contention No. 3.* The realism debate is properly conducted within the philosophy of language, or, more narrowly, within the theory of meaning.

This is perhaps the most contentious of the broad claims, and derives from Dummett. Metaphysics is to be subsumed by the philosophy of language. The provocative idea is that the philosophy of language will provide the conceptual resources and the theoretical constraints involved in stating what is at issue, and helping one to attain some settled and reasoned views on the matter. There may, indeed, be deeper reasons for agreeing with Dummett on this score than those that he himself urges, or that become manifest in the way he prosecutes the anti-realist programme. These deeper reasons have to do with the quandary one would be in when trying to make sense, within one's realism or non-realism, of what one is up to in maintaining that very doctrine.

One of our first orders of business in our 'taking stock' in this chapter will be to formulate key theses of realism in a way that draws freely on notions from metaphysics, epistemology and the philosophy of language. It will in due course be seen that those of these theses that are crucial—those that the anti-realist would refuse to accept, or even reject—are the ones that seem the most likely candidates for reconstrual as theses wholly within the philosophy of language. Whether such a metaphilosophical 'insulation' (within the philosophy of language) can be effected, though, is not a question on which the validity of any of our conclusions will turn. One virtue, however, of seeking thus to 'insulate' the formulations of these crucial theses is that we thereby have the best possible chance of attaining a formulation, within an acceptably neutral setting, that will convey the same content to both the realist and the anti-realist. For one of our worries has to be that any of the key 'realist' theses can appear to be wholly acceptable to the anti-realist, given only that the anti-realist can attain a suitable interpretation of it within the framework of his own thought about these deep and interconnected matters. One wants to forestall the possibility that the two sides of the debate might achieve homophonic agreement but really be talking right past each other; that they might fail to find any key thesis on which they genuinely disagree. One wants, that is, to ensure that the key theses are so anodyne in their theoretical presuppositions that they can serve as genuine points of contention between the realist and the anti-realist.[9]

> *Contention No. 4.* The issue of realism versus anti-realism is orthogonal to the issue of whether one is willing to maintain a supervenience or reductionist thesis with regard to any two areas of discourse.

Suppose the question is whether to regard some 'higher level' discourse (such as psychology) as reducible to some 'lower level' discourse (such as neuro-physiology), or whether to regard the 'higher level' of facts (such as mental states) as supervening on the 'lower level' of facts (such as brain states). Whether or not one's reductionist or supervenience views serve to make one an anti-realist about the higher-level discourse will depend on a closer consideration of the nature of the reduction or supervening that is bruited, and, if such is, on one's views about the lower-level discourse. In principle, all four positions are possible, and have adherents:

(i) the reductionistically-minded psychologist (such as the central state materialist) could be a realist about neurophysiological matters, and therefore, *via* the reduction, about the psychological ones;[10]

(ii) the anti-reductionistically-minded psychologist could be a realist about mental discourse;

(iii) the reductionistically-minded psychologist could be an anti-realist about neurophysiological matters, and therefore, *via* the reduction, about the psychological ones; and

(iv) the anti-reductionistically-minded psychologist could be an anti-realist about mental discourse (and perhaps even a realist about neurophysiological

---

[9] The importance of this was stressed by Robert Kraut in discussion.

[10] This is Dummett's own example, in his essay 'Realism', in *The Seas of Language*, Oxford University Press, 1993, pp. 230–76. Wright, therefore, was mistaken to hold that 'Dummett ... would be content to add ... that realism must be a view about what makes for the truth of statements *when they are literally and nonreductively construed*' (my emphasis). See his 'Realism, Antirealism, Irrealism, Quasi-Realism', loc. cit., at p. 27.

discourse).

The issue of reductionism (and supervenience) is therefore something of a red herring.[11]

> *Contention No. 5.* Anti-realists often argue that one important consequence of their anti-realism is that one ought, for the sake of reflective equilibrium, to adopt a non-classical logic as properly answering to those propositional contents, and their logical structures, that the anti-realist finds acceptable.

The driving idea is that logic depends, for its justification, only on the meanings of the logical operators.[12] That is, logic is epistemically analytic. Classical logic is in error by imputing illicit extra content to some of these operators, most notably negation, disjunction and existential quantification. If one were unable to exploit that illicit extra content, various strictly classical inferences would be invalid. That is, they would not be justifiable on the basis of considerations of meaning alone. A sentence is epistemically analytic just in case grasp of its meaning suffices for one to be warranted in asserting it (or justified in holding it true).[13] This formulation, however,

---

[11]The exceptions to this claim would be cases where: (a) reduction is proposed, (b) realism is entertained about the lower level, but (c) anti-realism for the higher level is induced by the failure of Referentialism (for which, see below). Dummett offers two examples where (a), (b) and (c) hold. One is classical phenomenalism, where the details of the proposed phenomenalist reduction make for truth-conditions for sentences about ordinary objects being specified without involving reference to those objects themselves—hence the failure of Referentialism. The other is Frege's abstractionist treatment of line-directions (the 'higher level'), where the 'lower level' discourse concerns lines, points and incidence. Here, likewise, only reference to lines and points is involved in the specification of truth-conditions for sentences involving apparent reference to directions.

[12] *Cf. Tractatus Logico-Philosophicus* 6.112: 'The correct explanation of the propositions of logic must assign to them a unique status among all propositions.'

[13]The notion of epistemic analyticity, as it applies to logic, is not new. McDowell, for example, expresses the matter as follows, when he says that the verificationist conception:

> requires a conception of the truths of logic, not as true solely in virtue of the senses of the logical constants—without assuming the principle of bivalence, there is no telling which sentences have that status—but as *knowable solely in virtue of the senses of the logical constants* ('Truth Conditions, Bivalence and Verificationism', in G. Evans and J. McDowell (eds.), *Truth and Meaning*, Oxford University Press, 1976, pp. 42–66; at p. 60; my emphasis).

The *term* 'epistemically analytic' comes from Boghossian's paper 'Analyticity', forthcoming in Crispin Wright and Bob Hale (eds.), *A Companion to the Philosophy of Language*, Oxford, Blackwell, 1997.

masks an important ambiguity.[14] We need to distinguish between grasp of meaning which suffices for the discovery of a warrant to assert, and grasp of meaning which suffices merely for the appraisal of a purported warrant to assert. The latter (weaker) notion is to be preferred. That is, a sentence ϕ is epistemically analytic just in case (a) there is a warrant Π for its assertion, and (b) grasp of ϕ's meaning suffices for one to appreciate that Π is indeed a warrant for ϕ's assertion. We would also argue that some areas of mathematics—such as number theory—contain epistemically analytic statements that carry existential commitments. These commitments are not vicious, though, since the (abstract) entities involved are necessary existents. Epistemically analytic statements need not be any of the following: decidable; obvious; free of existential commitments.[15] In Chapter 9 an account of analyticity is developed that warrants all of these claims.

The anti-realist, of course, will dispute whether there are truths of logic whose (logical) truth cannot be known without assuming the principle of bivalence. For to maintain this is to conceive of the classical logical truths as the logical truths; and one would need to establish one's entitlement to do that. But the anti-realist can at least avail himself of the useful conception according to which the truths of logic are true (and knowably so) solely in virtue of the senses of the logical constants. Indeed, it is precisely because of the deep constraints that the anti-realist acknowledges concerning manifestability of grasp of meaning, the exercise of appropriate recognitional capacities therein, and the compositionality of meaning, that he (the anti-realist) moves from this conception of the source of logical truth to a non-classical logic as the proper repository of such truth. The detailed case for such logical reform was put forward in $AR\&L$.[16]

Anti-realism, then, is held to entail logical reform. It is important, for the reflective equilibrium thus claimed, that the anti-realist also discharge the responsibility of showing what would thereby be lost, and what would thereby be retained. The new logic, if not classical, must at least answer to the main methodological concerns of truth theory, mathematics and nat-

---

[14]The ambiguity is neither noted nor appreciated by Boghossian, loc. cit.

[15]Anyone who maintained that first-order logical truths are analytic is already committed to the view that analytic statements need not be decidable or obvious. But it is decidable and obvious that analytic statements need not be free of existential commitments either: consider the analytic claim that the number of non-self-identical things is 0.

[16]Wright, also, if somewhat belatedly, has come round to the view that if we entertain any 'epistemically constrained conception of truth' then this will involve 'a willingness to undertake broadly intuitionistic revisions' ($T\&O$, p. 44). This, indeed, is a central claim of global anti-realism, the position defended here.

ural science. Will it do so? Or will it prove to be inadequate, in a way arguably worse than the way in which, according to the logically reforming anti-realist, classical logic itself errs by favouring certain non-analytically justifiable inferences? *AR&L* showed that the system of intuitionistic relevant logic answered to all the methodological concerns just mentioned. It should be unnecessary to reproduce that part of the argument here.[17]

2.3   Key theses

On offer below is a set of theses which, because of how they go beyond the Platitudes, should afford enough material to characterize realism from the standpoint of metaphysics and epistemology as well as the philosophy of language. It would be artificial to try to draw distinctions between the disciplines of metaphysics and epistemology and the philosophy of language in the initial stages of this investigation. Only later, when the issues are clearer, shall we be in a position to judge whether the characteristic theses can be rephrased in such a way as to lie uncontroversially within the philosophy of language. Not every one of the following theses is to be thought of as the exclusive theoretical commitment of the realist. Indeed, many of them (as is the case with the Platitudes) are accepted by the anti-realist, and ought to be; for anti-realism, though arresting, thought-provoking and revisionary, still has to save many, if not all, of the intuitive appearances in our account of mind, language and reality.

The realist, however, often thinks of himself as making philosophical mileage by advancing each thesis with a certain tone of voice: with a special 'realist' emphasis, say, on the notion of truth, or of reference. The trouble is, however, that these terms occur in the philosophical parlance of the anti-realist as well. And the theses in question really only have their realist bite if one can succeed in conferring on those terms their supposedly realist

---

[17]For further developments recently undertaken of the metatheory of intuitionistic relevant logic, see the following: *Autologic*, Edinburgh University Press, 1992; 'On Maintaining Concentration', *Analysis* 1994, pp. 143–52; 'Automated Deduction and Artificial Intelligence', in R.Casati, B.Smith and G.White (eds.), *Philosophy and the Cognitive Sciences: Proceedings of the 16th International Wittgenstein Colloquium*, Hölder-Pichler-Tempsky, Vienna, 1994, pp. 273–86; 'Intuitionistic Mathematics Does Not Need Ex Falso Quodlibet', *Topoi*, in a special issue on Intuitionistic Truth, 1994, pp. 127–33; 'Delicate Proof Theory', in J.Copeland (ed.), *Logic and Reality: Essays on the Legacy of Arthur Prior*, Oxford University Press; and 'Transmission of Truth and Transitivity of Proof', in D.Gabbay (ed.), *What is a Logical System?*, Studies in Logic and Computation Series, Vol. 4, Oxford University Press, pp. 161–77.

significance. Yet it is at least part of our project to try, independently, to pin
down that significance by setting out the very theses that are supposed to
invest the terms in question with that significance! The reader will forgive
any hint of methodological circularity here. It is inevitable. Indeed, part
of the robust appeal of anti-realism derives from its serious and principled
reconstrual of notions such as truth and reference, a reconstrual that corrects
current misconceptions and exaggerated notions of what it is that we can
truly grasp. Such reconstrual is then urged as the proper construal of the
key terms, leading to the anti-realist acceptability of several of the key theses
involving them. Still, all this would be effort entirely wasted if the list of
theses did not contain at least some theses that proved to be proper bones
of contention between realist and anti-realist, even after the sophisticated
reconstrual by the anti-realist that serves, in his view, to set the philosophical
record straight. It is therefore worth indicating, with each thesis, whether
it proves to be acceptable to the anti-realist, upon anti-realist (re)construal
of its key terms. If it does, the realist is barking up the wrong tree if he
thinks that the thesis in question really sets him apart from the supposedly
deluded herd. Such theses, though not yet on our list of Platitudes above,
nevertheless deserve to be called platitudes, since they do not provide genuine
bones of contention. That is, they do not succeed in investing their key terms
with the crucial content that the realist requires in order to make his realism
both understood and weighty (let alone: plausible) as a metaphysical view.

We shall be stating and explaining thirteen key theses of realism in what
follows. The first two are usually uttered in the same breath.

Key Thesis No. 1. Externalism[18]
Our declarative discourse involves reference to things which exist
independently of us

Key Thesis No. 2. Independence[19]
...and which are the way they are quite independently of us and
our beliefs.

It may be questioned why we distinguish Independence from Externalism.
This is, in effect, to make an ontology-ideology distinction. Are we not

---

[18]Wright ('Realism, Antirealism, Irrealism, Quasi-Realism', at p. 25; *T&O*, 1992 at
pp. 1–2) calls this not externalism, but 'modesty'. In Haldane and Wright (editorial
'Introduction', in *Reality, Representation and Projection*, Oxford University Press, 1993,
pp. 3–12) the terminology changes to 'deference'.

[19]'The truth is ...independent of human opinion, which is the key realist notion.' Thus
Wright, in 'Realism, Antirealism, Irrealism, Quasi-Realism', at p. 26.

neglecting the fact that ontology can only be 'read off' what we assert?[20]
The answer is negative. Not all of our assertions in an area of discourse are
needed in order to establish what its ontology is. A good case in point here
is the theory of natural numbers based on 0 and s (successor). The Peano–
Dedekind axioms for 0 and s already suffice to fix our discourse as being
about the natural numbers. Any extra theorizing (using plus and times)
serves only to contribute additional ideological superstructure, not change
our conception of what it is that we are talking about.

By claiming that the ontology-ideology distinction can be made, one is
not committing oneself to essentialism concerning the objects. For there
need be no privileged attributions of properties ('essences') that serve to
fix what the discourse is about. Moreover, even though, from the standpoint of a supervenience theorist, we can say that our assertions form the
supervenience base for attributions of ontology, it is nevertheless not required (for such supervenience) either that all the assertions be needed for
the supervenience base to fix the ontology, or that there be any privileged
or distinguished core of assertions that suffices as a supervenience base. The
moral that we can draw from this is: when in the process of radically interpreting the utterances of an alien community, we would do well to regard
our ontology-ideology distinction for their language as tentative and defeasible; but certainly as something it makes sense to try to draw. A similar
conclusion holds for the analytic-synthetic distinction. The inextricability of
fact and meaning is an epistemological problem for the radical interpreter.
Their extrication is always a matter at which our interpretive hypotheses
take a tentative stab. But the guiding assumption should be that there is
an analytic-synthetic distinction to be drawn, even though our drawing of
it is a highly defeasible matter, subject to continual revision in the light of
further data about linguistic behaviour.

The next two realist theses pay tribute to the imagined semantic power
of our propositional representations, and to the aloofness (or possible inac-
cessibility) of the world within which we try to learn how matters stand.

Key Thesis No. 3. Determinacy of External Reality
What we can say about these independently existing things is
rendered definitely true or false by (the meaning of what we say,
and) the way these things stand, that is, the way the world is,
this latter being independent of our means of coming to know
whether what we say is true, or false.

---

[20]Robert Kraut raised this question.

Consequently one is led to entertain a sceptical worry, the epistemological 'tails' to the metaphysical 'heads' set out so far:

> *Key Thesis No. 4. Potential Unknowability*
> The truth about these matters of independent fact could elude what we could possibly come to know about them.

Key Thesis No. 4 comes in a weaker and a stronger version. Let us assume that knowledge is what results, in the felicitous case, from applying our best methods to all the available evidence. (The precise analysis, if such be available, of the concept of knowledge need not detain us here. It is the *analysandum* which features in our expression of the following principle.) The weaker form is:

> *Key Thesis No. 4(a): Knowledge-Transcendence*
> All that we could possibly know—even in the form of an ideal theory 'in the limit', based on all possible and humanly accessible evidence, and put forward as the result of our applying our best methods to such evidence—could fall short of the whole truth.

Our formulation involving ideal theories in the limit is concessive. We do not presuppose that one can make sense of the notion, or that such theories exist.[21] We could reformulate 4(a) along the following lines: It is possible that there be some true sentence ϕ such that, whatever theory T ('knowledge') we may have at any stage, where T contains ϕ, we might, at some later stage, subscribe to a different theory T^* ('revised knowledge') that does not contain ϕ. That is, ϕ does not get 'stably into' our succession of theories. This formulation does not assume that there is any such thing as an ideal limit to the sequence of theories. The reason why the concessive form has been chosen is that if we allow ourselves the thought that such an ideal limit existed, it would seem even more compelling that, for the very reasons that it is the limit of a succession of theories, it is tracking as closely as possible the truths about our world and its organizational principles, reflected in the deductive structure of the theory itself. That such a theory could nevertheless fall short of the whole truth is therefore even more arresting. And this is the possibility that Knowledge-Transcendence maintains. But this is still weak by contrast with the following much stronger form of Key Thesis No. 4.

---

[21] It was Robert Kraut who asked whether such an objectionable presupposition was involved.

Key Thesis No. 4(b): Radical Error
Even an ideal theory 'in the limit', based on all possible and
humanly accessible evidence, and put forward as the result of
our applying our best methods to such evidence, may be radically
false.[22]

What is here called 'knowledge transcendence' is sometimes called 'verification transcendence' or 'evidence transcendence'. The phrase 'verification
transcendence', though, lays too much stress on verification. This stress
implies an overly exigent constraint on the methodology one might employ
to produce hypotheses worthy of holding true on the basis of the evidence.
And the phrase 'evidence transcendence'[23] is not altogether happy either,
because even hypotheses that we put forward as true, and that happen to be
true, can and indeed ought to transcend the evidence, in one obvious sense
of 'transcend', namely, of not being strictly entailed by the evidence. We
want to allow that what we know can go beyond the evidence; but the realist
wants to hold that our best methodologically constrained ventures beyond
the evidence may not capture the whole truth. The weaker form 4(a), therefore, holds that not all the truth need be knowable.[24] The stronger form
4(b) holds moreover that not all that is 'knowable' need be true.

For the realist, *Homo sapiens* is *not* the measure of all things. We may,
in certain cases, attain to the truth; but we do not ourselves *determine* it.
That is to say, our coming to know that *P* does not *make* it the case that *P*.
Rather, what we come to know would be the case even if we did not know it
to be so. By means of our representational powers, we reflect what is already
the case; we do not and cannot *bring to light* what is not already the case,
waiting for light to be cast upon it. We are mariners on a sea of uncertainty;
and when we reach a beach of knowledge, we know that a hinterland of as
yet uncharted truths awaits us.

Key Thesis No. 5: Discovery
When we come to know these truths we discover what is the case;
we do not ourselves in any way 'create' what is the case.

---

[22] Jack Smart is an ardent proponent of this thesis; there may well be others.

[23] Although it will be used below, with its standard metaphorical meaning of
(verification/falsification)-transcendence.

[24] Wright's way of putting this thought is: that truth is not 'essentially epistemically
constrained'. See Wright, 'Realism: The Contemporary Debate—W(h)ither Now?', at
p. 65.

The realist in the grip of the sceptical worry of 4(b) may succumb to an even deeper worry: the worry, not that the quarry might evade us though our tools be suited to it, but that our very tools might be incapable of leaving any telling marks:

> *Key Thesis No. 6: Ultimate Non-Affordability*[25]
> Reality may be ultimately constituted in such a way that its deepest secrets might elude our own very limited, cosmically provincial, perceptual and conceptual apparatus (which may be abbreviated to: 'cognitive apparatus').

Writers on evolutionary epistemology, such as Vollmer,[26] frequently describe their metaphysical and epistemological position as one of 'hypothetical realism'. But this is an ontological realism, and is orthogonal to the question of semantic realism. The semantic anti-realist can make sense of evolutionary epistemology as a branch of science. So Ultimate Non-Affordability makes sense to the anti-realist, who can even agree with it.

It is conceivable, for example, that alien creatures might communicate with a recursive syntax of chemical concentrations. Their 'linguistic' 'behaviour' would be highly non-observable for us. We would need a fully developed scientific theory before we could even begin to break into their 'language'. And vice versa, perhaps. They might not have anything like ears adapted to detect variable compressions in a gaseous medium, or eyes adapted to read our bodily movements. They might be deaf and blind to our words and gestures. If they were to have radically different modes of sensory awareness, attuned to the exigencies of their environments, they might even have developed different conceptual systems as a result. This worry about the cosmic provinciality of our cognitive apparatus can be both provoked, and somewhat allayed, by considerations from evolutionary epistemology. It is provoked by the consideration that we are cognitively adapted to a relatively narrow region of physical reality, and that certain deep truths may be both literally and metaphorically 'beyond us' and our capabilities.[27] We may not be able to apprehend them at all, since we have not evolved the requisite concepts or modes of sensory awareness. We could be cosmic hicks.

---

[25] This term is introduced here in the sense of Gibson's 'affordances', not in the sense that we could be thus afflicted no matter what resources and effort we might expend on the problem.

[26] Cf. *Evolutionäre Erkenntnistheorie*, Hirzel, Stuttgart, 1975.

[27] There is something of this line of thought in McGinn's belief that the mind–body problem may be insoluble *by us*.

The consideration from evolutionary epistemology that goes some way to allaying the worry is that our modes of sensory awareness, and our concepts, have been produced as a result of aeons of presumably optimizing (or at least 'satisficing') natural selection, and that they should, consequently, be tolerably well-adapted to the limited niche that we occupy. Both the later Wittgenstein and Davidson would urge that, in so far as our beliefs and values are our guides to life, and we are still here to form them and be guided by them, there must at least be some measure of truth in the former. (This must be the strongest consideration against any error-theoretic irrealism for a given discourse.) Moreover, in so far as the meanings of our sentences are their truth-conditions, and we grasp those meanings, there must be some considerable measure of truth in the sentences that we accept as true when we learn our language. These considerations alone—evolutionary adaptation of our cognitive apparatus to that part of the world that we inhabit, and the fact that we come to grasp the meanings of sentences of our language—go a long way to justifying our next five theses:

Key Thesis No. 7: Epistemic Accessibility[28]
Despite our possible cognitive shortcomings, we could in principle come to know, or achieve adequate (if defeasible) grounds for believing, some/many/most/almost all the truths expressible in our language (and have, indeed, perhaps already done so)

Key Thesis No. 8: Inter-Subjectivity
...and our knowledge can be intersubjectively appraised

Key Thesis No. 9: Communicability
...and communicated to fellow-speakers.

Key Thesis No. 10: Knowledge of Meaning is Knowledge of Truth-Conditions; K(M)=K(TC), for short
When that knowledge is communicated, we know what is meant, that is, what is claimed to be known, because we know under

[28]Wright ('Realism, Antirealism, Irrealism, Quasi-Realism', *Midwest Studies in Philosophy, Vol. XII: Realism and Antirealism*, 1988, pp. 25–49, at p. 25; *T&O*, 1992 at p. 2) calls this not epistemic accessibility, but 'presumption'. In Haldane and Wright (editorial 'Introduction', in *Reality, Representation and Projection*, Oxford University Press, 1993, pp. 3–12; at p. 3) the terminology changes to 'self-assurance'. They make the point that, just as modesty or deference give rise to worries of scepticism, so do presumption or self-assurance lure one in the direction of idealism. But does realism, as here characterized, represent the best resolution of these opposing tensions?

what conditions the sentence involved in the knowledge claim would be true.

Consequently,

> *Key Thesis No. 11: TM is TC*, for short
> An adequate theory of meaning for our declarative discourse (in which those knowledge claims are made) must be truth-conditional.

The next principle has been advocated by some realists, and opposed by yet others. It would, presumably, appeal to some anti-realists but not to others. It is on the list of Key Theses only in the interests of completeness. It need not be regarded as criterial for either realism or anti-realism. But one needs to come to a considered view on this thesis, whether one is a realist or an anti-realist. For in doing so one will be exploring the deductive reach and internal consistency of whatever position one holds.

> *Key Thesis No. 12: Progress*
> Science, if properly conducted, involves progress towards the truth; that is, later theories will explain and predict more salient truths, and explain and predict fewer salient falsehoods, than would have been explained and predicted by the earlier theories that they displace.

Some (but not all) scientific realists state their belief in Progress as expressive of their realism. But the anti-realist can have just as much interest in the notion, once one appreciates that one is working with a substantial, if not evidence-transcendent or bivalent, notion of truth. Suppose the target theory is the consistent theory T. T is the set of substantial truths expressible in one's language. Note that on an anti-realist account, T need not be logically complete. That is, it need not be the case that, for every sentence ϕ, either ϕ or $\neg\phi$ is in T. We need to explicate the ternary relation 'theory T_1 is closer than theory T_2 to theory T'. In the classical (realist) case, it is of course assumed that the theory T is complete (in that, for every sentence ϕ, T will contain exactly one of ϕ and $\neg\phi$). Thus there is a tendency on the part of the semantic realist to reduce the problem of verisimilitude to that of explicating a binary relation 'theory T_1 is closer-to-the-truth than theory T_2'. Instead, the latter should be taken as a special case of the former. If we were to speak of 'demonstrasimilitude' rather than 'verisimilitude' this might be clearer.

These brief remarks serve to underline an obvious connection that is seldom made in the literature on either theory revision or verisimilitude. Theory revisions aim to get us closer to the truth; and to get closer to the truth we have to revise our theories. Obvious though this connection is, it is extraordinary how the literature on theory revision ignores the problem of verisimilitude, and how the literature on verisimilitude offers no advice on the process of theory revision. A tandem treatment of these two topics cannot be undertaken here; but we note that it merits detailed investigation.[29]

The final realist thesis is what we shall call the thesis of Archimedeanism. It is on this thesis that much of Putnam's thinking about internal realism turns. Putnam is concerned[30] to show how illusory is the wanted Archimedean 'point of view' when one considers both Tarski's language hierarchy and the 'observer-system cut' that is called for in any application of quantum mechanics. There is no language strong enough to talk about absolutely everything, including the relationship that the language itself bears to the world; and there is no vantage point from which the quantum-mechanical observer would be able to observe the whole physical universe and all the interactions of things within it, including the observer himself and all the things he is trying to observe and measure.

> *Key Thesis No. 13: Archimedeanism*
> There is a perspective, or standpoint, or imaginary point-of-view, or view-from-nowhere, or God's-eye point-of-view, from which some logically possible extension of ourselves could be properly apprised of every matter of fact, both by being cognitively equipped to conceive of the truth-conditions involved, and by being able to marshal all the relevant evidence that would be decisive. Or, if there could not be some logically possible extension capable of dealing with every matter of fact, then at least: for every matter of fact, some possible and finite extension of ourselves would be able to deal with it in the way described.

Note that the stronger and the weaker readings both have the same initial existential quantifier:

Strong reading. There is a point of view V such that for some

---

[29] With an eye to such a tandem treatment a start was made, on theory revision, in N.Tennant, 'Changing the Theory of Theory Change: Towards a Computational Approach', in *British Journal for Philosophy of Science*, 1994, pp. 865–97.

[30] *Cf. Realism with a Human Face*, Harvard University Press, 1990.

extension E of ourselves, for all truths ϕ, E can be apprised of ϕ from V.

Weak reading. There is a point of view V such that for every truth ϕ there is some finite extension E of ourselves such that E can be apprised of ϕ from V.

In stating these key theses, we have helped ourselves to terminology such as 'object', 'matters of fact', 'reality', etc. Admittedly we have had to speak at times about the workings of language, but we have not sought to phrase the theses in terminology exclusive to the philosophy of language. Two of these theses, however, have been rephrased by Dummett so as to appear to sit squarely within the philosophy of language. First, for Dummett, the thesis of Externalism is to be rephrased as follows:

Key Thesis No. 1*: Referentialism
Any adequate semantics for our declarative discourse gives truth-conditions for sentences *via* appeal to an indispensable notion of reference for some of their constituent terms.

Note that this rephrasing of No. 1 does not involve any explicit requirement to the effect that the indispensable reference involved in those sentences' enjoying the truth conditions that they do is reference to things that exist independently of us. Nor, in fact, does Dummett think it necessary to saddle the realist with the further thesis of Independence, to the effect that the things referred to are the way they are quite independently of us. He seeks no 'semantic' analogue of this realist metaphysical claim about the objects. Arguably, however, it is subsumed by the second of Dummett's theses. This is the one that results from the metaphysical thesis of Determinacy of External Reality when it is rephrased as a 'semantical' thesis:

Key Thesis No. 3*: Bivalence
Every declarative sentence is determinately true or false, independently of our means of coming to know whether it is true, or false.

Naturally, we delimit the range of quantification over declarative sentences so as to exclude vague sentences, and sentences whose failure to acquire a truth-value is due to failure of certain of their referential presuppositions.

It is usually also thought that we have to rule out those paradoxical sentences whose construction is possible only in a semantically closed language.

Indeed, there is a criterion for showing that these paradoxical sentences are not strictly 'declarative'. Thus they can be left in the language (if it is semantically closed), and would demonstrably fall outside the intended scope of our statement of the principle of Bivalence.[31]

As remarked earlier, Bivalence may be thought of as subsuming Independence, although this could be controversial for some. Perhaps Bivalence could be true without 'the way things are' being independent of us. Note, however, that Bivalence makes no mention of how the world helps to determine the truth-value of a sentence. Whether or not the world (in the form of an external, independent and/or determinate reality) does so enter would presumably depend on the form of the semantical theory that one eventually adopts for one's language. Dummett can afford to state what, in his view, realism amounts to from the point of view of a philosopher of language, without having to saddle the realist with that extra conception of how the Central Platitude is to be sustained.

Wright, however, appeals to the workings of the Central Platitude to make out a 'more basic kind of realism' which can be characterized even for statements whose truth-values are decidable, and therefore not knowledge-transcendent.[32]   For these statements, Knowledge-Transcendence cannot capture the idea involved in this 'more basic kind of realism'. But we can

---

[31] This is a long and rather tangential story. The proof-theoretic criterion for paradoxicality was first put forward in 'Proof and Paradox', *Dialectica*, 36, 1982, pp. 265–96, and is developed further in 'On Paradox without Self-Reference', *Analysis*, 55, 1995, pp. 199–207. If one does opt for a semantically closed language, relying on the proposed test for paradoxicality to distinguish between those sentences that aim for the truth and those that make one go round in circles (or in spirals!), then one has to be prepared to deal with troublesome quirks like the following: could the Principle of Bivalence be the sole exception to itself? This will be left to the reader to work out.

[32] This more basic kind of realism consists in

> a sort of *mechanical* view of [the Central Platitude]. Truth-values are, so to speak, ground out on the interface between language and reality. What thought a particular sentence would express in a particular context depends only on the semantics of the language and germane features of the context. Whether that thought is true depends only on which thought it is and germane features of the world. *At neither point does human judgment or response come into the picture.* ...Thus, of any particular statement of sufficiently definite sense, it is determinate whether it expresses a truth in any particular context, irrespective of any judgment we may make about the matter. A basic realist thought is that wherever there is truth, it is, in this way, *investigation-independent.*

('Realism, Antirealism, Irrealism, Quasi-Realism', at p. 28; my first emphasis.)

comfortably reckon that the principle of Independence covers what he is after with his mechanical view of the operation of the Central Platitude.

In summary, then, our realist principles so far include the following. Asterisks indicate those theses that could be acceptable to an anti-realist upon anti-realist construal of the terms involved. Not every asterisked thesis has to be maintained by the anti-realist, though; a case in point is the thesis of Referentialism.

1.   Externalism/Referentialism*
2.   Independence*
3.   Determinacy of External Reality/Bivalence
4(a). Knowledge-Transcendence
4(b). Radical Error
5.   Discovery*
6.   Ultimate Non-Affordability*
7.   Epistemic Accessibility*
8.   Inter-Subjectivity*
9.   Communicability*
10.   K(M)=K(TC)*
11.   TM is TC*
[12. Progress*]
13.   Archimedeanism

It is fair to say that each of these theses has been advanced by at least one avowed realist in the past. But it does not follow that every such thesis is distinctive of realism. Only a few of them, as we see from the presence of so many asterisks, have that status. These are Determinacy of External Reality/Bivalence; Knowledge-Transcendence; Radical Error; and Archimedeanism.

Archimedeanism, however, may not be as essential to realism as are the three other 'distinctively realist' theses on the foregoing list. There is the prima-facie possibility of being an Archimedean moderate anti-realist. This character would be unmoved by the independent arguments against Archimedeanism, but not be willing to maintain that the world, from the imagined Archimedean vantage point, has to be determinate. Behind Archimedeanism one has more of a longing for objectivity, not determinacy. The idea seems to be that:

> if there are any propositions ϕ on which there can be epistemi-
> cally disciplined, intersubjective agreement among any suitable
> subjects, should they be placed at different points of view V_1, V_2:

$\exists \phi \; \exists V_1 \exists V_2 (V_1 \neq V_2 \wedge$

$\forall S_1 \forall S_2 (\text{Can-see-true}(S_1, V_1, \phi) \wedge \text{Can-see-true}(S_2, V_2, \phi)))$

(or $\exists \phi \; \text{ISA}(\phi)$, for short—where the acronym is for 'intersubjective agreement')

then there there should be some privileged point of view V from which any subject S, appropriately equipped, should, for any such ϕ, be able to be apprised of the fact that ϕ:

$\exists V \; \forall \phi \; [\; \text{ISA}(\phi) \rightarrow \forall S \; \text{Can-see-true}(S, V, \phi) \;]$

Archimedeanism, on this diagnosis, is no more than alleged objectivity-via-a-quantifier-switch. And the longing for objectivity to which it gives expression may be met by employing an appropriately substantial notion of truth (involving intersubjectively appraisable truth-makers etc.) without yet incurring commitment to either Evidence-Transcendence or Bivalence. Thus rejecting (or refusing to accept) Archimedeanism is not quite the same as refusing to accept Bivalence. The view from many a lofty peak, after all, is often misty. It follows that Putnam's internal realist is not to be confused with (or too readily identified with) the Dummettian anti-realist. This cautionary remark holds even if it turns out, on closer reflection, that the most attractive position involves accepting neither Archimedeanism nor Bivalence. For these two refusals will be, to some extent at least, independently motivated.

There are four 'global' remarks to make about the list of key theses above. These remarks are ventured without regard for Dummett's emended ways of expressing at least two of them as theses peculiar to the philosophy of language.

First, there is the question of logical relationships among the theses. There are, arguably, severe tensions among some of them. This leads, indeed, to the instability that the anti-realist(s) diagnose in the realist's position. Since the 'theses of realism' have been garnered from different sources, such tensions may be thought unavoidable. It may be thought that it is too much to expect any one realist to hold all of these theses. Nevertheless, there are some philosophers who would, over the course of time, allow each of the above commitments to be educed *seriatim*, and only subsequently be apprised of the internal tensions (if not outright inconsistencies) that are generated. Apart from possible inconsistencies, there is the question of entailments among some of the theses. Some of the key theses may be entailed by conjunctions of others. They need not all be logically independent.

Secondly, there is the observation that some of the theses appear to be so obvious that one could not imagine any philosopher, of whatever reasonably sane metaphysical or epistemological persuasion, wishing to deny them. If so, then well and good. It is not being claimed that every thesis is exclusive to realism. Realism may hold some common ground with various anti-realisms and irrealisms. The interest is in locating just where the differences are, and what these crucially amount to.

Thirdly, our theses above involve modalities, and modal discourse itself is fraught with realist versus anti-realist concerns in its interpretation. This gives rise to the following reflective worry.

Fourthly, we need to ask whether there is any difference between these theses of realism on a realist interpretation as opposed to the 'same' theses on a non-realist interpretation. The problem is to find some ground that is neutral within the realism debate, from which to apprehend the characteristic theses of realism to which one might wish to commit oneself (thereby avowing one's realism) or oppose oneself (thereby avowing one's non-realism). It is important that the same propositional contents be involved in order for those respective commitments to represent a genuine clash of philosophical opinion. Can one, therefore, interpret the theses above from a neutral position, as though one is as yet uncommitted within the realism debate? Better: as though one is, in some pristine way, unapprised of, and therefore essentially unaffected by—the realism debate? It is sensitivity to this demand that motivates Dummett's insistence that the key realist theses that are the subject of dispute should be formulated within the resources of the philosophy of language. Moreover, the theoretical framework involved (in the theory of meaning) should involve notions and principles that, even if controversial, at least carry the same sense for the disputants. Thus a behaviouristically based theory of meaning offers a common ground for discussion on which both realist and anti-realist can make themselves mutually understood. By keeping within the realm of the grossly observable we make it as likely as possible that realist and anti-realist can construe themselves as talking about the same things, in much the same terms. The trouble, however, is that semantical theory quickly ascends from its evidential base, both in the abstractness and generality of the key notions employed (reference, meaning, truth, understanding,...) and in the tenuous nature of the evidential support it marshals for its main principles. The latter feature is less worrisome than the former. After all, all theorizing of reasonably wide explanatory scope is tenuous to a certain degree, whatever the unproblematic nature of the evidence it seeks to account for. More to the point of our present concerns is the theoretical character of such notions as 'reference', 'truth', 'meaning', 'understanding', etc.

Any student of Tarski, Quine, Davidson, Grice and Dummett will be acutely aware of the prevalence and centrality of both intentional and semantic vocabulary in even the 'lowest levels' of our theorizing about the workings of language as an instrument of communication and as a means to represent the world. It is therefore vitally important that we not be lured into an irrealism about intentional and semantic discourse, if we wish to find, in the philosophy of language, a retreat from that metaphysical Babel that threatens to ruin the diagnostic function of certain of our key theses. The alternative is to be irrealist about intentional and semantic discourse and therefore, ultimately, an irrealist about the very terms in which the debate between realism and irrealism is to be conducted. To some, this might seem a stable, even welcome, outcome of the debate. To others, such as myself, it would represent a disastrous trivialization of all our philosophical endeavours. A key initial concern, then, has to be: can we avoid commitment to an irrealist view of semantic and intentional discourse?

There are at least two ways we can avoid such commitment. The first is to attempt to reject it out of hand; the second is to avoid it, by justifying a polite 'Yes, perhaps, but no, thanks.' The first way seeks to show that irrealism concerning our discourse about meanings and minds is incoherent. We shall call this the incoherence strategy. The second way—which we shall call the preference strategy—seeks only to fashion a better, more attractive way of regarding that discourse, than claiming that its subject matter is illusory or that the role of its apparent assertions is not to state facts of the appropriate kind. Irrealism, on this account, succumbs to an alternative, preferred view.

The incoherence strategy has been pursued by Boghossian.[33] We shall see that it does not succeed in the form in which Boghossian develops it; but one cannot rule out the possibility that a different *reductio* might succeed. We present in the next chapter detailed reasons why Boghossian's transcendental assault on irrealism about content ascription is not successful. The preference strategy is therefore to be preferred, in order that we may attain a substantial (albeit anti-realistically acceptable) theoretical account of meanings and minds. The account will ensure the substantial intelligibility of a theory of meaning, within which we shall then attempt to follow Dum-

---

[33] *Cf.* 'The Status of Content', *Philosophical Review* 99, 1990, pp. 157–84; henceforth, *SOC.*

mett, by formulating the cruces of realism in as neutral a fashion as possible. In developing our preferred account, we must, of course, counter Kripkean scepticism about meaning, which Kripke developed in his reflections on rule-following; and this we shall do below. Although Kripke's 'sceptical solution' appears to be an anti-realist one, it is really an irrealist one, which threatens (as already explained) to block our strategy in developing the debate and reaching an intelligible, well-argued conclusion.

2.4   Superassertibility

Wright thinks one can 'inflate' the deflationist notion of truth, and that the resulting 'inflated' notion, which he calls superassertibility, is not yet what is required for realism. One can agree, in so far as one concedes that superassertibility (if we can make sense of it) is a substantial notion of truth, but not yet a realist one. But can we, as anti-realists, make sense of superassertibility? Or is the earlier and simpler notion of warranted assertibility (with an appropriate account of warrant) the best that the non-realist substantialist can do?

A statement is superassertible just in case, according to Wright, we can understand reaching a point at which we are justified in asserting it, and would continue to be justified in so doing no matter how much more relevant evidence we might garner in the future.[34] This feature of eventual stability enables one, Wright thinks, to distinguish superassertibility from a Peircean notion of ideal assertibility in the limit:

> Rather than ask whether a statement would be justified at the limit of ideal empirical investigation, or under ideal empirical circumstances, whatever they are, we can ask whether an ordinary carefully controlled investigation, in advance of attaining any mythical limit, justifies the statement, and whether, once justified, that statement continues to be so no matter how much further information is accumulated ... A statement is superassertible, then, if and only if it is, or can be, warranted and some

---

[34] Compare the notion of a sentence's being 'stably true' in some theorists' treatment of the paradoxes that arise in a semantically closed language. Successive evaluations after the initial one make the truth-value of such a statement flip back and forth between truth and falsity, until eventually it settles down to the value True. Thereafter, no further evaluations affect that determination. Cf. H.Herzberger, 'Notes on Naive Semantics', *Journal of Philosophical Logic*, 11, 1982, pp. 61–102.

warrant for it would survive arbitrarily extensive increments to or other forms of improvement of our information.[35]

The superassertible, then, is the 'eventually monotonic'. Wright goes on to say

> This notion may be unclear in various respects, but they will be respects in which the relevant notion of warranted assertibility was already unclear.

Not so, however. There is an important respect in which warranted assertibility differs from the notion of superassertibility that is supposed, helpfully but harmlessly (for the anti-realist), to idealize it.

An assertion is warrantedly assertible just in case there is a warrant for its assertion. A warrant is a construction that can be recognized as such by a competent speaker of the language. In the presence of any warrant Π for ϕ, the speaker will know that ϕ is warrantedly assertible. But there is no analogue of this for superassertibility. There is no such thing as a 'super-warrant' for the assertion of ϕ, nor such a thing as a warrant for the 'superassertion' of ϕ. Indeed, if Wright is correct, and superassertibility is an appropriately beefier, but still anti-realistically acceptable surrogate for an otherwise realist notion of truth (without consummating a slide to realism), then superassertibility is what our assertions aim for. Our warrants, therefore, must recognizably give us a bead on the superassertibility of the sentences concerned. So our warrants for assertion have, all along (according to Wright's overly helpful proposal) been warrants for superassertion. But what can be so super about any warrant for erstwhile assertion that it somehow becomes a warrant for superassertion? The superness is what eludes one. There appears to be no chance for the allegedly discernible difference (between 'mere' warranted assertibility, and superassertibility) to manifest itself in the assertoric and argumentative behaviour of speakers of the language.

In the realm of defeasible discourse, arguments almost always take the form of one-upping or trumping the opposition's warrant. One's warrants may be in order with respect to a limited basis of evidence, and not otherwise deficient (fallacious) in their internal constitution. But they may be trumped with likewise non-deficient warrants that are based on more inclusive evidence. Sentences' fortunes vacillate. Any sentence subject to the potential

---

[35] *T&O*, at pp. 47–8.

vicissitudes involved in 'taking more evidence into account' is not, thereby, to be held as aimed (when asserted) at anything less than substantial truth. (Only remember: the substantiality of a notion of truth is no guarantee of its bivalence.) It is our very preparedness to revise our judgements in respect of a sentence that shows what we are aiming for when we assert it, and that what we are aiming for is of value, and that we are concerned, in asserting the sentence, to be 'telling it like it is'. It is our preparedness so to revise (according to communal norms) and no more.

It is in this respect that defeasible discourse (which is to say: empirical discourse generally) differs so markedly from logical and mathematical discourse. In logic and mathematics, truth is eternal.[36] Warrants are conclusive. The warranting relation is monotonic on its first term, which is the set of evidential premisses for the conclusion that is its second term. In logic and mathematics, if any state of information[37] I warrants the assertion of ϕ, then any expansion I^* of I warrants the assertion of ϕ. That much is known *a priori*. Therefore, any warrant for a mathematical statement ϕ is good enough. It secures the truth of ϕ. We have taken aim at the truth, and hit it.

In defeasible discourse, however, quite a different thing is known *a priori*. It is known that any warrant is only as good as the strictly underdetermining evidence that it marshals, and can be overturned by future warrants based on extensions or refinements of that evidence. We continually take aim at the truth, but it is a more elusive target. All the problems that the Dummettian anti-realist had with manifestability of grasp of realist truth-conditions will resurface now as worries about the manifestability of grasp of superassertibility-conditions. For there is no relation 'S is able to recognize Π as a warrant for the superassertibility of ϕ' on which to base an anti-realistically acceptable epistemology of linguistic understanding. By contrast, 'S is able to recognize Π as a warrant for the assertibility of ϕ' can render its yeoman service.

In Chapter 12 we shall be suggesting that a more appropriate central semantic concept for defeasible empirical discourse would be that of constructive falsifiability. It is our suspicion that many of the problems facing anti-realists in the area of empirical discourse stem from the fact that they are seeking, inappropriately, some soft empirical analogue of proof-based as-

---

[36] Hence the subtitle of *AR&L: Truth as Eternal*.

[37] In mathematics, a state of information may be thought of as a consistent set of axioms and rules.

sertability in mathematics. But what we have in the empirical case (if we have anything at all) is refutation-based deniability. Instead of working with epistemically diluted grounds for empirical assertion, we should work with epistemically undiluted grounds for empirical denial. This is not the place, however, to develop this idea in detail. More groundwork has to be covered before we can do that. At this stage we shall simply content ourselves with registering the point that, even if the criticisms of superassertability advanced above failed to convince a fellow anti-realist, there would still be value in exploring a radical alternative to the empirical assertabilism, super or otherwise, which seems to hold many anti-realists in its thrall. There may be, at some future date, more effective criticism than ours of the notion of superassertability. In that event it would be useful to have an alternative notion to explore for empirical discourse. But even if no effective criticism of superassertability were forthcoming—to the effect that the notion is explanatorily inadequate, or counterintuitive, or incoherent, or inherently realist—the very availability of an alternative notion, and a comprehensive semantics based on it, will induce the anti-realist to weigh the merits of the competing proposals very carefully. He may even make a final decision on pragmatic grounds, with an eye to uniformity of explanations, conceptual economy and clarity, logical elegance and so on.

2.5   Semantic anti-realism

Our key theses above provide enough materials for us to locate certain significant figures in the broadly anti-realist and irrealist camps. Dummett, for example, sees semantic realism as consisting, essentially, in the conjunction of Referentialism, Bivalence and $K(M)=K(TC)$.[38] Accordingly, there are different varieties of anti-realism, depending on which of these three principles is not accepted.

The 'mild' anti-realist refuses to accept Referentialism. An example is the Fregean on line-directions. A classical phenomenalist is a further possible example, depending on the details of the translations proposed of material-object statements into sense-data statements. If no constituents of the latter

---

[38] *Cf.* Dummett, 'Realism', essay 11 in *The Seas of Language*, Oxford University Press, 1993, pp. 230–76. One of our major tasks in ch. 6 will be to examine whether Dummett is right to focus thus on Bivalence, without any explicit mention of the potential recognition-transcendence of truth-values as constitutive of realism. For one can question whether Bivalence implies the possibility of recognition-transcendence.

'save the references' to material objects in the former, then Referentialism is violated.

The 'moderate' anti-realist refuses to accept Bivalence. Examples are the constructivist or intuitionist in mathematics, and the neutralist about the future.

The 'strong' anti-realist accepts neither Referentialism nor Bivalence. An example would be the phenomenalist who so translated material-object statements that the translations did not 'save the references' made in the former, and for whom the phenomena were such that one had no justification for maintaining, of the phenomenalistic translation of ϕ and the phenomenalistic translation of $\neg\phi$, that exactly one of these would be true.

The 'radical' anti-realist refuses to accept $K(M)=K(TC)$. An example is the later Wittgenstein on ascriptions of inner sensations.[39]

Dummett focuses on those three principles, then, as individually necessary and jointly sufficient for semantic realism. In characterizing the moderate anti-realist, however, merely as someone who refuses to accept one of these principles—Bivalence—he is not thereby offering his reader any clear insight into the deeper grounds for such refusal. These grounds can be spelled out, however, and have indeed been indicated by Dummett in other writings.[40] Chapter 1 of *AR&L* sought to lay these out clearly, and to place appropriate emphasis on the role played in Dummett's anti-realism by the notion of compositionality and by the *manifestation requirement*: that manifestation of grasp of meaning should be by the public exercise of certain recognitional capacities. Chapter 7 of the present work seeks to make the tension between the manifestation requirement and bivalence painstakingly clear.

The *molecularist thesis* is that we grasp determinate sentence meanings, even when the sentences are theoretical ones. Semantic anti-realism enjoins a molecular, as opposed to an holistic, theory of meaning. The anti-realist believes in determinate sentential contents. He adopts a compositional approach. One familiar ground for this comes from theoretical linguistics, which rightly stresses our recursive, generative or creative capacity to understand new sentences as we encounter them. Another ground is that the opposing holistic view simply cannot account for language learning. We do,

---

[39] *Cf*. Dummett, loc. cit., for fuller discussion of these types of anti-realism and their exemplars.

[40] Perhaps most cogently, for the case of mathematical intuitionism, in his essay 'The Philosophical Basis of Intuitionistic Logic', in *Truth and Other Enigmas*, Duckworth, 1978, pp. 215–47.

it would appear, master language fragments progressively as learners, and are able to isolate or excise them for theoretical study later on. Meanings of words remain relatively stable under increase of vocabulary and during developments in our ability to produce and understand more complicated utterances. These considerations point to a compositional approach.

Manifestationism and molecularism are principles in the epistemology of linguistic understanding. They are the principles fuelling the eventual (and derivative) refusal to accept Bivalence. They make anti-realism the natural starting-point for one's reflections on the relationships between (learnable) language, (substantial) thought and (determinable) reality. We shall discuss in some detail below the connections between manifestationism, undecidability and bivalence. Manifestationism and molecularism have as an immediate corollary a wider epistemological principle: that all truths are knowable. We shall defend this principle also, against the most powerful, and thus far unanswered, case against it.

One way to understand how natural and inviting a position semantic anti-realism is would be to consider how Quine and the anti-realist react to an argument on which they both agree. The argument has three premises and a conclusion that they both reject:

> Meaning is given by truth conditions;
> Meaning is determinate;
> Truth is bivalent; *ergo*,
> Grasp of meaning cannot be manifested fully
>   in observable behaviour.

Both Quine and the anti-realist agree on the first premiss. Quine holds that meaning (via translation) is indeterminate, but that truth is bivalent. The anti-realist, by contrast, holds that meaning is determinate, but that truth is not bivalent.

Precision about contents brings with it commitment to normative connections among them: their justification conditions, and their entailments. One of the main aims of semantic anti-realism is to give an accurate picture of such contents as the speaker or thinker can genuinely grasp or entertain in thought, and convey in language. This means that anti-realism has to have some answer to sceptical problems about the objectivity of rule-following. For it is only by conforming to, or keeping faith with, rules for the use of expressions that the speaker can claim to have mastered their meanings. We attempt to provide an answer to these sceptical problems below.

In empirical discourse, and especially statements about other minds, one has to attend closely to the criteria in accordance with which one ventures any informative claim. Here the situation (as already indicated) is very different from mathematics. For in mathematics, once a statement is proved it remains proved. In empirical discourse, however, statements are defeasible. That is, they can be justified on a certain amount of evidence; but may have to be retracted or even denied on the basis of new evidence accreting upon the old. (A modern way of putting this is to say that they are governed by a non-monotonic logic.) There is also the familiar problem from the philosophy of science, that no general claim about natural kinds can ever conclusively be proved. At best, such claims can be conclusively refuted; but no amount of humanly accessible evidence can entail them. The combination of defeasibility with this familiar asymmetry between proof and refutation makes particularly problematic the provision of a satisfactory anti-realist account of meaning for empirical discourse. This problem will be addressed below.

Anti-realism favours reformism rather than quietism. In particular, the anti-realist critique of genuinely graspable meanings can be brought to bear on the meanings of the logical expressions of our language: the connectives and the quantifiers. The observable conditions of their use (especially in mathematics) concern the discovery, construction, presentation and appraisal of proofs. Central features of the use of logical expressions—in particular, their introduction rules—serve to fix their meanings. Other features of use need to be justified as flowing from the central features. In mathematical discourse we can justify the elimination rules, because these are in harmony with the introduction rules. In the case of empirical discourse, as we shall presently see, it is the elimination rules that serve to fix their meanings. That it is nevertheless the same meanings with which we are concerned in each kind of discourse is secured by the fact that the principle of harmony holds for the introduction/elimination rule pairs. In empirical discourse it would be the introduction rules that were so justified.

On this model of meanings and how one comes to grasp them, there does not appear to be any justification for the strictly classical rules of reasoning, especially as they concern negation. There does not appear to be any justification for the law of excluded middle ($A \lor \neg A$) or for the law of double negation elimination (from $\neg\neg A$ infer A) or any of their equivalents. Thus the anti-realist response has been to favour logical reform: crucially, to drop the stricly classical negation rules and opt for intuitionistic logic. Thus intuitionism is the main form of mathematical anti-realism. When anti-realists generalize from the mathematical case, with its conditions of constructive proof, they usually look for appropriate conditions of warranted assertibility. That is, they seek analogues of the mathematical case of assertion backed by proof.

It is a major contention of this work that it is a mistake to seek such an analogue. Rather, one should attend to the main feature of natural scientific theorizing to which Popper drew our attention: our scientific theories can at best be falsified, not verified. Accepting this logical predicament, the anti-realist should seek to fashion a notion of warranted denial, or of constructive falsity, that appropriately complements the notion of warranted assertion, or of constructive truth, already developed for mathematics. We shall see below how this is to be done.

Most writers on anti-realism try to explore its strengths and weaknesses on particular areas of discourse: mathematics; statements about other minds; statements about the past; counterfactual statements; and so on. In each area one looks critically at the observational basis on which one can acquire grasp of meaning. One examines the criterial structure governing how speakers venture, and are taken at, their words. One tries (if necessary) to deflate any overly realist classical conception of how, in response to each such area of discourse, a mind-independent region of reality might inaccessibly yet determinately be. The realist sometimes complains that the anti-realist is guilty of epistemic hubris in taking the human mind to be the measure of reality. The anti-realist responds by charging the realist with semantic hubris in claiming to grasp such propositional contents as could be determinately truth-valued independently of our means of coming to know what those truth-values are.

Dummett construes this supposedly piecemeal nature of the enterprise as involving at most the application of the same 'general line of argument' to different discourses; and he represents himself as giving hostage to reflective (and empirical?) fortune in so doing.[41] This, however, is a little disingenuous on Dummett's part. What is important about the 'line of argument' in question is that it characteristically proceeds from the above foundational principles concerning meaning, principally Manifestationism, Molecularism and Compositionality. These are principles of very wide scope, which are not to be thought of as standing or falling depending on the discourse in question. There is therefore certainly enough depth and substance in the anti-realist's initial thoughts about meaning for it to be quite in order to

---

[41]See his Oxford valedictory lecture 'Realism and Anti-Realism', in *The Seas of Language*.

represent him as putting forward a global anti-realism. In particular, before
he even considers what is peculiar to any one discourse, the anti-realist will
be committed to the tenet that truth is in principle knowable. That is, he
will reject Knowledge-Transcendence across the board. For the principle of
Knowledge-Transcendence is incoherent. Consider what it says: that there
could be some truth ψ such that it be impossible to know that ψ. For the
anti-realist, however, the truth of such ψ would have to consist in there
being some truth-maker Π for ψ that we can recognize as such. Being able
so to recognize Π as a truth-maker for ψ, we would therefore know that
ψ. But precisely this knowledge is supposed to be beyond our reach!—a
contradiction. In every discourse the notion of truth will be epistemically
constrained. It has to be thus constrained, from the anti-realist's point of
view, in order to be able to play the role of that central concept T whose
distribution across sentence components is what allows a recursive theory of
T-conditions of sentences to be a theory not just, as for Davidson, of the
meanings of those sentences, but of graspable meanings of those sentences.
Whether it will then follow that, for the discourse in question, Bivalence will
be acceptable, will be the remaining hostage to reflective (and empirical?)
fortune.

2.6   A crescendo of concerns

Now that we have all the Platitudes and Key Theses before us, it is time to
consider how orderly one can make one's questions as to where the philosophical chips fall. This section presents a crescendo of concerns, each one
leading us, potentially, further down the primrose path to full-blown realism.
But this whole volume provides a sustained argument in favour of staying
on the straight and narrow, and finding a stopping-place in between the two
extremes.

Imagine oneself confronted with some discourse D, trying to decide what
the appropriate '-ism' is for D. Here we are indulging the 'piecemeal' theorist: the one who believes that one can have a little realism here, a little
anti-realism there, with details depending on the discourse in question. We
start from a philosophically neutral position, informed only by the core of
truths about truth.

It seems that the first and major question to pose, regarding the discourse
D, is the one which settles whether an irrealist view is appropriate for D:[42]

---

[42]In the next chapter we consider irrealism in greater depth, and semantic irrealism in

(1) are the declarative sentences of D to be understood as used
to make genuine assertions, or do those 'assertions' play some
other role within D—not a fact-stating role, but, perhaps, an
expressivist or projectivist one?

Wright's minimalist holds that merely being possessed of the appropriate
syntactic potentialities—grammatical embeddings—incurs commitment to
the genuineness of the assertions involved. One should, however, be able
in principle to keep this moot, and allow for the syntactic potentialities to
be displayed while yet the role of 'assertions' be other than fact-stating.
Suppose, though, that one is satisfied that the declarative sentences of D
are indeed used to make genuine assertions. So far, then, one's commitment
is only to there being some notion of truth satisfying the core of truths about
truth.

The next question should be:

(2) is the notion of truth involved in giving an account of these
assertions an epistemically substantial one?

This is where at least two of Wright's marks of non-minimal truth would fit
in. The first of these marks is

Convergence of Opinion
The members of a certain class of statements are candidates for
truth only if each of them will, under suitable circumstances,
command a convergence of opinion on its truth, or falsity.[43]

An evidence-transcendent notion of truth would still fail this test. Convergence fails if there are empirically equivalent but mutually conflicting theories. But convergence can hold even if our theoretical claims as to what is
true are undetermined by the evidence. Convergence of Opinion marks out a
'middle ground' for truth. It ensures that truth is more than minimal—that
there is some substance to the notion, by virtue of some assertoric discipline.
But convergence also ensures that truth is not too transcendent—that it can
be kept constrained by that assertoric discipline, and not be let off the epistemic leash. In this regard, Convergence of Opinion is not well-suited as a
mark of realist truth, even though Wright himself has not drawn attention
to this fact. A highly realist notion of truth at one end of the spectrum,

particular.

[43]loc. cit., p. 71.

just like a non-substantial notion of truth at the other end of the spectrum, will not pass the test of Convergence of Opinion. Too much Knowledge-Transcendence will ensure potential and critical divergences of opinion, not general convergence. And too little assertoric discipline likewise.

There is no problem, from an anti-realist's point of view, in conceding that theories may be underdetermined by the evidence. One can believe in underdetermination of theory by evidence without being committed to the existence of empirically equivalent but mutually conflicting theories. (To concede the existence of such theories would be to concede that truth is potentially evidence-transcendent, provided that, unlike the instrumentalist, or van Fraassen's constructive empiricist, we regard theoretical sentences as candidates for truth and falsity.) Thus success on Convergence, though it shows that truth is more substantial, hardly provides much motive for regarding the notion of truth involved as a realist one. Indeed, that very success on Convergence holds us back from regarding the notion of truth involved as a realist one.

The quoted formulation of the test of Convergence of Opinion given above involved the word 'command': we have to establish whether each statement of the disputed class commands a convergence of opinion on its truth, or falsity. In *T&O*, Wright naturally generalizes this idea and proposes a new test, which, one supposes, would simply take the place of the test of Convergence of Opinion. The new test is that of Cognitive Command.

> *Cognitive Command*
> It is *a priori* that disagreements, when not attributable to vagueness, are ultimately explicable in terms of cognitive shortcomings; specifically, some material ignorance, material error, or prejudicial assessment.[44]

Cognitive Command is, essentially, an ingredient in the *substantiality* of truth, which Wright has elsewhere conceded to be a licit part of the moderate anti-realist's conception of truth. All our earlier remarks about Convergence of Opinion apply with equal force to Cognitive Command. Cognitive Command is at odds with Knowledge-Transcendence. But subscribing to the underdetermination of theory by evidence (without commitment to the existence of empirically equivalent but mutually conflicting theories) is compatible with Cognitive Command.

The third of Wright's marks of non-minimal truth is

---

[44]loc. cit., p. 72.

Explanation of True Belief, and Wide Cosmological Role
... where the best account we can give of the epistemology of
statements of a certain kind represents the beliefs which they enable us to express as the products of interaction with the states
they describe—or anyway essentially adverts, one way or another, to those states of affairs in explaining why we hold those
beliefs—our conception of what it is for those statements to be
true crucially exceeds the minimal conception.[45]

Briefly: the best explanation of our true beliefs requires appeal to the truths
in question. Also,

the states of affairs which we regard our judgments as reflecting
enjoy a *width of cosmological role*, as it were, sufficient to force
us to regard their role as truth-conferrers in more than minimal
terms. They must therefore participate in other kinds of explanation besides those in which germane beliefs of ours are the
explananda.[46]

Again, this can quite properly be part of the anti-realist's conception of
truth. Failure of this constraint is a mark of irrealism rather than of anti-
realism! Conformity with the constraint is a mark of the substantiality of
truth, and does not imply that the notion of truth involved will be a realist
one.

Wright's marks concern the objectivity of the discourse. They are invoked in order to establish whether the notion of truth is more than the
minimal, deflationary one. The notion of truth might possess these marks,
and yet be neither knowledge-transcendent, nor bivalent. Note, however,
that satisfying Convergence makes it rather unlikely that the notion of truth
could ever turn out to be a realist one. Note further that the global anti-
realist, unlike the piecemeal theorist, denies Knowledge-Transcendence at
the very outset as incoherent.

In asking (2), and putting truth to these three of Wright's tests, we
want to know whether, behind the assertions, can be pedigrees that justify
them; whether truth consists in the existence of such pedigrees, or truth-
makers; whether there can be intelligible debate, among participants in the

---

[45]'Realism: The Contemporary Debate—W(h)ither Now?', at p. 73. Remember that
for Wright the 'minimal' conception is a slightly inflated version of deflationism; but in
this context any cavil based on this observation would be a trifle captious.

[46]loc. cit., p. 76.

discourse, over the quality and constitution of such pedigrees. We want to know whether intersubjectively available evidence or proof are notions with relevant application here, to the assertions in question. If the answers are affirmative, we have left minimal anti-realism behind, and we have entered the territory of possible substantial anti-realisms.

The next question (raised by the M-realist) will be:

> (3) Is the notion of truth such that a sentence's truth-conditions might obtain independently of our means of coming to know whether they obtain?

The M-realist holds that one can have Knowledge-Transcendence without Bivalence. Our view is that the M-realist who receives a positive reply to this question cannot (from the point of view of the moderate anti-realist) be distinguished from the full-blown realist. But for those who find the argument for this view unconvincing, the last question has been given its own discrete status within the crescendo of realist concerns. If the argument is wrong, then at least this will be the appropriate point at which to press the question of knowledge-transcendence.

The next two questions (raised by the Dummettian) will be:

> (4) Do we, in our account of how sentences acquire such truth, make indispensable appeal to the notion of reference of terms within the sentence?

> (5) Is one's knowledge of a sentence's meaning simply knowledge of its truth-conditions?

If we answer 'yes' to both these questions, we are in the territory of moderate anti-realism, which I regard as optimal. Dummett's further question, the high point of our crescendo, is:

> (6) Is the notion of truth bivalent?

With an affirmative answer to this final question, we would have reached full-blown realism. The alternatives that are negotiable are as follows:[47]

> (1) Assertoric?
>   No ⇒ irrealism;
>   Yes

---

[47] In this diagram, '⇒' mean 'implies', and '↓' means 'raises the next question'.

$\downarrow$

(2) Substantial?

    No $\Rightarrow$ minimalism

    Yes

    $\downarrow$

    (3) Knowledge-transcendent?

        No $\Rightarrow$ anti-realism *or* Gödelian optimism[48]

        Yes $\Rightarrow$ M-realism

        $\downarrow$

        (4) Referentialist? (5) K(M)=K(TC)?

            No to either $\Rightarrow$ possibly mild anti-realism

            Yes to both

            $\downarrow$

            (6) Bivalent?

                No $\Rightarrow$ moderate anti-realism

                Yes $\Rightarrow$ full-blown realism

2.7   Remarks on natural deduction

The logically sophisticated reader may omit this section entirely. It is intended to explain the formatting of natural deductions to the reader who might not be fully acquainted with them. For a fuller account, the reader is referred to my book *Natural Logic*.[49] A great deal that is useful, however, can be explained in just a few pages, so it is worth making a few of the most important points here, in order that this work might be as self-contained as possible.

---

[48]See Ch. 6.

[49]Edinburgh University Press, 1978; second, revised edition 1990. The aim of this book was to make the natural deduction systems of the proof-theorists Gentzen and Prawitz pedagogically accessible, and to show how all the major metalogical results (soundness, completeness, etc.) could be very elegantly proved with respect to systems of natural deduction. The tradition of natural deduction had (regrettably) been developed in a wholly self-contained way, without much concern for the link between proof theory and model theory. The aim of the book was to marry model theory to the best kind of proof theory.

2.7.1   Arguments and natural deductions

We take seriously the value of setting out arguments rigorously in the style of natural deduction. We shall be formalizing below some important passages of philosophical argumentation that call for close appraisal.

When an argument is set out in prose, there is no requirement that its premisses be stated first or that its conclusion be stated last. Often an author states first what is to be proved and then proceeds to provide the supporting justification. The ultimate premisses on which the conclusion of the argument depends may well be revealed last.

This rhetorical licence in the order of presentation of an argument is disallowed by logical regimentation. In any proof system there is a unique preferred format for the laying out of arguments. In the system of natural deduction, this format has a 'tree structure'. The tree structure may be made more or less explicit, according to the format used.

On the Gentzen–Prawitz approach, the chosen format makes this tree structure maximally explicit. Arguments are actually regimented as tree-like arrays of sentence occurrences. This may strike some readers as somewhat unusual if all they have ever encountered are the 'linear' arrangements of arguments as numbered lines incorporating references to earlier lines. In the Gentzen–Prawitz format, however, it is not necessary to number the lines or to resort to such back-reference when applying rules of inference. Instead, all is made clear within the tree-like array itself. The conclusion of the argument is at the root; and the premisses are at the 'tips of branches'. Steps of inference are 'branchings' within the tree. The direction of argument is represented as *downwards* on the page, *from* the premisses at the top, *to* the conclusion at the bottom:

Premisses
$\searrow \swarrow$
Conclusion

2.7.2   Accumulating arguments

We shall use the upper-case Greek letters Π, Σ, Θ, Ξ to refer to natural deductions. We shall use the letters A, B, C, D, ... and lower-case Greek letters ϕ, ψ, ... to refer to sentences. We shall in addition use X, Y, Z to denote sets of premisses of arguments; and sometimes also the upper-case Greek letters Δ, Γ. We need a convenient notation for speaking of a set of premisses of a natural deduction within which we wish to focus our attention on a particular premiss. Let us use the notation 'X, C' for this. C will be the premiss on which we wish to focus attention; while X will be the set consisting of all the other premisses of the deduction.

Suppose that an argument Π for the conclusion D has C as one of its premisses:

$$\underbrace{X\ ,\ C}$$
$$\Pi$$
$$D$$

One might offer further justification for C, in the form of yet another argument Σ, say, with premisses Y and conclusion C:

$$Y \text{—new premisses}$$
$$\Sigma \text{—new argument for } C$$
$$\underbrace{X\ ,\ C}$$
$$\Pi \text{—old argument}$$
$$D$$

The result, overall, is an argument for D from X, Y.

The opportunity thus to 'tack on' a new argument to one of the premisses of an old argument is crucial. It enables one to dig ever more deeply into the argumentative foundations of any discipline, unearthing the bedrock of sentential assumptions on which its assertions ultimately rest. One could speak of a process of 'accumulating' deductions, as exhibited by the scheme just given. C would be a 'point of accumulation'.

In mathematics, one often proceeds as follows. First, one proves a lemma C from axioms Y. Call this first proof Σ. Secondly, one proves a theorem D by appeal to the lemma C already proved, along with other premisses X. Call this second proof Π. Note that C is a premiss of Π. So here the lemma C is featuring exactly as C does in the schema above.

A crucial tenet is that the mathematical theorem D would depend, ultimately, only on the mathematical axioms Y used in the first proof Σ, and (via the lemma C) on the mathematical axioms X used in the second proof Π. This tenet is known as the *transitivity of deduction*; and on it all deductive progress in mathematics depends. Transitivity is vital both for unearthing new axioms (developing deeper foundations) and for settling difficult conjectures (building taller edifices). In the tree-format for natural deduction, transitivity is made vivid: joining the root of one tree to the tip of a branch of a second tree produces another tree.

2.7.3   Rules of inference

Primitive steps of argument

Arguments consist of *discrete* steps. Given any sentence within an argument, one can legitimately ask 'On what other sentences does this one *immediately depend*?'; and the answer should be forthcoming upon inspection of the argument.

A step that counts as primitive within an argument will be indicated by means of a horizontal inference stroke. Immediately above the stroke will be the premisses of the step; immediately (and centred) below it will be the conclusion of the step. Thus we shall render the step

> A , B; *therefore,* C

as

$$\frac{A \qquad B}{C}$$

Note that in general a step of inference could have any (finite) number of premisses. It is unusual, however, to have more than three premisses for any step in arguments that we shall encounter.

Depending on the level of logical analysis involved or insisted upon, a step that counts as primitive within an argument may eventually have to be 'filled out' in more detail. In an earlier context, a step R might be treated as primitive:

$$\frac{G \qquad H}{K} R$$

simply because no further detailed justification is offered for it by the author of the argument. But R might later be *derived*, by supplying more inferential detail:

$$\underbrace{G \qquad H}$$
$\qquad$ Π more steps filled in to justify the transition R
$\qquad$ K

Ideal rules of inference

The primitive steps (or rules of inference) of an argument that cannot be 'filled out' any further are, ideally, of two kinds. First, there are the so-called *logical* rules of inference, such as

$$\frac{A \qquad B}{A \text{ and } B} \qquad\qquad \frac{A \qquad A \text{ only if } B}{B}$$

whose correctness depends on how some salient logical operator (here, the word 'and' or the phrase 'only if') occurs in the immediate premises and/or conclusion of the rule. Secondly, there are rules that express meaning relations, such as

$$\frac{a \text{ is red}}{a \text{ is coloured}}$$

or that express entailments that we insist upon on philosophical grounds, such as

$$\frac{a \text{ knows that } P}{\text{it is true that } P} \qquad\qquad \frac{a \text{ knows that } P}{a \text{ believes that } P}$$

There are also rules that express requirements we would impose on ideally rational thinkers, such as the rule

$$\frac{a \text{ knows that } P \qquad a \text{ knows that } Q}{a \text{ knows that } (P \text{ and } Q)}$$

2.7.4 *Reductio ad absurdum*

One very important kind of argument, especially in philosophy, is *reductio ad absurdum*. This is a form of argument that brings out the incoherence, or internal contradictoriness, of a set of premises (and/or the primitive rules used in the argument). We shall denote absurdity by the symbol $\perp$. $\perp$ can be used as the conclusion of a rule to show that its premises are contraries:

$$\frac{a \text{ is red} \quad a \text{ is green}}{\perp} \qquad\qquad \frac{a \text{ knows that } P \quad a \text{ wonders whether } P}{\perp}$$

Reductio ad absurdum is the paradigmatic way of establishing the negation not-P of a proposition P. One assumes P 'for the sake of argument', and derives a contradiction by means of a *'reductio'* argument Ξ, say, whose other assumptions (besides P) form, say, the set X:

$$\underbrace{X\,,\,P}$$
$$\Xi$$
$$\bot$$

Having done that, one may immediately conclude that not-P:

$$X\,,\,\overline{P}^{(i)}$$
$$\Xi$$
$$\frac{\bot}{\text{not-}P}{}^{(i)}$$

The *reductio* is the sub-proof Ξ, with conclusion $\bot$. The undischarged assumptions of Ξ are X, P. After applying the rule of negation introduction, the conclusion not-P depends only on X, and no longer on P. The assumption P, having been made only 'for the sake of argument' within Ξ, has now been discharged.

The discharge notation here involves a stroke over each occurrence of the assumption being discharged, labelled with the same numeral as labels the step that discharges that assumption. This tells us clearly *which* steps discharge *which* assumptions 'made for the sake of argument' within a proof. The undischarged assumptions of a proof will then be those enjoying occurrences at tips of branches without discharge strokes over them. An alternative notation for indicating discharge of assumptions, especially when just stating rules rather than constructing proofs, is to enclose the discharged assumption in square brackets.

2.7.5   Regimenting philosophical arguments

We shall be focusing below on rules of analytic entailment, or rules that constrain certain notions of ideality or competence. These are the logical underpinnings that we shall be anxious to expose in various philosophers' argumentation about deep and complex matters to do with truth, knowledge, meaning, possibility, existence, etc.

When an argument has been rigorously 'regimented' as a partial ordering of steps in accordance with formally precise rules of inference, we speak of having a *proof*. Proofs carry conviction; they establish the deductive transition (from premises to conclusion) with as much certainty as the least certain of the rules used. But the conclusion of a proof remains as uncertain as any of its premisses, or any of its primitive steps of inference—at least, in so far as *that* proof is all that is offered in support of the conclusion.

The discipline imposed by the construction of a natural deduction helps us to attain a deeper understanding of the thrust of the philosophical argumentation concerned. It helps to reveal exactly what one's basic assumptions are, whether these are in sentential form (premisses) or in rule form (primitive transitions taken to be immediately justified by the meanings of the terms involved). Casting arguments into natural deduction form also helps to pinpoint passages of philosophical argumentation where one might have gone awry — where things don't (formally) 'fit together' as they should if the argument were to be ultimately convincing as a properly constructed proof in accordance with acceptable rules.

2.7.6   A plea for tolerance in matters logical

Some philosophers may baulk at the thought of going so far as to analyse a complex philosophical argument by casting it into 'natural deduction' form. But regimentation can provide logical insights into philosophical arguments that one would not otherwise come by.

Still, some might object, *Why go to all that bother?* Why set out arguments in these space-consuming tree structures? Why not just set them out (if you *have* to regiment them!) as do, say, those authors of well-known and widely used introductory logic texts, such as Lemmon, Mates, Fitch, Quine, or Kalish and Montague?

The response to *this* kind of objection is that those alternative systems of so-called 'natural deduction' are simply not as elegant or perspicuous as the system due to Gentzen and Prawitz. The tree-structures briefly described above serve to focus one's eye on the premisses, and make absolutely clear the argumentative transitions involved. They reveal logical relations in a vivid way. As soon as one has a little familiarity with this format for proofs, one will be loath to revert to any other format that one might have employed in the past. What is particularly useful about our preferred format for natural deductions is how one can see so effortlessly what assumptions a conclusion ultimately depends on, simply by casting one's eye up the 'branches' within the proof. *This* is the most important relation that the philosophical logician has to track. No other format for natural deduction is as helpful in this regard as the one we prefer.

Chapter 3

Irrealism

3.1   A survey of various kinds of irrealism

Without attacking any irrealist position or defending it against various objections, we shall briefly survey the variety of irrealisms in the philosophical literature. Then we shall discuss how they might best be understood and classified.

Irrealism in mathematics (more commonly called nominalism or materialism) is the view that there are no such things as numbers and sets, and no genuine mathematical relations among them, such as succession, addition, multiplication (in the case of numbers) or membership (in the case of sets).[1]

An irrealism in ethics (more commonly called expressivism or non-cognitivism) is the view that there are no objective moral facts, no substantial properties of goodness and evil, inhering in either characters or actions. Our ethical judgements would have to be understood as expressing an attitude or a stance, or making a prescription: condoning, commending, praising, or condemning various actions, policies, strategies, character traits, etc.[2]

An irrealism about causation (more commonly called projectivism) is the view that there are no objective causal connections among events, reflected more or less accurately in our ordinary causal discourse. Our causal discourse does not reflect, but rather 'gilds and stains' nature, showing no more than an attitude or habit of mind on our part: that we are prepared to

---

[1] For the best-developed recent account of such a view, see H. Field, *Realism, Mathematics and Modality*, Blackwell, Oxford, 1989.

[2] Cf. J. L. Mackie, *Ethics—Inventing Right and Wrong*, Penguin, Harmondsworth, 1977.

rely on like 'causes' supposedly 'producing' like 'effects'.[3] Closely allied to
this, an irrealism about even common-or-garden dispositional properties will
maintain that physical dispositions are really nothing more than complexes
of categorical properties. An example would be the categorical properties of
clusters of molecules in sugar, that ensure its solubility. (Whether a fundamental physics could make do with only such properties as are themselves
obviously non-dispositional is a question that makes this kind of realism
rather contentious.)

Irrealism about modality and possible worlds (more commonly called
actualism) could have one of two forms. The more radical form holds that
modal 'statements' cannot be construed in any way as to be apt for truth
(or falsity). The declarative sentences involving modal operators therefore
would not be allowed to be making statements at all. The less radical form
of modal irrealism allows that such sentences do make statements, and are
truth-apt, but that there are no such things as possible worlds—alternative
ways the world might be, but which it happens not to be; and there are
no such things as mere possibilia—unactualized possibles—for there are no
other possible worlds, or 'outer domains', in which they might be. Our
modal discourse is at best expressive of strong conventional undertakings
regarding rules for the use of our words, and of sentences that as a result
we feel obliged to assert come what may, once we have reflected on what
appears to be enjoined by those rules. Yet those conventions and rules are
themselves matters of contingent fact.

An irrealism in semantics (of which extensionalism is a very specific variety) is the view that there are no objective or determinate senses, contents
or meanings to be attached to our words and sentences. Discourse that
appears to attribute contents to expressions of our language should be understood as expressive of an undertaking to use those words according to
certain rules, or as a way of acknowledging another speaker as well-enough
versed in those communal patterns to be trusted as a participant in the
discourse in question—as an understander, as a grasper 'of meaning', even
though there be in reality no such things as meanings to be grasped. This
is Kripke's so-called 'sceptical solution' to the problem of rule-following.[4]
This irrealism about semantics is closely allied to irrealism about the contents of propositional attitudes on the part of human agents. The question

---

[3]The *locus classicus* is of course Hume, *A Treatise of Human Nature*, 1739, Book I,
Part III, Section VI.

[4]*Wittgenstein on Rules and Private Language*, Harvard University Press, Cambridge,
1982. Note that Kripke is not an extensionalist in canvassing these views.

of analytic or empirical connection between individual mental content and communal sentential content will not detain us here. Nor will the question of whether (and if so, how) individual mental contents, as realized in the human brain, might, in their occurrent causal succession, match patterns of logical or analytic connection among the contents in question. The foregoing remark provides only a segue into irrealism about the mental quite generally. The irrealist projection in the case of propositional attitudes is caught by Dennett's phrase 'the intentional stance'.[5]

Irrealism about the mental more generally can take two forms, commonly called eliminativism and reductionism.

The first, eliminativism, is the view that there are no such things as mental events, states or processes (be these sensations, percepts, beliefs, desires, inferences, rational reflections, etc.). There are only the physical happenings in the brain. The eliminativist holds that our mental discourse is fundamentally wrong or mistaken. As a theory it would, in a completed science, reveal itself as false. The only true theory to be had will be some neurochemical, neurobiological, quantum-mechanical story about what goes on in our grey matter.[6]

The second irrealism about the mental, reductionism, is the view that the vocabulary of mental description and explanation is definable in physical or behavioural terms, so that one can achieve at least extensional reductions of mental theorizing to purely physical or behavioural theorizing. Whether one availed oneself of the reduction would be a matter of convenience and taste. The reduction would in all likelihood be hopelessly complicated—the usual favourite phrase is 'chaotically disjunctive'—if possible at all. So one would probably stick to the mental theorizing as though it offered an autonomous level of description and explanation, while carrying at the back of one's mind the irrealist (because reductionist) conviction that it was not, in the final analysis, strictly necessary to do so.

To be a realist about the mental, by contrast, one needs to accord more serious weight to the explanatory significance of mental discourse. As a species of modest realism about the mental one may include supervenience accounts such as Davidson's anomalous monism[7] and (the early) Putnam's

---

[5]'Intentional Systems', *Journal of Philosophy*, 68, 1971, pp. 87–106.

[6]The classic statement of this position is in Paul Churchland, 'Eliminative Materialism and the Propositional Attitudes', *Journal of Philosophy*, 78, 1981, pp. 67–90.

[7]'Mental Events', in L. Swanson and J. W. Foster, eds., *Experience and Theory*, University of Massachusetts Press, Amherst, 1970.

functionalism.[8] These accounts combine ontological monism with attribute dualism. They maintain that mental events are token-identical to brain events, and that the physical facts fix the mental facts. But these accounts accord at least some importance or autonomy to mental discourse as explanatory in its own special way. So it is not just the physical that really exists. Even though the mental, according to these modest realisms, depends asymmetrically on a physical basis, the mental is not accorded only a shadowy sort of existence compared with the physical. A full-blown realism about the mental would maintain either that there are inherent and essential defects or omissions in any purely physicalistic account of the mental (the 'qualia freak')[9] or that the mind is a distinct substance from the body, and interacts with it (the Cartesian dualist). Either way, mental theorizing will be held to be indispensable and *sui generis*.

Irrealism about the social is more commonly called methodological individualism.[10] According to this view, it is only a crude and convenient fiction to think about socio-economic and political life in terms of groups (such as caucuses, cabals, committees, organizations, unions, guilds, professions, income groups, classes, castes, cliques, companies, corporations, families, clans, tribes, firms, etc.). All the apparently emergent phenomena at the social level are in principle explicable in terms of interactions among more or less rational individuals with different abilities, beliefs, desires and interests.

Irrealism about secondary qualities such as colours would follow from the claim that there is no categorical or dispositional physical property corresponding to any colour. There may be a dispositional relation rather than a property involved: namely, that of tending to produce a certain mental response in the observer. (Hence the current terminology of 'response-dependent concepts'.)[11] Suppose we hold that to be red is at best such a relational/dispositional property: roughly, that of tending under suitable conditions to appear, to suitably placed and properly functioning observers, to be red. It would follow that colours are only as real as their appearances. So if one were irrealist about the latter then one would be irrealist about the former.

---

[8] 'Psychological Predicates', in W. H. Capitan and D. D. Merrill, eds., *Art, Mind and Religion*, University of Pittsburgh Press, 1967, pp. 37–48.

[9] F. Jackson, 'Epiphenomenal Qualia', *Philosophical Quarterly*, 32, 1982, pp. 127–36.

[10] Cf. J. W. N. Watkins, 'Ideal Types and Historical Explanations', in H. Feigl and M. Brodbeck, eds., *Readings in the Philosophy of Science*, New York, 1953, pp. 723–43.

[11] Originally due to Mark Johnston; for an informative discussion of various subsequent developments of this notion, see *T&O*, pp. 108–11.

An irrealism in physics (more commonly called instrumentalism, or constructive empiricism)[12] is the view that there are no such things as electrons, photons, etc., or any of the unobservable fundamental particles posited by theoretical physics. Talk of such things has to be construed instrumentally, as conducing to reliable predictions about the observable phenomena, without its success in this regard being owed to the actual existence of the recondite entities in question.

That concludes the list of examples of irrealisms.

3.2 Non-factualist irrealism *v.* error-theory

We have seen that these irrealisms come in two varieties. First, non-factualist irrealism invites one to see the supposed reality postulated by the realist vanish before one's eyes. According to the non-factualist, that of which we take ourselves to be speaking, despite our well-meaning convictions to the contrary, is simply not there. And the terms in which we speak of it latch on to no genuine properties that are (or could possibly be) exemplified in the world. '[N]o real properties answer to the central predicates of the region [of discourse] in question.'[13] Our 'assertions' in the discourse in question, then, are not truth-apt. This is the case despite superficial syntactic appearances to the contrary. Non-factualist irrealism about properties, however, could be compatibly combined with an ontological realism towards the would-be bearers of those properties. Thus one could be a realist about actions (as a species of events) but a non-factualist about their moral properties, denying that they really have any. One could even be a realist about personalities or characters (at the intentional level) while, as a non-factualist, demurring over the attribution, to personalities or characters, of moral qualities such as virtues or vices. As another example of non-factualism about properties combined with realism about their would-be bearers, we have the Quinean attitude towards sentence-types and meanings. The Quinean is willing to go beyond sentence tokens to sentence types, the latter being not physical objects or events such as utterances or inscriptions, but rather abstract objects of a certain kind. Nevertheless the Quinean would be most unwilling to regard it as a factual matter that such-and-such a sentence type has a particular meaning, or determinately means that so-and-so. So we see that care is needed with non-factualism. We have to enquire whether it is just

---

[12]Cf. B. C. van Fraassen, *The Scientific Image*, Clarendon Press, Oxford, 1980.

[13]Thus Boghossian, *SOC*.

a denial of the 'reality' or 'robustness' of certain qualities, properties or relations; or whether it goes further, and denies also the reality or existence of those properties' would-be bearers—that is, of the individuals that would enjoy or instantiate them.[14]

Secondly, error-theoretic irrealism accepts the superficial syntactic appearances of our declarative sentences at face value, allows that our primitive assertions aim at the truth, but maintains that these assertions always miss their target. They are false. We can make sense of the way they represent the world as being; it is just that they misrepresent the world. They make an intelligible attempt to tell it like it is, but they get it wrong. They picture the world as being thus-and-so, but the world is not that way at all. The Platitudes of normativity and representation can be milked for all they are worth here. A notion of minimal truth, at least,[15] is in play; but the participants in the discourse systematically err (at least with every one of their primitive assertions).

Wright defines irrealism as the following view about the apparently declarative sentences of the discourse in question:[16]

> the world is [not] furnished to play the part required by the [Central] Platitude in the determination of truth-value; there really are no such states of affairs.

This is really the non-factualist conception, but one which is mute on the crucial distinction that we noted earlier between individuals and properties. Do those states of affairs fail to exist for want of the properties and relations involved in their constitution, or for want of the very individuals themselves? For the irrealist, says Wright,[17]

---

[14]Boghossian, in particular, does not appear to take much care over this distinction.

[15]No one seems to have pointed out the interesting possibility that one might have a semantically realist error-theoretic irrealism about a discourse D, in the sense that:
(i) one allows that the primitive predicates of D express genuine properties;
(ii) one maintains the falsity of all the primitive predications of D, but
(iii) one contends also that their falsity might be evidence transcendent!—as might be the truth-values of other (complex) sentences of D, which are nevertheless determinate.
Someone with the robust good intentions of a Jack Smart, but without the benefits of our modern scientific smarts, might have had the temerity to maintain all of this about witch-discourse at the time of the medieval witch-hunts. The spectre of (error-theoretic) irrealism accompanies us, then, all along the spectrum of more and more substantial kinds of truth, even unto (semantically) realist truth at the far end.

[16]'Realism, Antirealism, Irrealism, Quasi-Realism', *Midwest Studies in Philosophy, Vol. XII: Realism and Antirealism*, 1988, pp. 25–49; at p. 30.

[17]loc. cit., at pp. 29–30.

the range and diversity of our declarative discourse somehow out-
strips the categories of states of affairs that are genuinely exemplified by reality. We apparently talk as if there were moral, or
scientific theoretical, or pure mathematical states of affairs, but
in truth there are not.

Boghossian in turn[18] characterizes irrealism more liberally and disjunctively,
as the view that

> nothing possesses (or, perhaps, could possess) the sorts of prop-
> erty denoted by the characteristic predicates of [the fragment of
> discourse] F (if the predicates of F denote any sort of property
> at all).

This leaves the two avenues of irrealist argument noted above. The non-
factualist maintains that the predicates of F do not denote any sort of property at all; whereas the error-theorist concedes that the predicates of F do
denote real properties, but that 'their extensions (are) uniformly empty'.
Concerning any primitive predication $P(a)$ in F, then, the non-factualist
says that $P(a)$ expresses no kind of fact at all, since the predicate P denotes
no real property, whence the question of the truth or falsity of $P(a)$ cannot
even arise. (This involves what might be called a Strawsonian presupposition view—about properties expressed by predicates, rather than about
individual denotata of singular terms.) The error theorist says, by contrast,
that P expresses a real property, but — lo and behold!—nothing possesses
(or could possess) that property, whence $P(a)$ is false.

Care is needed, however, when we realize that there are two ways in which
all our primitive assertions in a given discourse could be systematically false.
One is that no genuine properties are expressed by the predicates, whence,
on a Russellian view, any primitive predication would be false.[19] But now
the systematic falsity is no reason to classify the view as error-theoretic,
since it is already non-factualist. On this view it is a defect in our primitive predications—namely, the failure of our primitive predicates to express
genuine properties—that is responsible for the subsequent, Russellian conclusion that those primitive predications are false. Thus the primary defect
is one which should incline us to assimilate the irrealist view in question to

---

[18] *SOC*, at p. 509.

[19] On the Strawsonian view mentioned in the previous paragraph, the question of truth
or falsity simply would not arise; so, to the extent that one was erring, it would be an
erring that fell short of saying something false.

non-factualism, rather than hold the view to be distinctly error-theoretic. At best, this kind of irrealism would be both non-factualist and error-theoretic; whence we see that the division of irrealisms into the non-factualist and the error-theoretic is not genuinely dichotomous. It is this kind of irrealism that is in fact espoused by Mackie regarding ethics—making it an unhappy exemplar to cite as the sole illustration of error-theoretic irrealism, when explaining the difference between non-factualist and error-theoretic irrealism.[20] The other source of systematic falsity is that while indeed the primitive predicates express genuine properties, nevertheless no individuals instantiate those properties. This latter view is the purely error-theoretic one; but there is no author who espouses any such view in the literature! One can see why it has no adherents: it would be especially difficult to make out a sense in which any primitive predicate could have a current meaning, in continuing established usage, and yet fail to be satisfied by any individual(s) whatsoever. How would one learn the fragment of language in question? How would one come to grasp a sense for the predicate if one were (as the view maintains) systematically in error in all one's basic judgements involving the predicates in question?

Is 'pure' error-theoretic irrealism for what we earlier called 'the reflective participant' in any discourse a tenable view to start with, before going into the details of the particular discourse concerned? Remember that the error-theorist is at least conceding that the discourse in question involves assertions aimed at the truth. It is just that (so he maintains) none of the primitive assertions can be true, even though they are made by means of predicates that express genuine properties. This broad claim of primitive falsity across the board, however, cannot be allowed to make much headway. It runs aground on the simple consideration, familiar from Wittgenstein and Davidson, that there is no way that we can learn the primitive predicates of a discourse except by exposure to at least some paradigmatic cases where the predications are true. Else, how would we ever form our conception of what it would be for the predicate to hold? This Wittgensteinian point is most telling against the error-theoretic claim in so far as it concerns the basic primitive predicates of the discourse—those predicates that are attuned most directly to observable conditions. Now there is of course still the possibility that a primitive predicate be introduced in such a way that it acquires its cognitive significance through certain sorts of logical linkages between hypotheses containing it and the basic sentences that are already significant by virtue of

---

[20]Boghossian cites no other example of error-theoretic irrealism in *SOC*.

being keyed directly to observable conditions.[21] Would the error-theoretic irrealist be on firmer ground when maintaining falsity-across-the-board for primitive predications involving these more 'theoretical' predicates?

It seems that the answer here is a cautious affirmative; but only provided that one is not a participant in the discourse, with theoretical allegiances involving those predicates. One could maintain falsity-across-the-board for primitive predications involving 'theoretical' predicates of a thoroughly discredited theory to which one no longer holds any allegiance. Is not 'x is phlogiston' just such a predicate, introduced into earlier scientific discourse via certain logical linkages with basic sentences such as 'This is burning', 'This is ash', etc., but (by present-day theoretical lights) failing to hold of anything in the real world? More generally, failed and discredited scientific theorizing is prone to error-theoretic irrealist reconstrual of all its non-basic terms. Notoriously, the eliminative materialists today would have us hold the same view of the 'theoretical' terms of folk psychology, such as 'x believes that it is raining', 'x wants to stay dry' and 'x intends to open his umbrella'. We do not *see* a person believing that it is raining, or wanting to stay dry, or intending to open his umbrella. Rather, we conjecture that the person is in these various states, states postulated by our folk-psychological theory. The problem, however (says the eliminative materialist) is that there are no such states in reality. Folk psychology is really a very poor explanatory and predictive theory as far as the behaviour of human beings is concerned, just as was the theory of phlogiston in its attempted explanation and prediction of the observable, measurable features of burning bodies. So the folk-psychological predicates fail to limn the way the world really is, just as the predicate 'x is phlogiston' failed to do. By contrast—so the eliminative materialist contends—a completed neuroscience will one day provide just the right conceptual equipment, marshalled in just the right theoretical superstructure, that will succeed in a way that folk psychology never could, in explaining and predicting significant stretches of human behaviour.

It is not the aim here to counter the eliminative materialist's charges against folk psychology with the obvious battery of objections concerning differences between folk psychology and properly discredited theories like phlogiston theory. At this stage one need only make room for the prima-facie consistency of an error-theoretic irrealist view of regions of theoretical discourse. According to the recommendation implicit in the examples, one

---

[21]An analysis of these logical linkages, and how they succeed in conferring cognitive significance on 'higher-level' theoretical terms and sentences, will be given below.

could (perhaps: should?) be an error-theoretic irrealist about any failed and discredited scientific theory, or at least that part of it that ventures beyond the basic, observational terms used in confronting the tribunal of experience. As soon as any theory is sufficiently widely falsified to be overturned and replaced by a new theory for the same (or a more inclusive) domain of phenomena, the discarded theory is to be seen as false in all key respects. Even though its theoretical predicates were meaningful (via the logical linkages they bore to basic, observational sentences) their extensions were uniformly empty. But then if those predicates' extensions are indeed uniformly empty, the meaningfulness of the predicates hardly secures genuine properties for those predicates to express. And in theoretical scientific discourse the existence of things such as electrons is very closely tied up with the predicate 'x is an electron' expressing a genuine property. As far as the ultimate natural kinds of theoretical science are concerned, it would seem that there is little distinction to be drawn between a non-factualist attitude and an error-theoretic attitude. There are not any witches (error-theory). The predicate 'x is a witch' fails to express a genuine property (non-factualism). There is not any phlogiston (error-theory). The predicate 'x is phlogiston' fails to express a genuine property (non-factualism). There are not any beliefs (error-theory). The predicate 'x believes that p' fails to express a genuine property of the individual x (non-factualism).

So the irrealist view we have been canvassing concerning 'theoretical' predicates of a discarded theory could also be interpreted as a non-factualist one. For one will hardly be willing to think of those primitive predicates as expressing genuine properties. By far the best explanation for the failure of a discredited scientific theory is that it failed to 'limn the structure of reality', in that it did not latch on to the right—or indeed any—genuine properties with its primitive predicates.

Wright thinks that appropriate syntactic conditioning of the discourse guarantees its truth-aptitude, and therefore makes non-factualism untenable. If the declarative syntactic appearances are thick and systematic enough, as it were, they cannot be as misleading as the non-factualist, at least, maintains. Assertions will be made by the declarative sentences involved. It would appear, then, that the only irrealist option left open to someone of Wright's Fregean persuasions in this regard would be the 'pure' form of error-theoretic irrealism, according to which predicates did express genuine properties but had uniformly empty extensions. We have seen above, however, that serious difficulties stand in the way of any such view.

In summary so far, we see that non-factualism may be a non-starter, on grounds of the assertoric character of the discourse; and error-theoretic irrealism may be a non-starter for the basic predicates of the discourse, on grounds of its learnability. Error-theoretic irrealism, however, may be a coherent view to take of the higher theoretical reaches of failed scientific theories; but then it tends to go hand-in-hand with non-factualism about the would-be properties expressed by the central theoretical predicates of the discourse in question.

What, though, about the following possibility? One might not regard even the primitive theoretical assertions of a failed theory as uniformly erroneous, and therefore not be an error-theorist. Some atomic tilts at the truth, even at the theoretical level, one maintains, found their mark, though (since the theory was falsified) some must have missed. So error-theoretic irrealism about the theoretical predicates of a rejected scientific theory should not be the immediate and obvious consequence of having rejected that theory. It is difficult, however, to see how one would distinguish, in a principled way, between those primitive theoretical predications that were true and those that were false, unless some of the discarded theory survived, with modifications (perhaps in the form of even higher-level hypotheses) that would preserve the original significance of the contested theoretical predicates but somehow newly constrain their extensions so as to eliminate the earlier troublesome instances.

Error-theoretic irrealism, then, would seem to be on firmest ground concerning the primitive theoretical predicates of a theory that is not transmogrified in this way, but is completely jettisoned in favour of a new theory with a wholly new system of concepts marshalled by a completely fresh set of explanatory hypotheses, and bearing the sorts of logical linkages to observational reports that are needed for all the new terms concerned to acquire cognitive significance. When old theories are badly wrong, when the anomalies have become overwhelming, and when their conceptual baggage has become completely unworkable, we may conclude, with the error-theoretic irrealist, that their primitive theoretical predicates must, after all, have had uniformly empty extensions. Thus too we would agree with the non-factualist that the central theoretical predicates could not have latched on to any genuine properties in the world. This, at least, seems the best line to take on past theories about witches and phlogiston.

One might agree with Wright about the truth-aptitude of a discourse (on the basis of its syntactic conditioning), and therefore not be a non-factualist; and decide on the appropriateness of error-theoretic irrealism on the merits and demerits of the displaced theories in question. What is still hard to imagine, however, is how one might hold an error-theoretic irrealist view of discourse in which one currently engages, in which one's current theory has not been jettisoned as false under the weight of many anomalies, and which is in no immediate prospect of being displaced by a new, alternative theory using completely different theoretical concepts. Error-theoretic irrealism concerning current theoretical allegiances would have to involve at least some sort of pragmatic inconsistency, like Moore's. It is a pragmatic paradox to say that one lives one's life by theory T, but that one doesn't really think that the theoretical terms of T are true of anything. 'There are electrons, but I don't believe in electrons' strikes one as of a piece with 'P, but I don't believe that P'.

Suppose, then, that non-factualism is put behind us, and that error-theoretic irrealism is in abeyance, at least for the discourse in which we currently engage. What sort of truth, then, is involved in the discourse in question? On the assumption that nothing further can be said about it than the usual platitudes, it must be minimal truth. Whether the notion of truth for that discourse is yet more substantial than minimal truth can be put to some or all of Wright's tests explained above. Wright himself thinks that when a notion of truth for a given discourse passes these tests, that is good reason to incline towards a more 'realist' view of the discourse, even though the 'realism' in question is not full-blown semantic realism in Dummett's sense. Little purpose is served by getting into terminological quibbles here. Wright's tests are important, in that their results tell us something important about the notion of truth for the discourse in question. But (with the exception of evidence-transcendence) Wright's tests do no more than secure the substantiality (or objectivity) of the notion of truth, which substantiality it behoves the moderate anti-realist to demand of the notion of truth anyway. For full-blown semantic realism, nothing less than Knowledge-Transcendence and Bivalence will do. At the very least, these two features are necessary for a realism worthy of the title (*pace* McDowell's so-called M-realist, who holds—erroneously, as will be argued below—that one can have Knowledge-Transcendence without Bivalence).

We should perhaps understand the irrealisms listed above as having more to say about the ontological (the supposed objects and properties in question) than about the semantic (the determination of truth-value by world plus content). For each of these (ontological) irrealisms would be combinable, in principle, with the original (semantic) realist outlook according to which every declarative sentence was determinately true or false, independently of our means of coming to know its truth-value. Realism, in the ontological sense in which it is opposed to these irrealisms, is the view that the sector of reality is mind-buffeting, or reflected in the mind. The things in question really are out there, and they will impinge on us if we are suitably aware and sensitive to them. The corresponding irrealism holds that the sector of 'reality' in question is at best mind-built, if it exists at all; and at worst non-existent.[22] The dubious sector of reality is populated by convenient fictions (social individuals; mathematical objects and relations), or by unjustifiable extrapolations (theoretical physical entities and processes), or by posits brought into the picture only in order to satisfy our craving for an objectivity that is, however, not to be had (causal relations, rules, meanings and values).

A comprehensive metaphysics, epistemology and philosophy of mind and of language would have to pick its way through this variety of local realisms and irrealisms in pursuit of an account that is coherent overall, that does justice to intuition and achieves reflective equilibrium, that is informed by our best current scientific theories, and within which, it is to be hoped, the various options on different domains (the logical; the mathematical; rules and meanings; sense and content; modality; causation; mental states and events; theoretical entities; secondary qualities; etc.) would be mutually supporting. In this kind of broad philosophical theorizing one is seeking such distant and comprehensively informed inferences to the best explanation that one is obliged to look at the ramifications of one's stance in any one local realism/irrealism debate, and assess how it affects one's stance on the others.

In conclusion, we shall now take a closer look at the most important kind of irrealism given our present concerns. This is semantic irrealism, both in the guise of content non-factualism and in the guise of deflationism about truth. We shall consider now the arguments offered by Boghossian purporting to establish the incoherence of each of these positions.

3.3 Notational preliminaries

We shall adopt the following regimentations:

ϕ—a significant declarative sentence
P—a predicate

---

[22]It would be rather difficult for the eliminativist to say that the domain of the mental is mind-built! Boghossian, as we shall see, tries (unsuccessfully) to show that irrealism (or what he calls non-factualism) about content is actually incoherent.

p—a content (that is, a truth condition)
$TC(\phi)$—ϕ is truth-conditional
$T(\phi)$—ϕ is true
$tc(\phi, p)$—ϕ has truth-conditions p
$R(P)$ —P is robust (that is, P expresses a property)

Note that

- P is in general a linguistic item;

- p is a semantic item (if it exists);

- $tc(\ ,p)$ is a metalinguistic predicate, which can be substituted for P in the last regimentation above; and similarly for the metalinguistic predicates $T(\ )$ and $TC(\ )$.

When making meta-metalinguistic predications about these metalinguistic predicates one should, strictly speaking, use some quotational device such as placing the metalinguistic predicate in question within a box. Thus if one wished to say that the metalinguistic predicate $T(\ )$ is Ψ (that is, $T(\ )$ has the property Ψ), a scrupulous way to do so would be to write

$$\Psi(\boxed{T(\ )}).$$

We shall not, however, be this scrupulous. Instead we shall allows ourselves the liberty of writing simply

$$\Psi(T).$$

Moreover, we shall abbreviate

$$\Psi(\boxed{tc(\ ,p)})$$

to

$$\Psi(tc_p).$$

These notational preliminaries are all we need in order to formulate certain philosophical theses succinctly and adequately, and to codify various logical moves involving them.

3.4   A *reductio* of semantic irrealism?

For Boghossian,[23]

- *content non-factualism* is the claim $\neg R(tc_p)$

  (the predicate 'has truth conditions p' does not refer to a property).

- *deflationism about truth* is the claim $\neg R(T)$

  (the predicate 'true' does not refer to a property).

- *deflationism about reference* is the claim $\neg R(P)$

  (the predicate P does not refer to a property).

Boghossian offers two *reductio* arguments in an attempt to refute irrealist views in semantics:

- one to the effect that content non-factualism is incoherent; and

- another to the effect that deflationism about truth is incoherent.

Our aim here is to examine these arguments in some detail. We shall identify those steps that count as primitive within them—those steps, that is, that are used to justify others but for which no further justification is offered. Obviously, any argument, once fully analysed, consists of such basic steps; our task is to identify them as they occur in Boghossian's arguments. We shall show how the arguments are built up from the basic steps; then we shall assess the steps themselves. It will turn out that they do not withstand critical scrutiny.[24]

3.5   Isolating the basic steps

3.5.1   The first basic step

Consider the following passage:[25]

---

[23] Cf. *SOC*, loc. cit.

[24] Boghossian's most vocal critic so far has (in our view mistakenly, and as Boghossian points out with satisfaction) acquiesced with his argument against content non-factualism. See Michael Devitt, 'Transcendentalism about Content', and Boghossian's reply 'The Status of Content Revisited', both in *Pacific Philosophical Quarterly*, 71, 1990.

[25] loc. cit., p. 161.

What all non-factualist conceptions have in common—what in effect is constitutive of such a conception of a declarative sentence of the form 'x is P'—is

(1) The claim that the predicate 'P' does not denote a property

and (hence)

(2) The claim that the overall (atomic) declarative sentence in which it appears does not express a truth condition.

Here we have the inference

(1) 'P' does not denote a property
hence
(2) 'x is P' is not truth-conditional

Now any inference of the form 'not-A, hence not-B' might just as well be expressed by the simpler contrapositive 'B, therefore A'. The only circumstance in which this is not so is where there are anti-realist scruples about classical negation moves, such as double negation elimination or classical *reductio*. Such scruples, however, have no place in this discussion, where the assumption is that these *a priori* conceptual issues are decidable.[26] We shall therefore take it that a basic rule of inference to which we may appeal in the reconstruction of Boghossian's arguments is

'x is P' is truth-conditional

ergo, 'P' denotes a property

which, given the explanations of notation above, we may regiment as follows:

$$\frac{TC(P(t))}{R(P)} \qquad \ldots\text{(I)}$$

Note that in (I) t is a placeholder for singular terms in general, including names of sentences. Also, P can be replaced in this inference scheme by any

---

[26] The reader will note, for example, the absence of any quantificational complexity in the arguments we shall be considering. The philosophical claims involved would appear to belong, then, to a decidable *a priori* fragment of our philosophical language. But even if this consideration were to fail to convince, the point remains that we have no reason to believe that Boghossian himself would not accede to the positive form of inference 'B therefore A' just as readily as to the negative form 'not-A, hence not-B'.

linguistic predicate, including such metalinguistic predicates as $T(\ )$, $TC(\ )$ and $tc(\ ,p)$.[27]

3.5.2 The second basic step

For Boghossian, the essential deflationist thesis is $\neg R(T)$; and for Boghossian's deflationist, any significant declarative sentence ϕ is automatically truth-conditional. He writes that[28]

> [the] requirements [of significance and of declarative form] would seem ...to be jointly sufficient for truth conditionality, on a deflationary understanding of truth.

We can express this view by the basic inference

$$\frac{\neg R(T)}{TC(\phi)} \qquad \ldots(\mathrm{II})$$

Note that in (II), while T is specifically the truth predicate, ϕ is a placeholder for sentences in general.

3.5.3 The third basic step

Boghossian writes:[29]

> the truth-value of a sentence is fully determined by its truth condition and the relevant worldly facts. There is no way, then, that a sentence's possessing a truth-value could be a thoroughly factual matter ("true" does express a property) if there is non-factuality in one of its determinants ("has truth condition p" does not express a property).

Using the terminology introduced above, we can regiment the relevant parts in parentheses within the last sentence, and distil the claim

There is no way ...that ...$(R(T))$ if ...$(\neg R(tc_p))$.

---

[27] Whether this is a good idea or sound semantics is a question we shall address below. For the time being, we simply note that Boghossian countenances such unrestricted usage for these rules.

[28] loc. cit., p. 164.

[29] loc. cit., p. 175.

The spade has turned. We have to see the following inference as primitive for Boghossian:

$$\frac{R(T) \qquad \neg R(tc_p)}{\bot} \qquad \qquad \ldots \text{(III)}$$

Note that in (III), tc_p is a complex placeholder with generality implicit in its subscript p.

3.6   Some simple arguments using the basic steps

The exegetical purist need only satisfy himself that we have correctly identified the *primitive* steps of inference of which Boghossian avails himself, and by means of which he would allow any philosophical interlocutor to reason. The quotations we have given above should satisfy him on this score. Once we have these rules of inference clearly laid out, Boghossian would have to concede the formal correctness of any argument built up by means of their correct application. Indeed, he would quite understandably be anxious to be credited with having discovered at least some of these arguments (and for having, to that end, isolated the primitive inferences involved). By the same token, however, it need be no concern of ours here to convince the exegetical sceptic that any argument that we might construct (according to Boghossian's own rules) is indeed an argument that Boghossian himself authored in *SOC*. In the interests of both brevity and perspicuity, we are happy to leave to the exegetical sceptic the question whether the formal arguments to be presented below really do faithfully regiment the prose arguments that occur in Boghossian's text. All that matters is that we have already shown above, with attention to his text, what primitive stuff his arguments are made of. So let us advance without further ado to the arguments we would like to present. We give credit to Boghossian where we believe credit is due.[30]

The two deflationisms are in conflict:

$$\frac{\dfrac{\dfrac{\neg R(T)}{TC(P(t))}\,(II)}{R(P)}\,(I) \qquad \neg R(P)}{\bot}$$

---

[30] Boghossian's arguments, remember, were in prose; what we would like him to realize, *pace* M. Jourdain, was that he was really only constructing the following nice, sparse natural deductions all along.

Indeed, by substituting T for P and ϕ for t in the foregoing, we see that deflationism about truth leads to absurdity:[31]

BOGHOSSIAN'S REDUCTIO OF DEFLATIONISM ABOUT TRUTH

$$\frac{\dfrac{\dfrac{\neg R(T)}{TC(T(\phi))}(II)}{R(T)}(I) \qquad \neg R(T)}{\bot}$$

Content non-factualism implies deflationism about truth:

$$\frac{\dfrac{\overline{}(1)}{R(T)} \qquad \neg R(tc_p)}{\dfrac{\bot}{\neg R(T)}(1)}(III)$$

So of course content non-factualism also leads to absurdity. The proof of this is obtained by putting the previous two proofs together and converting the result into normal form:[32]

CONSTRUCTIVE REDUCTIO OF CONTENT NON-FACTUALISM

$$\frac{\dfrac{\dfrac{\dfrac{\overline{}(1)}{R(T)} \qquad \neg R(tc_p)}{\dfrac{\bot}{\neg R(T)}(1)}(III)}{TC(T(\phi))}(II)}{R(T) \qquad\qquad \neg R(tc_p)}(I)$$
$$\bot$$

Interestingly, the *reductio* of content non-factualism that Boghossian himself presents boils down to a proof of slightly different form, containing a strictly classical negation move:[33]

---

[31] This argument is to be extracted from p. 166 and p. 181 of *SOC*.

[32] Boghossian appears to be unaware of the possibility of thus accumulating these two proofs.

[33] For reasons explained above, we spare the reader the exegetical mileage involved in substantiating the claim that this indeed is the essence of Boghossian's own argument against content non-factualism. If this exegetical claim is disputed, we do not mind the (undeserved) credit for having found the proof given here! The reader who is interested

BOGHOSSIAN'S CLASSICAL REDUCTIO OF CONTENT NON-FACTUALISM

$$\frac{\cfrac{\overline{\hspace{2cm}}\,(1)}{\neg R(T)}\,(II)}{\cfrac{TC(tc(\phi,p))}{\neg R(tc_p)\qquad R(tc_p)}\,(I)}$$

$$\frac{\cfrac{\bot}{R(T)}\,(1)\qquad \neg R(tc_p)}{\bot}\,(III)$$

It would appear that two apparently live philosophical options have fallen to a grim logical reaper—one of them, content non-factualism, to two strokes of the scythe. In what follows we shall focus on the *reductio* of deflationism about content and the constructive *reductio* of content non-factualism.

3.7   Evaluating the steps

Whenever a seemingly secure edifice is demolished by a couple of blows, however well directed, one suspects that a very heavy hammer or ball (or perhaps both) are being used. Which, if any, of the basic steps in the two main *reductio* arguments is questionable?:

(I) 'ϕ is true' is truth-conditional
ergo, 'is true' expresses a property

(II) 'true' does not express a property
ergo, 'ϕ is true' is truth-conditional

(III) there is no way that 'true' expresses a property and that 'has truth condition p' does not

(III) seems safe enough, and we shall grant it.

---

in seeing how Boghossian's argument boils down to the simple (classical) proof given here should read *SOC*, p. 175, referring back where necessary to pp. 161–66 of that paper. Note that Boghossian's classical *reductio* of content non-factualism was given in his text both earlier, and independently of, his *reductio* of deflationism about truth. This partly explains why he missed the constructive *reductio* of content non-factualism that we have provided.

3.7.1 A stratificationist objection to Boghossian will not work

It might be thought that one way to ward off Boghossian's *reductio* arguments would be to demur from Boghossian's implicit view of truth as univocal, and of our language (including that part of it in which we conduct our philosophical discussions about truth) as semantically closed. The concern to be explored here was foreshadowed in our earlier footnote about the unrestricted applications that Boghossian needed to be able to make of his rules. On inspecting rule (II), for example, any reader with a background in logical semantics will have misgivings about semantic closure:

$$\frac{\neg R(T)}{TC(\phi)} \qquad \dots (\text{II})$$

The conclusion $TC(\phi)$ attributes truth-conditionality to *any* sentence ϕ, no matter how many embeddings of occurrences of 'the' truth predicate T ϕ might contain. In particular, rule (II) has been applied in the *reductio* arguments above with 'semantically higher level' instances of ϕ. Let us look at how rule (II) is applied in each of these *reductio* arguments.

First, the constructive *reductio* arguments against deflationism about truth and against content non-factualism both contained the following instance of rule (II):

$$\frac{\neg R(T)}{TC(T(\phi))}$$

in which the substituend $T(\phi)$ is used in place of the place-holder ϕ in the statement of rule (II). The occurrences of TC and of T in the conclusion of this application of (II) put that conclusion on a semantically higher level than the premiss.

Secondly, in Boghossian's classical *reductio* of content non-factualism there is the following application of rule (II):

$$\frac{\neg R(T)}{TC(tc(\phi, p))}$$

in which the substituend $tc(\phi, p)$ is used, once again making the 'semantic level' of the conclusion of the application of (II) higher than that of its premiss.

The well-known semantic paradoxes, such as the Liar, arise from allowing such conflation of, or inattention to differences in, semantic levels. Why, then, should we not suspect that the *reductio* arguments above reach absurdity as their conclusions more by courtesy of semantic closure than because of the intrinsic incoherence of the philosophical theses to which their target premisses (such as $\neg R(T)$ and $\neg R(tc_p)$) give expression? Neither Boghossian nor any of his critics have thus far raised or considered such a misgiving. This is puzzling, given the semantic tradition. It is important, however, to see that such a 'confusion of levels' is *not* at work in Boghossian's argumentation; for this will help ensure that the search for the real fault-line can be properly focused.

Let us, then, explore a little further the worry just voiced about a possible confusion of levels. The suggestion is that we should adopt some device such as stratification of semantic locutions. In particular, there would have to be an ascending sequence $T^1, T^2, \ldots$ of truth predicates. (Sentences with no semantic locutions would appear at level 0.) Rule (II) would then have to be restricted so that the sentence ϕ embedded in its conclusion $TC(\phi)$ is lower in the stratification hierarchy than the predicate T^i occurring in the premiss, and with respect to which the predicate T^iC of (level i) truth-conditionality is to be construed. Moreover, since 'expression' is a semantic relation, the predicate R, which embeds it, would have to be one level higher than any argument to which it is applied. Thus rule (II) in its stratified form would have to read

$$\frac{\neg R^{i+1}(T^i)}{T^iC(\phi)} \qquad \text{where } \phi \text{ is of level less than } i \qquad \ldots (\text{II}_S)$$

Likewise for rules (I) and (III):

$$\frac{T^{i+1}C(P(t))}{R^{i+1}(P)} \qquad \text{where } P(t) \text{ is of level } i \qquad \ldots (\text{I}_S)$$

$$\frac{R^{i+1}(T^i) \qquad \neg R^{i+1}(t^i c_p)}{\bot} \qquad \text{where } p \text{ is of level } i\text{-}1 \qquad \ldots (\text{III}_S)$$

But would these stratificatory precautions render the applications made of rules (I), (II) and (III)—now thought of as rules (I_S), (II_S) and (III_S)—in the *reductio* arguments above formally incorrect? Would these applications violate the new stratification restriction?

Unexpectedly, perhaps, the answer is negative. Thus the suggested recourse to a standard Tarskian remedy is of no avail in averting a *reductio* of semantic irrealism. Even after this stratification, the *reductio* arguments marshalled against semantic irrealism remain formally correct.[34] Here are our three earlier proofs, duly stratified:

BOGHOSSIAN'S REDUCTIO OF DEFLATIONISM ABOUT TRUTH

$$\cfrac{\cfrac{\cfrac{\neg R^{i+1}(T^i)}{T^{i+1}C(T^i(\phi))}(II_S)}{R^{i+1}(T^i)}(I_S) \qquad \neg R^{i+1}(T^i)}{\bot}$$

CONSTRUCTIVE REDUCTIO OF CONTENT NON-FACTUALISM

$$\cfrac{\cfrac{\cfrac{\overline{R^{i+1}(T^i)}^{(1)} \qquad \neg R^{i+1}(t^i c_p)}{\bot}(III_S)}{\cfrac{\neg R^{i+1}(T^i)}{\cfrac{T^{i+1}C(T^i(\phi))}{R^{i+1}(T^i)}(I_S)}(II_S)}^{(1)} \qquad \neg R^{i+1}(t^i c_p)}{\bot}$$

BOGHOSSIAN'S CLASSICAL REDUCTIO OF CONTENT NON-FACTUALISM

$$\cfrac{\cfrac{\neg R^{i+1}(t^i c_p) \qquad \cfrac{\cfrac{\overline{\neg R^{i+1}(T^i)}^{(1)}}{T^{i+1}C(t^i c(\phi,p))}(II_S)}{R^{i+1}(t^i c_p)}(I_S)}{\cfrac{\bot}{R^{i+1}(T^i)}(1)} \qquad \neg R^{i+1}(t^i c_p)}{\bot}(III_S)$$

What these stratified proofs show is that if one wishes to fault the Boghossian line then one must find a different philosophical objection to his rule (I) or to his rule (II)—in either stratified or unstratified form. Since each of these rules finds application in each of the *reductio* proofs above, it would be enough to fault just one of them. Since the stratified proofs just given show that Boghossian's argumentation has been 'invisibly stratified' all along, we

---

[34] Comments from Stewart Shapiro on an earlier draft of this section helped me to get the stratificational strategem into proper dialectical perspective.

shall conduct the rest of our discussion without the subscript S that we
have been using to indicate stratification. Thus we shall be continuing on
the assumption of what might be called 'stratificational ambiguity'.

3.7.2   Objection to step (I)

A nominalist would object to (I) on the grounds that there are, in general,
no properties to be expressed. Thus any instance of

> (I) '$P(t)$' is truth-conditional
> *ergo*, 'P' expresses a property

would make the nominalist baulk, and not just those instances where $P(t)$
takes the form 'ϕ is true'. The nominalist might still be able to provide
an account of truth-conditionality that did justice to cognitively significant
discourse. Boghossian offers no arguments compelling allegiance to (I).

3.7.3   Objection to step (II) from a projectivist's point of view

A 'robust' deflationist would object to (II) on the grounds that 'true' does not
express a property, while yet not every significant declarative sentence (and
especially not those of the form 'ϕ is true'!) should be regarded automatically
as being truth-conditional.[35] The robust deflationist is thereby challenging
Boghossian at his most confident and insistent:

> on a deflationary conception any declarative sentence is automat-
> ically truth-conditional. Understanding this feature of deflation-
> ary truth is a *sine qua non* of understanding it at all. This is a
> point that is stressed equally by me and Devitt[36]

There would appear to be the following problem with the robust deflationist response here, albeit not one explored by Boghossian (since he did not
anticipate that response in the first place). The problem is that for this
response to bite, the robust deflationist must be envisaging the possibility of
a significant declarative sentence ϕ that might be a candidate for assertion
while yet the truth-predication 'ϕ is true' not be a candidate for assertion
(on pain of having to recognize conditions for the truth of ϕ—that is, of

---

[35]The most subtle statement that I know of this position is by Robert Kraut, in 'Robust
Deflationism', *Philosophical Review*, 102, 1993, pp. 247–63.

[36]'The Status of Content Revisited', p. 276.

conceding ϕ's truth-conditionality). This would put in jeopardy that half of Tarski's T-schema which allows one to infer 'ϕ is true' from ϕ. Perhaps the robust deflationist could bite the bullet here, and put 'ϕ is true' on a par with ϕ, and admit Tarski's inferential T-schemata in both directions. His strategy would then be to refuse to advance to the truth-conditionality of ϕ even when saddled with 'ϕ is true' as a candidate for assertion. Perhaps the picture on offer would be of a special kind of assertion (hence of assertibility), not automatically earned by ϕ solely on account of being a significant declarative sentence.[37]

It is not obvious how to develop the fine details of such a view; we are not claiming that it would be impossible to supply them. We are not, that is, party to Boghossian's dogmatic insistence quoted above. But there is a prima-facie problem with the robust deflationist's proposal as it stands. The problem is that Boghossian would be able to respond by pointing out that what is being bruited here is simply a new kind of dichotomy to replace the old one. The old one was the dichotomy between sentences that were genuinely truth-conditional and those that were not. Among the latter, according to the would-be non-factualist about content, were those sentences of the form 'ϕ has truth conditions p'. And this, Boghossian would say, had been shown to be unstable by the argument whose form has been analysed above. The new dichotomy now is between sentences that are 'substantively eligible for assertion (or denial)' and those that are not so, even though they are significant declaratives. So, the suggestion on Boghossian's behalf would go, *rerun the form of argument with this new dichotomy replacing the old one*. The result should be interesting and important: namely, the revised content non-factualist claim that it is incoherent to suppose that one can regard as not substantively eligible for assertion (or denial) sentences of the form 'ϕ has substantive assertibility conditions p'.

But a closer look at the form of Boghossian's first argument, reconstrued as suggested with this 'dichotomy shift', shows that the very same step—namely, (II)—is objectionable, as it was before. It suffices, for the purpose of rejecting the reconstrued argument, to sustain an objection against this step; so let us look at it more closely. On the reconstrual, (II) would become

(II′) 'is substantively assertible' does not express a property *ergo*, 'ϕ has substantive assertibility condition p' is substantively eli-

---

[37]This, at least, appears to be the (not altogether unproblematic) proposal of Robert Kraut, loc. cit.

gible for assertion or denial[38]

Kraut is one theorist who urges the new dichotomy and who opposes Boghossian's conclusion. Kraut claims that he has no reason to accept (II′). He claims to be able to assert the premiss of (II′) while denying its conclusion (or at least, while refusing to assert its conclusion—which suffices). Kraut's central claim is that one has to appreciate the coherence of being a projectivist about such locutions as 'ϕ is descriptive'.

Nor is Kraut alone in this response. Quite independently, Wright had formulated a parallel thought.[39] Boghossian's argument, says Wright, rests on

> the contention that the taxonomy of the distinction between merely correctness-apt discourses and those which are apt for truth should itself be a substantial matter: that the statements which classify discourses on one side or the other should be truth-apt.[40]

But the irrealist or meaning-minimalist could sidestep Boghossian by simply insisting that

> [the] distinction between the truth-apt and the merely correctness-apt is one whose details, since founded in semantic contrasts, may be recorded only by correct statements. 'ϕ is true', 'ϕ has the truth condition that p', 'ϕ is correct', 'ϕ has the correctness condition that p'—all these are statement-forms whose instances are, for the meaning-minimalist, only correctness-apt.[41]

A position such as the one mooted here by both Kraut and Wright no doubt needs to have much more detail filled in. But it shows, prima facie, that Boghossian's way with the deflationist cannot be so swift as his insistence on the validity of (II), now reconstrued as (II′). A defence of (II′) would seem to require, at the very least, an argument to the effect that there can be no projectivist construal of any significant declarative sentences as serving assertive purposes other than that of aiming to represent what is factually the

---

[38]The phrase 'substantively eligible for assertion or denial' is preferable to '(substantive assertibility)-conditional' on stylistic grounds, even though the latter would make the reconstrual induced by the dichotomy shift somewhat clearer.

[39] *T&O*, Appendix: On an Argument against the Coherence of Minimalism about Meaning, pp. 231–36.

[40]loc. cit., p. 233.

[41]loc. cit., p. 235. Wright's text has 'S' in place of 'ϕ'.

case.[42] To be sure, this presupposes some robust notion of truth (call it F), in order to make out the contrast between sentences that are to be construed descriptively and those that are to be construed projectively. But it simply does not follow from this (so the robust deflationist would argue) that any significant declarative sentence is automatically F-conditional. Least of all does it follow that sentences attributing F-ness or F-conditionality are themselves F-conditional.

This response allows the semantic irrealist to ward off Boghossian's *reductio*. Or, put slightly differently: one way to ward off Boghossian's *reductio* is to express one's semantic irrealism in this fashion, maintaining that with semantic ascent our attributions 'go soft', lacking substantive truth conditions and enjoying only much more anaemic correctness conditions for 'projective' assertion.

3.8   Conclusion

All the *reductio* arguments considered above contain two questionable steps of inference, namely (I) and (II):

(I) '$P(t)$' is truth-conditional
ergo, 'P' expresses a property

(II) 'true' does not express a property
ergo, 'ϕ is true' is truth-conditional

(where, in the conclusion of (II), ϕ may be any significant declarative sentence).

The nominalist objects to (I) because it involves commitment to properties. And the deflationist objects to having such a general commitment as (II) foisted upon him. His objection survives the suggestion that 'true' be replaced by whatever predicate F it may be that, for the deflationist, is to play the role of 'true' but which is also to be such that not every significant declarative ϕ is automatically F-conditional.

These would-be *reductio* arguments do not, then, provide one with any good reason to adopt an alternative to an irrealist view of content attributions, or to go beyond deflationism in one's theorizing about truth. Thus the objections that we have considered clear the ground for fresh considerations

---

[42]It is precisely such a projectivist construal that Robert Kraut has essayed in 'Robust Deflationism', loc. cit.

for or *against* content non-factualism, and *for* or *against* deflationism. Our consideration of Boghossian's transcendental attack has been dialectically necessary in order to justify the need to engage more directly with the arguments put forward by the content irrealist or meaning sceptic.

Our own view is that content attributions are themselves possessed of objective contents, and that there is more to truth than the deflationist permits. Content attributions feature pervasively as hypotheses arrived at by way of inference to the best explanation of human interactions, especially linguistic ones. Precisely because interpretive hypotheses can be put to the test of observable behaviour, the attributions of content that they involve are themselves cognitively significant. The burden of refutation is on the irrealist opposition. They have not yet, as we shall see in the next two chapters, effectively shouldered it; nor have they made any mileage with their attempted arguments *for* semantic irrealism. It would indeed have been most agreeable to us had Boghossian's arguments *against* semantic irrealism proved to be compelling. But honesty compels us to acknowledge their flaws, and to make do with what we can in our quietism about the objectivity of content.

Thus deprived of a would-be quick, transcendental antidote to content irrealism, we need now to explore other remedies for the cankerous doubts that the meaning sceptic tries to spread. The next chapter prescribes medicine intended to prevent any attack of the sceptical strain known as Kripkensteinianism.

Chapter 4

Against Meaning Scepticism

4.1 The impact of scepticism about meaning. The stress between materialist metaphysics and analytic intuition

The history of philosophy has been in large measure a history of its canni-balization by the special sciences. Philosophy now retains a powerful grip only on those areas where the *a priori* exercise of refined, reflective modes of intuition can reasonably claim priority over any empirical methodology. His-torically, this accounts for the fundamental importance of pure mathematics in all major Western systems of ontology and epistemology, from Plato to Kant.

Closely allied to the operation of pure arithmetical and geometric intu-ition are our intuitive, introspective convictions about the nature of content and consciousness. Russell once made a remark to the general effect that mathematics was the subject in which we laid claim to certain knowledge of necessary truths about we knew not what. One could make a similar claim today about what used to be called the theory of meaning, which is now, with widened attention on the link between the mental and the linguistic, called the theory of content.

A theory cannot face a more radical challenge than that at present con-fronting the theory of content: that its supposed objects do not exist, or that the most important properties and relations that the theory claims to hold turn out to lack any factual foundation. (This is the irrealist challenge described in the previous chapter.) Yet this threat of vanishing domain and vaporizing structure is what Kripke's meaning sceptic poses to the theorist about content. What is at issue is a correct understanding of the nature or status of content: mental content and semantic content.

Content stands at the confluence of two powerful intellectual stresses. The first of these is the range of (usually introspective) intuitions of thinkers and speakers about the exact meanings of their words or the fine-grained import of their thoughts. Our convictions about precise grasp are at odds with Quine's attack on the analytic-synthetic distinction and his associated thesis of indeterminacy of radical translation; with the holist's attack on the molecularity of sentence meaning; with extended Goodmanian questioning of what might be meant by 'green'; and with the eliminative materialists' threat to our folk scheme of shared views, differences of opinion, common objectives and conflicting desires.

The second stress, which conflicts with the first, is generated by our all-pervasive materialist metaphysics. Everything is (under a suitably chosen aspect) physical. Minds, ultimately, are naught but brains in reasonable working order. Every mental event is a physical event. All facts, whatever their prima-facie non-material nature, are fixed by the unalloyed physical facts. This is not to claim reducibility of the mental, or apparently non-physical, to the physical; it is only to claim that the former supervenes on the latter. It is these convictions about ultimate constitution that are so at odds with 'third realm' metaphysical theories, with substance dualism, and with idealism of all varieties.

The challenge, then, is to provide an account of content that does justice to a wide range of arguably correct intuitions and more sophisticated observations about its fine grain. We must at the same time be able to locate the account, at least in principle, as part of a wider discourse about facts that we can appreciate as being fixed, ultimately, by physical facts. (Under 'physical' here we include the causal, the teleological, the dispositional, and the functional: this is the legacy of Kant, Darwin, Ryle and the early Putnam.)

The orthodox opposition to Kripke's sceptic would have its cake and eat it. That is, they would argue both for the reality of rule-following and for the reality of content (though it is an interesting question whether the former entails the latter). They would claim to do justice to all our analytic intuitions about content, and claim to have accommodated the notion within a naturalistic world-view. It is important to appreciate, however, that merely being a naturalist need not impel one to naturalize content. Indeed, it was Wittgenstein himself who once wrote to Schlick that he, like Carnap, was a physicalist, 'nur nicht unter diesem scheusslichen Namen'; the Wittgenstein whose probings into rule-following and attribution of content led, if Kripke has it right, not to naturalistic accommodation, but to naturalistic eviction of content, and a face-saving reconstrual of our talk about it. Naturalism (or physicalism, or materialism) can go either way on content; it all depends on the extent to which the naturalist is prepared to go to salvage analytic intuitions, and his preparedness to let both science and philosophy reform his commonsense conception of what there is and how it is.

4.2 Theses about content, and some orthogonal issues

Any adequate theory of content has to do justice to the following intuitions and philosophical observations, or reform and rehabilitate them, or else accommodate them in some more oblique way. We shall call them the Theses about Content:

1. Content attaches to both expressions of a public language and mental states of individual thinkers and speakers.

2. Contents of declarative sentences, and the core contents of propositional attitudes such as beliefs and desires, are primary, in that they are truth evaluable.

3. These sentential or core contents are determinate.

4. They are also compositional—they are made up, at least in part, out of the contributed contents of their constituents. In the case of sentences, these will be the contents or meanings of sub-sentential expressions. In the case of core mental contents, these will be the constituent concepts involved.

5. They are indefinitely various—there is a potential infinity of distinct contents.

6. They are finitely generable—some inductive or recursive procedure, drawing on a finite basis of primitive conceptual resources, can deliver the full range of contents.

7. They are able, by virtue of their role in speech and thought, to represent the way the world is or may be, and it is in this connection that

they are truth evaluable (in context). They have normative or rational
acceptance conditions, or criteria for assertion, and once a speaker or
thinker accepts a given content or contents, he thereby commits himself to others that are logically, analytically or criterially linked with
them.

8. They are objective, in so far as one speaker or thinker can communicate
   them fully to another; agree or disagree on them; and debate about
   accepting them.

9. Membership in a linguistic community involves accepting a set of obligations
   or commitments to respect the meanings of expressions—to keep faith
   with them, or to follow the rules appropriate for the use of the words of
   the language. One has to remain party to the conventions of language
   use in order to use the language successfully—that is, to communicate
   effectively.[1]

10. Understanding a public language consists at least in part in knowing
    what content attaches to any given sentence of the language. Un-
    derstanding or interpreting another thinker or speaker—making his
    actions rationally intelligible—consists at least in part in being able to
    attribute contents to his sentences, and to attribute to the agent beliefs
    and desires with a selected range of contents, so as to make his actions
    (linguistic or otherwise) intelligible on the basis of what he means and
    what he happens to believe and desire.

11. Speakers can effectively grasp the meanings of sentences in context.

The theses above have been formulated as neutrally as possible, so as not
to take a stand on various issues which are arguably orthogonal to or independent of the question of our rich intuitions about content v. their possible
metaphysical vacuity. The orthogonal issues in question are as follows.

1. Should contents be reified, or could one get by with just the appropriate
   predicates of contentfulness? (Even semanticists of the propositional
   attitudes are divided on this question.)

---

[1]Naturally, if one makes linguistic innovations, or undertakes reforms, it will only be to
the extent that one carries others with one that one will be able to continue to communicate
effectively by means of the extended or newly disciplined medium.

2. Can there be thought without talk? Put another way, is mental content parasitic upon sentential content—or could a creature harbour mental contents without yet having mastered a public language? (Analytical philosophers from Frege to Davidson have tended to claim that there cannot be thought without talk. But theorists of language interested in evolutionary origins, primate communication systems, and comparative psychology tend to favour an account on which rational thought and ability to communicate might have coevolved in an intercalated way. For these theorists, the dogma of analytical philosophy—that thought requires talk—is at the very least problematic.)[2]

3. Could one attach contents to symbols in a wholly private way? Or does content attribution to symbols require that those symbols be in communal use? (The global anti-realist's answer to the latter question is affirmative. In this he follows the later Wittgenstein.)

4. Even conceding thesis (4) about content, might it be that a content could be fully individuated only by ineliminable reference to the whole system of contents in which it is embedded? (The holist answers affirmatively, the molecularist negatively.)

5. Is the notion of truth involved in theses (2) and (7) about content one that could attach to a content even though we might never in principle be able to come to know that it does so? Or, put another way, can truth-conditions properly extend acceptance conditions? (The global anti-realist's answer is negative.)[3]

6. Does the communication involved in (8) rely only on the observable behaviour of the speakers and hearers? (The global anti-realist's answer, like that of the Quinean, is affirmative.)

7. Does the interpretation involved in (10) have to make the theory of meaning for an individual's speech, and the folk-psychological theory of

---

[2]See my 'Intentionality, Syntactic Structure and the Evolution of Language', in C. Hookway, ed., *Minds, Machines and Evolution*, Cambridge University Press, 1984, pp. 73–103.

[3]I have countered an argument, due to Peacocke (see his book *Thoughts*, Blackwell, Oxford, 1986, ch. 2), for the contrary view, in 'Manifestationism without Verificationism?', a paper to the Ockham Society in Oxford in 1992 to honour Michael Dummett on the occasion of his retirement from the Wykeham Chair of Logic. This paper is forthcoming in a collection to be edited by M. Lievers.

his beliefs and desires, holistically interdependent? (The Davidsonian radical interpreter would answer affirmatively.)

8. Could the contents of our words and mental states depend, for their full individuation, on the nature and identity of the external objects and states of affairs that our words or thoughts are about? (The externalist such as Burge would answer affirmatively.)

9. Is there a privileged class of contents—say, those of ordinary perceptual judgements—from which all cognitively significant content can be generated in some orderly logical way? (The theorist who believes in a workable criterion of cognitive significance would answer affirmatively. We attempt to justify such an answer in the chapter on cognitive significance.)

10. Is there a system of representation in the mind/brain that could enable a thinker to have thoughts without a public language, and also ground the translation of any public language into any other? (The theorist of mentalese, such as Fodor, would answer affirmatively.)

11. Could 'meaning that p by uttering a sentence ϕ' be analysed in terms of beliefs and intentions, on the part of the speaker, concerning beliefs and intentions on the part of the hearer? (The intentions-based meaning theorist, such as Grice, would answer affirmatively; while yet conceding that the account needs supplementation in the form of a recursive theory of truth-conditions for the complex sentences involved. The Gricean maintains what we shall call the *thesis of intentional analysability of meaning*.)

12. Even if 'meaning that p by uttering a sentence ϕ' turns out *not* to admit of analysis in terms of beliefs and intentions, might not that 'meaning fact' (and all others) be somehow *determined by* facts concerning beliefs and intentions on the part of the members of the linguistic community in question? Put another way, do semantic facts *supervene on* other, intentional, facts? (The claim that they do will be called the *weak thesis of determination of content*. The thesis is *weak* because it *allows* appeal, in the determining basis, to intentional facts—e.g. facts about beliefs and intentions.)

13. If semantic facts do not supervene on other, intentional facts (say, because both semantic and intentional facts are coeval or holistically

interdependent), might it nevertheless be the case that both semantic and intentional facts are theoretically reducible to other, non-semantic and non-intentional facts? (The claim that they are would be the *thesis of physicalistic reductionism*.)

14. If semantic facts do not supervene on other, intentional facts and cannot be reduced to non-semantic and non-intentional facts, might it be the case that both semantic and intentional facts *supervene on* other, non-semantic and non-intentional facts? (The claim that they do would be the *strong thesis of determination of content*. The claim is *strong* because it *eschews* appeal, in the determining basis, to intentional facts.)

4.3 What semantic determination thesis does the Kripkean sceptic try to undermine?

In order to bring Kripkean scepticism into clear focus, it is important to appreciate that the 'neutral' theses about content or meaning cut across the aforementioned issues of reifiability, linguistic priority, the possibility of a private language, constitutive holism, verification-transcendent truth-conditions, behavioural manifestability of grasp of meaning, holism of radical interpretation, intentional analysability, wide *v.* narrow content, constitutive foundationalism, language of thought, intentional analysability, weak determinationism, physicalistic reductionism and strong determinationism. The Kripkean sceptic tries to uncover an irresolvable tension between the *normativity* of content and even *weak* determinationism concerning content. The argumentative strategy adopted is this:

> Whatever meaning or content may be, it has to be normative; BUT there is no possible factual basis to normativity, even if one includes non-semantic but intentional facts in such a basis; SO there is no possible fact of the matter about meaning or content.

It is important to appreciate the full force of the scepticism. Kripke is out to challenge or undermine even the *weakest* form of confidence in the status of meaning. That is why he chooses as his target for refutation (or at least for the instilling of sceptical doubt) that version of semantic determination according to which

1. the determining basis is allowed to contain non-semantic but *intentional* facts, and

2. the 'determining' in question is that of mere *supervenience* rather than analysability or theoretical reducibility.

If we were to interpret Kripke himself as attempting only to undermine some *stronger* thesis, how then could we make sense of Kripke's claim[4] that

> Wittgenstein has invented a new form of scepticism. Personally I am inclined to regard it as the most radical and original sceptical problem that philosophy has seen to date, one that only a highly unusual cast of mind could have produced.

For this reason an anti-sceptic such as Scott Soames is not countering Kripke on the intended ground when he claims that Kripke equivocates between *metaphysically necessary consequence* and *a priori consequence* in the course of setting out the sceptical argument.[5] Soames's complaint is that, as he reconstructs Kripke's argument, he finds that at least two of its premisses contain the notion of 'determination'. Neither one of the two distinguished senses of determination, however, can, according to Soames, sustain the joint truth of those premisses.

We would maintain, on the contrary, that Kripke had always intended his reader to appreciate that his sceptical argument bore directly on what we have called the *weak* thesis of determination of content. In this thesis, determination is conceived as metaphysically necessary consequence (or, conversely, as supervenience). With that disambiguation of the alleged equivocation in mind, Soames needs to re-evaluate the intended force of the argument. It is directed against a conception of determinate content supervening on a range of facts that is rich enough to include even facts about the subject's history of mental states. By 'history of mental states' Kripke of course countenances past *content-laden* states of the subject's mind. He explicitly allows such states into the determining basis, in his remarks on pp. 14, 21 and 56—among others—of his monograph. Soames's anti-sceptical response, once he had diagnosed the alleged equivocation, was simply to assert the weak thesis of determination. But on our view it is precisely that thesis which is under sustained attack in Kripke's monograph. Accordingly, much

---

[4] op. cit., p. 60.

[5] *Cf.* his paper 'Scepticism about Meaning: Indeterminacy, Normativity and the Rule-Following Paradox', Chapel Hill Philosophy Colloquium, 1995.

more is needed by way of anti-sceptical response to Kripke's arguments. Such a response has to proceed by looking at the argumentative details, in order to discover what, on closer reflection, is suspect about the way Kripke tries to refute, or at least instil doubt about, any claim of semantic determination; and that is what we try to do in what follows.

We shall use the symbol $\leadsto$ to represent that form of determination that corresponds to supervenience , and the symbol $\Rightarrow$ to represent the stronger form of determination that would involve analysability or theoretical reducibility. One could read

$$\mathcal{F}_1 \leadsto \mathcal{F}_2$$

as

'All the facts in $\mathcal{F}_2$ supervene on the basis of facts $\mathcal{F}_1$'

or, equivalently, as

'The basis of facts $\mathcal{F}_1$ has, as metaphysically necessary consequences, all the facts in $\mathcal{F}_2$';[6]

and one could read

$$\mathcal{F}_1 \Rightarrow \mathcal{F}_2$$

as

'All the facts in $\mathcal{F}_2$ can be analysed in terms of, or theoretically reduced to, the facts in the basis $\mathcal{F}_1$'

or, equivalently, as

---

[6] Note that nothing said thus far commits us to an account of supervenience in terms of possible worlds. But, in case a possible worlds theorist cares to appraise in 'possible worlds' terms the ensuing anti-Kripkean dialectic, it would be worth pointing out at this stage that a distinction might be drawn between 'intra-world' and 'inter-world' forms of supervenience. The *inter*-world supervenience claim is that any two individuals sharing the same $\mathcal{F}_1$-properties thereby share the same $\mathcal{F}_2$-properties, *regardless of what (possibly different) worlds they happen to be in*. The *intra*-world supervenience claim, by contrast, is that the sharing of $\mathcal{F}_1$-properties guarantees the sharing of $\mathcal{F}_2$-properties only when the two individuals are in the *same* world. If one makes this distinction, it should be noted that the Kripkean sceptic is denying even the *intra*-world form of supervenience of facts about meaning on such 'basis' facts as the sceptic would allow one to invoke. Whether one would in this case still want to call the converse of supervenience 'metaphysical necessitation' is doubtful.

'The basis of facts $\mathcal{F}_1$ has, as *a priori* consequences, all the facts in $\mathcal{F}_2$'.

With this notation, the last four theses mentioned above can be represented as follows:

Thesis of intentional analysability of meaning

| Basis of [non-semantic, but possibly intentional] facts | $\Rightarrow$ | Meaning facts |

Weak thesis of determination of content

| Basis of [non-semantic, but possibly intentional] facts | $\rightsquigarrow$ | Meaning facts |

Thesis of physicalistic reductionism

| Basis of [non-semantic, non-intentional] facts | $\Rightarrow$ | Meaning facts |

Strong thesis of determination of content

| Basis of [non-semantic, non-intentional] facts | $\rightsquigarrow$ | Meaning facts |

It is the weak thesis of determination of content that is the weakest of all four of these claims, and hence the most plausible for the quietist about semantic facts to believe. It therefore also must be the target of Kripke's sceptical argument, if the resulting scepticism is to be as radical and unsettling as Kripke claims it is. How, then, does Kripke's sceptic proceed?

4.4   On past and future applications of rules

The sceptic lays before the advocate of rule-following an observation, and a demand. He tries to show that they are in irreconcilable tension. The *observation* is that, for any rule-formulation R, purportedly representing the rule $\mathcal{R}$ that one is following or applying in a given instance:

> R has been applied only finitely often in the past.

This, of course, is an inherent feature of the human predicament. The *demand* is that one should ground the claim that

> Applying the rule represented by R in this new instance ought to yield the result r.

It is a *normative* demand. As Kripke spells it out, it has a little more detail than provided above. As he puts it (op. cit., p. 13)

> The sceptic doubts whether any instructions I gave myself in the past compel (or justify) the answer [r] rather than [some other answer r'] ... the sceptic holds that no fact about my past history—nothing that was ever in my mind, or in my external behaviour—establishes that I [intended to follow R] rather than [some different rule R'].

The result r is thus an 'unjustified leap in the dark' (p. 15); one's inclination to give that answer in the present instance is 'brute'. 'Nothing justifies' it. The central reason for the sceptical challenge is the point about finitude. Only finitely many applications—fewer than n, say—of what we suppose to be the rule $\mathcal{R}$ are available from the past. Therefore any continuation of the purported $\mathcal{R}$-sequence $r_1, \ldots, r_n$ as $r_1, \ldots, r_n, r'$ is as good as the supposedly 'correct' continuation $r_1, \ldots, r_n, r$. We have stated the problem thus generally, speaking schematically of rules $\mathcal{R}$, rule-formulations R and results r, to bring out only the essential features.

The doubt is infectious; the rot spreads. If it can be sustained, the sceptical attack broadens its front to include also theses (1), (3), (6), (7), (8) and possibly also (10). That is, the sceptic would call into question also the claims of inherence, determinacy, generativity, representation, objectivity and mutual understanding. As Wright has put it:[7]

> to sustain the skeptical argument is to uncage a tiger whose depradations there is then no hope of containing.

Kripke conducts much of his discussion by focusing on a specific example, namely the interpretation of the arithmetical sign '+'. It will be argued presently that Kripke's sceptic faces a number of constraints in trying to reinterpret '+' as representing *quaddition* (for which, see below). The constraints force him continually to reformulate the reinterpretation in a way that sacrifices uniformity—and with it, conviction. It will be shown further how Kripke is forced in the end to make possibility claims (concerning reinterpretations) as unfounded as those made by Quine concerning the possibility of alternative translation manuals. The sceptic's alternative interpretations turn out to be will o' wisps. *Pace* Kripkenstein and Quine, meaning is determinate; or at least, determinate enough for the moderate anti-realist's manifestation requirement on grasp of meaning to pose to the realist a challenge that he simply has to face. The ensuing difficulties will be

---

[7] Cf. 'Kripke's Account of the Argument against Private Language', *Journal of Philosophy*, 81, 1984, pp. 759–78; at p. 771.

examined in the next three chapters, once we have disposed here of Kripke's sceptic.

4.5   The sceptic is a non-factualist

What is remarkable about Kripkean scepticism, quite apart from its perverse ingenuity, is this: the argument Kripke employs to instil the doubt about meaning crucially exploits intuitive discriminations among contents in order to show not just that contents cannot be naturalized—cannot, that is, be located as some nexus of physical fact—but that there are no facts of the matter about (normatively imbued) content at all. By 'no facts of the matter' here the Kripkean sceptic means no facts whatsoever, physical or mental, be they behavioural, dispositional, functional, teleological, causal, intentional, or historical. The upshot is doubly bizarre: it is not just the non-factuality of content-attribution that surprises us; it is the paradoxical reliance on exquisite intuitions about individuation of content on which the sceptical argument is based.

The non-factuality of content-attribution has to be understood in a particularly strong way with Kripke's challenge. He is not allowing any dispositional facts about language-users to ground claims that they ascribe this content rather than that content to any particular expression. Therefore, as the sceptic raising the problem, he cannot help himself to a conception of the problem whereby there are two or more competing interpretations (each one definite or sharp in its own way) with equally good claim to being 'the' correct interpretation. For if he did help himself to such a conception, one would have to be able to make sense of the claim that differing contents were attached to an expression in advance of any decisively revelatory evidence as to their being competing interpretations: in advance, as it were, of any speaker revealing himself as 'deviant' in grasp of meaning. Thus one would be entitled to ask what it was about speaker S that made it the case that he attached content C to expression E, and what it was about speaker S^* that made it the case that he attached the different content C^* to the same expression E. This question is being posed before the divergent behaviour alerting us to the very fact that they do indeed interpret the expression E differently. The answer could only be that in such-and-such circumstances (the revelatory ones) the two speakers would, respectively, answer thus-and-so.

We can then press for grounds for such (thus far) counterfactual claims.

They cannot, *ex hypothesi*, be evidential grounds. Nor can such counterfactuals be *barely true*, with their truth-values discoverable no earlier than the fulfilment of their antecedents. There has to be some 'fact of the matter' concerning speakers S and S^* to ground the truth of the counterfactuals in question. But then this would be just the kind of factual basis that the sceptic is concerned to deny in the case of our grasp of meanings in general. That a speaker attaches a certain meaning to an expression is *not*, according to the Kripkean sceptic, something that is grounded in any fact about the speaker (or indeed in any fact about the speaker-within-the-community). So it would appear then that this construal of the sceptic's claim (namely, that different speakers may be attaching distinct contents to the same expression, but as yet undetected in doing so) is self-undermining, *if* the upshot is then to be that there can be no fact of the matter as to what speakers of one and the same language mean by their words. Once distinct and competing interpretations (and speakers' grasps) are in the picture, grounded in dispositions supporting counterfactual claims about language use, we are moving in a space of possibilities that includes their fortuitiously, or perhaps even as an evolutionary outcome, having the same dispositions by virtue of enjoying the same constitutional structure as human beings.

Thus the sceptic is forced to move to a conception of non-factuality that does not turn on there being *competing interpretations* of one and the same expression. Yet the Kripkean sceptic seems precisely to be relying on finely honed competing interpretations of familiar expressions in order to induce the scepticism in others! For this reason we can place the burden of proof on the Kripkean sceptic. The conclusion he wishes to force upon us is that there is no fact of the matter that could ground the (undisputed) normativity of meaning. In the course of doing so he arrives at a lemma denying the determinacy of meaning. The lemma claims that at any point in time our words can be bizarrely reinterpreted while yet doing justice to all available evidential facts concerning our use of the language. It is important to appreciate that the reinterpretability in question could ground the sceptic's conclusion only on the further assumption that the reinterpretation attaches a distinct but deviant range of contents to our sentences. The sceptic does not challenge unique interpretability by showing that no interpretation exists; rather, he challenges it by purporting to show that an embarrassing variety of exact interpretations exists. It is multiplicity, not non-existence, of interpretations which is the problem he wishes to foist on the orthodox content theorist. But if one can help oneself thus to contents so finely and intuitively discriminated, so can the orthodox opposition. And the orthodox opposition can make so bold as to insist on a firm and unique co-ordination of contents with sentences, consonant with common-sense expectation and practice, failing convincing sceptical proof to the prolific (not empty) contrary.

4.6   Kripke's dialectic of reinterpretation

Kripke's example of quaddition is a variation on Wittgenstein's original example (*PI*, §185) of the pupil who continues the series +2 by writing 1000, 1004, 1008, 1012. For our purposes Kripke's is the more instructive to concentrate on, so let us restate it. The sign '+' stands for addition, or the plus function—so we assume. But, says Kripke, there is an alternative possibility posed by the sceptic. The sign '+' stands rather for *quaddition*, or the *quus* function. The operation • of quaddition is defined as follows:

$$x \bullet y = x + y \text{ if } x, y < 57$$

$$x \bullet y = 5 \text{ otherwise}$$

Let us go along with Kripke in all the background assumptions needed, concerning the paucity of past additions. The subject has never before dealt with numbers greater than 57, etc. Thus, according to his sceptic, we have no guarantee that he now means addition rather than quaddition when he uses the sign '+'. The crunch comes with, say, the problem '68+57=?'

The unreflective person thinks there is a fact, or facts, about himself that make it the case that he ought to respond with '125'. For these facts determine that he means (the operation of) addition by his present use of the sign '+', that he intends to apply the same rule (to compute sums) that he had done in the past when using the sign '+'. If he is to keep faith with his past intentions in using the sign '+', then the answer must be 125. Against this, Kripke's sceptic suggests that, compatibly with all such purported facts about the computing subject, he might just as well respond with '5'—the *quum* of the two numbers 68 and 57, rather than their sum. This is not to say that an observer would find the prediction that he would answer '5' just as likely or plausible as the prediction that he would answer '125'. The point has to do rather with whatever justification the subject would have for his answer, in so far as it turned on associating one meaning rather than another with the plus sign. According to the sceptic, he would be just as justified in quadding as he would have been in adding.

So far so good. One can imagine how we could discover that there was a 'hidden quadder' in our midst—should the 'bending point' be accessible.[8] Such a person would agree with us in our computations up to a certain point—say, during all his training and early 'independent' computing—and then suddenly 'go awry'. It would only be this 'deviant' behaviour that provided the first shred of evidence that he meant quaddition, rather than addition, by the plus sign.

The first objection that Kripke considers (and rejects) to the sceptical possibility just outlined consists in a specification of

> a *rule* which determines how addition is to be continued. What was the rule? Well, say, to take it in its most primitive form: suppose we wish to add x and y. Take a huge bunch of marbles. First count out x marbles in one heap. Then count out y marbles in another. Put the two heaps together and count out the number of marbles in the union thus formed. The result is $x + y$.

He goes on to say (p. 16)

> Despite the initial plausibility of this objection, the sceptic's response is all too obvious. True, if 'count', as I used the word in the past, referred to the act of counting (and my other past words are correctly interpreted in the standard way), then 'plus' must have stood for addition. But I applied 'count' to only finitely many past cases. Thus the sceptic can question my present interpretation of my past usage of 'count' as he did with 'plus'. In particular, he can claim that by 'count' I formerly meant *quount*, where to 'quount' a heap is to count it in the ordinary sense, unless the heap was formed as the union of two heaps, one of which has 57 or more items, in which case one must automatically give the answer '5'. It is clear that if in the past 'counting' meant quounting, and if I follow the rule for 'plus' that was quoted so triumphantly to the sceptic, I must admit that '68+57' must yield the answer '5'. Here I have supposed that previously 'count' was never applied to heaps formed as the union of sub-heaps either of which has 57 or more elements, but if this particular upper bound does not work, another will do. For the point is perfectly general:

---

[8]I take the terminology of 'bending' from Blackburn; *cf.* 'The Individual Strikes Back', *Synthese*, 58, 1984, 281–301; and *Spreading the Word*, Oxford University Press, 1984.

if 'plus' is explained in terms of 'counting', a non-standard interpretation of the latter will yield a non-standard interpretation of
the former.

Note the definitional dialectic emerging in this long move by Kripke (a dialectic endorsed, incidentally, by Blackburn).[9] We have on the left the standard
interpretations or meanings, and on the right the sceptic's proposed alternatives, defined in terms of the bounds indicated:

1. *plus*   *quus*   57
   addition *quaddition*   57
   sum   *quum*   57
2. *count*   *quount*   possibly $>> 57; 10^6 + 1$, say

There is a first word, or family of words, and these are sceptically reinterpreted by reference to a first bound (here, 57). The opponent then links
the first word, or family of words, with a second word, bringing out important meaning-constituting links between them. The sceptic in turn offers a
reinterpretation of the second word, but now, importantly, with the bound
possibly very different. This would have been the case in our example of addition and counting if, say, the subject in question was a seasoned marathon
counter who was known to have counted up to one million as a playground
stunt. With that piece of evidence about his past usage, the sceptic would
be forced to reselect the 'bending point' of the reinterpretation, making it
greater than one million. The corresponding reinterpretation of '+' would
now have to differ from that originally proposed, in order to overcome the
problem of the meaning-constituting link to the word that had the much
bigger bound associated with it.

Apparently satisfied with this strategem, Kripke goes on to say[10] that
the same objection (namely, offering a deviant interpretation for any new
word offered in a meaning-constituting link with the original one) 'scotches
a related suggestion':

> It might be urged that the quus function is ruled out as an inter-
> pretation of '+' because it fails to satisfy some of the laws I accept
> for '+' (for example, it is not associative; we could have defined
> it so as not even to be commutative). One might even observe
> that, on the natural numbers, addition is the only function that

---

[9] loc. cit., p. 288.
[10] In a very important footnote—no. 12 on pp. 16–7.

satisfies certain laws that I accept—the 'recursion equations' for $+$: $(x)(x+0 = x)$ and $(x)(y)(x+y' = (x+y)')$ where the stroke or dash indicates successor; these equations are sometimes called a 'definition' of addition. The problem is that the other signs used in these laws (the universal quantifiers, the equality sign) have been applied in only a finite number of instances, and *they can be given non-standard interpretations that will fit non-standard interpretations of* '$+$'. Thus for example '(x)' might mean for every $x < h$, where h is some upper bound to the instances where universal instantiation has hitherto been applied, and similarly for equality. (My emphasis)

Thus we have yet a third word or family of words—here, the universal quantifier—involved in meaning-constituting links with the original; and again, Kripke's method of saving the sceptic is to impose a reinterpretation determined by a bound h arising from past usage of the new word in question. Our table above has grown longer:

1. *plus*	*quus*	57
addition	*quaddition*	57
sum	*quum*	57
2. *count*	*quount*	possibly $>> 57; 10^6 + 1,$ say
3. $\forall x$	$\forall x < h$	h

where $h =$ upper bound of $\{n|$the subject has in the past inferred '$A(n)$' from '$\forall x A(x)$'$\}$

Now this bound h may be very large indeed, even if the subject's applications of the rule of universal elimination have been relatively rare. But again, it is the tail that is wagging the dog. One finds the bound h for the third link of the meaning chain, and then the other two links are reforged with sceptical reinterpretation on the strength of the bound h chosen. What we do not have from Kripke is a satisfyingly uniform way of sustaining the original reinterpretation on the very first word on which the sceptic tried to ring the changes.

But that, one might say, is how one would expect it to be. After all, interpretation is a global or holistic affair, and evidence can be brought to bear on the proposed interpretation of a word from all sorts of unexpected directions. The important point, surely, (so this line of thought continues) is that the subject has mastered only finitely many individual words, and has applied each of these only finitely often in the past; thus, in the light of the total evidence concerning his past usage, the 'bending' can be done for all the words that have to be bent if any chosen one of them (like 'plus') is to be bent to start with.

We shall argue against this reinterpretability claim. The need to do so is highlighted by the way in which a writer hostile to Kripkean scepticism, such as Blackburn, has nevertheless acquiesced in the claim. Blackburn too readily concedes[11] that by '$x + y$'

> I might yesterday have meant ... the sum of x, y, except when $x=57$ and $y=68$ and 5 otherwise. This hypothesis is not refuted by my present staunch denial that I had any such thought in mind yesterday, or that if asked I would have used words like these to explain myself. For the sceptic will urge that as well as having a bent interpretation of '+' yesterday, *I could have had a bent interpretation of these other terms as well.* (My emphasis)

4.7   Uniformity of reinterpretation requires globality

What is to be challenged in this nonchalant accommodation of any new meaning constraints produced to discomfit the sceptic is the very idea that a global reinterpretation is to be had. Kripke has simply not supplied the details of any full reinterpretation once all the evidence is in. All he has done is provide local, piecemeal reinterpretations of individual words and phrases, and shifted his ground (or his bound) in response to objections as they were raised. The sceptic's strategy is just this: to any objection of the form 'But what about such-and-such a meaning connection (or operational constraint, or whatever) with X?' the sceptic replies, 'Well, how do you know that in the past you meant $\mathcal{X}$ by 'X', and not qu-$\mathcal{X}$?'

Thus, for example, to illustrate his method further: Suppose we challenge him on the reinterpretation of 'for every x'. We point out that it is not only universal eliminations that have to be reckoned with, but universal introductions also. We are accustomed to inferring 'for every x $F(x)$' when we have a proof of $F(a)$ from assumptions that do not involve the parameter a. Kripke would reply that on every occasion that we have inferred that for every x $F(x)$, we could just as well have been inferring that for every

---

[11]Cf. 'The Individual Strikes Back', at pp. 287–8.

$x < h$, $F(x)$. 'True', we retort, 'but it is clear that that would not be the strongest conclusion possible in the circumstances.' 'So what?' the sceptic replies. Then we point out to him the reason, inherent in the schematic subproof, why we take the quantified formula with, so to speak, the full universal force. This is that we can take *any* term t (here, a numeral say) and substitute it for appropriate occurrences of a in the subproof of $F(a)$, to produce a proof of $F(t)$. 'Aha!', says the sceptic. 'Let us then simply reinterpret your "any" in this gloss along the same lines as before. It looks just like the metalinguistic version of the object-language universal quantifier that has already been qu-ed as "for every $x < h$, $F(x)$".' The problem, however, is that the bound variable of quantification in the metalinguistic phrase ranges over terms, not their denotations. And there is no obvious ordering of all terms by means of which the reinterpretation can be stated, which will mesh with that proposed for the numerical universal quantifier. Of course, the sceptic might say that the metalinguistic quantifier is simply to be reinterpreted as 'for every term t that denotes a number less than h', but still this is interestingly different from the first reinterpretation of the object-language quantifier prefix. The difference is enough to raise doubts as to whether 'all', 'every', 'each' and 'any', in their 'universal' uses, are being uniformly reinterpreted. And one wonders whether there might not be other connections, with universal quantifications over items other than terms, where the reinterpretation that would have to be exacted on the new material would display the same sort of sortal sensitivity as we have just seen in the case of terms.

The point about the substitution of terms for a parameter could be put thus: Given a subproof $\Pi(a)$, of the conclusion $F(a)$, whose assumptions do not involve the parameter a, and given any term t, there is an operation $[a/t]$ that one can perform on the proof to turn it into a proof $\Pi(t)$, of conclusion $F(t)$, from the same assumptions. Call the operation 't-for-a-substitution'. If the sceptic were dissuaded, by the considerations given above, from pursuing his line of reinterpretation of the quantifier phrase 'any term t', he might try to shore up his reinterpretation 'for every $x < h$' by reinterpreting 't-for-a-substitution' as meaning t-for-a-*quub*stitution, where . . . .

Now it is conceivable that substitution of terms in contexts other than proofs would also have to be re-construed as we pursued the qu-ing strategy with Kripke's sceptic. And it is possible that the reinterpretations of these other kinds of substitution would involve different bounds, or indeed wholly different kinds of bound. Substitution becomes context-specific for its (re)interpretation, just as universal quantification became sortal-specific for its own (re)interpretation.

So far the only meaning-constituting links that we have explored for 'plus' are:

1. the connection with counting heaps

2. the connection with laws of arithmetic such as associativity, and in particular the occurrences of the universal quantifier within those laws

3. the connection between the universal quantifier within object-language sentences, and the universal quantifier in the metalanguage, especially the ones ranging over terms and proofs

We have seen the bounds-for-bending shifting retrospectively as each new link has been adduced for consideration; or the sortal context emerging as crucial for the reinterpretation of what is usually taken to be an applicative with uniform meaning. Let us not beg the question, however, with this last phrase; the sceptic need only claim *quuniformity* in his own usage!

There is a fourth kind of meaning-constituting link constraining our interpretation of '+' that has not yet been mentioned. It is of a purely mathematical nature, albeit metamathematical. If someone were to have produced the following proof as part of the finite evidential basis to which the Kripkean sceptic is responsible when framing his reinterpretations, then we are not at all sure that quaddition (with whatever bound) is even a starter: Note the following pattern for addition. The sum of the first two digits in each row is the third in the row.

0 0 0

0 1 1
1 0 1

0 2 2
1 1 2
2 0 2

0 3 3
1 2 3
2 1 3
3 0 3

```
0 4 4
1 3 4
2 2 4
3 1 4
4 0 4

0 5 5
1 4 5
2 3 5
3 2 5
4 1 5
5 0 5
```

In general there are $(n + 1)$ distinct addition sums with result n:

```
0          n          n
1          n − 1      n
.          .          .
.          .          .
.          .          .
n − 1      1          n
n          0          n
```

Definition: $\underline{n}$ is the numeral for n—that is, the term '$sss\ldots s0$', with n occurrences of s; or the canonical representation of n in decimal notation.

Theorem: For every n, there are exactly $(n + 1)$ distinct addition sums with result $\underline{n}$, including, for every $p < n$, the sum '$\underline{p} + \underline{(n − p)}$' and the sum '$\underline{(n − p)} + \underline{p}$'.

Proof: By induction.

Basis: There is 1 sum with result 0, namely '0+0'

Inductive hypothesis: There are exactly n distinct addition sums with result $(n−1)$, including, for every $p < n$, the sum '$\underline{p} + \underline{(n − 1 − p)}$' and the sum '$\underline{(n − 1 − p)} + \underline{p}$'.

Inductive step: Write down all the sums guaranteed by inductive hypothesis. Change the second summand $\underline{m}$ of each sum '$\underline{k} + \underline{m}$' to $\underline{m + 1}$. There result n distinct addition sums with result $\underline{n}$, including, for every $p < n$, the sum '$\underline{p} + \underline{(n − p)}$' and the sum

'$(n - 1 - p) + (p + 1)$'. There remains only one outstanding addition sum with result n not yet on this list: namely, '$\underline{n}+0$'. The result follows.

Kripke's quadder would be embarrassed by this result. For there are not exactly 6 quaddition sums with result 5. Yet that the user of '+' should have the disposition to accept the theorem just given is surely a reasonable precondition for attribution of competence with that sign.

Another constraint to explore is a refinement of (1), Kripke's operation on heaps of marbles. This constraint makes a very general connection between numbers as mathematical objects (positions within the series of natural numbers) and the numerosity of predicate extensions. We call it Schema C:

> For every natural number n
>
> there are n F's
>
> if and only if
>
> the number of F's = $\underline{n}$

As one counts the F's, passing through the numbers (or numerals) 1,2,3,4,5,... one is assured that there are at least correspondingly many F's at each stage. When one reaches the final number (or numeral) $\underline{n}$, with no more F's to count, one knows that there are exactly n F's. This may appear banal, but it is important in connection with Kripke's sceptical reinterpretation of 'count' as *quount*. Another way of putting the schema above is as follows (call it the Operational Schema C):

> If one correctly counts the F's,
>
> one gets the answer $\underline{n}$
>
> if and only if
>
> there are n F's

Now let us concentrate on what is meant by 'There are n F's'. One can recursively define '(There are at least n)x Fx':

(There is at least 1)x $Fx =_{df} \exists x Fx$

(There are at least $(n + 1)$)x $Fx =_{df}$

$$\exists x(Fx\wedge(\text{there are at least } n)y(x \neq y \wedge Fy))$$

Then one can define 'There are exactly n F's' as 'There are at least n F's but it is not the case that there are at least $(n+1)$ F's.'

Kripke is now in trouble from a different direction with his interpretation of 'count' as quount. Before, he was exercised by the constraint that one can interpret addition in terms of heaps—putting a heap of n marbles together with a different heap of m marbles to get a heap that, so one must be able to tell, by counting, consists of $(n$ plus $m)$ marbles. In this context quounting was forced to yield the automatic answer '5' if either 'quummand' heap had more than 57 marbles. But let us now make addition subject to a more general schema:

> If there are exactly n F's and exactly m G's, and nothing is both
> F and G, then there are exactly $(n+m)$ things that are F or G.

We shall be making use of the schema presently. For the time being, note that Schema C links the adjectival use of number words to their substantival use as numerals. It introduces an important conceptual control on the use of numerals. For example, when '12' is used as a numeral—as a name of a number, or position in the series of numbers—to 'give the number' resulting from counting the F's, it has to correspond, *via* Schema C, to a sentence in first-order notation saying that there are exactly twelve F's. This sentence does not involve the numeral '12' at all. Rather, it is constructed using the appropriate number of quantifier occurrences according to the recursive definition given above. In order to illustrate, let us take a smaller number such as 2. The canonical sentence, on the definition above, that says there are exactly two F's is

$$\exists x(Fx \wedge \exists y(Fy \wedge \neg x = y)) \wedge \neg\exists x(Fx \wedge \exists y(Fy \wedge \neg x = y \wedge \exists z(Fz \wedge \neg x = z \wedge \neg y = z)))$$

which is logically equivalent to

$$\exists x\exists y(Fx \wedge Fy \wedge \neg x = y \wedge \forall w(Fw \supset (w = x \vee w = y)))$$

In the latter sentence we see more clearly the twofold occurrence of the existential quantifier, and the action of the universal quantifier that, as it were, limits those occurrences to two. The formula shows something about the two-ness of F, rather than saying anything about the number 2.

Now consider how such formulae feature in the 'conceptual control' via our new schema above for addition. Suppose the number of F's is 68 and the number of G's is 57. Suppose also that nothing is both F and G. Then $(68+57)$ is the number of things that are F or G. If we get our addition right, we have that 125 is the number of things that are F or G. That is (according to Schema C) there are 125 things that are F or G. This latter claim says nothing about the number 125 (the sum of 68 and 57); rather, it shows the 125-ness of $(F$ or $G)$:

$$\exists x_1 \exists x_2 \ldots \exists x_{125}((Fx_1 \vee Gx_1) \wedge (Fx_2 \vee Gx_2) \wedge \ldots \wedge (Fx_{125} \vee Gx_{125}) \wedge$$
$$\forall y((Fy \vee Gy) \supset (y = x_1 \vee y = x_2 \vee \ldots \vee y = x_{125})))$$

Now Kripke's quadder, if he accepts Schema C—which he must—will have a very different formula here. It will have only the first *five* existentials, and will be truncated accordingly within. Yet he will have to maintain that it follows logically from the two formulae saying, respectively, 'There are exactly 68 F's' and 'There are exactly 57 G's', along with the premiss 'Nothing is both F and G'. Thus the sceptic is faced with a very difficult logical gerrymander indeed. Either recursive definition goes haywire when the bound gets big enough, so that we are dealing with *requursions* (but how, exactly?); or the syntactic properties of formulae change suddenly upon over-accretion of quantifiers—and we have to develop a theory of *quyntax* (but how, exactly?); or logic gets fitted out with a *quonsequence* relation (but how, exactly?).

At this point we would be quite right to baulk at the (now most casual-seeming) claim that the sceptic 'need only reinterpret' such-and-such other expressions in a correspondingly deviant way in order to sustain the fit with the (admittedly finite) evidence, including now, as it does, the conceptual controls provided by closer philosophical analysis. Kripke has not shown, in any convincing way—with appropriate detail—just how the changes would have to be rung on our normal understanding of number, logical structure, logical consequence, recursive definition and so on, for it to be plausible that anything in the spirit of the original definition of quaddition can sit on the evidence about usage as happily as addition can.

We say 'anything in the spirit... ', because, as already pointed out, the actual bounds that would have to be chosen for the bending of predicates and other expressions (such as the universal quantifier) appear to depend on all our past usage of any and every expression of our language. A settled deviant interpretation of '+' appears to be possible only when *all* the facts about usage are in. We have already noted how, if we do not get all those facts in first, the pile-up of constraints via semantically neighbouring expressions forces us continually to revise our original choice of bending point for the sceptical reinterpretation.

4.8   Kripkean scepticism compared with Quinean indeterminacy: the new dogma of post-empiricism

At this point we see that Kripke's sceptical claim is very closely akin to Quine's thesis about the radical indeterminacy of translation. According to that thesis,

> *given any* translation manual f from Junglese to English, compatible with all possible behavioural evidence—past, present and future—*there will be another* manual g (indeed, an indefinite multiplicity of manuals), likewise compatible with all the evidence, such that for some Junglese sentence ϕ, speakers of English will agree that $f(\phi)$ and $g(\phi)$ 'stand in no plausible relation of equivalence, however loose'.

This $\forall\exists$-claim that, given any f, there will be such rival g, has never been given detailed proof.[12] But it remains one of the most influential dogmas of contemporary philosophy of language, supplanting the two dogmas of empiricism identified and rejected by Quine. These were the 'dogma' of the analytic-synthetic distinction, and the dogma of reductionism.[13] The new dogma on offer from Quine deserves a title: let us call it the Π_1-dogma, because of its $\forall\exists$-form. It appears in Kripke in the following form:

> *given any* interpretation (rule) for a term that accords with all (finite) past usage, *there will be another* rule (indeed, an indefinite multiplicity of rules) that accords equally with that past usage, but which differs from the first rule in some as yet unencountered instance or application.

The only methodological (or metaphysical) differences here between Quine and Kripke are these:

1. *Individual v. community*

---

[12] For an extensive justification of this claim, see *AR&L*, ch. 4.

[13] In the philosophy of language, it seems, it's a dogma-eat-dogma world.

Kripke, in setting up the sceptical paradox, focuses on just one individual language-user (not on the usage of the whole community—that features only later, in his 'sceptical solution').

2. *Nature of evidence*

Kripke would be prepared to let his opponent count as evidence (as to meaning) not only the individual's observable behaviour, but all his mental states as well, whether or not these issue in observable behaviour.[14] In this way he is more generous than Quine. But in another way Kripke is less generous than Quine. Kripke considers not all *possible* evidence — past, present and future, as Quine does — but rather all *past* evidence.

3. *Fact of the matter*

For Kripke, f is normal and g is 'bent'—'bizarre', 'crazy', 'insane', as he himself has sympathetically put it. For Quine, f is no better nor worse than g—all that counts for him is that there is an ineliminable multiplicity of conflicting translation mappings, none of them privileged in any way; and that multiplicity reveals that there is no semantic fact of the matter.

4. *Centrality of logic*

For Quine, a constraint on translation (hence interpretation) is that one should represent the native as using the same logic as we do (that is, according to Quine, classical logic); for Kripke, however, everything is up for reinterpretation, including logic.[15]

The force of Kripke's sceptical paradox is precisely that, even when allowed God-like access to all (past) facts about a given individual, if one proposes the normal interpretation (call it f) there will allegedly be a sceptical, deviant, 'bent' interpretation (call it g) such that ... [and here would follow a specification of how the bent interpretation would conflict with the normal one but only in respect of some hitherto unencountered circumstance, of a kind not yet encountered in the past evidence.] The circumstance could be, for example, one's first-ever attempt to add numbers one of which is greater than 57.

---

[14] As Kripke stresses at p. 14 and p. 56.
[15] I owe this observation to John Martin.

Now despite the four differences between Kripke and Quine just stated, there is hardly any difference at all in the dogmatic nature of their conditional existence claims: they both claim that, *given any f* (satisfying certain conditions), *there will be some g* such that ... without providing the substantive details that would be required in order to show exactly *how* one gets one's *g* from the given *f*. It is instructive to see how this is borne out in their writings. The following quotations from Chapter 2 of *Word and Object* give, in their various ways, the content of Quine's conclusion, without the preceding or surrounding text providing anything like a proof of that conclusion. In each quotation the emphasis is on the part that requires but does not receive proof.

> The thesis is then this: manuals for translating one language into another *can be set up in divergent ways*, all compatible with the totality of speech dispositions, yet incompatible with one another. *In countless places they will diverge* in giving, as their respective translations of a sentence of the one language, sentences of the other language which stand to each other in no plausible sort of equivalence however loose. (p. 27)

> We could equate a native expression with any of the disparate English terms 'rabbit', 'rabbit stage', 'undetached rabbit part', etc., and still, *by compensatorily juggling the translation of numerical identity and associated particles, preserve conformity* to stimulus meanings of occasion sentences. (p. 54)

> Both analytical hypotheses ... *could doubtless be accommodated by compensatory variations in analytical hypotheses concerning other locutions*,[16] so as to conform equally to all independently discoverable translations of whole sentences and indeed all speech dispositions of all speakers concerned. And yet countless native sentences admitting no independent check ... may be expected to receive radically unlike and incompatible English renderings under the two systems ...

---

[16] As Jay Rosenberg has pointed out, this 'bland assurance ...does not constitute an *argument* [for the indeterminacy thesis]'. See his *Linguistic Representation*, Reidel, Dordrecht, 1974, at p. 70.

There can be no doubt that rival systems of analytical hypotheses can fit the totality of speech behaviour to perfection, and can fit the totality of dispositions to speech behaviour as well, and still specify mutually incompatible translations of countless sentences insusceptible of independent control. (p. 72)

rival systems of analytical hypotheses can conform to all speech dispositions within each of the languages concerned and yet dictate, in countless cases, utterly disparate translations; not mere mutual paraphrases, but translations each of which would be excluded by the other system of translation. Two such translations might even be patently contrary in truth value, provided there is no stimulation that would encourage assent to either. (pp. 73–74)

another bilingual *could have a semantic correlation incompatible with the first bilingual's* without deviating from the first bilingual in his speech dispositions within either language, except in his dispositions to translate. (p. 74)

Our advantage with a compatriot is that with little deviation the automatic or homophonic ... hypothesis of translation fills the bill. *If we were perverse and ingenious we could scorn that hypothesis and devise other analytical hypotheses that would attribute unimagined views to our compatriot, while conforming to all his dispositions to verbal response to all possible stimulations.* (p. 78)

Compare now Kripke's similarly confident but detail-deficient claims, quoted earlier, about sceptical reinterpretability of our words. Again, the emphases are ours:

If 'count', as I used the word in the past, referred to the act of counting... , then 'plus' must have stood for addition. But I applied 'count', like 'plus', to only finitely many past cases. Thus the sceptic can question my present interpretation of my past usage of 'count' as he did with 'plus'. In particular, *he can claim that* by 'count' I formerly meant *quount*, where to 'quount' a heap is to count it in the ordinary sense, unless the heap was formed as the union of two heaps, one of which has 57 or more

items, in which case one must automatically give the answer '5'.
It is clear that if in the past 'counting' meant quounting, and if I
follow the rule for 'plus' that was quoted so triumphantly to the
sceptic, I must admit that '68+57' must yield the answer '5'. ...
the point is perfectly general: if 'plus' is explained in terms of
'counting', *a non-standard interpretation of the latter will yield
a non-standard interpretation of the former.* (p. 16)

The last claim that we have emphasized here really needs more careful formulation. Kripke should say 'a non-standard interpretation of the latter, if it
be available, will yield a non-standard interpretation of the former (though
not necessarily the original non-standard interpretation of the former that
we started out with)'. Yet his formulation invites the reading 'for the original non-standard interpretation of the former, there will be a non-standard
interpretation of the latter that sustains it'; and it is this stronger reading
that is so starkly similar to Quine's claims about the the existence of rival
translation manuals. But even if Kripke cleaves to the more careful reading we have given, he is doing no better than Quine. For the claim would
be that, once all the evidence concerning all words is in, there will be a
simultaneous sceptical reinterpretation of those words severally, which will
support one another mutually so as to do justice to the evidence. In effect,
the global reinterpretation here proposed is a rival translation manual set
up against the standard, homophonic one: needing perversion and ingenuity,
perhaps, as Quine said, but allowing us nevertheless to scorn the standard
interpretation of our words.

As already noted above, in a footnote to the quoted passage on p. 16,
Kripke attempts to 'scotch' the 'related suggestion' that the law of associativity constrains the sceptic's reinterpretation of 'plus' in a way similar to that
in which the link with counting heaps was supposed to do. We have already
seen that Kripke's way of dealing with this particular meaning-constituting
link is to reinterpret the universal quantifier. For present purposes, all that
needs to be amplifed is the by now familiarly dogmatic ring to his claim that

The problem is that the other signs used in these laws (the universal quantifiers, the equality sign) have been applied in only a
finite number of instances, and *they can be given non-standard
interpretations that will fit non-standard interpretations of '+'.*
(My emphasis)

And again, on p. 17:

It is tempting to answer the sceptic by appealing from one rule
to another more 'basic' rule. But the sceptical move can be
repeated at the more 'basic' level also. Eventually the process
must stop—'justifications come to an end somewhere'—and we
are left with a rule which is completely unreduced to any other.
How can I justify my present application of such a rule, when a
sceptic *could easily interpret it so as to yield any of an indefinite
number of other results?* (My emphasis)

4.9 Anti-sceptical responses emphasizing the first-person case

Bearing in mind the four points of contrast noted above between Quine and
Kripke, it is interesting to see how anti-sceptical responses, from Searle[17] and
Wright[18] respectively, have been framed. Quine occupies an anti-mentalistic,
third-person standpoint, allowing only observable behaviour as evidence for
a theory of translation:

> All the objective data (the linguist) has to go on are the forces
> that he sees impinging on the native's surfaces and the observable
> behavior, vocal and otherwise, of the native.
> (*Word and Object*, p. 28)

Given the

> fugitive nature of introspective method, we (are) better off theo-
> rizing about meaning from the more primitive paradigm: that of
> the linguist who deals observably with the native informant (op.
> cit., p. 71)

At best he will allow dispositions to verbal behaviour, in response to external
stimuli, into the evidential basis. But still he maintains

> in all positivistic reasonableness that if two speakers [of the same
> language] match in all dispositions to verbal behaviour there is
> no sense in imagining semantic differences between them. (op.
> cit., p. 79)

---

[17]'Indeterminacy, Empiricism and the First Person', *Journal of Philosophy*, 84, 1987,
pp. 123–46.
[18]loc. cit.

And of any such disposition he says (pp. 33–4) that it is

> a disposition to assent to or dissent from (a sentence) S when variously stimulated. The disposition may be presumed to be some subtle structural condition, like an allergy and like solubility; like an allergy, more particularly, in not being understood. ... we are familiar enough in a general way with how one sets about guessing, from judicious tests and samples and observed uniformities, whether there is a disposition of a specified sort.

Quine 'argues'—better, asserts—that, given this anti-mentalistic third-person standpoint, indeterminacy follows. Searle agrees: for him, as for Quine, behaviourism plus determinacy leads to absurdity. Quine holds on to behaviourism, concluding to indeterminacy. Searle, possessed of the inviolable intuition that 'I know what I mean' (p. 141), holds on to determinacy and rejects the behaviourism. He concludes (p. 146) that

> when we understand someone else or ourselves, what we require—among other things—is a knowledge of intentional contents. Knowledge of these contents is not equivalent to knowledge of the matching of public behaviour with stimuli nor to the matching of utterances with conditions in the world. We see this most obviously in the first-person case, and our neglect of the first-person case leads us to have a false model of the understanding of language.

But of course even this appeal to the first-person standpoint is not enough, on Kripke's view, to secure determinacy. For Kripke, the sceptical challenge

> purports to show that *nothing in my mental history or past behavior*—not even what an omniscient God would know—could establish whether I meant plus or quus. (p. 21) (My emphasis)

So whereas Quine maintains, and Searle agrees, that

> No behavioural evidence secures determinacy

while yet Searle claims that

> Behavioural evidence supplemented by introspective evidence secures determinacy

we have Kripke claiming that

Not even behavioural evidence supplemented by introspective evidence secures determinacy.

Finally, against Kripke, Wright puts forward the view—congenial, one should imagine, to Searle—that

Behavioural evidence supplemented by introspective evidence (to wit: precise recall of one's previous intentions, to whose content one has authoritative and non-inferential access) secures determinacy.

Wright candidly admits that

The (intuitive notion of intention) is not unproblematic. It could be that it is radically incoherent.

Nevertheless, he ventures to claim that

[t]he fact remains that it is available to confront Kripke's sceptic, and that, so far as I can see, the sceptical argument is powerless against it. (p. 776)

It cannot be said, however, that Wright's further discussion[19] produces the suasive details needed to back this claim. The difference between Searle and Wright appears to be negligible. What Wright says in more philosophical jargon, Searle comes out with directly: 'I know what I mean.' Both stray uncomfortably close to a position whence but a step or two would deliver the possibility of a private language. Both are moving to much more fertile ground for an epistemology of linguistic understanding; but by the same token both will have to hack at a rank abundance of weeds.

4.10 On Goodman's Paradox

A hidden gruester is one who attaches to the word 'green' the concept *grue*. Now there are well-known moves in the debate over Goodman's new riddle of induction[20] that show how elusive is any supposed asymmetry between

---

[19]'On Making Up One's Mind: Wittgenstein on Intention', in *Proceedings of the 11th International Wittgenstein Symposium, 1986, Kirchberg*, Hölder-Pichler-Tempsky, Vienna, 1987, pp. 391–404.

[20]*Cf. Fact, Fiction, and Forecast*, 3rd edn., Bobbs-Merrill, Indianapolis, 1973; at pp. 72–81.

the 'normal' concepts and their 'gruified' counterparts. It will not do to try to exploit nomological links with, say, wavelengths of reflected light. For the gruester will be conceiving of *lavewengths*. Nor will it help to appeal to meter readings—for the gruester will be making meter *greadings*; and so on. To sustain the original symmetry of definition (of 'grue' and 'bleen' in terms of 'green' and 'blue'—and vice versa—see below) one rings the definitional changes all the way up through the conceptual scheme. It would appear so far that the discussions of Goodman's paradox in the literature have conspicuously failed to serve up a single impossibility proof to quash the gruester's wholesale gruifiability claim.

But it must also be conceded that we are not yet possessed of a satisfactory *possibility proof* either. The best we can do is piecemeal handwaving of the kind just gone through, concerning wavelengths and meter readings. Just as Quine has failed to provide proper proof of the Π_1-dogma of indeterminacy, and Kripke has failed to provide proper proof of the Π_1-dogma of non-unique interpretability, so too have Goodman and his successors failed to provide proper proof of the Π_1-dogma of wholesale gruifiability. But the Goodmanian strategy of reinterpretation is interestingly different from Kripke's, in one respect at least. This is that as the ripple of reinterpretation spreads, the original plop stays the same. It is still *grue*, as originally defined, that is on offer as the reinterpretation of 'green' when we advance to reinterpret 'wavelength' as *lavewength*; and so on through the widening web of reinterpreted logical siblings, semantic cousins and nomological neighbours. But as we have seen above, Kripke's reinterpretation of '+' itself has continually to be revised in the light of the bending points chosen for the reinterpretation of other terms involved in meaning-constituting links with '+'; and ultimately the Kripkean alternative has to be advanced wholesale, only once all the evidence about past usage of all expressions is in.

Why is this? Why is Goodman's bizarre reinterpretation sustainable by thus ringing the changes without, as it were, any corrective feedback to the deviant reinterpretation of the original expression? It may have something to do with the sheer simplicity of the gruification formula. *Grue* is defined in terms of green (G) and blue (B) with respect to a cut-off predicate (T). We may abbreviate 'grue(x)' as $[G, B, T](x)$, defined as follows:

$$[G, B, T](x) =_{df} (Gx \wedge Tx) \vee (Bx \wedge \neg Tx)$$

Likewise we may abbreviate 'bleen(x)' as $[B, G, T](x)$, defined as follows:

$$[B, G, T](x) =_{df} (Bx \wedge Tx) \vee (Gx \wedge \neg Tx)$$

The irksome feature of Goodman's definitions is that they are symmetrical as between the normal concepts and their gruified counterparts. Thus we have $G(x)$ coming out as

$$[[G, B, T], [B, G, T], T](x),$$

that is, as [Grue,Bleen,T](x); and we have $B(x)$ coming out as

$$[[B, G, T], [G, B, T], T](x),$$

that is, as [Bleen,Grue,T](x). It is this symmetry that the gruifier seeks to sustain in order to make Goodman's problem into the paradox it is. It is built into Goodman's dialectic of reinterpretation that the original deviant reinterpretations (of 'green' and 'blue') will stay the same. For if they did not, the symmetry would probably be broken, and the gruifier's opponent would be able to exploit the new asymmetry to ground a preference for the normal interpretation over the deviant one. With Kripke, however, matters stand somewhat differently. It was no part of Kripke's brief so to frame his deviant interpretation of '+' that addition would be definable in terms of quaddition in a completely symmetrical fashion. Let us try it for a moment:

$$x \text{ plus } y =_{df} x \text{ quus } y \text{ if } x, y < 57$$

$$= ?? \text{ otherwise}$$

By ignoring the need for symmetry at the outset, Kripke launches himself on to a destabilized path of ever more bizarre reinterpretations to shore up the original. But he explores only a very short initial segment of this path. He does not venture on to any of the territory that, we have argued, is subject to strong conceptual controls, controls whose circumvention would force him finally to undertake the most bizarre imaginable feats of reinterpretation (much more bizarre even than those he offered at the outset). It is at this point that the anti-sceptic can claim with justification that *the burden of proof has been shifted back onto the sceptic*. So monumentally bizarre is the reinterpretative feat now required, that to claim it can be accomplished is simply to assert the Π_1-dogma.

4.11   The proper way to meet the sceptical challenge

It is better to refuse at the outset to accept the Π_1-dogma in the absence of any compelling proof. This is the proper beginning for a better line of resistance to Quinean and Kripkean scepticism about determinacy. It is one that still rests on (appropriately liberal) behaviouristic assumptions about meaning, and sticks to the third-person standpoint. It would allow the evidence of introspection, but only in the form of first-person reports, to be treated as evidence alongside all other utterances. It would not commit one to infallible or authoritative access to one's own linguistic intentions, or knowledge of meaning—indeed, it may even deny it on occasion.[21] Yet it would remain uncommitted to indeterminacy—and so by default, as it were, it would rest content with the assumption of determinacy. It would do this simply by pointing out that the Quinean 'argument'—to which, ultimately, Kripke's must be assimilated by the 'change of bending points' considerations pursued above—remains one of the most celebrated theses in the literature of the philosophy of language still begging for proof of a kind that it is appropriate to demand for any statement of its logical form.[22]

It is time now to provide a more positive account of what we mean by what we say: an account immune to the depradations of the tiger that Wright fears to have let loose, that Blackburn allows to stalk in the grounds, and from which McDowell can only seek refuge in the 'whirl of organism'.[23] Some writers[24] have canvassed the possibility of appealing to dispositions in ways that can overcome Kripke's initial objections. But Blackburn concedes defeat on the question whether a revived dispositional account can ground the normativity involved in following a rule. We shall provide in the rest of

---

[21] See this possibility developed in *AR&L*, ch. 15: 'Do We Know What We Mean When We Mean What We Say?'

[22] For an extensive defence of this claim, against all published 'proofs' to the contrary, see *AR&L*, ch. 4: 'The Behaviourist Method in Semantics and the Alleged Indeterminacy of Meaning'.

[23] Here Cavell might cavil that he had said 'whorl'—an observation I owe to Mark Johnston.

[24] e.g. S. Blackburn, 'The Individual Strikes Back', *Synthese*, 58, 1984, pp. 281–301; P. Horwich, 'Critical Notice: Saul Kripke: *Wittgenstein on Rules and Private Language*', *Philosophy of Science*, 51, 1984, pp. 163–71; W. Goldfarb, 'Kripke on Wittgenstein on Rules', *Journal of Philosophy*, 82, 1985, pp. 471–88; and J. J. C. Smart, 'Wittgenstein, Following a Rule and Scientific Psychology', Lecture given at the Van Leer Jerusalem Foundation, Israel, February 1986.

this chapter a strong enough dispositional account both to select the rule meant and to explain what it is to be faithful to a rule.[25] Furthermore, we shall locate the normativity essentially in the interpersonal character of communication, thereby providing a response to Blackburn's challenge to 'identify the fugitive fact'[26] that helps the community bypass the sceptic when the individual cannot do so. If we can succeed in what follows, the overall position reached will be:

1. a grounded refusal to grant indeterminacy or global reinterpretability as claimed by the Π_1-dogma;

2. a liberal behaviourist methodology in the study of meaning;

3. a physicalistic explanation of faithfulness to a rule, and of the normative dimension of meaning generally; and

4. a principled asymmetry between the so-called 'private' case—the case of the individual considered in isolation—and the so-called 'public' case—the case of a community of mutual understanders.

We shall thus avoid Wright's and Searles's extreme appeal to authoritative access to one's own intentions, or knowledge of what one means. These ingredients cannot manifest themselves publicly except by means of words that are themselves up for interpretation; which ventures uncomfortably beyond even what is allowed by (2).

The main reasons for other anti-sceptical writers' failing to occupy the position described by (1), (2), (3) and (4) above appear to be as follows:

- they acquiesce in the Π_1-dogma; so

- they seek to augment the materials from which determinacy or unique interpretability can be forged (Wright, Searle);

These two points have been borne out in our discussion so far. Alternatively,

- they attempt to counter the effects of the Π_1-dogma with further considerations about the manifestation of dispositions (Blackburn).

---

[25]These are both requirements laid down by Blackburn—Cf. 'The Individual Strikes Back', at p. 291; and he thinks that a dispositional account fails on the second score.
[26]loc. cit., p. 292.

But these further considerations either do not do justice to the very hypotheses built into that dogma itself;[27] or (as we shall see below) they lead to a collapse of the private/public distinction. Finally

- they do not adequately explore the resources of a dispositional account, and of the supervenience basis to which a dispositionalist can appeal, to achieve a naturalistic accommodation of normativity.

The last two claims will be borne out in due course, as we accomplish (3) and (4) in accordance with (2).

4.12   A parable

Imagine being given a machine—a black box—with a tape passing through it. It looks just like a physical realization of those little diagrams of Turing machines that one is used to seeing in advanced logic books. It turns out that it is. One can dismantle and reassemble the machine quite easily. Pieces clip in and out of place, or slide into grooves to dovetail nicely together. Axles spin smoothly, little doors flap through ninety degrees. The tape is perforated along both edges, and the perforations engage perfectly around the little cogged wheels that guide it through the machine in both directions. The wheels have reversible ratchets. There is a magnetizing- and demagnetizing-head, positioned to scan and operate on just one cell of the tape at a time.

You spend some hours taking the machine apart and putting it together again. You explore thoroughly the possible configurations of its inside parts, and eventually satisfy yourself that the machine is capable of being in any one of exactly n states, for a reasonably small number n. You may even prove this by cleverly applying some theorems of solid geometry. Further painstaking investigation reveals to you exactly what transitions between states the machine, by virtue of its internal construction, is able to make. Moreover, you find out what can trigger such transitions. It turns out that the state of the scanned cell, plus the present state of the machine, causes the machine either to magnetize the cell, or to demagnetize it; upon which it either moves the tape one cell to the right, or one cell to the left; and then enters a new state. What your investigations reveal is, in effect, the finite machine table of this little Turing machine you have been given. The table

---

[27] Cf. my critique of Blackburn on this score: 'How is Meaning Possible?', *Philosophical Books*, 26, 1984, pp. 65–82.

consists of finitely many ordered quadruples, with each quadruple having one of the eight forms

$$(S_i, 0, 0, S_j), (S_i, 0, 1, S_j), (S_i, 0, R, S_j), (S_i, 0, L, S_j),$$
$$(S_i, 1, 0, S_j), (S_i, 1, 1, S_j), (S_i, 1, R, S_j), (S_i, 1, L, S_j)$$

$(S_i, 0, 1, S_j)$, for example, represents the description

'If the machine is in state S_i and the scanned cell is unmagnetized, then it will magnetize it, and enter state S_j.'

$(S_i, 1, R, S_j)$ represents the description

'If the machine is in state S_i and the scanned cell is magnetized, then it will move the tape one cell to the right, and enter state S_j.'

In due course you become so familiar with the workings of the machine that, for each state that the machine may be in, and given the condition of the scanned cell, you can predict—infallibly, given your knowledge now of the internal geometric constraints of the machine's construction—what the machine will do. That is, you can predict what the scanning head will do, how the machine will move the tape, and what new state the machine will enter. Indeed, you manage, given idealizing assumptions about the impenetrability of parts, the elimination of friction, the absolute inelasticity of the materials used, the uniform density of components, the immortality of its power cell, and so on, to give a Newtonian–Maxwellian–Euclidean proof of each tuple in the machine table. Each tuple describes or predicts what the machine will do when the tuple's first couple of entries apply. The table, in this sense, is a theoretical description of the machine. You took the machine apart in order that you might arrive at its table as the result of empirical investigation. Given the idealizing assumptions mentioned, you are happy to acquiesce in the description of your conception of it as 'super-rigid'. Let us, for the sake of argument, suppose that the machine table turned out to be that of the doubling function in the standard way. That is, if fed a sequence of m neighbouring magnetized cells from the left, the machine goes through a series of steps before halting with an output of $2m$ neighbouring magnetized cells on the right.

One day your partner, fed up with your endless tinkerings, puts the machine down the garbage disposal unit. It turns out that your idealizing assumptions were wrong. It was not perfectly rigid. It bent and buckled and got eaten up. Worse still, you are so upset that you forget how the machine was made. Once upon a time you could have conjured up in your mind's eye a picture of the internal configuration of parts for any of its states; but now no more. All you have left is the machine table, written down as before.

So you set about designing a new machine to instantiate the machine table. It has to have exactly n states, and be capable of transitions between them, upon triggers of the appropriate kind (registrations of cells), as the table says. You find, perhaps, that there are many ways of doing this. You settle on one of them. The incident with the garbage disposal unit incidentally blew the fuses on your street, so you do not design an electrical device. Instead, you go for a Heath Robinson machine. It runs on the kinetic energy you will generate by peddling on an exercise bike. The scanning head will not be electronic either. Instead, you will have a spindle that engages in a slot in the cell (the slot representing 1) and that fills it in with woodfill (if it has to 'bear the entry' 0). If the spindle finds no slot, it 'registers' that too (by being slightly higher in its supporting tube), and a diamond-edged cutter goes through one rotation to make a slot if the entry 1 is needed according to the machine table. Your new idealizing assumptions are a little different when you come to prove that your new machine is correctly described by the machine table. For now you have to assume an unlimited supply of woodfill, a non-erodable blade and an immortal pedaller in the saddle. Still, on the new assumptions a suitably different Newtonian–Euclidean proof goes through. The machine table is the true description of this machine, given these idealizing assumptions about its workings.

Old machine and new were both described by the same table. In the first case, you got the table by looking at the machine. In the second case, you made the machine by looking at the table. It is in cases like the second— where the machine is fashioned on the basis of a pre-existing table—that it is clear why one usually speaks of the table being a set, or programme, of instructions. It derives that status from the background intention to construct a machine (or deploy an existing one) in order to realize the table. The machine is to be made or configured so that the table, descriptively, is true of it. Any machine so made or configured counts as a realization. Because of the variety of realizations that are physically possible for any given programme, one speaks of such 'machines' only indirectly, via the equivalence class, as it were, given by the programme that they variously realize.

It is this detachment from actual machines, when we talk about what they are to do, that generates what look remarkably like normative claims about their operations. Let us return to the first machine, which your partner junked. You knew it so well that, when asked what the machine would do if given the input 5, you could confidently reply 'It will give the output 10.' You deduced that from your idealizing assumptions about its material make-up, and your knowledge of its internal geometry. Admittedly, real components wear out and go on the blink. They fuse, they melt. But when everything is going all right—and you are quite clear in your own mind, concerning this machine, what would count as 'all right'—it will compute the answer 10. And if you actually try it with input 5, and it does not compute the answer 10, then you exclaim 'Why, it ought to have computed the answer 10; something must have gone wrong!' And you open it up and look for the culprit parts.

So cantankerous does your partner become, and so regularly does she consign new physical realizations of your favourite programme to the garbage disposal, that you grow tired of physical realizations and just keep a note of the machine table. When one of your friends visits to reminisce about the old days—when it was all 'hands on', and one got down to the 'nuts and bolts' of it all—you are still able to give answers to her questions about what your original machine (or indeed any of its successors) would have computed as output for any given input. Only now you do this not by imagining, in your mind's eye, the sequence of transitions that Mark 1 would have made. Instead, you deduce it from the machine table. That was the programme that Mark 1 executed (and which the successors of Mark 1 were designed also to execute); therefore the answer to input 435, say, *ought to have been* 870.

4.13   From dispositional facts to normativity of meaning

For a materialist, the difference between your machines and your mind is only a matter of degree. When you learn new words, some part of your mind/brain is being redesigned to compute communally approved outputs for a given range of inputs. Within the parameters of plasticity granted by our evolutionary past, only certain end-results (mature configurations of neurons) are possible. Conditioning prunes down the possibilities drastically, to within uniqueness (in the sense of computational equivalence). Given a mature speaker, one could in principle open his head, as one did with Mark 1 of the machine, and discover his sub-programme for '+', or 'green'.

Idealizing, we can say that she ought to respond to '58+67=?' with '125'.

At this stage the objector will say 'Don't be crazy! How on earth could you ever read off from the wiring in someone's head how he would respond to isolated tasks like this, when so little is known about where the competences are localized in the brain?' We can concede this point. But we can rejoin with the invitation to let a little machine do duty for us in our computations using '+'. First, let us write down a machine table for addition. Presumably we can agree on it, even if you are a hidden quadder. Indeed, we have such agreement *ex hypothesi* by the sceptic's lights. It forms part of the evidence in the face of which which the global reinterpretation is allegedly to be had. Secondly, let us build a machine to instantiate the machine table that we have written down. We now have a physical realization that operates independently of our own unpredictable whims—but for which, admittedly, the question might at some time have to be faced as to whether it had functioned correctly, or malfunctioned, in the execution of its programme. In the ideal case we shall arrive at the machine table both *a priori* and, in principle, empirically. *A priori*, by devising a machine table for addition in a thought experiment; empirically (in principle) by opening up heads, discovering their sub-programmes, and finding that in the great majority of cases these coincide with the *a priori* specification. This would not be so much a matter of finding 'physical states that can, on internal grounds, be distinguished as competency states',[28] as finding modules or neuronal configurations which, by virtue of their occupancy of a variety of states, can carry out the computing operations in question.

Having written down the machine table for addition, let any question as to how one *ought* to respond to an addition sum be answered by reference to that machine table, and its physical realization—or, if you like, by reference to the (idealized) operations of any actual physical realization of that machine table that we might construct. (We would of course have constructed something like Mark 1—a pure adder—rather than a chunk of neural network in the horrendously complex environs of an actual brain.) If the goings-on in your head are so complicated and electroscopically cacophanous that it would be impossible to tell proper functioning of your addition sub-module (should you have one) from malfunction, then we can retreat to the machine table, or the actual machine that realizes it. We can use it to say what the sum of two numbers *is*—what anybody's answer *ought to be*. Indeed, it is plausible that with enormous computational tasks we would be willing

---

[28] Goldfarb, loc. cit., at p. 477.

(communally) to let a properly designed machine be the arbiter as to what the answer should be. The following, it seems to me, is quite conceivable:

1. We are confronted with a computational task—a numerical calculation or a proof search—that we can prove to be computationally intractable for ourselves. Yet

2. we can agree on a programme for a supercomputer as embodying 'the rules' to be followed in the calculation or the search; and

3. the programme can be run on the supercomputer so as to yield a result. Moreover,

4. we can check the answer by rerunning the programme, and by employing different supercomputers to do so.

It seems that something like this situation obtains in the recent proof of the four-colour conjecture. Quite apart from how actual historical examples might fit the description we have given, we need only establish the possibility in principle of our acquiescing in artefactual exploration of the realm of (Fregean) sense. This is what decides between $\mathcal{R}$ and qu-$\mathcal{R}$. To reuse a well-known image: we can inspect the tracks, make the machine, and then let the machine run. We can be nomological parasites in executing our design intent. Should the machine ever malfunction, we would have in principle independent access to evidence that it has done so. This is evidence over and above the bare production of a 'quomputational' result.

At this point we should consider an objection that might have been pressing the reader for some time: how can one be sure that the machine table on which we have agreed is not being read in a deviant way by the other party to the 'agreement'? How can we be sure that, for example, the symbol S_1 is being taken by him to denote the same state as we take it to denote? How can we be sure that he does not conceptualize the operation of the machine in terms of 'quates'? Or, again, how can we be sure that he intends the symbols R, L, H (for 'move one cell to the right', 'move one cell to the left', 'halt') to have constant those operational meanings? Might he not, at some bending point that might be reached one day as a computation proceeds, suddenly 'permute' these symbols over the set of actions that they respectively describe? Similarly, how can we be sure that for him, three successive one's on the tape coming in from the left will always represent the input 3? and that six successive one's on the tape as it comes out on the right will always represent the output 6?

The proper response to this deepening of the coding problem is to shift the burden of proof once again on to the sceptical opposition. Let them show now how such deviant interpretations of machine-table symbols can sit coherently with the deviant interpretations originally offered by the sceptic for the function symbol (such as '+') for which the machine table was agreed upon. And let the opposition also show that each state transition envisaged for the actual machine on the deviant interpretation of the machine table is one which the actual machine (agreed on as the physical realization of the machine table) is causally capable of making. But it is difficult to believe the sceptic could do this in general. The example brings the incredibility of the II_1-dogma into the starkest possible relief. Indeed, it now brings within the horizon of envisaged possibilities the prospect that one might also have to attribute to the sceptic deviant beliefs about the operations of the physical world in order to shore up the proposed deviant interpretation of his language. Perhaps, for the Quinean, this is just as it always is; but in the example just discussed we would prefer, charitably, to fix on agreed beliefs about the machine's possible operations, and solve for meaning. Perhaps, in the end, the principle of charity is just the guiding methodological belief that one's interlocutor cannot be that poorly constructed a human being.

4.13.1   On going wrong: competence v. performance

In general, every computation (by a human individual, by a group of human individuals, or by a programmed machine) suffers from two potential limitations:

(i) there may not be enough time (or computing 'space'—memory storage, tape, etc.) to do the calculation;

(ii) the human computer may make a mistake; the mechanical computer may 'malfunction'.

Ordinary English usage inclines one to describe the human and machine cases in (ii) differently; but on the physicalistic conception there is no essential difference. We shall talk in both cases of malfunction. Let us call (i) the problem of *duration*, and (ii) the problem of *reliability*.

The problem of duration is something we simply have to learn to live with. No one will seriously maintain that one cannot make sense of a computation proceeding according to plan up to any given point in its execution, despite the fact that we shall never live to register the final result.[29] The problem of duration really arises out of the problem of reliability, which is the more fundamental. The worry is that with non-feasible computations (ones that would only terminate, say, billions of years from now) the probability of malfunction is so high that anyone around billions of years from now to read the result would have good reason to doubt its accuracy. The two problems manifest themselves together when we are dealing with barely surveyable computations that 'might have gone wrong'. The thought is that one would really like to be able to 'go over every step by hand' and check for errors. But it is not humanly possible to do so. One has to rely on the computer having functioned properly—having followed the rule we programmed into it, only much faster than we ourselves could ever do.

The practical way to eliminate anxiety or scepticism about the result in such a case is to increase reliability by harnessing machines in parallel. That way we can greatly increase our confidence that the agreed-on result is correct. There is von Neumann's well-known result[30] that from unreliable components reliable machines can be constructed. They will perform to within any degree of reliability, on all inputs. There is also a less widely known result, due to Rabin,[31] to the effect that if we are prepared to accept a minuscule probability of vast error, we can dramatically speed up computations within given problem spaces. (There is reason to believe that our brains can accomplish what they do by virtue of having been subjected to this sort of selective constraint; rather than requiring constant accuracy within a specified limit, and thereby requiring much more computing 'space' or 'time'.) The neurological evidence is that our brains are designed with an enormous amount of 'distributed parallelism' built in (in order to increase reliability). This suffices, in a normal range of cases, to make the individual reasonably self-sufficient in 'applying rules' on his own (albeit rules learned from others). But there again, if for whatever reasons the individual is not too reliable, there is recourse to the wider 'distributed parallelism' of his community. If he is not too adept at large computations (even though he

---

[29] Possible objection, owed to Mark Johnston: proceeding according to plan or proceeding according to *qu-lan*? Reply: at this stage it does not matter. *Ex hypothesi* the bending points have not yet been encountered; the human computer and the Kripkean quomputer both agree that everything is proceeding according to what happens to be (coextensive initial segment of plan and qu-lan).

[30] J. von Neumann, 'Probabilistic logic and the synthesis of reliable organisms from unreliable components', in C. E. Shannon and J. McCarthy, (eds.), *Automata Studies*, Annals of Mathematics Studies, no. 34, Princeton University Press, 1956, pp. 43–98.

[31] M. Rabin, 'Probabilistic automata', *Information and Control*, VI, 1963, pp. 230–45.

has mastered the basic steps, on more tractable instances, that are involved in the computation), then he can have recourse to others in the community in an attempt to arrive at the correct answer. The problem of reliability at the individual level, on individually tractable cases, is in practice resolved by recourse to the wider community. But it would be a mistake to infer from this that it is only by reference to the wider community's responses that one can find what an individual's correct application of rules consists in.

If the individual's understanding (that is, his intention to follow this rule rather than that) has to consist in anything, then it is reasonable to hold that it is a supervening, but not necessarily a reducible consisting-in, that is in question. Neurological (dispositional) facts about a person can suffice to determine what his understanding of, say, '+' is. But it is too much to demand as well that in the schema

X understands '+' to mean addition

the predicate here applied to X can be translated into a complex expression, employing only physicalistic vocabulary, describing precisely the 'isolated configuration', as it were, of those more basic physical, functional or causal-dispositional facts about X on which his thus understanding '+' supervenes. It is not necessary, therefore, to go along with Goldfarb and Horwich in their suggesting (on behalf of the reductionist) a double-barrelled dispositional account according to which there might be[32]

> two mechanisms, separable on scientific grounds. States of the first amount to a person's linguistic competence, and would, if untrammeled, always cause correct responses; states of the second are identifiable with interfering features, which explain why on particular occasions the first mechanism does not issue in an appropriate response (and the person errs).

Against this background, how can we answer the demands of normativity— or, rather, the demand that our account of how an individual means his words imposes a normative demand on him to apply his words one way rather than another in new cases? It seems to me that there are two ways in which we can say that X ought to apply an expression E thus-and-so in a new case C. One is to say that X ought by now to have understood expression E as meaning M; and that, as a matter of constitutive fact, application of E in accordance with meaning M goes thus-and-so in case C. The other is to say that X

---

[32]Goldfarb, loc. cit., p. 477.

does understand E as meaning M, and is thereby bound (in a contractual sense) to apply E thus-and-so in C; that is, given his grasp of meaning M for E, X ought to apply E thus-and-so in C. Not to satisfy the first obligation is to fail to have the required competence with the expression E; not to satisfy the second obligation is to fail in one's performance with case C. The latter failure highlights once again the problem of reliability. The former failure is the failure to have acquired (on the account offered here) the correct dispositions in which understanding consists. On an opposed account, such as Kripke's, it would be the failure to have acquired such facts about oneself as are to ground the attribution of grasp of meaning.

In general, a problem for interpretation is to separate out the respective contributions of these two components — non-fidelity and non-felicity — into which deviant usage can factor. But one would have the same problem simply watching an actual physical Turing machine in action, and trying to work out what function it is computing. And this is still an epistemological problem only. We can make sense of the machine as a matter of 'design' fact being one that instantiates or realizes the machine table for the doubling function, while as a matter of historical fact malfunctioning during a given computational episode.[33] In the same way, we can make sense of a person's neurological patterns as a matter of 'design' fact constituting his taking '+' to mean addition, while yet subject to disturbances during an act of addition that produce the wrong result. Reading 'physical state' as 'neurological pattern' we do not, it seems to me, need to agree with Goldfarb's reductionists[34] who

> reject Kripke's demand that a physical state identifiable with meaning have a reasonably tight (although not necessarily exceptionless) causal relation to the potential infinity of future correct responses.

Underlying both kinds of 'ought' that were described above is the bond that binds a group of individuals into a linguistic community. Sharing a form of life involves sharing goals and beliefs, and engaging in co-operative actions. It is clear that language has evolved to further this co-operative achieving of goals. In its assertive use its main function is to transmit information, or reliable beliefs. Individuals are by now pretty much hard-wired to pick up mastery of whatever local code it is that allows them to participate in that

---

[33] Cf. Smart, loc. cit.
[34] loc. cit., p. 478.

form of life. As one learns words to the satisfaction of other members of the community, one acquires the obligation to use them faithfully—that is, in accordance with their meanings. Otherwise, as a receiver and transmitter of messages one would subvert the flow of information. If one misunderstands, then one's own perceptual beliefs cannot be transmitted by one's own testimony to others; and the testimony of others cannot be put to good effect in the choice of one's own actions. This is the contractual element of meaning. It is no accident that one's discharge of those obligations requires essential recourse to the consensus of the community.

How, then, may we approach the question of the normativity of meaning? How may we accommodate normativity within a naturalistic framework? What has to be explained is what it is to have an *obligation* to use a word in one's language in a certain way.

In answering this question we intend to help ourselves to the very notion of an expression in a language (such as English) having the meaning that it does. In so doing we concede no circularity! We cannot be accused of illicitly helping ourselves to the notion of content, or of correct rule, or of unique interpretation, as that notion has been under challenge from the sceptic. For we have met the sceptical challenge, and have offered a physicalist account, based on neurological and behavioural dispositions, of what it is for the words of a language to have the meanings that (or to mean what) they do. That account involved the notions of nomological parasitism, artefactual exploration of the Fregean realm, and distributed parallelism.

4.13.2 Alleged problems for a dispositional account: the argument from finitude

Kripke's first objection to a dispositional account is that our dispositions are 'finite', whereas an arithmetical operation such as addition covers a potential infinity of instances. How, then, can our dispositions be up to the challenge of gearing us to do what we ought to be able to do when adding arbitrarily large numbers? This 'finitude argument' against a dispositional account has been, in my view, bought far too cheaply by supporters of Kripkean scepticism. It suffers from the same sort of flaw as will be exposed in the argument for strict finitism, examined in the next chapter. Kripke is in effect demanding of the dispositionalist that he specify or identify some disposition on the part of the subject, which will enable the subject to cope with the following demand:

> Given any two numbers m and n, no matter how large, compute their sum $m + n$!

That his demand is indeed this crude is evident from the following clear statement of it:[35]

> First, we must state the simple dispositional analysis. It gives a criterion that will tell me what number theoretic function ϕ I mean by a binary function symbol 'f', namely: The referent ϕ of 'f' is that unique binary function ϕ such that I am disposed, if queried about '$f(m, n)$', where 'm' and 'n' are numerals denoting particular numbers m and n, to reply 'p', where 'p' is a numeral denoting $\phi(m, n)$.

Kripke's summary dismissal of this dispositional proposal proceeds as follows:

> The dispositional theory attempts to avoid the problem of the finiteness of my actual past performances by appealing to a disposition. But in doing so, it ignores an obvious fact: not only my actual performance, but also *the totality of my dispositions, is finite.* It is not true, for example, that if queried about the sum of any two numbers, no matter how large, I will reply with their actual sum, for some pairs of numbers are simply too large for my mind—or my brain—to grasp. When given such sums, I may shrug my shoulders for lack of comprehension; I may even, if the numbers involved are large enough, die of old age before the questioner completes his question. [My emphasis]

The emphasized claim in this passage, even if conceded, need not entail that such dispositions as we do have, even if we concede their finitude *in Kripke's sense*, cannot suffice to ground the normativities of addition. Why should one accept the implicit presupposition that the dispositionalist is committed to having the subject be able to carry out every command to add two numbers, no matter how large they be? Clearly this is too extravagant a demand. Why not rather say that the way to check a subject's 'correct' dispositions with regard to addition is to present him with any (stretch of) a computation of the sum of two numbers, and then, with respect to any surveyable aspect of such a computation, ask him whether it is in order?

---

[35] op. cit., p. 26.

This would allow us to direct his attention to any one 'column' of an addition sum in decimal notation, say, and ask whether it is in order, on the assumption that everything from the extreme right up to the column in question were in order. In response to *this* kind of test of correct grasp, any ordinary subject should be able to acquit himself perfectly well, provided only that he could be said by normal criteria to understand what '+' means. This is what we call in the next chapter the 'factorizable' way of understanding the anti-realist's manifestation requirement. Just as it arrests the threatened slide to strict finitism, it forestalls also Kripke's argument from finitude against the possibility of dispositions grounding the normativity of arithmetical meanings.

4.13.3   Alleged problems for a dispositional account: the argument from error

Kripke's other main argument against the dispositional theory is the argument from error. As he puts it:[36]

> Most of us have dispositions to make mistakes. For example, when asked to add certain numbers some people forget to 'carry'. They are thus disposed, for those numbers, to give an answer differing from the usual addition table. Normally, we say that such people have made a *mistake*. That means, that for them as for us, '+' means addition, but for certain numbers they are not disposed to give the answer they *should* give, if they are to accord with the table of the function they actually *meant*. But the dispositionalist cannot say this. According to him, the function someone means is to be *read off* from his dispositions; it cannot be presupposed in advance which function is meant.
> ...where common sense holds that the subject means the same addition function as everyone else but systematically makes computational mistakes, the dispositionalist seems forced to hold that the subject makes no computational mistakes, but means a non-standard function ('skaddition') by '+'.
> ...the difficulty cannot be surmounted by a *ceteris paribus* clause, by a clause excluding 'noise', or by a distinction between 'competence' and 'performance'. No doubt a disposition to give the true

---

[36]op. cit., pp. 28–30.

sum in response to each addition problem is part of my 'competence', if by this we mean simply that such an answer accords
with the rule I intended, or if we mean that, if all my dispositions
to make mistakes were removed, I would give the correct answer.
...But a disposition to make a mistake is simply a disposition to
give an answer other than the one that accords with the function I
meant. To presuppose this concept in the present discussion is of
course viciously circular. If I meant addition, my 'erroneous' actual disposition is to be ignored; if I meant skaddition, it should
not be. Nothing in the notion of my 'competence' as thus defined
can possibly tell me which alternative to adopt.

Kripke here assiduously ignores the recourse that the dispositionalist would
have to the wider consensus to be obtained within a *community* of understanders. He focuses just on the single subject, considering only *his*
dispositions to carry out a given computation, including such dispositions as
he might also have to make mistakes in so doing. But of course part of true
understanding on the part of any speaker or subject is a principled willingness to defer to communal correction. Such correction is usually adjudicated
by a minority of experts if need be; but still it involves *other understanders*
and *their* dispositions to compute (for such, it is being maintained, is all that
there is to ground the normativities in question). Let us call *idiosyncratic*
any disposition of the computing subject that can be characterized without reference to the corrective influences that could be exercised by fellow
understanders. Instead of being downhearted at the apparent impossibility
of giving a non-circular account of exactly what idiosyncratic dispositions
might ground a subject's normative grasp, we should be willing to consider
non-idiosyncratic dispositions and the whole hierarchical governance of both
idiosyncratic and non-idiosyncratic dispositions within the subject's psychological make-up. The pig-headed maker of mistakes who refuses ever to be
corrected can indeed be said (by the dispositionalist) to mean skaddition
rather than addition. But the fallible adder who is willing to have his mistakes pointed out to him, and accept corrections as called for, may by virtue
of those very dispositions be said to be a true understander of addition. In
this way the communal dimension so essential to the thought of the later
Wittgenstein can be brought to bear on the problem of what a given individual might really mean by his words. What he means will depend not only on
what goes on inside his own head, but how some of those goings-on incline
him to keep in step with what is going on in other people's heads. We have

here the beginnings of a dispositional account of the normative dimension of meaning: one which pays attention to the crucial role to be played, in the account of any one speaker's grasp, by the dispositions of fellow speakers.

What now remains to be done is to round off this picture with an account of *our obligation to keep faith with the meanings of our words*. On the view put forward here, this is a challenge over and above accounting for *what those meanings are*, and accounting for *what it is that grounds their ascription to the expressions of a language*. The normativity of meaning arises out of the constellation of speaker, hearer, expression and meaning. Meaning is normatively imbued because of how it is involved in that quartet. Speakers *ought* to use the meaningful expressions of their language, for the benefit of their hearers, in certain ways. The claim that you (as an English speaker) *ought* to call this pencil 'green' breaks into the following components:

(i) the pencil is green, and you ought to be able to perceive that;

(ii) in English, 'green' means green (note our analytical disclaimer above!);

(iii) as a speaker of English, you ought to know that (ii) is true; that is, you ought to understand 'green' (and of course you ought also to be able to pronounce the word 'green'!).[37]

(iv) given (iii), you ought, if prompted in a situation where clearly the correct English word is required of you, to call this pencil 'green'.

(i) requires you only to be a properly constructed member of the species. (ii) is a constitutive fact that supervenes on the behaviour (and the underlying, happily co-functioning, neurological patterning) of members of a community. Remember, no questions of normativity are being begged here. (ii) is embedded in (iii), and (iii) conditionalizes (iv). It is this fourth and final strand of obligation that provides the contractual element in our mutual understanding as speakers of English—an obligation that can be assimilated to moral obligation generally.

Thus, on our account, there is essential reference to a wider community in order to ground the normativity of meaning in the sense that involves a

---

[37]Note that you are not required to know *what it is, physicalistically, that grounds this fact*; language-learning involves other epistemic routes than that of metaphysical underpinning.

contractual bond. But the ability of any given individual to discharge the obligations in question, as a speaker of the language, can be ontologically self-contained, as it were. His own understanding of expressions of the communal language can supervene on underlying physical facts about him and him alone. Meaning is communal; grasp of meaning is individual. If one functions properly within a linguistic community, it is still by virtue of the cogs in one's own machinery, not by virtue of being a mere cog in a communal machine.

Chapter 5

Avoiding Strict Finitism

5.1 Knowability in principle

Whether one is talking about the remote past, or what it is like to be a bat, or the interior of black holes, or very large cardinal numbers in set theory, the only licit notion of truth, for the moderate anti-realist, is knowable truth. But knowable by whom? And by what means? The moderate anti-realist's opponents (of realist or of even more extreme anti-realist persuasion) will complain that the formula is uninformative or misleading as long as the suffix '-able' remains unexplicated. Although this is not as problematic as the first modality involved in the realist's claim that the truth could transcend what is knowable, we nevertheless concede that we owe an account of the second modality at least.

First, let us dismiss the two extremes. The truth does not have to be knowable by all and sundry, regardless of their competence to judge. That is, we do not require that for any true proposition ϕ, and any subject S, S could be positioned so as to come to know (within his lifetime) that ϕ, by the exercise of such cognitive capacities as S actually happens to possess. This would be to hostage too much of what is true to individual misfortune. At the very least we have to abstract or idealize away from the limitations of actual individuals, and their proneness to mistakes, where these limitations or pronenesses are the result of poor natural endowment or maturation or training, or any other disadvantage in their position as investigators. At the very least, then, we have to imagine that we can appeal to an ideal cognitive representative of our species. Call such an idealized individual H (for 'human being'). It does not matter if we think of H as a particularly gifted and conscientious individual, or as a personification of some communal, co-operative enterprise among experts. The latter would involve the exchange of views, sharing of perspectives, mutual challenges to inferences made, etc. The verdict of the idealized individual on any issue, one may suppose, would agree with the consensus that would emerge in such a community of investigators, from the pooling of information and the (sometimes adversarial) exercise of different individuals' critical acumen.

A first approximation, then, of the moderate anti-realist's principle concerning knowability is this:

> for any true proposition ϕ, H could be positioned so as to come to know (within his lifetime) that ϕ, by the exercise of such cognitive capacities as we think of H as ideally possessing and deploying on our behalf.

This is not yet weak enough; but before we considejr further weakenings of this principle, let us hasten to dismiss too weak an extreme. Consider the principle

> for any true proposition ϕ, an omnipotent, omnipresent God would (be able to) know that ϕ.

Note that the adjective 'omniscient' is omitted in this characterization of the God invoked by this extreme principle, since this adjective would add nothing. The sequence of questions that it would naturally provoke would be:

> What does 'omni-' in 'omniscient' range over? That which is true? But are we not trying to characterize truth in an epistemically constrained way? So, until one knows what the constraints are, is it not unhelpful to be told that what is knowable is that which could be known by one who knows every truth?

It therefore behoves us, at this other extreme, to make mention only of omnipotence and omnipresence (but not: omniscience) on the part of the God whose knowledge is supposed to be coextensive with what is true. Having got at least that clear about the suggested characterization of divine knowability, it should be evident that this would be completely unacceptable to the anti-realist. The truth is not to be taken as what is knowable by an omnipotent, omnipresent God. For, even prescinding from obvious difficulties concerning the alleged mode of access to the truth that would be enjoyed by an omnipotent and omnipresent God, one can see that the well-intentioned replies would only serve to fix the truth in such a way that for every proposition ϕ, either ϕ would be true or its negation $\neg\phi$ would be true. For the point would be that God would have to have been less than omnipotent, or less than omnipresent, if, for some proposition ϕ, He could not make up His mind that ϕ held, or that $\neg\phi$ held, as the case may be. To explicate the suffix '-able' in 'knowable' in this way, then, is to evacuate the principle that all truths are knowable of any interesting content.

So: '-able' must not be interpreted in too strong a fashion (by appeal to all and sundry), nor in too weak a fashion (by appeal to God).

We were considering the formulation that

> for any true proposition ϕ, the ideal cognitive representative H could be positioned so as to come to know (within his lifetime) that ϕ, by the exercise of such cognitive capacities as we think of H as ideally possessing and deploying on our behalves.

Even this is too strong. There should be no upper limit on how long H might have to live to prosecute his inquiries. This is especially the case if our best theory about matter, energy, space and time imposes limits on how short a time a basic step of computation (data transfer or inference) can take. In such a world, no matter how long a period of time one fixed, there would be infinitely many prime numbers whose primality could be determined only by a computation lasting yet longer.

Nevertheless one would want to say that the primality of any given number is surely knowable, in the sense of 'knowable' that we are concerned here to explicate. For no conceptual leap is involved when we try to conceive what kind of fact it would be that such a huge number were prime. It would be the same sort of fact, essentially, as the fact that 17 is prime. It is just that it would take much longer to establish it as a fact, that is all. (And: given sufficient time, it would eventually be established whether the number in question was prime.) One does not have to imagine any essential change to the human cognitive repertoire, or new modes of sensory access to the external world, or telepathic ability, or anything incongruous or out of keeping with our current cognitive apparatus. We are equipped, right now, to perform tasks such as applying Eratosthenes' sieve. The sheer size of the number whose primality is in question is neither here nor there when it comes to our ability to conceive of the kind of fact that it is (or would be) for some gargantuan number N—so gargantuan that Eratosthenes' sieve, as a matter of physical law, could never reach it before the Big Crunch—to be prime.

It is not just a matter of our being able to conceive of the kind of fact that it is for N to be prime. It is also a matter of our knowing that the fact itself would be accessible to the exercise of the very cognitive abilities that we possess, had we but enough time to exercise them in pursuit of a decision in the matter.

We are invited to think, then, of a simple linear compression of the time-line; this suffices to bring the eventual determination of N's status as prime or otherwise closer to hand. The sheer size of N can be compensated for by supposedly spectacular speed in computation. The speed may be that of a superendowed human subject, or that of some supercomputer that an ordinarily endowed human subject may be able to use to perform the computation. This helps to blur the distinction (if there ever was one) between that which is knowable in principle and that which is humanly, feasibly knowable.

Now the same kind of idealization must and can take place with the other resource for computation besides time, namely space. We mean here memory space, whatever its physical realization within physical space may be. Some (indeed almost all) kinds of computation consume ever-increasing amounts of space before terminating, as the length of their inputs increases. Thus one of the misgivings someone may have about the knowable in principle (where the knowledge is to be arrived at by applying some effective procedure) is that, for some particular truth, the actual physical universe may not contain enough fundamental particles or arrangements of them to realize the memory requirements of even the most efficient computational course of events that will yield knowledge of that truth, even if it is assumed to proceed perfectly free of such errors as may arise from random physical events.

Again, the advocate of knowability in principle undertakes a thought experiment invoking a certain kind of scaling. We are invited to conceive of there being no limit to the degree of miniaturization that could be effected on the physical wherewithal by means of which we store and transform information. Thus we can think of either a superendowed human subject with much more neuronal circuitry in his head, the faster to think with, or of an ordinary human subject who is able to use a supercomputer that has ever more highly compressed hardware for the storage and transformation of data in the course of a computation.

Our thought experiment about the scalings of time and of physical components can therefore be of two kinds. The first keeps constant our notion of the ordinarily endowed, but competently performing, human subject, and vests in his artefacts, such as computers, the imagined increase in computing power necessary to bring the otherwise non-feasibly computable within the range of the newly feasibly computable. The second allows us, rather, to imagine the human subject himself, without recourse to such artefacts, as endowed with much greater computational power: as a finite extension of his earlier self, in respect of the salient cognitive capacities.[1]

There may, of course, be actual physical limits on the extent to which the time-line may be compressed, or on the extent to which physical components may be miniaturized, whether in human heads or in computers. The world may not be able to co-operate with us in our thought experiments. That is why they are thought experiments. But the actual limits to effective human thought, with or without the aid of artefacts, that we are thinking of ourselves as transcending here are not limits to the kind of thinking we may do, but only limits on how much of that kind of thinking one could do. The thinking is all of one uniform kind. Moreover, such actual limits are not limits of which we are remotely aware, as ordinary learners or as theorists of the learning process. Such limits are dictated only by arcane and high-level theories such as quantum mechanics and relativistic cosmology.[2] There is no reason why the contingent truth of such theories (should they be true) should be allowed to invalidate our explanation of how we are entitled to conceive of the sorts of finite extensions, bruited here, of the ordinary cognitive capacities whose very finitude gives rise to the worry we are trying to meet. That worry, remember, is that any particular finite limit to what we can do must feed into, and adversely affect, our desired account of the knowable, the computable, and the decidable-in-principle.

Given any number N, no matter how large, there is some combination of

---

[1] No doubt the explication of 'finite extension' here will ultimately invoke the notion of 'natural number'; but this will not make it viciously circular. For the Peano–Dedekind axioms for successor give us an adequate characterization of the concept of a natural number. For the purposes of being able to frame a principle invoking arbitrary finite extensions of our cognitive capacities, it is enough for us to have an intellectual hold on the numbers themselves, and their potential infinity. It is not necessary that we should already be able to ward off a threatened slide to strict finitism that takes the form of restricting bivalence to some indeterminate range of 'feasibly decidable' sentences of arithmetic rather than those that are decidable in principle.

[2] For the limits entailed by the values of Planck's constant $\hbar$ and the speed of light c, see D. Mundici, 'Natural Limitations of Algorithmic Procedures in Logic', *Atti dell'Accademia Nazionale dei Lincei. Classe di Scienze Fisiche Mathematiche e Naturali.* Rendiconti (Series 8) 69 (3–4), pp. 101–05.

temporal and physical scaling of the kinds imagined that would enable the ideal cognizer H to determine, within a reasonable period of time, whether N was prime. The scalings would involve finite scaling factors. The scalings help to put within ordinary, competent cognitive compass those propositions that are in principle effectively knowable, even though perhaps not feasibly so (without the scaling) for ordinarily endowed human thinkers enjoying normal lifespans. We are concerned to explicate a sense of 'knowable' according to which such propositions are indeed knowable. The concern, now, should be whether the sorts of idealizations involved in bringing such propositions within (linearly scaled) human or artefactual 'reach', could also allow within such modified reach other propositions that should not count as effectively knowable.

5.2   The strict finitist's worry

It is not plausible that our idealizations so far bring in their wake this un-wanted prospect. No finite linear scaling of the kind entertained above could ever make it possible to survey, within a finite time, the 'grounds of truth' for a numerically quantified statement of the form $\forall x F(x)$, unless these grounds possess the uniformity across instances encapsulated in the inductive step of a proof by mathematical induction. Suppose, then, that we have no such proof by induction of $\forall x F(x)$. Then the alleged grounds for its truth would encompass those of all its infinitely many instances of the form $F(n)$. No amount of finite scaling could bring these within cognitive compass. Thus there is a principled difference between the non-effectively decidable quanti-fied sentences of arithmetic and the effectively decidable ones. Our scalings do not alter the logical topology of our language here. At most they deform the 'effectively or feasibly knowable' side of the divide, leaving this region of discourse, in the appropriate metaphorical sense, disconnected from the un-decidable. The scalings show how arbitrary and vague would be any attempt to demarcate, and disconnect, the feasibly knowable from the non-feasibly but in principle effectively knowable. What is in principle effectively know-able becomes feasibly knowable, case by case, via an imagined linear scaling. We conclude, then, that the only worthwhile distinction to maintain here is that between what is in principle effectively knowable and that which is not.

So far we have conducted the discussion of knowability against the back-ground of examples from arithmetic, where the sentences concerned have admitted of decision procedures to establish whether they were true. But it should be stressed that not all knowable propositions need be of the kind to which a decision procedure may be applied. Instead, one could settle the question of the truth of some proposition ϕ by producing a proof Π of ϕ through the exercise of inspiration and ingenuity. This could happen even though one did not have at one's disposal any decision method of which one could say, in advance of applying it, that its application would in principle yield an answer on the question whether ϕ. Nevertheless, the proof Π of ϕ establishes the truth of ϕ. Thus the question of how ϕ is knowable becomes the question of how one could grasp the fact that Π was indeed a proof of ϕ. The algorithm here is that of checking Π for proofhood. If Π is so long that qualms would be in order as to the feasibility of checking Π for proofhood, then we would enter the same idealizing considerations as before. We would imagine linear scalings of time and physical resources so as to make the proof-check feasible, whether this be by an intrinsic or an artefactual extension of ordinary human competence. The scalings once again allow us to distinguish between those propositions that do admit, in principle, of finite proof or disproof, and those that do not. The sheer size of a finitary truth-maker must not be allowed to strip it of its truth-making capacity.

Still, one has to proceed cautiously with the notion of propositions that do not admit, in principle, of finite proof or disproof. This is to explain matters from a rather realist perspective. We have to avoid committing ourselves, as anti-realists, to the existence of any proposition that does not, in principle, admit of finite proof or disproof. The point of our discussion is not so much to drive a wedge between the decidable and the undecidable, making it a decidable matter which side of this divide a given sentence falls; but rather to emphasize the homogeneity of the class of sentences that do admit of finite proof or disproof. Our target for attack is the pair of ideas that the distinction between the feasibly knowable and the non-feasibly knowable is both

(i) as stable as the distinction between that which is in principle knowable and that which is not, and

(ii) the more appropriate of the two distinctions for the application of the manifestation requirement within the anti-realist's theory of meaning.

The manifestation requirement, which will be discussed in much greater detail in the next two chapters, is that every aspect of a subject's grasp of the meaning of a statement should be able to be manifested in his observable behaviour—in particular, in the exercise of his recognitional capacities. Our attack must not be thought of as issuing in a claim, concerning any proposition ϕ, that ϕ is neither knowably true nor knowably false. All truth is knowable; but this does not entail that every proposition is either true or false. Indeed, one who holds that all truth is knowable will, for that very reason, be disinclined (pending closer scrutiny of the discourse in question) to assert that every proposition is either true or false.

5.3 Recognitional capacities and compositionality

AR&L argued that it was a profound mistake to view the modern anti-realist as holding the naïve verificationist criterion of meaningfulness that the Logical Positivists employed to their discredit. The concern was to make room for the meaningfulness of statements for which we happened (as understanders) to possess no effective method that we could recognize as issuing, once applied to the statement, in a decision as to its truth or falsity. Thus, it would be anti-realistically acceptable to attribute to even a relatively ungifted mathematician a full understanding of, say, Goldbach's conjecture, even though he did not have much of a clue as to how to set about finding a proof or a disproof of Goldbach's conjecture. Rather, all that is required of such a person is that (ideally and counterfactually) he would be able to recognize a proof (or disproof) of the conjecture if he were presented with one. That is, we require of an understander not the ability to decide the statement of whose meaning his grasp is in question, but only to decide the question of proofhood (or disproofhood) of any purported proof (or disproof) of that statement. It would not be up to him to find the latter; but only to pronounce on their status once he were presented with them. The contention was that such an ability could be attributed to a human speaker on good criterial grounds, concerning his grasp of the constituents of the statement in question, and his grasp of the way those constituents are put together within the statement. That is, grasp of constituents within, and grasp of manner of construction, should suffice for grasp of any statement. Compositionality had a very important role to play.

Understanding a sentence, then, is to be understood as factorizable: as consisting in one's understanding of the various component parts of the sentence, which understandings then combine or co-operate to produce one's understanding of the whole sentence. A speaker's understanding of the primitive constituents of a given sentence can be displayed, crucially, with regard to their occurrences within other sentences. In particular, one can arrange for their occurrence in prominent and salient positions in other sentences that provide canonical contexts for the testing of a speaker's competence with them. Once one is satisfied that the speaker grasps these primitive expressions in these canonical contexts of use, one can extrapolate the postulated understanding of those expressions to new syntactic contexts—such as, say, undecided conjectures like Goldbach's—along with a postulated understanding of the latter's pattern of composition, and thereby justifiably attribute to the speaker an understanding of the new sentence even though he may be at a loss as to how one might set about proving or disproving it.

The crude verificationist made the crucial mistake of taking the sentence as a whole, and not fully seizing on the opportunities that are afforded by seeing it as composed out of its parts. The mistake was to think of the speaker as having to be able to take the whole sentence and come up, all on his own, with a verdict as to its truth or falsity. We have seen that this would be to require far too much. The more modest, and anti-realistically licit requirement is only that the speaker should be able to take the sentence, along with a given piece of discourse purporting to be a proof or a disproof of that sentence, and decide whether that piece of discourse was indeed what it was claimed to be with respect to the sentence in question. In this way, only the recognitional (not: divinational) capacities of the speaker would be engaged in the required manifestation of his understanding of the sentence. The conditions of correctness of proofs (and disproofs) are intimately bound up with the compositional structure of the sentence in question. Its breakdown into immediate sub-sentential constituents will be reflected in the breakdown of the proof (or disproof) into its immediate subproofs. The latter breakdown will have a specific form, according to the logical operator that may be dominant in the sentence. And the relationship between sentence structure and the structure of subproofs is a rule-governed, recursive one. Compositionality is the crucial key. By its means the anti-realist can sidestep any imputation of an overly crude verificationist account of meaning.

5.4 Feasible verifiability

There still lingers, however, even on the part of anti-realist writers (such as Wright)[3] a defective understanding of the workings of the manifestation requirement. The defect stems from their reluctance to appeal to another kind of factorizability. The defect is apparent in the misgiving that the manifestation requirement, properly pursued, would allow for the meaningfulness

---

[3]See his 'Strict Finitism', *Synthese*, 51, 1982, pp. 203–82.

only of such sentences as are actually verifiable (practically, feasibly verifiable) rather than of sentences that are verifiable in principle though perhaps not feasibly so. They conceive of the verification as having to be carried through to completion, no matter how long it might be. They also think that, since there are obviously finite limits (however vague these may be) to what human subjects could actually achieve in this regard, so too, then, there must be sentences that are decidable in principle but whose meanings could not be regarded as graspable. For these sentences would admit only of verifications that were too long to be recognized as such. And this could happen even for sentences that themselves were relatively short and surveyable, such as the claim that

$$(2^{2^{2^{2^{2^2}}}} + 1) \text{ is prime}$$

There is an adequate proper response to these finitist misgivings about such drastic consequences of the manifestation requirement.[4] So far, however, it has not been made clear by anti-realist writers, even when they do not make the mistake of espousing too crude a verificationist criterion of meaning. Let us see how the finitist misgiving is located even when crude verificationism has been disposed of.

5.5 Aspectual recognition: competence as factorizable

The anti-realist's proposal would be as follows:

> (R) for a speaker S to be credited with a grasp of the meaning of a sentence ϕ, we should have good grounds for believing that, if presented with some finite piece of discourse Π, S would be able to recognize whether Π was a proof or a disproof of ϕ.

So far, this proposal avoids the crude verificationist's mistake of insisting that S be able to discover for himself some proof or disproof Π, in order

---

[4]These misgivings are most forcefully essayed by Wright, loc. cit. The misgiving is that the manifestation requirement, as pressed by the moderate anti-realist or intuitionist, entails a slide all the way to strict finitism. That is, we can justify bivalence only for feasibly decidable sentences, rather than for all those sentences that are decidable in principle. Here we are proposing a solution to Wright's worries that effectively sidesteps the dialectic he launched himself into. Wright did not exploit the opportunities presented by the aspectual dispositional conditionals to be described below.

to be credited with an understanding of ϕ. But there is still the risk, in the formulation (R) just given, of making the further but related mistake of under-appreciating the force of factorizability. Some surveyable sentences ϕ might be decidable in principle but not feasibly decidable. Their shortest proofs (or disproofs) might be too long for ordinary, competent human beings to inspect and check and judge to be correct. But we are not, just for that reason, to be deprived of our alleged understanding of the sentence ϕ.[5]

For, first, ordinary speakers would still be able to dismiss various surveyable pieces of discourse II as non-proofs and as non-disproofs of ϕ. In so doing, they would exercise their recognitional capacities in precisely the way required by the manifestation condition in our theory of meaning. Secondly, suppose they were presented with a non-surveyable proof- (or disproof-) token: one that is too long for them actually to complete their check of it as a proof (or disproof). Nevertheless, there is still a *factorizable* way that they could exercise their recognitional capacities with respect to it, even though (*ex hypothesi*) the total exercise of those capacities within any one speaker's lifetime would not suffice for a verdict as to the proofhood (or disproofhood) of the token in question. The factorizable way is to direct their attention to various aspects of the token, and to ask them whether those aspects are locally in order.[6] Imagine that we received sensible replies to such queries. These replies may, of course, be hedged with respect to supposed outcomes of checks of, say, subproofs, that the speaker knows he cannot actually make, but could 'in principle' imagine having been made. The contention is that,

---

[5]Nor, even for unsurveyable sentences ϕ, should we be deprived of our alleged 'potential' understanding of ϕ, provided that ϕ is composed out of constituents that we understand, and in a manner that we understand.

[6]This idea is owed to Jon Cogburn. He first thought of it in connection with a defence against Kripkean scepticism as to whether '+' meant addition or quaddition for a given speaker. The Kripkean worry was that with a long addition sum carried out in decimal notation, a sum too long to be exhaustively checked by the speaker in his lifetime, the dispositionalist would be unable to derive from the imputed understanding of '+' (on the part of the speaker) any true claim about how the speaker would be disposed to respond to the addition sum in question. Cogburn's idea was to limit the manifestation requirement for the dispositions that the speaker had to have, so that these dispositions concerned only local requirements of correctness-in-context. Thus, the speaker would have to be able only to check each 'column' of the addition sum, to ensure that, with the digit carried from the previous column, the correct digit was written below the line and the appropriate digit was carried to the next column. This provided a factorizable sense in which the speaker's dispositions would embrace the whole addition sum, even if it were unsurveyable.

Clearly, the idea generalizes to the checking of pieces of discourse for proofhood. We pursue this generalization here.

under such circumstances, we should not be so uncharitable as to withhold attribution of full understanding.

The inadequate, *non-factorizing* way of understanding (R) above is as follows:

> (R_{NF}) for a speaker S to be credited with a grasp of the meaning of a sentence ϕ, we should have good grounds for believing that, if presented with some finite piece of discourse Π, S would actually be able to deliver a correct verdict either of the form 'Π is a proof of ϕ' or of the form 'Π is a disproof of ϕ' or of the form 'Π is neither a proof nor a disproof of ϕ'; that is, after some time S would have checked all aspects of Π for correctness in the appropriate regards.

Contrasted with this is the more adequate, *factorizing* way of understanding (R):

> (R_F) for a speaker S to be credited with a grasp of the meaning of a sentence ϕ, we should have good grounds for believing that, if presented with some finite piece of discourse Π, S would be able to deliver a correct verdict on any aspect of Π that is relevant to arriving at a correct judgement of the form 'Π is a proof of ϕ' or of the form 'Π is a disproof of ϕ' or of the form 'Π is neither a proof nor a disproof of ϕ'; that is, for any such aspect α, S would, after some time, be able to judge whether α was as it ought to be, in order for Π to have the status in question.

(R_F) is less exiguous than (R_{NF}), because of the quantifier switch involved. The speaker's understanding, on this account, is conceived somewhat along the line of a (potentially unsurveyable) host of true dispositional conditionals, one for each aspect of the piece of discourse Π:

> if S were to have his attention directed to aspect α_1 of Π, then S would be able to determine whether α_1 was as it ought to be in order for Π to be a proof/disproof/neither;

> if S were to have his attention directed to aspect α_2 of Π, then S would be able to determine whether α_2 was as it ought to be in order for Π to be a proof/disproof/neither;

> . . .

if S were to have his attention directed to aspect α_n of Π, then
S would be able to determine whether α_n was as it ought to be
in order for Π to be a proof/disproof/neither;

. . .

We can have good grounds for believing that each of these conditionals is
true of S, even while conceding that S is perforce unable, given the sheer
size of Π, to pronounce on the correctness of all aspects of Π. Understanding
is projective and productive, and, on the reading given by (R_F), comprehensive; and understanding can be attributed even when we know that the
speaker's manifestational performance could not, in the nature of things, be
exhaustive.

5.6 Finding the right dispositional conditionals

Grasp of meaning, on the model given here, consists in the truth of a set
of dispositional conditionals. The set is determined by the range of possible
aspectual tests of a speaker's ability to tell whether a piece of discourse
counts as a proof, or a disproof, or neither. Even with a surveyable sentence ϕ
that has a surveyable proof Π, the set of dispositional conditionals associated
with ϕ will itself be unsurveyable. This is because one has to allow for other
possible proofs of ϕ besides Π, which, unlike Π, may be unsurveyable; and
in general for unsurveyably long pieces of discourse that are not proofs of
ϕ, but which, presumably, the speaker has to be 'able to rule out' (in the
aspectual sense) as proofs of ϕ.

The set of dispositional conditionals associated with any sentence ϕ will
therefore in general be unsurveyably large. Hence we cannot expect their
antecedents ever to be co-realized for any speaker. That is, we cannot expect
any speaker ever to have his attention directed to all the aspects of all
pieces of discourse whose proofhood he is supposed to be able to appraise.
This, however, is a very contingent limitation. The dispositionals in question
are nevertheless more happily co-criterial for grasp of meaning than other
dispositionals can sometimes be, even when they are true of the same thing.
For, take some physical object a, with two dispositional properties F and G.
Suppose F-ness consists in manifesting F_2-ness in test conditions F_1, and
G-ness consists in manifesting G_2-ness in test conditions G_1. That is,

$$F(a) =_{df} F_1(a) \Rightarrow F_2(a)$$
$$G(a) =_{df} G_1(a) \Rightarrow G_2(a)$$

where $\Rightarrow$ is the subjunctive conditional. The intended sense of $F_1(a) \Rightarrow F_2(a)$ is 'if a were to be subjected to test conditions F_1 then a would manifest F_2'. Now it is quite possible for the test conditions F_1 and G_1 to be 'mutual blockers'. That is, when the *ceteris paribus* clauses in the conditionals

$$F_1(a) \Rightarrow F_2(a)$$
$$G_1(a) \Rightarrow G_2(a)$$

are properly spelled out, we get

$$(F_1(a) \wedge \neg G_1(a)) \Rightarrow F_2(a)$$
$$(G_1(a) \wedge \neg F_1(a)) \Rightarrow G_2(a)$$

This can be illustrated with an imaginary example from folk physics. Suppose F is solubility in paraffin and G is elasticity under compression. $F_1(x)$ means 'x is immersed in paraffin' and $F_2(x)$ means 'x dissolves'; $G_1(x)$ means 'x is compressed' and $G_2(x)$ means 'x springs back to its former shape'. It may be that being immersed in paraffin causes the body a to become non-elastic and non-deformable; and that being compressed causes a to become insoluble in paraffin. (All we have to accept is that this is a possibility; we do not have to think that it is actually so.) Thus the realization of the test condition of either one of the dispositional conditionals

$$F_1(a) \Rightarrow F_2(a)$$
$$G_1(a) \Rightarrow G_2(a)$$

thwarts the other conditional. Yet, before such realization, both conditionals are (relatively unproblematically) true of the object a. The object a could have a micro-structure that makes both dispositionals true, even though their testing, in the nature of the case, is bound to be mutually exclusive. When the *ceteris paribus* clauses are spelled out more clearly to take account of the mutually thwarting tendencies described, we get something at least as explicit as the pair

$$(F_1(a) \wedge \neg G_1(a)) \Rightarrow F_2(a)$$
$$(G_1(a) \wedge \neg F_1(a)) \Rightarrow G_2(a)$$

in which it is clear that the test conditions are not co-realizable. Thus we see that in general we could have a set of true conditionals (holding of an object a) whose antecedents are not co-realizable, and for reasons having to do with the very nature of the dispositions truly and simultaneously ascribed to a.

If we are entitled to such a conception of mutually thwarting conditionals holding simultaneously of an object, then we should be even more willing to entertain the conception suggested above of a set of criterial ('aspectual') conditionals holding of a speaker S with respect to a proposition ϕ. Here, the difficulty in realizing all the antecedents (test-conditions) 'together' derives only from limitations on time and physical resources, and not in any mutually thwarting character of the conditionals themselves. First, they cannot be realized simultaneously, unless the speaker is capable of massively parallel 'direction of attention' to various aspects of a construction presented to him. So we have to imagine, rather, that the antecedents are realized sequentially. Still, for any surveyable subset C^* of the set C of conditionals, it may be possible to realize the antecedents of members of C^* within the lifetime of the speaker S. The realization of the antecedent $H_1(S)$ of any one conditional $H_1(S) \Rightarrow H_2(S)$ in C^*, when testing for the claimed manifestion $H_2(S)$, need not thwart the appropriate manifestation $K_2(S)$ claimed upon the realization of the antecedent $K_1(S)$ of any other conditional $K_1(S) \Rightarrow K_2(S)$ in C^*. It is just that, in the case of the conditionals that are criterial for speaker S's grasp of a sentence, there are too many conditionals in the whole set C for us to be able to realize all their antecedents within the lifetime of S. Nevertheless, the speaker S could be so constructed or internally constituted that all of those conditionals in C were true of S; just as the object a of our little example could be so constituted that both the conditionals

$$F_1(a) \Rightarrow F_2(a)$$
$$G_1(a) \Rightarrow G_2(a)$$

or their precisifications

$$(F_1(a) \wedge \neg G_1(a)) \Rightarrow F_2(a)$$
$$(G_1(a) \wedge \neg F_1(a)) \Rightarrow G_2(a)$$

were true of it.

In general, there is no reason why we should not attribute a plurality of dispositions simultaneously to an object, even though it is nomically impossible for the object to manifest its possession of all those dispositional properties. Hence we should be even less reluctant to attribute a plurality of dispositions simultaneously to a speaker, even though it is (merely) practically impossible for the speaker to manifest his possession of all those dispositional properties. Those dispositions, as remarked earlier, are happily co-criterial, and not even mutually thwarting. This provides strong reason for thinking that they hold by virtue of the same generative base for general linguistic competence. Provided only that the appropriate set of dispositional conditionals (determined by the sentence ϕ) is true of the speaker S, S should be credited with an understanding of ϕ. His grasp of ϕ is fully manifestable, in the sense that for any criterial test of such grasp, he can pass it; not in the sense that he can pass all the criterial tests of such grasp. Just as compositionality prevents moderate anti-realism from collapsing into naïve verificationism, so too does factorizability prevent moderate anti-realism from sliding into strict finitism.

Having saved moderate anti-realism from being undermined by an overly zealous application of its own foundational requirements (concerning speakers' manifestation of grasp of meaning), we turn in the next two chapters to an examination of how the moderate anti-realist prosecutes those requirements. Most importantly, we examine the reasons why, in the light of the manifestation requirement, the phenomenon of effective undecidability leads the anti-realist to eschew the classicist's principle of bivalence.

Chapter 6

The Manifestation Argument is Dead

> If, as I believe, there is a way to do justice to our sense that
> knowledge claims are responsible to reality without recoiling into
> metaphysical fantasy, then it is important that we find that way.
> — Hilary Putnam[1]

6.1 A summary by way of introduction

This chapter and the following one will get clear about four major competing viewpoints: Orthodox Realism, M-Realism, Gödelian Optimism and
Moderate Anti-Realism. These positions will be characterized by the different combinations of Yes/No answers that they respectively provide to
two *independent* questions concerning the nature of truth: 'Could there
be recognition-transcendent truths?'; and 'Is truth determinately bivalent?'
That these are indeed independent questions is often not appreciated.

Our task in this chapter will be part exegetical, part clarificatory, and
part critical.

The exegetical part will find fault with Dummett for his insufficiently
discriminating account of the four possibilities just mentioned. He discerns
only two of them. We shall show that Dummett conflates our two questions
about truth, and in effect sees the dialectic as involving only the 'Yes, Yes'
position and the 'No, No' position (that is, Orthodox Realism and Moderate

---

[1]The Dewey Lectures, Lecture I: *The Antimony of Realism*, in *Journal of Philosophy*
91, 1994, at p. 446.

Anti-Realism, respectively). Dummett appears to be blind to the prima-facie distinct possibilities of M-Realism and of Gödelian Optimism (the 'Yes, No' and 'No, Yes' options respectively).

The clarificatory part of our task in this chapter will mainly be concerned with distinguishing properly among these four *prima facie* distinct possibilities. This will give us a clearer understanding of just what the argumentative task would be for the Moderate Anti-Realist, who is concerned to rule out the three competing possibilities, thereby leaving his own position as the only tenable one.

The critical part of these investigations will take Dummett to task over the formulation of his famous 'manifestation argument', in so far as he intends to direct it against the principle of bivalence. We have no quarrel with this argument as a refutation of the alleged possibility of recognition-transcendent truth; for that is its properly confined role. But in Dummett's hands the manifestation argument has been supposed to establish something more—namely, the incoherence of asserting bivalence 'across the board' for the discourse in question. Dummett's formulation of the argument is what we shall call the 'single sentence' argument.[2] The label adverts to the fact that the argument involves as an intermediate conclusion an existential quantification over sentences, which serves as a premiss for an existential elimination in the remainder of the argument. Crucial though this more ambitious argument has been to the modern rehabilitation of anti-realism as a form of generalized intuitionism, it is, in Dummett's repeated presentations, fallacious through and through. Indeed, we are tempted to echo that ringing phrase of Strawson's in his criticism of Kant, and say that Dummett's manifestation argument, *in so far as it is directed against bivalence*, is, when properly regimented, revealed as embodying 'a non-sequitur of numbing grossness'. But that would be an overly harsh judgement, since the logical moves Dummett was making are prima facie more subtle and complex than the ones Strawson was addressing in Kant's writings. Nevertheless, it turns out that on the only two possible exegetically sensitive ways one can see of regimenting Dummett's 'manifestation argument' carefully and in full detail, Dummett is made to keep company with St Thomas Aquinas. We are referring, of course, to the latter's cosmological argument for the Existence of God, and the well-known quantifier-switch fallacy that it contains. On our analysis, Dummett commits the same fallacy—on two different ways of construing him. Unlike the cosmological argument, however, which is an argument in name only,

---

[2] This label is due to Jon Cogburn.

the manifestation argument *can* be rehabilitated; but that task is deferred to Chapter 7, where we shall finally attain a proper grasp of the philosophical potency of the manifestation requirement, properly understood.

6.2 Decidability, knowability and truth: picturing the positions

We need an overall idea of the possible pictures on offer from various philosophical quarters on the interconnections among the decidable, the knowable, the true and the theoretically complete. Let us start from scratch, as it were, trying to chart the various possibilities. As promised above, we shall invoke subsequent results to narrow these down to just a few; from among which only Moderate Anti-Realism will emerge as tenable, given all the considerations that will have been entered by then.

To make sense of the variation among the pictures, the reader ought to adopt at the outset only what we called earlier the 'philosophically neutral core of truths about truth'. In particular, this would involve not making any commitment—just yet—either way, regarding either the bivalent character, or the epistemically unconstrained character, of truth. These further realist ingredients of truth are precisely what will be at issue as we pursue the investigations below.

We shall use the following defined symbols:

$\mathcal{D}$ $=_{df}$ the set of sentences whose truth can be established by the application of an effective decision method[3]

$\mathcal{K}$ $=_{df}$ the set of sentences which are in principle knowable as true, even if not by way of application of an effective decision method[4]

$\mathcal{T}$ $=_{df}$ the set of true sentences

Each of these sets is of course consistent; that is, from none of them can one deduce $\bot$ (absurdity). Our task below will be to examine how, on different competing accounts, these sets are interrelated (by identity or inclusion).

---

[3]This $\mathcal{D}$ is to be distinguished from the domain of discourse D! The former is of course a proper subset of the latter.

[4]Note that we say *knowable*, not 'known'.

But first we have to define one more kind of set, which we shall call a *completion*. In what follows, all sets will be sets of sentences.

When Δ is consistent, we shall denote ambiguously by Δ^+ any *completion* of Δ: that is, any consistent set Γ such that $\Delta \subseteq \Gamma$ and for every ϕ either ϕ is in Γ or $\neg\phi$ is in Γ. In general Δ can have more than one completion.

$\Delta^- =_{df}$ the set of sentences whose negations are in Δ.

Obviously, Δ^- is unique. We shall call it the *undoing* of Δ.

LEMMA: For every ϕ, either ϕ is in Δ^+ or ϕ is in $(\Delta^+)^-$.

Proof. By definition ϕ is in Δ^+ or $\neg\phi$ is in Δ^+. In the second case ϕ is in $(\Delta^+)^-$. The result follows.

Our Lemma tells us that for any consistent set Δ, any completion Δ^+ and its undoing $(\Delta^+)^-$ form a partition of the language. The picture would be:

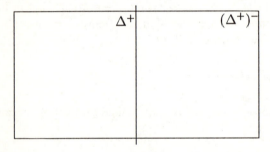

where the rectangle represents the set of sentences in the language. The dividing line down the middle shows the partition effected by the completion Δ^+ (the left square) and its undoing $(\Delta^+)^-$ (the right square).

Now in general every decidably true sentence is knowable as true; every sentence knowable as true is true; and every true sentence will be in any completion of the set of true sentences. Thus we know we have the containments

$$\mathcal{D} \subseteq \mathcal{K} \subseteq \mathcal{T} \subseteq (\mathcal{T})^+,$$

which will govern all the possibilities to be explored below.

This chain of containments gives us what we may call the Prima-Facie picture:

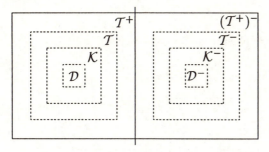

The dashed boundaries might be thought of as still rubbery, as it were.

In the 1920s the Logical Positivists of the Vienna Circle entertained a rather naïve picture, one that involved a bold answer to the question of whether any of the preceding containments might be proper:

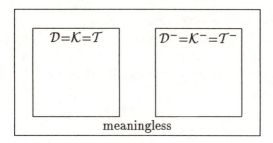

The Logical Positivists' principle of verifiability was tantamount to the requirement that any meaningful (that is, true or false) statement should have its truth-value determinable by the application of some decision procedure. Any statement for which a truth-value could not be so determined would be meaningless. Quite apart from various conceptual difficulties inherent in this position (especially from the principle of compositionality), the naïve picture could not withstand the discoveries of Gödel's completeness theorem[5] and Church's undecidability theorem[6] for first-order logic. Logical truth was undecidable—despite the fact that it was axiomatizable, hence knowable. This gave us the firm proper containment $\mathcal{D} \subset \mathcal{K}$. So the chain above had

---

[5]'Die Vollständigkeit der Axiome des logischen Funktionenkalküls', *Monatshefte für Mathematik und Physik*, 37, 1930, pp. 349–60.

[6]'A note on the Entscheidungsproblem', *Journal of Symbolic Logic*, 1, 1936, pp. 40–1; *Correction, ibid.*, pp. 101–2.

become

$$\mathcal{D} \subset \mathcal{K} \subseteq \mathcal{T} \subseteq (\mathcal{T})^+$$

which gives us a slightly firmer picture as follows:

The Metamathematical Limitativist's picture:

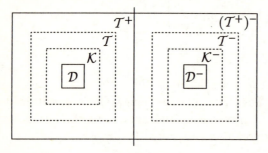

We must now enquire whether any of the other containments is proper. We must be careful, however, when we talk of proper containment. Suppose we already have that $\Delta \subseteq \Gamma$, that is, that $\forall\phi(\phi \in \Delta \rightarrow \phi \in \Gamma)$. For the classicist, the following are logically equivalent ways of stating that Δ is a *proper* subset of Γ ($\Delta \subset \Gamma$):

(1) assert $\exists\phi(\phi \in \Gamma \wedge \neg(\phi \in \Delta))$

(2) assert $\neg\forall\phi(\phi \in \Gamma \rightarrow \phi \in \Delta)$

For the intuitionist, however, (1) implies but is not implied by (2).[7] Even in

---

[7] The following sort of objection is in error, and betrays ignorance of the logical fundamentals of intuitionism: 'The intuitionist is supposed to be a constructivist; therefore, when denying a universal claim he should be prepared to provide a constructive counterexample.' All that is required for the denial of a universal claim is a constructive *reductio ad absurdum* of the universal claim itself. Such a *reductio* might well proceed by making *several* instantiations of the universal claim, whose results, collectively, lead (constructively!) to absurdity. This would suffice for the constructive *reductio* of the universal claim, without any one of those instantiations being identifiable as 'the' false one. In the same way, the intuitionist can deny a conjunction $(A \wedge B)$ without being committed either to $\neg A$ or to $\neg B$ (that is, without being committed to $(\neg A \vee \neg B)$). One can show that two propositions contradict one another without being justified in denying either of them. To be sure, in order to justify an *existential* claim, the intuitionist is required to be able to provide a constructive instance; but positive existentials are *not* straightforward duals of

the absence of (1) and (2), the intuitionist could

(3) refuse to assert $\forall \phi (\phi \in \Gamma \rightarrow \phi \in \Delta)$

without yet denying it. For certain choices of Δ and Γ, (1) would be intuitionistically incoherent, leaving (2) and (3) as the only options.

Suppose $\Delta \subseteq \Gamma$. When (3) is the only option on the question whether this containment is proper, we shall write $\Delta \sqsubset \Gamma$. With Brouwer[8] came the option of type (3) just discussed, that $T \sqsubset T^+$. This is the simple refusal to assert Bivalence. The undecidability of Robinson's arithmetic Q, as we shall in due course see, strengthened this.[9] It gave the *anti-realist* (even if not the realist) the option of type (2) just discussed: $T \subset T^+$.[10] The chain of containments

$$\mathcal{D} \subset \mathcal{K} \subseteq \mathcal{T} \subseteq (\mathcal{T})^+$$

could now, it seems, be firmed up only in a limited number of ways, each one corresponding to a distinctive philosophical position.

As it turns out, making all the containments potentially proper yields the picture favoured by McDowell's so-called M-Realist.[11]

The M-Realist's picture:

---

negative universals. The quoted objection from our imaginary objector is therefore based on a thoroughgoing and elementary misunderstanding. This misunderstanding of the intuitionist's obligations in respect of a denied universal no doubt stems from the confusion, easy for a classicist, of $\neg \forall x F(x)$ with $\exists x \neg F(x)$. But there, precisely, lies the rub.

[8] L. E. J. Brouwer, *Intuitionisme en Formalisme*, Amsterdam, 1912. English translation in *Bulletin of the American Mathematical Society*, 20, 1913, pp. 81–96.

[9] Cf. A. Tarski, A. Mostowski and A. Robinson, *Undecidable Theories*, North-Holland, Amsterdam, 1968.

[10] As will be shown below, if Δ is any arithmetical theory consistent with Q, then Δ is undecidable; whence one can deny Bivalence for the discourse of arithmetic. We are not here making the mistake of identifying knowable arithmetical truths with the theorems of any particular formal system.

[11] J. McDowell, 'Truth Conditions, Bivalence and Verificationism', in G. Evans and J. McDowell (eds.), *Truth and Meaning*, Oxford University Press, 1976, pp. 42–66.

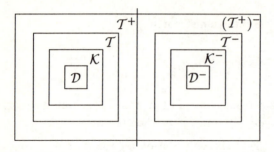

The M-Realist wishes to countenance as coherent a combination of intuitionistic logic (with its refusal to grant Bivalence — $T \sqsubset T^+$) with 'a conception of truth conditions as possibly obtaining, or not, quite independently of the availability of appropriate evidence' ($K \sqsubset T$). Such a position, he maintains, would be 'essentially realist'. So he is challenging the claim that realism entails the acceptance of Bivalence. He holds to Knowledge- or Recognition-Transcendence, but not Bivalence. We shall consider this position more closely below, and argue that one should reject it. Meanwhile, we shall continue our survey of possible positions.

From now on, we can ignore the right half of each picture, since it is obtained by reflecting the left half. The remaining philosophical positions are as follows.

The Gödelian Optimist's picture:

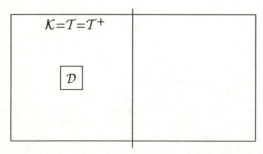

Gödelian Optimism consists in the view that truth is both bivalent and knowable. Our equation $T=T^+$ expresses bivalence. Bivalence is in effect the claim that the truths form a logically complete theory. The equation just given is a handy way of saying this. It claims that the inclusion $T \subseteq T^+$ is not a proper inclusion—that is, that the set T of truths is identical to (any of) its completion(s) T^+. Likewise, our equation $K=T$ expresses the principle of knowability (that every truth is knowable). According to the Gödelian Optimist, whatever it is that makes for the (classical, bivalent) truth of a given sentence, it could in principle yield to our intellectual insights.[12] These insights might have to await further intellectual developments — discoveries of as yet unknown proofs, and formulation of as yet unthought-of methods of proof—but they could not remain, in principle, forever beyond human appreciation. That is not to say that we would ever have at our disposal a system or set of methods that would generate all the truths—for that, as we know from the essential incompleteness of arithmetic, would be impossible. The Gödelian Optimist is saying only that each truth should be knowable by some means or other; not that there is some means by which every truth can be known.

The Orthodox Realist, by contrast, is gloomier about the prospect of ever being able to establish any given truth that is deep or elusive enough. Not only does he concede that no one system could encompass all the truth; he believes, unlike his more sanguine Gödelian colleague, that some truths might never fall prey to any method of detecting them—they might escape the compass of every system. His picture is as follows.

The Orthodox Realist's picture:

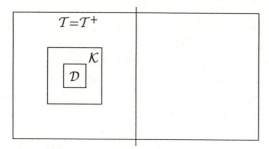

For the Orthodox Realist, every sentence is determinately true or false (i.e.

---

[12]I take the term 'Optimism' from Stewart Shapiro's 'Anti-Realism and Modality', in J. Czermak (ed.), *Philosophy of Mathematics*, Proceedings of the 15th International Wittgenstein-Symposium, Part 1, Hölder-Pichler-Tempsky, Vienna, 1993, pp. 269–87; at p. 283. Shapiro calls a proposition *absolutely decidable* if 'either there is a rationally compelling argument establishing [it] or a rationally compelling argument refuting [it]'; and he defines *optimism* as 'the belief that every sentence of every unambiguous mathematical theory, or at least, say, arithmetic and analysis, is absolutely decidable.' Note that he is not assuming that the means of constructing all rationally compelling arguments are captured in any one formal system.

Bivalence holds; in the picture, $T=T^+$) and there are truths that are in principle unknowable (Knowledge-Transcendence; in the picture, $K \subset T$).

The Moderate Anti-Realist opposes both of these views. For him, all truth is knowable ($K=T$); and he denies Bivalence ($T \subset T^+$). His picture is therefore as follows.

The Moderate Anti-Realist's picture:

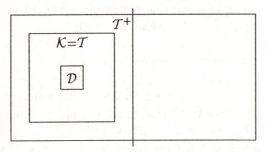

6.3 Dummett's construal of realist truth, and his blindness to Gödelian Optimism

We owe to Dummett the very idea of construing realism as a doctrine about the nature of truth. We owe to him also the idea that one could try to justify intuitionism by appeal to considerations of meaning that are informed by an appropriately substantive and epistemically constrained notion of truth.

It must be pointed out, however, that Dummett has consistently conflated two separable strands in the realist's notion of truth: determinate bivalence, and recognition-transcendence. One representative quotation will suffice, in which we employ boldface to indicate the strand of **determinate bivalence,** and italics to indicate the strand of *recognition-transcendence.*[13]

> What is a realistic interpretation of statements of some given class? It is, essentially, the belief that we possess a notion of

---

[13] For similar claims, the reader is referred to 'Realism', 1963, in *T&OE*, p. 146; 'The Reality of the Past', 1969, in *T&OE*, pp. 358, 361, 364; Postcript (1972) to 'Truth', in *T&OE*, p. 23; *Frege: Philosophy of Language*, Duckworth, 1973, 'Can Truth be Defined?', p. 466; 'The Philosophical Basis of Intuitionistic Logic', 1973, in *T&OE*, pp. 228–9; 'Realism', 1982, in *The Seas of Language*, pp. 230, 235–6; 'Realism and Anti-Realism', 1992, in *The Seas of Language*, p. 465.

truth for statements of that class under which every statement is **determinately either true or not true**, *independently of our knowledge or our capacity for knowledge*.[14]

Note that Dummett consistently fails to appreciate the option of Gödelian Optimism. He either passes over it altogether,[15] or is wholly dismissive of it as a possibility:[16]

> there is no intelligible anti-realist notion of truth for mathematical statements under which a statement is true only if there is a proof of it, but may be true because such a proof exists, even though we do not know it, shall never know it, and have no effective means of discovering it. The reason is evident: we can introduce such a notion only by appeal to some platonistic conception of proofs as existing independently of our knowledge, that is, as abstract objects not brought into being by our thought. But, if we admit such a conception of proofs, we can have no objection to a parallel conception of mathematical objects such as natural numbers, real numbers, metric spaces, etc.; and then we shall have no motivation for abandoning a realistic, that is, platonist, interpretation of mathematical statements in the first place.

Note that at this stage the phrase 'anti-realist notion of truth' is potentially ambiguous, given that we can identify two different strands in the realist's notion of truth.[17] A notion of truth may be considered anti-realist because it is subject to the principle that all truths are knowable. In that sense, the Gödelian Optimist is an anti-realist. Alternatively, a notion of truth may be considered anti-realist because it is not claimed to be subject to the principle of (determinate) bivalence. In this second sense, the M-Realist would count as an anti-realist.

The passage from Dummett just quoted above merely invites that rejoinder 'Quite so!' from the Gödelian Optimist; who would be correct in going on to point out that the passage is no more than a *petitio* of the question at hand, to wit, whether an insistence that truth cannot transcend the reach of recognizable truth-makers can consistently be combined with an

---

[14]'Is Logic Empirical?', 1976, in *T&OE*, p. 274.

[15]For example, see *The Logical Basis of Metaphysics*, Harvard University Press, 1991, pp. 314–5.

[16]'Realism' (1982), reprinted in *The Seas of Language*, at pp. 258–9.

[17]See next section.

insistence that truth is, nevertheless, determinately bivalent. If that consistent combination then entails a realistic or platonistic understanding of mathematical statements, *Well, then, so be it!* would be the appropriate answer. For one is still wanting, from Dummett, a philosophical *refutation* of the position (Gödelian Optimism) that does not depend on a premiss that in effect denies its possibility.

Dummett begs the question further against the Gödelian Optimist[18] when he goes on to say

> If we wish to say that a mathematical statement can be true only if there exists a proof of it, we have ... only two choices. We can interpret 'exists' as meaning concrete existence, our actual possession of a proof;... Alternatively, we may construe 'exists', and therefore 'is true', as tenseless. *We shall, in this case, have to interpret 'exists' constructively*[19]

'Not so!' rejoins the Gödelian Optimist. 'I am entitled to a non-constructive interpretation of the existential quantifier, equating (timeless) truth with the (non-constructive) existence of a proof, pending a refutation, which has yet to be presented, of the incoherence, or unsuitability (on, say, explanatory grounds), of holding the essential tenets of my position—namely, the knowability of truth (via proof), and the determinate bivalence of truth.'

Having noted that Dummett has not given independent grounds for ruling out Gödelian Optimism, we shall return later to the question of whether it *can* be ruled out, and, if not, what grounds there might be for eschewing Gödelian Optimism in favour of an anti-realist position.

6.4   Understanding the dialectic of debate

There are four positions in contention: Orthodox Realism, M-realism, Gödelian Optimism and Moderate Anti-Realism. They are generated by taking different views on two independent matters: the determinate bivalence of truth, and the possible recognition-transcendence of truth.

Dummett, as we have seen in the previous sections, tends to conflate these two strands so characteristic of Orthodox Realism. For him it is a monistic position, and Moderate Anti-Realism is diametrically opposed to it. For Dummett, the manifestation argument is at once an attack (presumably

---

[18]loc. cit.
[19]My emphasis.

successful) on both the bivalent and the recognition-transcendent character of realist truth. Carried to its conclusion, that argument leaves the anti-realist, or so he thinks, in full possession of the field:

Manifestationism
intended by Dummett to
rule out this position

↓

```
┌─────────────────────┐
│                     │
│     Orthodox        │
│     Realist         │
│                     │
│    (Truth is        │
│     bivalent,       │
│   transcendent)     │
│                     │
│          ┌──────────────────────┐
└──────────┤                      │
           │      Moderate        │
           │    Anti-Realist      │
           │                      │
           │    (Truth is         │
           │  neither bivalent    │
           │  nor transcendent)   │
           │                      │
           └──────────────────────┘
```

But this is to move too swiftly to the spoils. This picture is blind to the possibilities of M-Realism and of Gödelian Optimism. We have to ponder more carefully just what it is exactly, in the full-blown realist's notion of truth, that runs foul of the manifestation challenge. It will be argued here that manifestation is directed against the *recognition-transcendent* character of truth. It would be only derivatively (say, by showing that bivalence implied recognition-transcendence) that the manifestation challenge would count against bivalence as well. Until such further argument has been furnished, however, the two strands are, prima facie at least, independent of each other, as shown in the following diagram, with all the possibilities revealed:

Manifestationism
rules out only this column

↓

	Transcendence $\mathcal{K} \sqsubset \mathcal{T}$	Anti-Transcendence $\mathcal{K}=\mathcal{T}$
Bivalence $\mathcal{T}=\mathcal{T}^+$	Orthodox Realist	Gödelian Optimist
Anti-Bivalence $\mathcal{T} \sqsubset \mathcal{T}^+$	M-Realist	Moderate Anti-Realist

An *aggressive* defence of Moderate Anti-Realism will establish $\mathcal{K} = \mathcal{T}$ (all truths are knowable) and $\mathcal{T} \subset \mathcal{T}^+$ (truth is not determinately bivalent). Dummett's defence was trying to be of the aggressive type. A *tolerant* defence of Moderate Anti-Realism would proceed from the principle (as an assumption) that all truths are knowable, and offer various grounds for consequently refusing to be drawn into asserting bivalence ($\mathcal{T} \sqsubset \mathcal{T}^+$) or going so far as to reject it ($\mathcal{T} \subset \mathcal{T}^+$). The tolerant defender would also have to counter realist arguments purporting to reduce to absurdity the foundational assumption of knowability; and it would have to deflect or defuse realist complaints to the effect that the anti-realist would be methodologically deprived as a result of refusing to assert bivalence.

In this chapter and the next two, we shall be setting out what amounts to a tolerant defence of Moderate Anti-Realism. For the time being we shall be occupied with the questions of recognition-transcendence, bivalence, manifestationism and undecidability. When enough lessons have emerged to justify the diagram of the dialectical situation given above, we shall eventually turn, in Chapter 8, to a novel defence of the anti-realist's knowability principle $\mathcal{K} = \mathcal{T}$ against the transcendent realist's attack on it. Note, however, that on our diagnosis above of the dialectical situation, the anti-realist is joined in this defence of knowability by the Gödelian Optimist![20] The Gödelian Optimist will be sharing a trench with the anti-realist in Chapter 8. In the end, however, it will be an uneasy and short-lived alliance: for the Gödelian Optimist will come under attack when we broach the other topic, namely bivalence.

6.5   Bivalence and Decidability

Let us assume throughout that we are dealing with discourses D in which there are no vague or ambiguous expressions, and whose sentences are not structurally ambiguous either. Let us assume, that is, that the sentences of D have sharp and clear meanings.

The principle of bivalence for sentences in a discourse D is:

(Biv_D) $\forall \phi (\phi \text{ is in } D \ \rightarrow \ (\phi \text{ is true} \lor \neg(\phi \text{ is true})))$

This definition will be accepted by both the realist and the anti-realist. For the realist, it holds across the board—that is, for every discourse D. For the anti-realist, however, it could hold or it could fail, depending on the discourse D. One should not simply assume it without further justification. Justification would turn on details of the discourse D in question. Nor, according to the anti-realist, would the *failure* of Bivalence be in any way due to vagueness or ambiguity—for, as just stipulated, these defects of declarative language will not come into consideration at all.

The best way to justify bivalence for a discourse D is to show that D is *decidable*. A discourse is decidable just in case there is an effective method (that is, a mechanical procedure) for determining, given any sentence of the discourse, what its truth-value is. Thought of as a function defined on the sentences of the discourse D, such a method or procedure μ is *total*—that is, μ is 'everywhere defined' on its domain D. So: for *every* sentence ϕ of D, the value $\mu(\phi)$ exists. And the range of μ is the two-member set $\{T, F\}$ of truth-values. So: for *every* sentence ϕ of D, $\mu(\phi)$ is *exactly one* of the values T, F. Thus when a discourse is decidable, it is also *bivalent*. That is, every

---

[20]I owe this observation to Roy Cook.

one of its sentences is determinately true or false. This informal reasoning now invites closer scrutiny to see exactly why and how it is correct.

The claim that D is decidable is to be regimented as follows:[21]

(Dec_D) $\exists$ effective method $\mu(\mu$ is total on $D \wedge$
$$\forall \phi(\phi \text{ is in } D \rightarrow$$
$$(\mu(\phi) = T \rightarrow \phi \text{ is true}) \wedge$$
$$(\mu(\phi) = F \rightarrow \neg(\phi \text{ is true}))))$$

Here we are saying that the method μ correctly detects the truth-status of any sentence ϕ to which it is applied. If ϕ is true, then μ will yield the value T; otherwise, it will yield the other value F. Now, because μ is *total*, it follows *constructively* from (Dec_D) that:

(†) $(\phi \text{ is true} \rightarrow \mu(\phi) = T) \wedge (\neg(\phi \text{ is true}) \rightarrow \mu(\phi) = F)$

To see why this is so, we shall give the detailed reasoning that establishes the first conditional; the reasoning for the latter conditional is similar. So assume the antecedent ϕ *is true*. We know that $\mu(\phi)$ is well-defined and is either the value T or the value F. We cannot have $\mu(\phi) = F$, since by (Dec_D) this would imply $\neg(\phi$ *is true*), contrary to assumption. Thus $\mu(\phi) = T$.

The conjunction (†) of conditionals, then, follows constructively from (Dec_D). But (†) could not *replace* the conjunction of converses

$$(\mu(\phi) = T \rightarrow \phi \text{ is true}) \wedge (\mu(\phi) = F \rightarrow \neg(\phi \text{ is true}))$$

in (Dec_D) as just stated, and still yield a satisfactory definition of decidability. This is because (†) is too weak, constructively, to entail the first of the conditionals

$$\mu(\phi) = T \rightarrow \phi \text{ is true}$$

appearing in (Dec_D). Admittedly, the entailment in question would hold for the *classical* logician; but this would not be enough. For the point is that we need a formulation of (Dec_D) that will enable us to establish *constructive* inferential links with other important theses, such as (Biv_D) and others to be stated below. This is because we must avoid begging any questions against the anti-realist, who refuses to accept certain classical moves of inference as universally valid. To see how classical logic would be needed in order to derive from (†) the conditional

---

[21] We 'stagger' the display of the logical formula across several lines in order to make it easier to grasp its logical structure.

$$\mu(\phi) = T \;\rightarrow\; \phi \; is \; true$$

appearing in (Dec_D) we need to follow carefully how the reasoning would go:

> Assume the antecedent $\mu(\phi) = T$. It follows that $\mu(\phi) \neq F$. Contraposing constructively on the second conditional of (†), we can conclude $\neg\neg(\phi \; is \; true)$.

To extract from *this* that $\phi \; is \; true$ we would need the classical rule of double negation elimination. And it would entirely beg the question to be told that we could help ourselves to this rule, on the grounds that the discourse is decidable anyway! For the whole point is to be able to provide a constructively acceptable derivation of (Biv_D) from (Dec_D). Thus we must exercise great care in choosing our precise formulation of (Dec_D). The formulation we have chosen has the further virtue of being a plausible representation of the order of inference involved when applying a decision procedure μ to a sentence ϕ. The basic idea is that a mechanical process leads to a formalistic answer—either $\mu(\phi) = T$ or $\mu(\phi) = F$, where T and F are for the time being uninterpreted symbols. *Then* we move to the semantic conclusion, respectively, that $\phi \; is \; true$ or that $\neg(\phi \; is \; true)$.

(Dec_D) implies (Biv_D). To see this, assume that (Dec_D) holds. Now the function μ mentioned in (Dec_D) is total, thereby determining, for each sentence ϕ in D, exactly one of the truth values T or F as the value of ϕ. If μ determines T as the value for ϕ, then (so (Dec_D) tells us) ϕ is true; but if μ determines the value F for ϕ, then (so (Dec_D) tells us) $\neg(\phi \; is \; true)$. Either way, it holds that

$$\phi \; is \; true \;\; \vee \;\; \neg(\phi \; is \; true).$$

Thus (Biv_D) holds.

The difference between a semantically realist conception and a semantically anti-realist conception of a realm of discourse cannot be made out if the discourse in question is decidable.[22] If an effective method is available

---

[22] We use the qualifier 'semantically' here for good reason. Part of the interest of Wright's *T&O* was his proposal concerning how one might effect another kind of 'realist' *v.* 'anti-realist' contrast even within the realm of the decidable. He proposes what he calls the Order-of-Determination test, by means of which one can establish whether our judgements in the decidable discourse in question play a 'projective' or a 'detective' role; that is, whether they *determine* the extensions of the concepts involved in them, or *reflect* the extensions of those concepts. The test is intended to make more rigorous the basic Eu-

for deciding, of any sentence of the discourse, whether it is true or false, then even the would-be platonist will be able to manifest fully his grasp of the meaning of any sentence of that discourse. Given any sentence, all he need do is apply the effective method in question. This will yield a determinate answer as to its truth-value. The speaker will thereby have recognized what its truth-value is. If the sentence is true, he will be able to recognize it as true; if it is false, he will be able to recognize it as false. Either way, he will have manifested fully his grasp of what the truth-conditions of the sentence are. The anti-realist, in posing his characteristic demand that the speaker be able fully to manifest his grasp of the meaning—that is, the truth-conditions— of every sentence that he understands, will not be able to fault the realist on a decidable discourse. In fact, on a decidable discourse the anti-realist himself will accept bivalence, and hence regard as justified, within that discourse, any of the inferential moves of classical logic—including the 'strictly classical' ones not available within intuitionistic logic.

6.6 Manifestationism

6.6.1 The original 'manifestation challenge'

There is a demanding 'manifestation challenge' that the Orthodox Realist (and the M-Realist) must face.[23] The challenge, that is, is directed against those who espouse the possibility of recognition-transcendent truth-value, even if they do not espouse determinate bivalence.[24] Consider the principles

(A) The meaning of a declarative sentence is its truth-conditions.

---

thyphronic contrast: are matters thus-and-so merely because best opinion takes them to be thus-and-so, or does best opinion take them to be thus-and-so because they really *are* thus-and-so? The judgement that an object is red might be an example of the former (projective, extension-determining) kind; while the judgement that it is square would be an example of the latter (detective, extension-reflecting) kind. While this topic of 'response-dependent' judgements is of considerable independent interest, it is orthogonal to the main concerns of this inquiry. The idea of distinguishing in this way between projective and detective roles is originally due to Mark Johnston. Cf. 'Objectivity Refigured: Pragmatism without Verificationism', in J. Haldane and C. Wright (eds.), *Reality: Representation and Projection*, New York, Oxford University Press, 1992.

[23] Cf. Crispin Wright, *Realism, Meaning and Truth*, 2nd edn., Blackwell, 1993, pp. 246–50.

[24] It is an important part of our purpose here to distinguish these two strands of realist thought, and to inquire more pointedly which of them is infirmed by which considerations brought forward by the reforming anti-realist who insists on making the manifestation challenge.

(B) To understand a sentence is to know its meaning.

(C) Understanding is fully manifestable in the public exercise of recognitional skills.

It follows that knowledge of a sentence's truth-conditions is fully manifestable in the public exercise of recognitional skills. But suppose now, with the realist, that some sentence is *undetectably* true. Suppose, that is, that the truth of the sentence transcends any possibility of verification. We all agree that the sentence[25] is understood. Thus we supposedly know what its truth-conditions are. Now comes the disarming manifestation challenge, first formulated by Dummett and widely applied since. Perhaps the best-known source for the manifestation challenge is Dummett's 'first, big book' on Frege:[26] The challenge is to explain how a notion of potentially recognition-transcendent truth could itself be intellectually accessible. In posing the challenge, of course, the anti-realist believes that it cannot be met. It would follow that the supposed notion of potentially recognition-transcendent truth cannot help explain how we grasp meaning, if that grasp is both acquired and manifested only via responses to recognizable situations. Here is how Dummett posed the challenge:[27]

> The fundamental tenet of realism is that any sentence on which a fully specific sense has been conferred has a determinate truth-value independently of our actual capacity to decide what that truth-value is.
>
> ...for our language, in general, containing as it does many sentences whose truth-value we have no effective means of deciding, the possession of a truth-value is, on a realist interpretation, divorced from our actual means of recognizing truth-value; although an ultimate connection still remains as embodied in the principle that any true statement must be capable of being recognized as such by some hypothetically placed being with sufficiently extended powers.

---

[25] Note how in setting out the argument in English, one is inclined to use the phrase 'the sentence' with anaphoric back reference to the grammatical antecedent 'some sentence' within an earlier existential claim. When such an argument is regimented in formal notation, one finds that the phrase 'the sentence' corresponds to a parameter for an application of the rule of existential elimination. This is a common experience for logicians. The arguer using the phrase 'the sentence' need have no particular sentence in mind; hence it would be wholly inappropriate to think of this phrase as needing to be regimented in accordance with, say, Russell's theory of descriptions. That would be seriously to misunderstand the *inferential* role of the *only apparently* descriptive phrase.

[26] *Frege: Philosophy of Language*, Duckworth, 1973, 'Can Truth be Defined?', pp. 466–9.

[27] Similar statements of the challenge will be found at 'The Philosophical Basis of Intuitionistic Logic', 1973, in *T&OE*, pp. 223–5; 'What it a Theory of Meaning? (II)', 1976, in *The Seas of Language*, at pp. 46, 92; 'What does the Appeal to Use Do for the Theory of Meaning?', 1979, in *The Seas of Language*, p. 116; and *The Logical Basis of Metaphysics*, Harvard University Press, 1991, pp. 314–6.

A realistic conception of this kind is open to attack [with respect to its recognition-transcendence element—NT] from anyone who holds that the sense which we confer on the sentences of our language can be related only to the means of recognition of truth-value that we actually possess. ... In the case of a sentence for which we have no effective means of deciding its truth-value, the state of affairs which has, in general, to obtain for it to be true is, by hypothesis, one which we are not capable of recognizing as obtaining whenever it obtains. Hence a knowledge of what it is for that sentence to be true is a knowledge which cannot be fully manifested by a disposition to accept the sentence as established whenever we are capable of recognizing it as true: it is a knowledge which cannot, in fact, be fully manifested by actual linguistic practice; and therefore it is a knowledge which could not have been acquired by acquiring a mastery of that practice. ...

An undecidable sentence is simply one whose sense is such that, though in certain effectively recognizable situations we acknowledge it as true, in others we acknowledge it as false, and in yet others no decision is possible, we possess no effective means for bringing about a situation of one or other of the first two kinds. ...

The truth of such a sentence can consist only in the occurrence of the sort of situation in which we have learned to recognize it as true, and its falsity in the occurrence of the sort of situation in which we have learned to recognize it as false: since we have no guarantee either that a situation of one or other kind will occur, or that we can bring about such a situation at will, only a misleading picture of what we learned when we learned to use sentences of that form can give us the impression that we possess a notion of truth for that sentence relative to which it is determinately either true or false.

The manifestation challenge may be summed up in a single sentence:[28]

precisely because a realistic theory forces so large a gap between what makes a statement true and that on the basis of which we are able to recognize it as true, the theory has difficulty in explaining how we derive our grasp of the latter from a knowledge of the former.

And this is the thought which Wright unreservedly endorses also. How, Wright asks,[29]

could that knowledge [of truth-conditions] consist ... in any ability whose proper exercise is tied to *appreciable* situations?

---

[28] *The Interpretation of Frege's Philosophy*, Duckworth, 1981, ch. 4, 'Idealism', p. 71.
[29] loc. cit., p. 248.

Our three principles (A), (B) and (C) above implicitly constrain truth to be epistemic. They turn truth into *knowable* truth. And they do appear to render illegitimate the notion of recognition-transcendent truth. This is the notion according to which the truth of a sentence may be undetectable in principle, completely transcending any possibility in principle of establishing it by appeal to what is sensible and/or recognizable.

The manifestation challenge, in its original simplicity, is disarmingly effective, but only against the notion of *recognition-transcendent* truth. It dispatches the Orthodox Realist and the M-Realist, both of whom insist on recognition-transcendence.[30] But it does not yet touch the Gödelian Optimist. The Gödelian Optimist might reply that, compatibly with our three principles above, one could deploy a notion of truth that was bivalent even if not recognition-transcendent. Truth would consist in the non-constructive existence of a truth-maker, but at least the truth-maker itself would be effectively recognizable as such, even if we have no effective means for discovering the truth-makers for ourselves. Thus truth, for the Gödelian Optimist, would always be in principle detectable, even though our best systems of proof at any one time might be incomplete, and even though we have undecidability

---

[30] Although he may be reluctant to concede the point, the manifestation challenge also disposes of the 'reformed realist' represented by the Putnam of Lecture III of the 1994 Dewey Lectures. Putnam makes so bold as to claim (loc. cit., p. 516) that

> truth is sometimes recognition-transcendent because what goes on in the world is sometimes beyond our power to recognize, even when it is not beyond our power to conceive.

But this claim has the persuasive appeal that it does by the end of Putnam's 'journey ...back to the familiar' only because of the seductively familiar senses with which he deploys the words within it. *Of course*, in the ordinary sense, not all killers can be recognized as such! (cf. p. 511). And *of course* we can hold that 'there are certain determinate individuals who are or were killers and who cannot be detected as such by us' without having thereby to hold 'a belief in magical powers of the mind'! But this does not dislodge the denial of the possibility of recognition-transcendent truths, when that denial is properly understood for our present purposes of philosophical discussion. To drive this point home, consider what that denial really amounts to: it is the denial that *any possible* course of experience, or *any possible* evidence that might come to light, or *any possible* pieces of discourse directed to support the intended conclusion, could *in principle* render that conclusion true. Without believing in magical powers of the mind, one might wring one's hands over the outcome of the O.J. trial, and despair of ever being able to reach forensic certainty; but this would be quite compatible with holding the *philosophical* view that whether or not O.J. killed one or both of the two victims is not a 'potentially recognition-transcendent' matter. For one could imagine any number of various bits of evidence later coming to light that might settle the matter conclusively. *Mutatis mutandis* for Putnam's own example of Lizzie Borden.

theorems for certain (incomplete!) theories and their consistent extensions.

The dialectical position now reached is that *bivalence*, that other central strand of realism, would appear to survive the manifestation challenge. This would be a disappointing result for Dummett, who, in his paper 'The Philosophical Basis of Intuitionistic Logic', sought to apply the manifestation requirement so as to produce a *reductio* of the principle of bivalence. That *reductio* was to motivate the choice of intuitionistic logic as the logic that correctly reflected the meanings of the logical operators.

6.6.2   Does Bivalence entail the possibility of recognition-transcendent truth?

In the classic paper just mentioned, Dummett's attempted *reductio* of the principle of bivalence ran as follows:

> Suppose D^* is a discourse for which we possess no effective decision procedure for determining truth or falsity of its sentences. Assume nevertheless, for the sake of *reductio*, that bivalence holds for D^*. Then there will be an undecidable sentence in D^*. Call such a sentence ψ. Assume now that ψ is true. Then ψ's truth transcends any speaker's capacity to recognize it (since, so we are assuming, ψ is undecidable). But this would contradict the manifestation requirement (since we are assuming that ψ is understood). Hence it is *not* the case that ψ is true. Hence $\neg\psi$ is true. Then $\neg\psi$'s truth transcends any speaker's capacity to recognize it (since, to repeat, we are assuming that ψ is undecidable). Once again, this would contradict the manifestation requirement.

The overall logical form of this argument is as follows, involving a terminal step of $\exists$-elimination:

$$\cfrac{\begin{array}{c}\text{Bivalence for } D^* \\[2pt] \Pi \\[2pt] \exists\phi \in D^*\ \phi \text{ is undecidable}\end{array} \qquad \cfrac{\overbrace{{}^{(1)}\overline{\psi \text{ is undecidable}}\ ,\quad \begin{array}{c}\text{Manifestation}\\ \text{Requirement}\end{array}}^{\Sigma}}{\bot}}{\bot}\ (1)$$

In this (not yet fully detailed) regimentation of Dummett's argument,[31] the parametric sub-argument Σ for $\exists$-elimination[32] is in effect the argument given in the quote from Dummett above, by means of which the manifestation requirement rules out the possibility that any sentence ψ might enjoy recognition-transcendent truth. In the argument, the phrase 'the sentence' corresponds to our use of the parameter ψ for existential elimination.

Note that Σ, on Dummett's own understanding of the course of argument, would not *itself* rely on the principle of bivalence as a premiss. The reasoning that we would be regimenting as the argument Σ is intended by Dummett to bring out an inconsistency between just the two premisses displayed in the argument schema above, namely, the Manifestation Requirement and the assumption that ψ is an undecidable sentence. The Dummettian reasoning regimented by Σ began by assuming, for the sake of argument, that ψ was true. ψ's undecidability then entailed that ψ's truth could not be recognized. This contradicted the Manifestation Requirement. Hence (by intuitionistic reasoning) one could conclude that ψ would *not* be true. But then $\neg\psi$ would be true. Once again, ψ's undecidability would entail that the truth of $\neg\psi$ could not be recognized; and this would once again contradict the Manifestation Requirement. The reasoning is intuitionistic throughout. That makes the principle of bivalence *irrelevant*, hence not a premiss of Σ. Thus the 'single sentence' argument must incorporate the principle of bivalence (Biv_{D*}) as a premiss of its *other* sub-argument, namely Π, if it is to gain any refutational purchase on (Biv_{D*}) at all.

Σ is reasonably short and constructive, then; and does not even speak to the question of bivalence for the discourse in question. There is little point in regimenting it any further. Σ simply brings out a direct contradiction between saying, on the one hand, that a sentence ψ is undecidable (in

---

[31] Because of the way Dummett's argument invites one to contemplate some sentence ψ that is true but not recognizably so (or that is beyond the reach of any effective method for determining its truth-value), we are calling this the 'single sentence' argument. The 'single sentence' argument is to be distinguished from the 'whole discourse' argument, to be given below, of what we shall be calling the central inference. In Dummett's argument and ours, the principle of bivalence plays very different roles as a premiss.

[32] Note that while we are considering the extent to which one might be able to regiment Dummett's argumentation, we shall use the more neutral terms 'argument' and 'sub-argument' rather than 'proof' and 'subproof'. The latter terms would carry the connotation that they had been successfully constructed and were formally correct. They are what one might call 'success nouns'. An *argument*, by contrast, is something whose very designation as such preserves the needed whiff of skepticism as to its ultimately kosher status.

the sense that its truth-value, should it possess one, would transcend any speaker's ability to recognize it, even in principle) and saying, on the other hand, that any speaker who understands a sentence should be able, in principle, to recognize the sentence as true when it is true (and recognize it as false when it is false). The latter premiss, which we have called the 'manifestation requirement', is therefore the straightforward contradictory of the claim that there exists an undecidable sentence in the sense just explained.

Now 'x recognizes ψ as true' is equivalent to 'x knows that ψ'. Let us assume further that anyone who discovers grounds for ψ's truth (and therefore comes to know that ψ) could communicate those grounds to any other competent speaker. Then the manifestation requirement just expressed would be tantamount to the requirement that every truth (as expressed by a sentence that can be understood) is knowable. In the 'single sentence' manifestation argument, then, the premiss playing the role of the manifestation requirement is just the principle of knowability. This principle is held in common by both the Moderate Anti-Realist and the Gödelian Optimist. We shall be revisiting it as (KT) below.

On our account of the matter, Σ amounts to no more than a simple clash between the knowability of the truth of any sentence (manifestationism) and the potential recognition-transcendence of the truth of that sentence (which Dummett calls its 'undecidability'). That immediately puts one in mind of the general question whether a '$reductio$' that reduces a claim to absurdity simply by stating its contradictory as a premiss can carry much conviction.

Even if one were to disagree with this assessment of Σ's simplicity, the reader can rest assured that, in Dummett's writings anyway, the other sub-argument, called II in the argument schema above, consists of but a single step. Here, for example, is how he makes the move himself:[33]

> When the sentence is one which we have a method for effectively deciding, there is ...no problem [in espousing bivalence — NT] ... But, when the sentence is one which is not ... effectively decidable, as is the case with the vast majority of sentences of any interesting mathematical theory, the situation is different. Since the sentence is, by hypothesis, effectively undecidable, the condition which must, in general, obtain for it to be true is not one which we are capable of recognizing whenever it obtains, or of getting ourselves into a position to do so.

---

[33] 'The Philosophical Basis of Intuitionistic Logic', 1973, in $T\&OE$, p. 224–5.

Dummett takes it as immediately obvious (through his use of the phrase 'the sentence') that bivalence guarantees the existence of some sentence ψ for which

> there is no (or at least, we possess no) effective method for determining ψ's truth-value.

This necessary absence, or at least present unavailability, of any such method he takes to license one's thinking of the sentence in question as follows:

> ψ is not recognizably true, if it is true, and is not recognizably false, if it is false.

It is this latter way of thinking of the supposed sentence ψ that runs into trouble (via sub-argument Σ above) once one brings the Manifestation Requirement to bear upon it.

There is much to untangle here, and much to think through more carefully. We shall enter three main criticisms of the moves that Dummett attempts.

The first criticism is implicit in our last clarificatory remarks. This is the criticism that Dummett equivocates between two distinct technical construals of 'ψ is undecidable'. The first construal is that there is no (or at least, we possess no) effective method for determining ψ's truth-value. This we shall call the *effective undecidability* construal. The second construal is different. It is that ψ is not recognizably true, if it is true, and is not recognizably false, if it is false. This latter construal might be called the *recognition-transcendence* construal. The first criticism, in full detail, is that Dummett uses the 'effective undecidability' construal in order to accomplish the sub-argument Π; but then resorts to the 'recognition-transcendence' construal in order to accomplish the sub-argument Σ.

Now to avoid this objection, Dummett has to convince us that he is *not* thus equivocating on the construal of 'ψ is undecidable'. Can he do so? Let us explore what can be done here on Dummett's behalf.

What about avoiding the alleged equivocation by opting for the 'effective undecidability' construal of 'ψ is undecidable' in both the sub-argument Σ and the sub-argument Π? The would-be argument schema would then look like this:

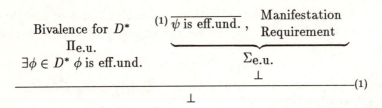

$$\text{Bivalence for } D^* \qquad \overset{(1)}{\overline{\psi \text{ is eff.und.}}}, \quad \begin{array}{l}\text{Manifestation}\\ \text{Requirement}\end{array}$$

Bivalence for D^*

$\Pi_{\text{e.u.}}$

$\exists \phi \in D^* \; \phi$ is eff.und.

$\overbrace{}$

$\Sigma_{\text{e.u.}}$

$\perp$

——————————————————————————————(1)

$\perp$

This strategy, unfortunately, would be confounded by the simple (and, in this context, rather tart) *tu quoque* that even intuitionistic arithmetic is effectively undecidable—whence, in so far as it would make any sense to say of any particular sentence that it was effectively undecidable in *classical* arithmetic, it would make just as much sense to say that is was effectively undecidable in *intuitionistic* arithmetic. Yet the Dummettian is supposed to be wielding the manifestation argument in favour of intuitionistic arithmetic. It would therefore be a howler to suggest, on his behalf, that $\Sigma_{\text{e.u.}}$ be constructed with the underlying notion of deducibility embedded in the predicates involved being *intuitionistic* rather than classical deducibility! The 'manifestation argument' would thereby have backfired—the anti-realist would be hoist with his own petard.

We have reason to doubt that $\Sigma_{\text{e.u.}}$ could be constructed. In order to contradict the Manifestation Requirement, we need a premiss for $\Sigma_{\text{e.u.}}$ at least as strong as 'ψ is recognition-transcendent', rather than the present, weaker, 'ψ is effectively undecidable'.

So avoiding equivocation by resorting to a uniform 'effective undecidability' construal simply will not work. It follows, then, that Dummett would have to avoid the equivocation by sticking to the 'recognition-transcendence' construal. The would-be argument schema would then look like this:

$$\text{Bivalence for } D^* \qquad \overset{(1)}{\overline{\psi \text{ is rec.-trans.}}}, \quad \begin{array}{l}\text{Manifestation}\\ \text{Requirement}\end{array}$$

Bivalence for D^*

$\Pi_{\text{r.t.}}$

$\exists \phi \in D^* \; \phi$ is rec.-trans.

$\overbrace{}$

$\Sigma_{\text{r.t.}}$

$\perp$

——————————————————————————————(1)

$\perp$

Certainly, on the 'recognition-transcendence' construal of 'ψ is undecidable', the sub-argument $\Sigma_{\text{r.t.}}$ is (even intuitionistically) watertight. But then on this same construal the sub-argument $\Pi_{\text{r.t.}}$ looks less convincing; and this misgiving will be developed in our second and third criticisms below.

Note that II would be more palatable on the 'effective undecidability' construal than on the 'recognition-transcendence' construal—that is, we are more likely to be able to construct the argument $II_{e.u.}$ than the argument $II_{r.t.}$. Why is this so? Well, think for a moment of the Gödelian Optimist. He does not believe in the potential recognition-transcendence of truth, but he would not for a moment demur from any of the known results about effective undecidability in logic and arithmetic. It is, presumably, on such results that the existence of 'single undecidable' sentences of arithmetic would somehow be taken to rest. Reflect also on the fact that

> ψ is recognition-transcendent

entails

> there is no (or at least, we possess no) effective method for determining ψ's truth-value,

whereas the converse implication fails, even when the premiss is taken as the unqualified

> there is no effective method *at all* for determining ψ's truth-value.

6.6.3 Dummett's quantifier-switch fallacies

The second criticism will show that *even on the more favourable 'effective undecidability' construal* of 'ψ is undecidable', the would-be sub-argument $II_{e.u.}$ cannot be constructed. So this would be fatal also for the prospects for the more ambitious sub-argument $II_{r.t.}$ on the 'recognition-transcendence' construal, whose conclusion, as already noted above, would be even stronger.

The second criticism is as follows. Let us grant to Dummett, as any-one must, that there is no decision method for (intuitionistic) arithmetic. That is, where D is the discourse of arithmetic (membership in which is of course decidable!) and the quantification over functions is understood to be quantification over *effective* functions,

$$\neg\exists f\forall\phi \in D((f(\phi) = 1 \;\rightarrow\; \phi \text{ is true}) \wedge (f(\phi) = 0 \;\rightarrow\; \neg\phi \text{ is true}))$$

Let us abbreviate

$$(f(\phi) = 1 \;\rightarrow\; \phi \text{ is true}) \wedge (f(\phi) = 0 \;\rightarrow\; \neg\phi \text{ is true})$$

as

f correctly decides ϕ

Now from the premiss

$\neg \exists f \forall \phi \in D \; f$ correctly decides ϕ

it does not follow that

$\exists \phi \in D \; \forall f \neg (f$ correctly decides $\phi)$

To think otherwise would be to commit a quantifier-switch fallacy. What *does* follow from the premiss stated is

$\forall f \neg \forall \phi \in D \; f$ correctly decides ϕ

By means of classical logic[34] we can then infer further that

$\forall f \; \exists \phi \in D \; \neg (f$ correctly decides $\phi)$

But not even classical logic will license the further conclusion that

$\exists \phi \in D \; \forall f \; \neg (f$ correctly decides $\phi)$

This would be the quantifier-switch fallacy foreshadowed above. The theorem on undecidability of arithmetic does not guarantee the existence of any particular sentences that are effectively undecidable in the sense that *no* effective method will correctly decide them.

Nor is any such guarantee forthcoming from any theorem in recursive function theory, in the neighbourhood of the result that there can be no recursive enumeration of all total recursive functions. Here, for example, is a prima-facie possibility that would be embarrassing for the Dummettian trying to pass from bivalence to the existence of recognition-transcendent truths. Note first that the discourse of arithmetic has many different *effectively decidable* syntactic fragments. Thus, there is the fragment of 'computations', namely, statements of identity $t = u$ containing only functional terms t, u built up from numerals using the function signs for addition and multiplication. There is also the Presburger fragment, namely, the set of sentences lacking any occurrence of the function symbol for multiplication.

---

[34]One could even tolerate such a strictly classical move at this point, since the aim is to perform a *reductio* of the realist's own principle of bivalence. If strictly classical moves help one to do this, one could say that the realist is simply digging his own grave.

Likewise, what might be called the Skolem fragment consists of those sentences devoid of any occurrences of the addition sign. Then there is the fragment of 'bounded arithmetic', none of whose sentences involves an unrestricted quantification over all the natural numbers. These examples could be multiplied. The point, in the current context, is that for various decidable linguistic fragments D_0, D_1, D_2, ... there are respective decision methods f_0, f_1, f_2, ... which, applied to any sentence in the respective fragment, will correctly decide its arithmetical truth or falsity.

Now the possibility bruited here is not that one could *effectively* enumerate a sequence of fragments D_0, D_1, D_2, ..., each equipped with its respective decision method f_0, f_1, f_2, ..., and have the union of those fragments exhaust the whole language of arithmetic. For that would fly in the face of the known undecidability of suitably strong theories of arithmetic. But what is to refute the (classical) suggestion that there is perhaps a sequence of fragments D_0, D_1, D_2, ..., each equipped with its respective decision method f_0, f_1, f_2, ..., but that that sequence of fragments is *not* effectively enumerable—and, indeed, that their union exhausts the whole language of arithmetic? The devil's advocate suggestion here is that the realist proponent of bivalence could invoke *this* alleged possibility to put the kybosh on Dummett's overly swift move, on the realist's behalf, from bivalence to the existence of some sentence ψ for which

there is no effective method for determining ψ's truth-value.

Indeed, one can show (albeit in an artificial and rather degenerate way) that a sequence of decidable linguistic fragments as mooted above, each with its own decision procedure, and collectively making up the entire language, is perfectly consistent and possible. The example that follows is owed to Warren Goldfarb.[35] Let ϕ_1, ϕ_2, ... be an effective enumeration of all sentences of the language. If ϕ_i is true, let D_{2i-1} be the 'fragment' consisting solely of ϕ_i and let D_{2i} be empty; but if ϕ_i is false, let it be the other way round, that is, let D_{2i-1} be empty and let D_{2i} be the 'fragment' consisting solely of ϕ_i. Now define the effective function f_i on D_i as follows:

if i is odd, f_i is the constant function T on D_i;

if i is even, f_i is the constant function F on D_i.

It follows that for every i, f_i is a decision procedure for truth or falsity of members of D_i.

---

[35] Private communication.

That, then, provides an easy positive solution to the question whether the language might be covered by a union of decidable fragments each of which has associated with it a decision procedure for truth or falsity of its member sentences. One might now ask whether there is any way of making a positive solution harder, but still possible. For example, what if one imposes some grammatical closure requirement[36] on the fragments in the sequence—so that the associated decision procedure really has to do some work?[37] These are admittedly vague suggestions, but it would be interesting if they could be made precise and still allow a positive solution.

The possibility sketched above, and confirmed by the Goldfarb example, infirms Dummett's sub-argument (or single step) II above. One should not infer too swiftly from the assumption of bivalence to the existence of an effectively undecidable sentence, even given the effectively undecidability of truth for the discourse as a whole. One cannot, that is, dispose of the Gödelian Optimist that easily.

Here we have been interpreting 'ψ is undecidable' to mean 'ψ is effectively undecidable'. ψ is thought of as lying beyond the reach of any effective decision procedure: the sentence is not (decidably) a member of any linguistic fragment D_i for which there is an effective method f_i for determining the truth-value of any sentence within the discourse.

We have been undermining Dummett's entitlement to the subproof II even when the existential conclusion of II involves the weaker of the two readings of the predicate '... is undecidable'. Our third and final criticism will now be directed against such II as might aspire to involve the stronger of the two readings in its existential conclusion. That is, we shall now provide further reasons why II cannot be constructed as a would-be passage from the principle of bivalence to the conclusion that there are sentences whose truth-values are potentially recognition-transcendent.

So we return now to the other sense of 'ψ is undecidable', which we said above was better suited for the purposes of the manifestation challenge. In this other sense, the sentence ψ's truth-value would be 'recognition-transcendent'—nothing could possibly count as a proof or a refutation of ψ. That is, no finite piece of discourse could decide ψ as true, or as false, whatever may be the acceptable formal system (of axioms and of rules of inference) by means of which proofs may be constructed. It is in *this* sense

---

[36] Note that the Presburger fragment, for example, is closed under all its logico-grammatical operations.

[37] Again, note how the decision method via quantifier elimination for the Presburger fragment really does some work.

of 'ψ is undecidable' that the Gödelian Optimist will *deny* that bivalence implies that there are undecidable sentences. So, even if there were effectively undecidable sentences in the *first sense* discussed above (involving effectiveness), the (alleged) fact that there are no undecidable sentences in the *second* sense (involving recognition-transcendence) means, says the Gödelian Optimist, that he will be perfectly able to meet the manifestation challenge while still maintaining bivalence. For, the claim would be, all that the speaker has to be able to do is display his ability to recognize proofs and disproofs when presented with them; and also to determine, of any given construction, whether it is a proof, or a disproof, or neither. That is, the Gödelian Optimist will insist on having to meet only what we shall call below the 'weak, passive' form of the manifestation requirement. But more of this in due course; for the time being we can safely say that Dummett's subproof II is not at all convincing. That was our main objection against his 'single sentence' version of the manifestation argument regimented above.

Let us grant to Dummett, as anyone must, that no formal system of first-order arithmetic can be complete—not even a classical one. Put another way, there is no recursive enumeration of the would-be 'truths of classical arithmetic'. (Thus even the categorical set of second-order Peano–Dedekind axioms will not do the trick, since second-order logical truth is perforce unaxiomatizable.) Put succinctly:

> No acceptable formal system can capture all the truths of classi-
> cal arithmetic.
> $\neg \exists S \forall \phi (\phi$ is true $\rightarrow \ S \vdash \phi)$

To infer from this the claim

> there is some truth of classical arithmetic that no acceptable
> formal system can capture (that is, there is some recognition-
> transcendent truth of classical arithmetic)
> $\exists \phi (\phi$ is true $\wedge \neg \exists S \ S \vdash \phi)$

would be to commit yet another quantifier-switch fallacy.[38]

---

[38] Compare the related point made by Wright, in 'Realism, Bivalence and Classical Logic', in *Realism, Meaning and Truth*, 2nd edn., Blackwell, 1993, at p. 460:

> anyone—realist or anti-realist—should demur at the form of transition
> ...from 'There is no guarantee that P' or 'We have no reason to suppose
> that P' to 'It is a possibility that not-P'...

Yet Dummett somehow thinks that this last claim is entailed by the principle of bivalence when applied to the discourse of arithmetic. Nowhere does he give any argument to justify the claim, or to show how it allegedly follows from bivalence. Dummett appears ready to rule out, without any detailed consideration of the reasons for doing so, the possibility of Gödelian Optimism.

The strong existential claim just given would be especially difficult to establish on a constructive interpretation of the existential quantifier. Indeed, the constructivist would argue that it would be impossible to do so. For, on a constructive account, if one can show of a given arithmetical sentence that it could never be established in any acceptable formal system, then one would in effect have established its negation, and thereby settled the question of its truth or falsity (in the wrong direction!).

Even on a classical interpretation, however, the strong existential claim does not follow, even given the undecidability of sufficiently strong theories of arithmetic and the unaxiomatizability of classical arithmetical truth. It would be enough, classically, to obtain the result

> not every truth of classical arithmetic can be captured in an acceptable formal system
> $\neg \forall \phi (\phi$ is true $\rightarrow \exists \mathcal{S}\ \mathcal{S} \vdash \phi)$

But there is no *reductio* in the offing of the optimistic assumption

> $\forall \phi (\phi$ is true $\rightarrow \exists \mathcal{S}\ \mathcal{S} \vdash \phi)$.

6.6.4 Independence results are no help to Dummett

What about a more direct approach on behalf of Dummett? Why not point to the famous unsolved conjectures of arithmetic, as examples of (possibly true) statements that we are not in a position to settle either way? The trouble with this strategy is that it cannot satisfy the present logical need; for it gives too much hostage to mathematical fortune. If one had pointed to, say, Fermat's Last Theorem as an instance of a possibly recognition-transcendent truth, it would immediately have failed to serve that purpose upon being proved by Wiles and his associate. If instead one points to, say, Goldbach's conjecture (which is still neither proved nor refuted), a small stretch of the imagination makes one realize that it, too, cannot do what it's supposed to do in this context. Who can rule out the possibility that the Field's Medal for the year 2000 will go to some young mathematician who furnishes an elegant proof, from entirely acceptable principles, of the conclusion that every even number greater than 2 is the sum of two prime numbers?

What about a more stratospheric approach on behalf of Dummett? Harvey Friedman has recently proved an exceptionally strong form of an independence result, arguably of the strongest possible kind. Independence results become stronger when either or both of the following two conditions are met:

1. the sentence whose logical independence is established is as elementary and intuitively graspable as possible;

2. the mathematical system from which its independence is established is as strong as possible, both in terms of its all-encompassing nature and in terms of the existential strength of its axioms.

Beginning with Gödel's incompleteness theorem for first-order arithmetic,[39] logicians have been improving their independence results in stages. Gödel's independent sentence was extremely long and cumbersome, obtained by the method of coding syntax in arithmetic. It made no intuitively graspable arithmetical claim; rather, its interest lay in what it could be thought of as 'saying' (concerning itself) via the coding: to wit, 'I am unprovable in the present formal system.' And the formal system concerned was only that of *Principia Mathematica*. Gödel's result could, of course, be indefinitely generalized, in the sense that, given any extension of the system, one would be able to find yet another sentence independent of the extended system. But note that the choice of independent sentence depended on the system.

Moreover, the peculiar nicety about Gödelian incompleteness of arithmetic is that the proof of the metatheorem itself furnishes an argument to the effect that the independent sentence is indeed *true* in the intended model of the natural numbers. The independent sentence has the form

$\forall n \mathcal{G}(n)$

where $\mathcal{G}(n)$ is so constructed that, via the Gödel numbering, it 'says' that (i.e. it is interdeducible with the claim that) n is not the Gödel number of any proof, in the system, of the sentence $\forall n \mathcal{G}(n)$ itself. Thus, if the system is consistent, we have

---

[39]K. Gödel, 'Über formal unentscheidbare Sätze der Principia Mathematica und verwandter Systeme I', *Monatshefte für Mathematik und Physik*, 37, 1931, pp. 173–98.

$\vdash \mathcal{G}(0), \vdash \mathcal{G}(1), \vdash \mathcal{G}(2), \ldots$

whence (by soundness) we have

$\mathcal{G}(0)$ is true, $\mathcal{G}(1)$ is true, $\mathcal{G}(2)$ is true, $\ldots$

From 'outside' the system, one is therefore justified in inferring that

$\forall n \mathcal{G}(n)$

But this is precisely what Gödel's theorem shows to be unprovable within the system. The metatheorem states that, if consistent, the formal system under investigation cannot itself contain a proof of this last result. The formal system could be *extended*, however, so as to enable us to codify within the *extended* system a formal proof of the formerly independent sentence. This extension would be effected by adopting a primitive truth predicate for the unextended language, thereby making available new instances, within the language thus extended, of the axiom scheme of mathematical induction. Of course, because of the essential incompletability of formal arithmetic, this extended system will, in turn, be unable to settle the truth or falsity of yet another independent Gödel sentence. Nevertheless, the point is that each independent Gödel sentence, at any stage of formalization, succumbs to proof at the next stage. So the Gödel sentence for any particular formal system of arithmetic is clearly *not* a case of utterly verification-transcendent truth of the kind that Dummett is seeking to establish as flowing from the adoption of bivalence.

We conclude, then, that Gödel's first incompleteness theorem for arithmetic is of no avail to the Dummettian in search of a single undecidable sentence of arithmetic. But we said earlier that there has been a succession of increasingly stronger independence results since Gödel's theorem. Could one of the more recent results provide Dummett with what he needs for the single-sentence argument to be compelling? Let us return to that story.

The next advance came when Gödel and Cohen between them proved the independence of the axiom of choice and of the continuum hypothesis from the axioms of Zermelo–Fraenkel set theory.[40] Here was a reasonably all-encompassing theory, and here were two deep and interesting foundational claims shown to be independent of that theory.

---

[40] K. Gödel, *The consistency of the axiom of choice and of the generalized continuum-hypothesis with the axioms of set theory*, Annals of Mathematics studies, no. 3, Princeton University Press, 1940; P. J. Cohen, 'The independence of the continuum hypothesis', *Proc. Nat. Acad. Sci. USA.*, 50, 1963, pp. 1143–8.

Later, Paris and Harrington proved the first so-called 'natural independence result'.[41] They found a simple arithmetical statement, which had reasonably sophisticated but mathematically 'combinatorial' content, and showed that it was independent of Peano–Dedekind arithmetic.

Friedman has now accomplished what may be regarded as virtually the culmination of the lines (1) and (2) above.[42] He has found an *exceptionally* simple, elementary statement ϕ about numbers, which is about functions on and into finite sets of vectors of integers. He has shown this sentence ϕ to be independent, not just of Zermelo–Fraenkel set theory with the Axiom of Choice (ZFC), but of its extension by certain large cardinal existence axioms. In the present stage of development of Friedman's foundational programme, ϕ is provable upon the additional postulation of the existence of yet larger cardinals (those which are 'k-subtle for all k'). Modulo ZFC, the sentence ϕ is equivalent to the consistency of these deciding cardinals. Nothing smaller will do for the purposes of settling the truth of ϕ. Friedman is confident that his programme can be prosecuted even further. He conjectures that he will be able, with the methods he has already developed, to find an exceptionally simple number-theoretic claim ψ that would be immediately understood by any college-level algebra student; and that he will be able to show that ψ is decided only by postulating the largest cardinal ever considered, namely, that associated with an elementary embedding of the set-theoretic universe into itself. The existence of the latter cardinal is known to be inconsistent with ZFC, but not with ZF. The truth of ψ would thereby have been consigned to a region where even the best mathematicians no longer had any clear intuitions.

Now what has all this to do with the possibilities being canvassed on behalf of Dummett? The suggestion is that the Dummettian might be able to point to the (promised, or threatened!) Friedman sentence ψ as a welcome example of the sort of 'recognition-transcendent truth' (if it *is* true!) (or 'recognition-transcendent falsity', if it is false) whose existence the principle of bivalence is supposed to secure. For, applying bivalence to Friedman's sentence ψ, the realist will say that either ψ is true, or $\neg\psi$ is true. If ψ is true, then, by Friedman's independence result, it cannot be recognized as true. On the other hand, if $\neg\psi$ is true, then, by that same result, it cannot be

---

[41] Cf. J. Paris and L. Harrington, 'A Mathematical Incompleteness in Peano Arithmetic', in J. Barwise (ed.), *Handbook of Mathematical Logic*, Amsterdam, North-Holland, 1977, pp. 1133–42.

[42] Harvey M. Friedman, 'Finite Functions and the Necessary Use of Large Cardinals', unpublished, 132 pp.

recognized as true. Either way, we get a recognition-transcendent truth—or so it would seem.

Nevertheless, despite the impressive nature of Friedman's present result, and the unsettling implications of its conjectured future strenghtening, it cannot be pressed into the sort of logico-philosophical service here that Dummett needs in order to establish that bivalence implies the existence of recognition-transcendent truths. The trouble is that we have no guarantee that the particular extension of Zermelo–Fraenkel set theory involved in Friedman's best possible independence result would have to be the 'last word' on the matter of a foundational starting-point on which to base eventual recognition of truth. We cannot second-guess what new sorts of axioms, or families of principle, might be devised or divined by mathematicians in the future, and appended to the current 'cardinal existence' extensions of Zermelo–Fraenkel set theory. After all, not too long ago even those cardinal existence axioms would not have been foreseen by the best mathematicians. The large cardinal axioms gathered up and extended the impact of the earlier so-called reflection principles, which emerged only after people had pondered long and hard the overall structure of the cumulative hierarchy. Later still, the axiom of determinacy shed new light on the nature of the continuum (even if it also brought out tensions with other candidates for axiomhood). We have no way of foreclosing on future extensions of our collective intellectual insight. Who knows what new principle might not emerge within the next few years, and settle the truth-value of Friedman's 'most independent' (and simplest) sentence? The impressive character of his ultimate (but still only conjectured) independence result derives from the way it would appear to use up *all* our current intellectual resources in the specification of the system from which independence is proved; and also from the exceptionally simple character of the sentence shown thus to be independent. All that, however, still fails to make the desired logical transition available to the Dummettian: the transition, that is, from bivalence to the existence of recognition-transcendent truths.

Chapter 7

Long Live the Manifestation Argument

7.1 A summary by way of introduction

In this chapter, we shall be seeking clarification of what exactly is meant by various important principles, most notably the principle of bivalence and the manifestation requirement itself. We shall distinguish various readings of these principles to see what argumentative weight they can bear. Then we shall seek to eliminate the three competing positions of Orthodox Realism, M-Realism and Gödelian Optimism. That would, if successful, leave Moderate Anti-Realism as the sole surviving option.

We shall be offering a careful formulation of a completely new argument proceeding from the Manifestation Requirement, in order to understand why it is that the anti-realist regards as justified the rejection of the principle of bivalence. This argument we shall call the 'whole discourse' argument. This label adverts to the fact that the argument invokes the effective undecidability of the whole discourse, and does not at any stage appeal to some imagined single undecidable sentence. The 'whole discourse' argument establishes what we shall be calling below 'the central inference'. It is *this* inference, we submit, that Dummett himself should have exploited when trying to show how manifestationism ruled out bivalence. Our newly attained precision in the formulation of the underlying principles, however, puts into sharp relief the differing possible responses of the realist and of the anti-realist to the central inference itself. The anti-realist may have to concede that the intended rout of realism is incomplete. Perhaps he ought to resign himself

to never achieving the sought *reductio* of determinate bivalence. He may
have to content himself, instead, with arguing as persuasively as he can that
his own position, all things considered, makes better sense overall than does
the other surviving (because still consistent) competitor—namely, Gödelian
Optimism.

7.2   A more convincing manifestation argument

7.2.1   The problem of undecidable sentences

Being able fully to manifest one's grasp of the meaning of a sentence ϕ does
not entail that one has a decision procedure for some language fragment to
which ϕ belongs, and of which it is known in advance that it will yield a
determinate answer to the question: 'What is the truth value of ϕ?'

Dummett may appear to invite this construal of the manifestation requirement when he writes[1]

> When the sentence is one which we have a method for effectively
> deciding, ... a grasp of the condition under which the sentence
> is true may be said to be manifested by a mastery of the decision
> procedure, for the individual may, by that means, get himself
> into a position in which he can recognise that the condition for
> the truth of the sentence obtains or does not obtain ...

The invitation, however, would be misascribed. All that Dummett is saying
here is that it is an *option* for the speaker to meet the demands of the
manifestation requirement on a given discourse D by exhibiting mastery of
a decision procedure for D, should one be available. But it is not *incumbent
upon* the speaker that this should be the way that he meet those demands,
even if a decision method be available for D.

Note first that although the generic 'we' might have a decision procedure
for D, it might not be in the repertoire of the particular speaker whose
manifestation of understanding of the sentences of D is in question. Thus,
there was a time at which I did not know that there was a decision method
for sentences in the language of arithmetic without multiplication (so-called
Presburger arithmetic). In particular, I did not know that there was a
complete axiomatization of that theory; and I certainly did not know about

---

[1]'The Philosophical Basis of Intuitionistic Logic', in *Truth and Other Enigmas*, Duckworth, London, 1978, pp. 215–47; at p. 224.

the method of quantifier elimination. I would not have known how to set about effectively deciding the truth-value of a sentence involving only 0, $s( )$ and $+$. Yet, for all that, I certainly *understood* perfectly well what even quite complicated sentences involving 0, $s( )$ and $+$ *meant*.

I could have manifested fully my grasp of their meaning in ways other than effectively deciding their truth-values. I could, for example, have appraised certain constructions correctly as proofs (or disproofs) of those sentences, when presented with those constructions, but without necessarily being able to discover them myself. I could have identified correct inferential patterns in which those sentences and their constituents could be embedded; I could have displayed my grasp of the primitives by citing the definitive axioms governing them; and I could have convinced anyone that I knew how the sentences were constructed out of their constituent expressions. I could also have expounded on the operational meanings of the primitive arithmetical expressions 0, $s( )$ and $+$, saying how they are used for counting members of empty or disjoint collections. All this, I am sure, would have been enough to justify my claim (or that of any reasonable and proficient bystander) that I knew what was meant by the sentences in question. Why should I be convicted of lack of grasp (or of inability fully to manifest my grasp) of the meaning of some arithmetical sentence simply on account of my lack of familiarity with some arcane and complicated decision procedure for Presburger arithmetic that I learned about only when I went to university?

Note, second, that when we encounter sentences for which we have no known effective means for deciding their truth-values, the equation

knowledge of meaning $=$ mastery of a decision procedure

will have to be abandoned. And this is just as much the case for the intuitionist as it would be for the classical mathematician against whom the manifestation challenge is supposed to be such a potent weapon. Even the intuitionist will often lack any effective method for determining truth-values of given mathematical sentences. Given an *intuitionistic* mathematical conjecture C, say, involving quantification over the natural numbers, the intuitionist can be just as much at an 'effective' loss as the classical mathematician when trying to determine from scratch what the truth-value of C is. Yet no one can reasonably take the absence of a decision procedure for determining intuitionistic truth as reason to deny the intuitionist mathematician a grasp of meaning, or to deny him in principle the possibility of fully manifesting that grasp.

We are not denying here that anyone who *did* possess an effective method for determining the truth-values of sentences of Presburger arithmetic could well lay claim to have discharged the obligations imposed upon him by the manifestation requirement of the anti-realist theory of meaning.[2] Mastery of a decision procedure (with suitable *caveats*—see last footnote) might be *sufficient* for attribution of grasp of meaning; but can it be *necessary* for such attribution? In the light of the foregoing, it is fair to think not. It would be overly exigent to equate knowledge of meaning with mastery of a decision procedure. How, then, might we improve on this mistaken equation?

7.2.2 The manifestation requirement made more precise

The manifestation requirement is as follows:

> (*MR*) Any speaker should be able fully to manifest his grasp of the meaning of any sentence ϕ that he understands, by a suitable exercise of salient recognitional capacities in connection with ϕ.

Each of the terms 'fully', 'suitable', 'salient', 'recognitional capacity' and 'in connection with' appearing in (*MR*) needs to be qualified and explained further. In cases where the requirement is discharged by the speaker's competent and complete application of an appropriate decision procedure, we can agree with Dummett that in the terminal position (when a verdict is returned) the speaker 'displays by his linguistic behaviour his recognition that the sentence is, respectively, true or false'.[3] The speaker will have manifested his grasp of meaning *fully*; the process of applying the decision procedure to the bitter end will have been a *suitable exercise* of a *salient recognitional capacity*; and this exercise will have been *directly in connection with* the sentence ϕ.

Let us return to something we said earlier:

---

[2]Ironically, though, one *could* complain that someone might be able to master the method of quantifier elimination *purely mechanically*, and be able to apply it *mindlessly*, without engaging his *understanding* at all. Even a suitably trained *idiot savant* could perform the quantifier manipulations and other moves in the procedure without having a clue as to what was really involved 'semantically'. Indeed, even full understanders, when applying such methods, can lapse into 'clerical mode' in which they are shunting symbols accurately without any concern at all for their meaning. Thus we see that the appeal to effective decision procedures is a somewhat double-edged sword. We can repair to our Chinese Rooms to swing it.

[3]loc. cit., p. 225.

> If the sentence is true, [the speaker] will be able to recognize it as true; if it is false, he will be able to recognize it as false. Either way, he will have manifested fully his grasp of what the truth-conditions of the sentence are.

This could suggest a narrower construal of the manifestation requirement set out above. It is the construal that is particularly suited to the *molecularist*[4] in the theory of meaning. The molecularist insists that the speaker's competence be manifested sentence-by-sentence, since these are the units of discourse by means of which one makes minimal moves in the language game of assertion and denial. Let us consider then the following narrower principle that makes (*MR*) more precise:

> (*M*) For all ϕ that the speaker understands: if the condition for the truth of ϕ *does* obtain, then the speaker should be able to recognize that it obtains, or at least be able to get himself into a position where he can so recognize; but if the condition for the truth of ϕ does *not* obtain, then the speaker should be able to recognize that it does not obtain, or at least be able to get himself into a position where he can so recognize.

It is important to appreciate that (*M*) is *not* in and of itself a requirement of decidability (by either the speaker or his linguistic community) for the sentences that the speaker understands. *For we are not assuming in advance that all these sentences are determinately true or false.* (*M*) can hold for a discourse without its being decidable and without its sentences being bivalent. The logical form of (*M*) is:

$$\forall \phi (X \ understands \ \phi \ \rightarrow$$
$$((\phi \ is \ true \ \rightarrow \ X \ can \ recognize \ that \ \phi \ is \ true) \ \wedge$$
$$(\neg(\phi \ is \ true) \ \rightarrow \ X \ can \ recognize \ that \ \neg(\ \phi \ is \ true))))$$

The reason why (*M*) in the form just given is so acceptable to an anti-realist is that the anti-realist thinks that he is entitled to interpret ϕ's being true in a constructive fashion. If ϕ is true, then there is (that is, for the anti-realist: *there can effectively be found*) an *effectively checkable something* in virtue of which ϕ is true;[5] and if ϕ is *not* true (where the negation is understood

---

[4]For more on whom, see below.

[5]Note once again that we are not yet imposing any requirement to the effect that that the effectively checkable something itself be constructed according only to intuitionistically acceptable rules of logic and mathematics. This further requirement would at best follow later, from one's subsequent analysis of what constitutes the right logic.

constructively), then there is likewise an *effectively checkable something* in virtue of which it cannot be true—that is, a *reductio ad absurdum* of the assumption (of the truth of) ϕ. This being so, it naturally follows that the two conditionals embedded in (M) should hold. For in each case the effectively checkable something can be presented to the speaker and he should be able to inspect them for correctness and deliver a correct verdict as to their probative status. (Call this the 'tandem method'.) All this can hold across a discourse D, it should be stressed, without every one of its sentences being determinately true or false, and without D itself being effectively decidable.

What if ϕ's being true is interpreted non-constructively? —that is, if the existential quantifier in

> ϕ's being true consists in *there being* an effectively checkable truth-maker for ϕ

is not interpreted constructively? On such a weaker interpretation, the truth-maker requirement could be acknowledged as licit by the Gödelian Optimist—who, as we have seen, believes that every classically true statement of arithmetic will in principle admit of (finitary) proof, albeit perhaps only a strictly classical proof. Such a proof might have to use axioms or rules of inference not yet acknowledged as valid, even by the classicist. These principles, moreover, might *never* be acknowledged as valid by the intuitionist. But what happens now with (M)? Could the Gödelian Optimist acknowledge it as a legitimate demand on speakers' grasp of meaning? If we interpose the acronym 'GO' at a crucial point to remind us that it is the Gödelian Optimist about whom we are talking, we would have something like

> (M_{GOD}) For all ϕ that the speaker understands: if the condition for the truth of ϕ *does* obtain—that is, if 'there is' (non-constructively) some truth-maker for ϕ—then the speaker should be able to recognize that the condition for ϕ's truth obtains, or at least be able to get himself into a position where he can so recognize; but if the condition for the truth of ϕ does *not* obtain—that is, if 'there is' (non-constructively) some truth-maker for $\neg\phi$—then the speaker should be able to recognize that the condition for ϕ's truth does not obtain, or at least be able to get himself into a position where he can so recognize.

But the average speaker certainly is not God; this would be to require too much. The non-constructive character of the Gödelian Optimist's existential quantification over truth-makers blocks application of the earlier 'tandem' effective method. The first part of that tandem method will be wanting, for we cannot *effectively* find a proof to present to the speaker; even though the speaker would be able to tell of any given construction, once presented with it, whether it is a proof of the sentence in question, or a disproof, or neither. A less demanding requirement, which the Gödelian Optimist is likely to demand that we be content to impose, would be

> (M_{GOOD}) For all ϕ that the speaker understands: if the condition
> for the truth of ϕ *does* obtain, then the speaker should be able, *if*
> *given the opportunity* to inspect any (future, possibly classical)
> truth-maker for ϕ, to recognize that the condition for ϕ's truth
> obtains, or at least be able to get himself into a position where he
> can so recognize; but if the condition for the truth of ϕ does *not*
> obtain, then the speaker should be able, *if given the opportunity*
> to inspect any (future, possibly classical) truth-maker for $\neg\phi$,
> to recognize that the condition for ϕ's truth does not obtain, or
> at least be able to get himself into a position where he can so
> recognize.

The trouble now, however, is that it is entirely unclear how one might adjudicate the question of whether a given speaker meets the demand posed by this more God-fearing version of the manifestation requirement. The worry stems from the fact that such future, classical truth-maker as ϕ might enjoy in fulfilment of the Gödelian Optimism here indulged could well involve new methods and rules of inference governing the constituent expressions in ϕ. These new methods and rules, in making good the known logical shortcomings of any present formal system, cannot be guaranteed not to have changed the meaning of the sentence ϕ. And we cannot say of our speaker at present that he would necessarily be able to grasp that future, changed meaning of ϕ, even were he adequately to grasp its present meaning. He just might not be inclined to recognize those new methods and rules as licit. And indeed why should he? Indeed, how *can* the Gödelian Optimist make so bold as to suggest not only that every one of the alleged truths to be found in *any* given pair $\{\phi, \neg\phi\}$ will in principle admit of finitary (albeit possibly classical) proof, but also that in doing so the new methods of proof would be justified by appeal only to the *present* meanings of ϕ and its constituent expressions?

The conclusion we draw from these worries is that the simpler version (M) of the manifestation requirement ought to be preferred to either of those designed to indulge the Gödelian Optimist. We would, however, as anti-realists, accept the following modification of our statement of the manifestation requirement, provided that the proofs mentioned therein are constructive ones, which exploit only such rules as are already justified on the basis of the meanings of the expressions involved:

> (wpM) For all ϕ that the speaker understands: if the condition for the truth of ϕ *does* obtain, then the speaker should be able, *if given the opportunity* to inspect any truth-maker for ϕ, to recognize that the condition for ϕ's truth obtains, or at least be able to get himself into a position where he can so recognize; but if the condition for the truth of ϕ does *not* obtain, then the speaker should be able, *if given the opportunity* to inspect any truth-maker for $\neg\phi$, to recognize that the condition for ϕ's truth does not obtain, or at least be able to get himself into a position where he can so recognize.

(wpM) gives expression to a weaker, more 'passive' form of the manifestation requirement, and is to be contrasted with the more 'active' form that would demand of the speaker that he be able simply to take the sentence and effectively determine whether it was true, or false. Truth is being interpreted, constructively, in terms of the existence of a truth-maker. The speaker is merely able effectively to recognize a truth-maker as such, when presented with it and with the sentence that it makes true. The effective method implicit in the existential quantification over truth-makers, combined with the effective method implicit in the speaker's ability to appraise a construction as a truth-maker, yield what we are here calling the ability effectively to recognize that the truth-conditions of the sentence obtain. It is the combined strength of the constructivity of truth (as that notion features in the Principle of Bivalence) and the speaker's passive recognitional capacity (which is all that is required by (wpM)) that will be exploited below to show that Bivalence and Manifestationism jointly entail the decidability of the discourse in question.

Provided that truth is construed as consisting in the constructive existence of an effectively checkable truth-maker (or proof), this 'weak, passive' version of the manifestation requirement is all that one needs for the proof of that 'central inference' to be established below. We shall be using the central inference to try to improve on Dummett's attempt to wield undecidability to threaten bivalence, in the shadow of manifestationism. Our argument will scrupulously avoid the quantifier-switch fallacies pointed out earlier; but whether it delivers a knock-down refutation of bivalence remains to be seen.

Let '$Ux\phi$' abbreviate 'x understands ϕ'. Our principle (wpM) just formulated has the following consequence, which we shall call 'Recognition of truth-value':[6]

(R) $\forall x \forall \phi (Ux\phi \rightarrow$

$\qquad ((\phi$ is true $\rightarrow \forall \Pi(x$ is presented with $\Pi \rightarrow$
$\qquad x$ will be able to recognize whether Π is a proof of $\phi))$

$\qquad \wedge$

$\qquad (\neg(\phi$ is true) $\rightarrow \forall \Sigma(x$ is presented with $\Sigma \rightarrow$
$\qquad x$ will be able to recognize whether Σ is a disproof of $\phi))))$

Contrast now with the manifestation requirement the requirement elucidated in the previous chapter that the discourse D be decidable:

(Dec_D) $\exists$ effective method $\mu(\mu$ is total on $D \wedge$

$\qquad \forall \phi(\phi$ is in $D \rightarrow$
$\qquad (\mu(\phi) = T \rightarrow \phi$ is true)$\wedge$
$\qquad (\mu(\phi) = F \rightarrow \neg(\phi$ is true))))$

As our earlier quote from Dummett shows, (Dec_D) clearly *implies* (M) (for sentences in D),[7] which in turn implies (wpM). And we saw earlier that (Dec_D) implies (Biv_D).

7.2.3   The principle of knowability made more precise

Truths (and falsehoods) are eternal sentences, or sentences-in-context, or propositional contents, depending on one's ontological tastes.[8] The important thing is that what comes to be licensed as a truth is something *that can be grasped or understood.*

---

[6] Note once again that the phrase 'proof of' could be replaced by 'truth-maker for'; and the phrase 'disproof of' could be replaced by 'falsity-maker for'. In the statement of (R) and similar principle we prefer the proof/disproof form of expression on stylistic grounds.

[7] Without making *too* fine a point of it, we should realize, though, that we are assuming, in order to sustain this implication, that any decision procedure available within the community is actually made available to the speaker whose competence is being tested. Otherwise, we could have decidability, while yet the particular speaker under scrutiny had the misfortune to remain in the dark, as it were, about the decision procedure. That is why Dummett is careful to say only that *if* the speaker has mastery of the decision procedure in question, *then* he will be able to meet the demands of the manifestation requirement.

[8] Famous though the debate over the exact nature of truth-bearers has been, it is actually somewhat orthogonal to our present concerns.

To say that all truths are knowable is to say that an idealized competent understander would have access to the grounds for their truth. This means, even despite the idealization of competence involved, that the truth of any sentence must consist in there being some *finite truth-maker*,[9] which could, in principle, be surveyed, effectively checked, and therefore recognized as such.

For those who hold the knowability principle, then, 'ϕ is true' is equivalent to '*There is* an effectively checkable truth-maker for ϕ'. This equivalence holds for both the Moderate Anti-Realist and the Gödelian Optimist. For the former, but not for the latter, the notion of truth is moreover constructive. That is, the Moderate Anti-Realist insists on a constructive reading of that initial existential quantifier. We advert here only to the initial existential quantifier just italicized. It would be a matter for further debate as to whether the truth-maker itself would be allowed to contain only so-called 'constructive' steps of inference. For that would turn on, among other things, what logic was decided upon as the correct logic. The Gödelian Optimist would allow the finitary truth-makers to contain strictly classical steps of inference, such as appeals to the Law of Excluded Middle or applications of classical *reductio*; the Moderate Anti-Realist would not.

Recall that 'x understands ϕ' is abbreviated as $Ux\phi$. With the understanding that the knowledge in question must be based on the recognition of some finitary truth-maker, the knowability principle could be expressed formally as follows:

$$(KT) \quad \forall x \forall \phi (Ux\phi \rightarrow$$

$$((\phi \text{ is true} \rightarrow \text{ it is possible for someone}$$
$$\text{to know that } \phi \text{ is true})$$

$$\wedge$$

$$(\neg(\phi \text{ is true}) \rightarrow \text{ it is possible for someone}$$
$$\text{to know that } \neg\phi \text{ is true})))$$

The last consequent could have read instead 'it is possible for someone to know that ϕ is false'. Dealing with the negation of ϕ allows us to keep truth as our only semantic predicate throughout, thereby justifying the name we have adopted for this principle—'knowability of truth'. Note also that, for any given speaker x who understands ϕ, it is no entailment of (KT) that it

---

[9] Note that we use 'truth-maker' and 'proof' interchangeably. It must be appreciated, however, that in so doing we are not delimiting in advance the methods whereby a proof may be constructed. We are *not* equating truth-makers with proofs in any particular formal system.

should be possible for x herself to know that ϕ is true, should it be so. All that (KT) requires is that it be possible in this circumstance for someone or other (not necessarily x) to know that ϕ is true.

We do not call our principle one of 'knowability of truth *for discourse D*', for the simple reason that the knowability principle is a global one, applying to all discourses. There is no need to 'specify down' to any discourse D. The same holds for the Manifestation Requirement. It too is a global principle, a philosophical precondition concerning meaning that is to be applied across the board. Realism or anti-realism 'for a discourse D' results from seeing whether the global requirement forces one to give up, or even reject, the Principle of Bivalence for D (which, with an eye to this potential specifity, we took care to label (Biv_D) earlier). And whether or not Bivalence is thought to hold for discourse D will depend, crucially, on whether D is decidable — that is, whether (Dec_D) holds. Accounting for how this is so will be our main expository and argumentative task in this chapter.

7.2.4   The principle of bivalence made more precise

Recall that the principle of bivalence for sentences in a class D is:

$$(Biv_D) \quad \forall\phi(\phi \text{ is in } D \;\rightarrow\; (\phi \text{ is true} \vee \neg(\phi \text{ is true})))$$

This principle too can be made more precise, by attending to the constructive character of truth adverted to earlier, on behalf of the anti-realist. The extra precision reveals whether the embedded notion of truth is interpreted constructively or neutrally. For those who hold the knowability principle, as mentioned above, 'ϕ is true' is equivalent to '*There is* an effectively checkable truth-maker for ϕ'. Suppose now, with the Moderate Anti-Realist, that we insist that the initial existential quantifier is to be understood constructively. When the embedded notion of truth is thus constructive, the principle of bivalence will be designated as $(cBiv_D)$. When one is neutral on this further possible demand for constructivity 'up front', or perhaps even indifferent to the demands of the knowability principle itself (and thus allowing even for the possibility that truth might transcend all possible proof), we shall designate the principle as $(nBiv_D)$ instead.

7.3 Logical relationships among theses; the central inference

(Dec_D) implies (M) (on D) but not conversely. In the absence of bivalence—the principle that every sentence in the class D in question is determinately true or false—(M) on D, as we have now seen, is strictly weaker than (Dec_D). But, in the *presence* of bivalence for sentences in D, and on the assumption that every sentence in D is understood by at least one speaker, (wpM) on D is *equivalent to* (Dec_D). To see this, note that we already have that (Dec_D) implies (wpM) on D. Here now is a proof of (Dec_D) from (wpM) plus $(cBiv_D)$ *plus* the assumption that every sentence[10] in D is understood by at least one speaker.[11]

THE REAL ANTI-REALIST MASTER ARGUMENT[12]

Assume

$$(cBiv_D) : \forall\phi(\phi \text{ is in } D \rightarrow (\phi \text{ is true } \lor \ \neg(\phi \text{ is true}))).$$

---

[10] Here, the quantifier prefix in the claim 'For every sentence ϕ in D there is some speaker who understands ϕ' is to be understood constructively: given any sentence ϕ, *we can find* some speaker who understands ϕ.

[11] This manifestation argument is very different in its general thrust from that attributable to Dummett and followers such as Wright. Our purpose here is to try, eventually, to focus on Bivalence as a vulnerable premiss in a *reductio*. We saw above reasons not to be convinced by Dummett's method of attack on Bivalence, which we called the 'single-sentence' argument. In the sustained argument that we shall now provide, we attempt to avoid making any fallacious inferences about the existence or non-existence of sentences or effective methods; and we draw only on undecidability results for mathematical theories whose logical forms render them appropriate for application within our argument.

[12] Opponents of semantic anti-realism often misconstrue exactly how the Manifestation Requirement is wielded in the 'master argument' of the anti-realist. A case in point is A. Brueckner, 'The Anti-Realist's Master Argument', *Midwest Studies in Philosophy*, XVII, 1992, pp. 214–23. Brueckner thinks (pp. 217–8) that what he understands as the 'master argument' for anti-realism can be blocked by the following claim:

> if for unproblematic [that is, decidable] sentences, knowledge of their truth-conditions consists in [an] evidential recognitional capacity.., so should knowledge of [bivalent] truth-conditions consist in such a capacity in the case of problematic sentences. This would block the master argument ...

It will be seen below how this rejoinder is simply to no avail. The only knowledge of 'truth-conditions' that one could possibly have in the case of the problematic (that is, undecidable) sentences is knowledge of their *epistemically constrained, substantive, hence anti-realistically licit* truth-conditions. And for *these* truth-conditions a convincing manifestationist-recognitional story can, as we shall presently see, be told.

where, note, the embedded notion of truth is constructive. We shall now prove (Dec_D); that is, we shall exhibit an effective method μ that will apply to any sentence ϕ in D in such a way that it will yield either the value T or the value F, and such that

$$(\mu(\phi) = T \rightarrow \phi \text{ is true}) \wedge (\mu(\phi) = F \rightarrow \neg(\phi \text{ is true})).$$

The method μ in question is this:

> Given any sentence ϕ in D, find a speaker who understands it. *Ex hypothesi* we can do this. Set this speaker the recognitional task, with our presentational help, of telling whether ϕ is true. (This is the first step of the tandem method.) If the speaker says that ϕ is true, record him as delivering the verdict T. If he says that it is not the case that ϕ is true, record him as delivering the verdict F. Take the speaker's verdict as the output of μ on ϕ. (This is the second step of the tandem method.)

We have to show, of the tandem method μ as here defined, that

1. μ is *total*;

2. μ is *effective*; and

3. $(\mu(\phi) = T \rightarrow \phi \text{ is true}) \wedge (\mu(\phi) = F \rightarrow \neg(\phi \text{ is true}))$.

Ad (1): By $(cBiv_D)$,

ϕ is true $\vee \neg(\phi$ is true$)$

Assume first that ϕ is true. Thus there is (constructively) some truth-maker Π for ϕ. Find it, and present it to the speaker. By (wpM), the speaker is able to recognize Π as showing that the truth-condition for ϕ obtains, or at least is able to get himself into a position where he can so recognize. That is, the speaker will be able to return the verdict T on ϕ. Therefore

ϕ is true $\rightarrow \mu(\phi) = T$

Now assume that it is not the case that ϕ is true. Thus there is (constructively) some falsity-maker Σ for ϕ. Find it, and present it to the speaker. By (wpM) again, the speaker is able to recognize Σ as showing that the truth-condition for ϕ does not obtain, or at least is able to get himself into a position where he can so recognize. That is, the speaker will be able to return the verdict F on ϕ. Therefore

$$\neg(\phi \; is \; true) \;\rightarrow\; \mu(\phi) = F$$

It now follows by $(cBiv_D)$ that μ as defined is total.

Ad (2): We now enter an explicit metaphysical assumption that is all too often suppressed in discussions of bivalence and decidability. The assumption in question is that speakers' recognitional capacities supervene on some physiological reality (their brains and nervous systems); and that their exercise of those capacities, in so far as it consists in some causally conditioned sequence of states of that physiological reality, could be simulated by a suitably programmed computer. We are assuming, that is, the truth of the computationalist view of mind. *This* is what permits us to say that the method μ as here defined is an *effective* method. To the objector who refuses to grant the metaphysical assumption just made explicit, we can only say: treat the speaker as a 'black box' about whose internal workings you make no metaphysical assumptions. On the assurance, however, that this block box is a reliable indicator of truth and falsity, you have what will pass muster for an 'effective method': namely, set the black box running on the problem ('What is the status of $\Pi\;(\Sigma)$?') and await its answer. The answer will be given within a finite time.[13]

---

[13]Stewart Shapiro has raised the objection that 'physiological computability' need not entail effective computability in the sense which, by Church's thesis, is captured by the notion of a recursive function, or a function computable by a Turing machine (cf. his paper 'Reasoning, Logic and Computation', *Philosophia Mathematica*, 3, 1994, pp. 31–51; at p. 40 ff.). At present, the suggestion that what the brain may be able to do may be non-algorithmic in its ultimate nature is a piece of highly speculative metaphysics. But even if one were to concede the point, the present argument could be carried through. Its conclusion Dec_D would simply have to be understood as a claim to the effect that the discourse D admitted of some 'physiologically effective' decision procedure (which might not be algorithmic in the standard sense). In that event, the contrapositions envisaged below would have to exploit a slightly stronger negative thesis, namely, one to the effect that the discourse D did not admit even of such a more liberally conceived decision procedure. Such a negative thesis would not be provable in the same way as, say, the effective undecidability of Robinson's arithmetic Q is to be proved below; but it would still be far more

Ad (3): It now only remains to show that

$$(\mu(\phi) = T \to \phi \text{ is true}) \wedge (\mu(\phi) = F \to \neg(\phi \text{ is true})).$$

Suppose now that $\mu(\phi) = T$. This means that the speaker's recognitional act was to the effect that ϕ *is true*. 'Recognition' is a *success* verb. One recognizes that something is a proof of ϕ only when it is indeed a proof of ϕ. So ϕ is indeed true. Likewise, if $\mu(\phi) = F$ then $\neg(\phi \text{ is true})$. QED

To summarize, then: while conceding that

$(Dec_D) \vdash (M)$ on D; and
$(Dec_D) \vdash (Biv_D)$,

we have nevertheless that

$(M) \nvdash (Dec_D)$.

Furthermore, on the background assumption that the speaker understands the sentences of D, we have that:

$(wpM), (cBiv_D) \vdash (Dec_D)$.

Thus

$(cBiv_D) \vdash (wpM)$ on $D \leftrightarrow (Dec_D)$.

In the presence of bivalence for constructive truth, then, the manifestation requirement (wpM) is in effect the requirement that the sentences of the discourse concerned be decidable. Thus we see how easy it might be, in the *absence* of any assurance of bivalence, to confuse the manifestation requirement with the requirement that the discourse be decidable. But, as we have been at pains to point out, these two requirements are not in general equivalent. *Only* in the presence of (constructive) bivalence do they become so.

Let us focus for a while on the main result above:

---

plausible, for certain discourses D, than its contradictory. In those cases the anti-realist argument for contraposing so as to refuse to accept Biv_D would stand.

$$(wpM), (cBiv_D) \vdash (Dec_D)$$

for this is the nub of the conflict between the reforming anti-realist who advocates a constructive logic and the quietist realist who is content to carry on with full classical logic. Crucially, the principle of bivalence is at stake, and with it all the strictly classical laws and rules of classical logic—the law of excluded middle, the rule of dilemma, the rule of classical *reductio ad absurdum*, and the rule of double-negation elimination—as applied to sentences in the discourse D.

(wpM) is the passive, weaker, 'recognitional' version of the manifestation requirement, according to which the understander is not required to be able to *find* proofs or disproofs, but only to be able to recognize presented constructions as being proofs or disproofs (or neither). This makes (wpM) independently plausible, and immune to any *reductio* arising from any refutation Θ of (Dec_D) for a given discourse D. This would mean that such a *reductio* would, prima facie, be targeting the more vulnerable premiss $(cBiv_D)$. Such would be the upshot of the completed 'whole discourse' argument, whose overall structure would be as follows:

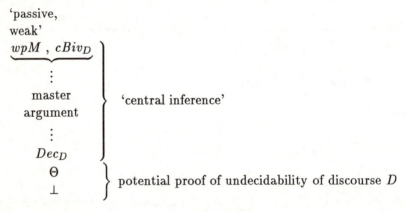

'passive,
weak'

$\underbrace{wpM \ , \ cBiv_D}$

⋮

master
argument   } 'central inference'

⋮

Dec_D

Θ } potential proof of undecidability of discourse D
$\bot$

While (wpM) is thus passive and weak, however, we were exploiting some hidden logical strength in the *other* premiss $(cBiv_D)$ when proving that (Dec_D) followed. This logical strength derives from the fact that in $(cBiv_D)$ the embedded notion of truth is being interpreted *constructively*, in terms of the *constructive* existence of an effectively checkable truth-maker. This helped us to carry out the first step of the tandem method. If truth were interpreted *non*-constructively, then our proof above would not go through. For then we would have $(nBiv_D)$ in place of $(cBiv_D)$ as a premiss. Thus we would have to strengthen the other premiss, namely, the manifestation requirement, in order for the effective method μ still to be forthcoming. But such a strengthening of the manifestation requirement would in effect require the ordinary competent understander to be an *oracle*, able to tell effectively, just by looking at the sentence ϕ, what its truth-value was. And that, we are prepared to concede, would be highly implausible.

The 'stronger, active' form (saM) of the manifestation requirement here contemplated would be:

> (saM) For all ϕ that the speaker understands: if the condition for the truth of ϕ *does* obtain, then the speaker should be able to recognize that it obtains, or at least be able to get himself into a position where he can so recognize—and do so by finding a truth-maker by himself; but if the condition for the truth of ϕ does *not* obtain, then the speaker should be able to recognize that it does not obtain, or at least be able to get himself into a position where he can so recognize—and do so by finding a falsity-maker by himself.

More formally, the principle is as follows:

(saM) $\forall x \forall \phi (U x \phi \rightarrow$

$\quad\quad ((\phi$ is true $\rightarrow$ if set the task, x will find some proof
$\quad\quad\quad\quad\quad\quad\quad\quad\quad\quad\quad$ on the basis of which x will be able
$\quad\quad\quad\quad\quad\quad\quad\quad\quad\quad\quad$ to recognize ϕ as true)

$\quad\quad\quad\quad\quad\quad\quad\quad\quad$ $\wedge$

$\quad\quad (\neg(\phi$ is true) $\rightarrow$ if set the task, x will find some disproof
$\quad\quad\quad\quad\quad\quad\quad\quad\quad\quad\quad$ on the basis of which x will be able
$\quad\quad\quad\quad\quad\quad\quad\quad\quad\quad\quad$ to recognize ϕ as false)))

Contrast (saM) with our earlier principle (R). (saM) could be simplified a little further, on the understanding that 'it is possible *for x to A*' means that it is possible for x to perform feat A all by herself. In the case where A is *coming to know that ϕ on the basis of proof* Π, this will involve x herself finding Π, and not simply being presented with it by others. With this made clear, the simplification in question would be

(saM) $\forall x \forall \phi (U x \phi \rightarrow$

$\quad\quad ((\phi$ is true $\rightarrow$ it is possible for x to know that ϕ)

$\quad\quad\quad\quad\quad\quad\quad\quad\quad$ $\wedge$

$\quad\quad (\neg(\phi$ is true) $\rightarrow$ it is possible for x to know that $\neg\phi$)))

We have cast the 'strong, active' manifestation requirement in this form so as to be able to compare it now with the earlier knowability principle. That principle, recall, was

(KT) $\forall x \forall \phi \in D(Ux\phi \rightarrow$

$((\phi$ is true $\rightarrow$ it is possible for someone
to know that ϕ is true)

$\wedge$

$(\neg(\phi$ is true) $\rightarrow$ it is possible for someone
to know that $\neg\phi$ is true)))

What is interesting to note here is how the difference between (saM) and (KT) consists in the presence of existential quantifications in the latter, whereas in the former one has the same variable bound by the initial universal quantifier. (saM) is therefore the stronger claim; it implies, but is not implied by, (KT). We noted earlier that the principle of constructive bivalence $(cBiv_D)$ presupposed the principle of knowability, in that it required the (constructive) existence of a proof for any truth. The more neutral bivalence principle $(nBiv_D)$, by contrast, does not presuppose the principle of knowability. It is therefore weaker than $(cBiv_D)$. This would suggest that, if in our proof above of the 'central inference', we tried to use $(nBiv_D)$ as the bivalence premiss instead of $(cBiv_D)$, we might have to look for some strengthening of the premiss expressing the manifestation requirement. And indeed we do need such a strengthening; and (saM) will do.

The reader will easily be able to rework our proof above of the 'central inference' by using the different pair (saM), $(nBiv_D)$ of manifestation and bivalence premisses, in place of (wpM) and $(cBiv_D)$ respectively. It will be found that the load of effectiveness shed by insinuating a non-constructive notion of truth into the statement of the principle of bivalence is compensated for by the greater oracular effectiveness of the understander as posited by the 'strong, active' manifestation principle. One will thereby be able still to exhibit an effective method μ as required in the proof. It will be more of a penny farthing, though, than a tandem.

The quandary is now that the conclusion (Dec_D) of our so-called 'central inference' above follows from each of the following two combinations of premisses:

(i) *Weak, passive* manifestation requirement (wpM) plus principle of bivalence $(cBiv_D)$ with a *constructive* embedded notion of truth (the tandem);

(ii) *Strong, active* manifestation requirement (saM) plus principle of bivalence ($nBiv_D$) with a *neutral* embedded notion of truth (the penny farthing).

(i) is the combination we actually used in the proof above.

The conclusion (Dec_D) does *not*, however, follow from the following combination of premisses:

(iii) *Weak, passive* manifestation requirement (wpM) plus principle of bivalence ($nBiv_D$) with a *neutral* embedded notion of truth.

This is a great pity. For we could have declared an apodeictic victory for the anti-realist if (Dec_D) had been derivable from this third combination. For then no philosophical issues would be begged. Bivalence would involve a neutral notion of truth, presupposing no commitment to any anti-realist view; and manifestation would be in its weak, passive form, which is highly plausible. It would then follow that any refutation of (Dec_D), for a given discourse D, would demand the outright rejection of ($nBiv_D$) (since the other premiss of the central inference, namely (wpM), would have been secured).

But this is a manifestationist pipe-dream. For the central inference is not to be had with combination (iii) of premisses (neutral bivalence and weak, passive manifestationism).

Nor will combination (ii)—strong, active manifestationism plus neutral bivalence—really suit the anti-realist's purposes here, since the stronger version of manifestationism is not independently plausible. Any subsequent *reductio* of (Dec_D), for a given discourse D, would fail to focus the blame entirely on ($nBiv_D$). The realist would be able to object that the fault must lie as much (if not exclusively) with the overly strong form (saM) of the manifestation requirement.

The anti-realist can only secure the central inference by using combination (i) of the premisses (constructive bivalence and weak, passive manifestationism). Since he wishes to hold on to manifestationism in the event of any subsequent *reductio* of (Dec_D) (for a given discourse D), he must have independent justification for the precise form of the manifestation requirement that he uses. This means that he must opt for the weak, passive form of manifestationism. That in turn forces him to apportion some of the 'effective load' required for the proof of the central inference on to the principle of bivalence. In order to secure the *effectiveness* of the function μ, the principle of bivalence must be ($cBiv_D$), understood as involving a constructive notion of truth. In other words, the anti-realist must presuppose, in order to establish the central inference, that *all truths are knowable*. It is the principle ($cBiv_D$), in light of the (weak) manifestation requirement (wpM), that one is ultimately forced to abandon for effectively undecidable discourses.

7.4 Decidability: demurral v. denial

Having clarified just which anti-realist cards have to be out on the table, let us see now how the anti-realist prosecutes his case once he has established the central inference above.

(Dec_D) is the claim that a decision procedure is available that will yield a verdict as to the truth-value of *any* sentence in the discourse D. On the face of it, this is a bold claim indeed. Its truth naturally depends on the discourse D in question. The anti-realist is prepared to be persuaded by a *proof* of (Dec_D), for any given discourse D, should he be presented with one. Naturally, he expects such a proof, should one exist, to depend on the details of D.

Such a proof may be short, and more or less immediately available, on reflection, to anyone competent in D. An example would be the case where D consisted of all truth-functional compounds of atomic sentences of the language of arithmetic. Each such atomic sentence is of the form $\underline{n} = \underline{m}$, where the terms $\underline{n}$ and $\underline{m}$ are formed from numerals by using the signs for addition and multiplication. A moment's reflection shows that one can effectively determine the truth-value of any truth-functional compound of these atomic sentences. A more complicated example would be the one mentioned earlier, namely, the language of Presburger arithmetic. Here the quantifiers are allowed, but no mention is made of multiplication. There is a decision procedure for Presburger arithmetic, but some sophistication is required to follow a proof of this fact. Nevertheless, once furnished with this proof of decidability, the anti-realist would be happy to grant (Dec_D) and hence also (Biv_D), where D is the first-order arithmetical language based on 0, $s(\ )$ and $+$.

In general, whenever an anti-realist is provided with an *ungrounded* universal claim of the form $\forall x(Fx \supset Gx)$, he can react in any one of three possible ways. First, he can simply *demur*. That is, he can refuse to assert the claim himself, but not say anything more on the matter. Secondly, he can *deny* the claim. That is, he can assert $\neg\forall x(Fx \supset Gx)$. If pressed for a justification for this denial, he would be obliged to respond with a *reductio ad absurdum* of the claim $\forall x(Fx \supset Gx)$. Such a *reductio* might proceed by means of several distinct universal instantiations, thereby establishing the falsity of the universal claim but without serving up any particular counter-example to it. Finally, he might be in a position to show, of some particular t, that $F(t)$ but $\neg G(t)$. This is the strongest response possible, serving up a definite counter-example t.

Now let us consider the possible responses when an anti-realist is provided with an *ungrounded* existential-universal claim of the form

$$\exists y(Hy \wedge \forall x(Fx \supset Rxy)).$$

First, as with the previous case, he can simply *demur*. Secondly, he could *deny* the claim. Justification for such a denial would take the form of a *reductio ad absurdum* of the 'parametric' claim

$$Ha \wedge \forall x(Fx \supset Rxa).$$

Here the parameter a would have been brought in to represent, in one's reasoning, a supposed 'arbitrary instance' that would serve to make the existential claim true. By $\wedge$-elimination, we reduce the target of the *reductio* to the pair of claims

$$Ha, \forall x(Fx \supset Rxa).$$

The latter has the earlier form $\forall x(Fx \supset Gx)$. Thus we can outline the two further alternatives for justified denial as before. The weaker form of denial is simply to use the premiss $\forall x(Fx \supset Rxa)$ several times for universal instantiation in a *reductio*. The stronger form of denial is to use that premiss in the *reductio* for only one instantiation, with respect to some term t, thereby making t a definite counter-example.

Now consider the general claim

$$(Dec_D)\ \exists\ \text{effective method } \mu(\mu \text{ is total on } D\ \wedge$$
$$\forall\phi(\phi \text{ is in } D\ \rightarrow$$
$$(\mu(\phi) = T\ \rightarrow\ \phi \text{ is true})\wedge$$
$$(\mu(\phi) = F\ \rightarrow\ \neg(\phi \text{ is true}))))$$

It has the logical form that we have just discussed, namely,

$$\exists y(Hy \wedge \forall x(Fx \supset Rxy)).$$

So, if (Dec_D) is ungrounded by proof, the anti-realist can react in any one of the three distinct ways just outlined. He can demur; he can deny without any particular counter-exemplary sentence ϕ^* on offer, but by way of a *reductio* none the less; or he can deny by way of a particular counter-examplary sentence ϕ^* used in a *reductio*.

7.5   The undecidability of arithmetic

When D is the language of arithmetic, justified denial of the first kind would be the appropriate response here, in light of the well-known proofs of the undecidability of particular mathematical theories, such as Robinson's arithmetics R and Q, Peano arithmetic, and (classical) $Th(N)$ (where N is the standard model of arithmetic).

At this point we might have to entertain a naïve objection along the following lines.

> Those undecidability proofs concern undecidability *of theorem-hood within a particular formal system*, or of classical truth in an intended model itself. But it is supposed to be an important part of the anti-realist outlook that (a) one should be unwilling to delimit formally and in advance all the methods of proof that one could ever regard as licit and compelling, and (b) one cannot guarantee that the set of truths is logically complete (that is, contains, for each sentence ϕ, either ϕ or $\neg\phi$). To be shown that theoremhood in a particular formal system is undecidable is not yet to be shown that the intuitionistic *truth* of claims formulable in the language of that system is itself undecidable. And to be shown that the set of *classical* truths is unaxiomatizable, hence undecidable, is not yet to be shown that the *intuitionistic* truth of claims formulable in the language of that system is itself undecidable.

So, the naïve objector concludes, the anti-realist does not yet have any reason to *deny* (Dec_D) when D is the language of arithmetic.

This naïve objection is wholly mistaken. The fact is that one can prove constructively that the *intuitionistic* deductive closure of Robinson's single axiom Q[14] manages to represent all recursive functions.[15] By representing all recursive functions, it follows (by Church's thesis)[16] that Q succeeds in being *strongly representing*: that is,

> for any decidable property P of natural numbers, there is a formula $\psi(x)$ in the language of arithmetic such that for any natural number n if $P(n)$ then $Q \vdash \psi(\underline{n})$ and if not-$P(n)$ then $Q \vdash \neg\psi(\underline{n})$.

It should be stressed that this last statement holds even when the turnstile $\vdash$ is taken to represent *intuitionistic* deducibility.

Now Q is most certainly acknowledged by the intuitionist to be consistent. Thus it follows that Q is *representing*: that is,

> for any decidable property P of natural numbers, there is a formula $\psi(x)$ in the language of arithmetic such that for any natural number n, $P(n)$ if and only if $Q \vdash \psi(\underline{n})$,

where, again, $\vdash$ may be taken to represent *intuitionistic* deducibility.[17] It now follows that (intuitionistic) theoremhood in Q is undecidable. This is a

---

[14] The important point about the theory Q is that it is finitely axiomatizable; hence we can take the single axiom to be the conjunction of the finitely many axioms that are usually provided. Cf. A. Tarski, A. Mostowski and A. Robinson, *Undecidable Theories*, North-Holland, Amsterdam, 1968.

[15] The proof is given in my *Natural Logic*, Edinburgh University Press, 1978, pp. 152–59. The reader will note that nowhere in that proof does one ever appeal to a strictly classical move within the object language; so that $\vdash$ can be read as intuitionistic deducibility throughout. Moreover, the proof itself is by mathematical induction on the pedigrees of recursive functions. These are defined inductively from certain basic functions by composition and minimization of regular functions; see op. cit. for details. Thus the proof of the representability of all recursive functions in intuitionistic Q is wholly constructive.

[16] A decidable property of natural numbers is one whose characteristic function is effective. Church's thesis is involved here in the move from the claim that the characteristic function of a property is effective to the claim that it is recursive.

[17] Note that the apparently classical move in the proof of the conclusion that Q is representing from the premises that Q is strongly representing and that Q is consistent, is intuitionistically acceptable since P is, *ex hypothesi*, a decidable property of natural numbers. The 'apparently classical' move in question is the final step of *reductio* labelled (1) in the following:

$$\frac{\dfrac{\dfrac{\overline{\hspace{2cm}}^{(1)}}{\neg P(n)}}{Q \vdash \neg\psi(\underline{n}) \qquad Q \vdash \psi(\underline{n})}}{\dfrac{Q \vdash \bot \qquad\qquad\qquad Q \not\vdash \bot}{(CR)\dfrac{\bot}{P(n)}{}^{(1)}}}$$

special case of the following general result.

THEOREM
Intuitionistic theoremhood in any representing theory is undecidable.

> *Proof*: Let Γ be any representing theory. Suppose for *reduc-tio* that Γ is decidable. Then the property $\Gamma \nvdash \psi_n(\underline{n})$ of natural numbers would be decidable, where $\psi_0, \psi_1, \ldots$ is an effective enu-meration of all formulae with one free variable in the language of arithmetic; and where $\vdash$ represents intuitionistic deducibility. Since Γ is representing, there would be some such formula ψ_k, such that for all n, $[\Gamma \nvdash \psi_n(\underline{n})$ if and only if $\Gamma \vdash \psi_k(\underline{n})]$. In particular, we would have $[\Gamma \nvdash \psi_k(\underline{k})$ if and only if $\Gamma \vdash \psi_k(\underline{k})]$, a contradiction.

COROLLARY
Any theory intuitionistically consistent with Q is undecidable.

> *Proof*: Let Δ be any theory intuitionistically consistent with Q. Since Q is strongly representing, its extension Δ, Q is strongly representing; whence, since this extension is *ex hypothesi* consis-tent, Δ, Q is representing. So, by the previous theorem, intu-itionistic theoremhood in Δ, Q is undecidable. Now if intuition-istic theoremhood in Δ were decidable, then by testing whether $\Delta \vdash Q \supset \phi$ we could decide whether $\Delta, Q \vdash \phi$. Thus intuitionistic theoremhood in Δ is undecidable.

Remember, all we have been assuming about Δ is that it is intuitionistically consistent with Q. But this is a truly minimal requirement on any theory Δ as far as the intuitionistic arithmetician, in search of intuitionistic arith-metical truth, is concerned. It follows now that the intuitionist will most definitely be in a position to *deny* the general claim (Dec_D) for the discourse D of arithmetic, thereby obliterating the naïve anti-realist objection outlined above. The proof on which this denial is based, however, takes only the an-odyne form of a *reductio* that does not necessarily provide, for any supposed decision method μ, any particular counter-exemplary sentence ϕ of arith-metic that would be demonstrably beyond the reach μ. So the anti-realist's

---

The first step is justified by Q's being strongly representing; the second step is justified by the presence of $\neg E$ in the underlying logic of Q; and the premiss $Q \nvdash \bot$ expresses the consistency of Q. It was Geoffrey Keene who raised the worry of which this observation disposes.

response to the unfounded (indeed: false) claim (Dec_D) in this case is of the second kind explained above: denial, but without specific counter-example.

7.6 Responses to undecidability

7.6.1 The anti-realist's response

Recall that we were considering above reactions to the crucial inference

$$(wpM), (cBiv_D) \vdash (Dec_D)$$

stemming from the particular kind of reaction one might have to its conclusion (Dec_D). We have now seen that where the discourse D is that of arithmetic, this conclusion (Dec_D) will be denied (and with warrant). It therefore follows, by contraposition on the very argument establishing the inference just displayed (an argument which is, as we have already seen, constructively acceptable) that the conjunction of its premises (wpM) and $(cBiv_D)$ will have to be denied. Given the anti-realist's entitlement to the principle (wpM) and his constructive construal of what is meant by any sentence's truth-condition obtaining, he has no alternative, then, but to deny $(cBiv_D)$. Note, however, that his denial of $(cBiv_D)$ is only of the weaker of the two forms discussed above. In denying $(cBiv_D)$ he is only asserting a 'negated universal', not necessarily asserting an 'existential negation'. Thus he is asserting only

$$\neg \forall \phi (\phi \text{ is in } D \;\rightarrow\; (\phi \text{ is true} \vee \neg (\phi \text{ is true})))$$

He is, however, refraining from asserting the more specific

$$\exists \phi (\phi \text{ is in } D \wedge \neg (\phi \text{ is true} \vee \neg (\phi \text{ is true})))$$

The latter would indeed follow *classically* from the former, but it is crucial to realize that it does not follow *intuitionistically* from it.

For an anti-realist, it is incoherent to maintain, of any particular sentence θ, that θ is *not* bivalent. For to do so is to assert

$$\neg (\theta \text{ is true} \vee \neg (\theta \text{ is true})) \; ;$$

and in intuitionistic (relevant) logic one can derive absurdity from any claim of the form $\neg (\sigma \vee \neg \sigma)$.

Without any proof of $(cBiv_D)$, therefore, the anti-realist can react to any assertion of $(cBiv_D)$ in only one of *two* (not three) possible ways: simply demur, or else deny (but without offering any putative counter-example). By contraposition on the intuitionistic result

$$(wpM), (cBiv_D) \vdash (Dec_D)$$

we would have to allow his grounded denial of (Dec_D) to translate into a denial of $(cBiv_D)$ (where D is the discourse of arithmetic), *modulo* the other premiss (wpM). But both these denials, remember, are of the 'non-counter-exemplary' kind.

Not every domain D of discourse need be like that of arithmetic, however, in furnishing a constructively acceptable *reductio* of the claim that D-truth is decidable. What happens, then, in a discourse D in which we have, as yet, no such disproof of decidability, but also have no constructive proof of it? For the anti-realist, it is simply unsafe to acquiesce in the decidability claim (Dec_D) before constructive proof of it is available. That course, after all, would have led to disaster in the case of arithmetic! So the most sensible policy to follow would be that of *demurral*, as outlined above.

What happens, accordingly, with the inference

$$(wpM), (cBiv_D) \vdash (Dec_D)?$$

For the discourse D under consideration, we are supposing that the anti-realist is now only demurring on its conclusion (Dec_D). It follows that he must therefore demur on at least one of (wpM) and $(cBiv_D)$. Otherwise, commitment to both of these would translate, via the intuitionistic proof of the inference, into a commitment to (Dec_D), which is unwanted. As before, (wpM) is absolutely secure on an anti-realist construal of its main terms. Thus the anti-realist must now merely demur on $(cBiv_D)$. That is, he must refuse to accept it; but, also, refrain from denying it. Bivalence must remain *moot*, until such time as he has either a constructively acceptable *proof* or a constructively acceptable *disproof* of the claim (Dec_D) that D-truth is decidable. $(cBiv_D)$ is definitely *not* a principle that the anti-realist will be prepared to adopt as a matter of meaning, or logic, across the board. Its status depends on the discourse D in question. It might be settled *a priori*, as it was (negatively) in the case of arithmetic; or it might be settled by reflection on various broad features of our empirical experience, as one might attempt in the case of statements about the future. Whether, in the latter case, the resulting determination is one that should be counted as *a priori*, one hesitates to say; for it may be difficult to say with confidence that one's actual knowledge of certain features of the world, as they might impinge on our senses, had not intruded in one's determination either way. Nevertheless, the point stands: eschewing (Dec_D), in the absence of either a proof or a disproof of it, is the only defensible position, from the standpoint of both logic and the theory of meaning; whence the same goes for $(cBiv_D)$.

7.6.2   The realist's response

From the realist's standpoint, the matter is very different. For the realist is committed to $(nBiv_D)$ *across the board*, claiming (very contentiously) that this is a central principle of (either one of, or both) logic and the theory of meaning. How, then, does the realist respond to the inference loosely expressed as

$$(M), (Biv_D) \vdash (Dec_D)?$$

Bear in mind that we have to distinguish the following two pairs of premiss-readings:

(i) *Weak, passive* manifestation requirement (wpM) plus principle of bivalence $(cBiv_D)$ with a *constructive* embedded notion of truth;

(ii) *Strong, active* manifestation requirement (saM) plus principle of bivalence $(nBiv_D)$ with a *neutral* embedded notion of truth.

That is, the loosely expressed inference firms up as one or other of the following two:

$$(wpM), (cBiv_D) \vdash (Dec_D);$$
$$(saM), (nBiv_D) \vdash (Dec_D).$$

Let us consider the realist's response first in the case where the discourse D admits of a proof of (Dec_D); secondly, in the case where (Dec_D) is still moot; and thirdly, in the case where (Dec_D) has been refuted.

When (Dec_D) has been proved, (M) is acceptable (on D); we noted earlier that

$$(Dec_D) \vdash (M) \text{ on } D.$$

Indeed, even the anti-realist would accept that

$$(Dec_D) \vdash (Biv_D).$$

so the realist would simply have some weak confirmation for his commitment to bivalence across the board. From the anti-realist's point of view, however, this would cut no ice at all so far as *other* discourses D were concerned, for which (Dec_D) had not been proved (or had even been refuted). Where

(Dec_D) *has* been proved, however—and especially when its proof should be obvious to any speaker—we see that the realist can grudgingly accept (M) (on D).

Now consider the realist's response in the second case, where (Dec_D) is still moot. Reflect on the inference

$$(saM), (nBiv_D) \vdash (Dec_D)$$

on construal (ii) of the premises. It cautions the realist at least to refuse to assert (saM); indeed, he may even be tempted to go further, and deny (saM). His reason would be that, in the present absence of any known decision procedure for D-truth, but with speakers manifestly (!) understanding all sentences in D, the strong, active reading of (saM) simply cannot be true. If, *later*, a proof of (Dec_D) were to be found, this would hardly make any concession of strong (saM) (on D) on the realist's part any the less grudging. A proof of (Dec_D) supports strong (saM) on D only in so far as immediate access to that proof deserves to be counted as part of one's very understanding of the terms of the discourse. But if, as is here being assumed, the proof of (Dec_D) was not immediately accessible upon any competent speaker's reflection, but rather could be found only after the exercise of considerable ingenuity, and *some time after* speakers had been communicating competently by means of sentences of D, then (according to the realist) (saM) (on D) should hardly count as a plausible claim concerning that competence as already made manifest before the proof of (Dec_D) was found.

Still in the second case, where (Dec_D) is moot, consider the realist's response to the central inference

$$(wpM), (cBiv_D) \vdash (Dec_D)$$

on construal (i) of the premises. Here it is the constructive embedded notion of truth in the postulated understanding of $(cBiv_D)$ to which the realist will take exception.

Finally, consider the realist's response when (Dec_D) has been *refuted*. Such is the case with the language of arithmetic. The realist too knows about the undecidability results for various true arithmetical theories[18] — so in the case where D is the discourse of arithmetic, he too will deny (Dec_D).

---

[18]These theories will now be closed under *classical* deducibility. Provided they are classically consistent with Q, they will of course be intuitionistically consistent with Q; hence, by our corollary above, undecidable.

Hence, since he hangs so determinedly on to $(nBiv_D)$ (construal (ii)), he chooses to deny the strong manifestation principle (saM) on this discourse D. Alternatively, if it is the weak manifestation principle (wpM) that is used as a premiss (construal (i)) then once again he takes exception to having a constructive notion of truth embedded in $(cBiv_D)$.

The realist's complaint, then, either takes the form that the strong principle (saM) is simply too demanding a requirement on linguistic competence to be imposed on every discourse D; or that his principle of bivalence was never meant to have a constructive notion of truth embedded in it. From his point of view, truth is bivalent (for *every* discourse D); but he should not be asked to be able to *construct* truth-makers for each and every truth—that is, to be able effectively to find a truth-maker for any given truth. That is not to say, however, that the realist's truth-makers themselves might not always be effectively checkable, once found. This is especially so for the Gödelian Optimist. Thus it would be too swift a conclusion to say that the ability to recognize, for any sentence in D, that the condition for the truth ϕ obtains, when it does, and does not obtain, when it does not, would have to be a *superhuman, transcendent* ability when the discourse D is effectively undecidable! *That* complaint can only be levelled legitimately against the Orthodox Realist, not the Gödelian Optimist. Not all realist proponents of Bivalence can be tarred with the transcendentalist brush here.

In summary, then, we see that the realist and the anti-realist respond to a disproof of (Dec_D) by jettisoning a different assumption in each of our central inferences

$$(wpM), (cBiv_D) \vdash (Dec_D);$$
$$(saM), (nBiv_D) \vdash (Dec_D).$$

The realist hangs on for dear life to $(nBiv_D)$ on *every* discourse D, insisting on a non-constructive construal of truth. Thus when, for a particular discourse D^*, (Dec_{D^*}) is refuted, he rejects (saM). The anti-realist, by contrast, insists on (wpM) for *every* D. Thus when, for a particular discourse D^*, (Dec_{D^*}) is moot or is refuted, he respectively demurs on, or rejects, $(cBiv_{D^*})$ as a principle governing his constructive notion of truth.

What we have here is a Janus-like instance of the Poincaré–Duhem–Quine problem writ into the very foundations of logic and the theory of meaning. Given the distinct readings (i) and (ii) of the premises for the central inference, the realist and the anti-realist are not really disagreeing with one another as to how to react to the undecidability of a particular discourse. It is rather as though they were *talking past* one another. Each proceeds from a set of foundational assumptions within whose logical scope everything else seems to make clear sense. The central inference, we are forced to conclude, does *not* adjudicate decisively between them.

7.7   Realist reconstruals of manifestation?

We have been careful to stress that it is the *weak, passive* version (wpM) of the manifestation requirement to which the foregoing considerations on behalf of the anti-realist apply. Truth boils down to (constructive) existence of (constructive) grounds for assertion; so *recognition* of truth is no more than *recognition that a given construction is indeed a proof*. But for the character we are calling the *Orthodox* Realist, for whom truth can be knowledge-transcendent, the (classical, bivalent) truth of a sentence might not in the same way *consist in* (the existence[19] of) any effectively checkable construction, *even if* the construction in question is allowed to contain strictly classical steps of inference! The truth of a sentence might, rather, *transcend* or *forever elude* our abilities to come to know of it. The condition for the truth of a sentence might be in principle undetectable—yet still obtain, for all that. Similarly, for McDowell's so-called M-Realist, who does not insist on bivalence but who does insist on the possibility of certain truths being recognition transcendent. Given this radically non-epistemic conception of truth on both these realists' parts, can they nevertheless recover something both plausible and theoretically significant from the manifestation requirement (MR) as originally stated above?

The Orthodox Realist and the M-Realist share the strand of recognition-transcendence of truth-value; but they differ on realism's other strand, the one of determinate bivalence. It is recognition-transcendence that is properly the immediate target of the manifestation challenge. Let us concede that the challenge is successful. The residual question, then, especially for the Gödelian Optimist, is: might there be other ways for one who claims determinate bivalence of truth to meet the manifestation requirement on a reasonable construal of its several important terms?

What, for example, about the ways of manifesting grasp canvassed above?

---

[19]This remark holds whether one construes *this* existence constructively or non-constructively. The whole remark is intended to apply to what we are calling the Orthodox Realist who, unlike the Gödelian Optimist already described above, thinks of truth as potentially transcending all means we might ever have for coming to know it.

The linguistic competent need not be a scientific genius, or inspired mathem-atician. He need not be able to take any sentence ϕ and settle for himself (except in the grammatically simplest and epistemically most obvious cases, which would be criterial for grasp of the constituent terms of ϕ) what the truth-value of ϕ is or would be. But should he not be able to respond appro-priately to someone else's suggestion of grounds for believing or disbelieving ϕ? Should he not be able to *appraise* purported proofs or disproofs of ϕ, and pronounce correctly on their probative quality? This seems plausible, especially in those cases where the proofs and disproofs in question are easily surveyable and suitably 'predicative'—that is, where they do not involve sen-tences containing terms from stretches of discourse with which the speaker is unfamiliar. The latter might be the case with a proof of Fermat's Last Theorem that involved a long excursus into the arcane upper reaches of set theory and algebraic topology. If the speaker were being tested for grasp of meaning simply as an arithmetician, it would be asking too much of him that he be able to appraise such a difficult 'theoretically impredicative' proof correctly.

One could maintain that one understood full well what was meant by Fermat's famous arithmetical claim that for no $n > 2$ is it the case that there are natural numbers a, b, c such that $a^n + b^n = c^n$; while yet confess-ing a complete inability to assess the recent proof of that theorem offered by Wiles and his associate. Of course, *ideally* the competent understander should be able to absorb the extra criterial axioms needed to furnish senses for the terms of the arcane theoretical extension within which the proof makes its excursus. Provided only that the proof were *fully formalized*, with every step turning, for its correctness, on the meaning of just one symbol occurrence at a time, the competent understander should, in principle, be able to 'recognize' whether Wiles's proof is indeed a proof.[20] But for under-standing as we usually understand it, this would be to ask too much of the understander of Fermat's Last Theorem. This would be true even if all that were being required were the ability to check each step, without necessarily having a global grasp of 'how the proof is proceeding' or 'where the argu-ment is leading'; and without being able, after exposure to the proof and even checking it, to reproduce it—or even its general strategic lines—upon request. All understanders are equal, in so far as they may grasp the same sentence meanings; but some are just a little more equal in that grasp than

---

[20] Here, of course, on behalf of the realist, we would have to allow the proof to contain strictly classical steps of inference.

others, when it comes to constructing and following proofs!

Once we have been cautious enough to stipulate that it is only 'theoretically predicative' and fully formalized proofs that the understander should be able to recognize as such, it remains to be settled whether we should also set limits on the length and complexity of proofs that could fall within the legitimate ambit of our testing of his competence. It is usual to idealize away the limitations on actual speakers by speaking of their being able 'in principle' to check whether a given construction—no matter how long or complex — constitutes a proof of the given sentence. If we follow this path, then we must be clear in our own minds that we are now dealing with a model of *idealized* competence, and expect that there will be many points of imperfect fit between the requirements of that model and the everyday logico-linguistic competences of actual speakers.

On the suggested model, then, one would be requiring (on behalf of the realist) that the speaker be able to recognize of *any* purported proof or disproof, no matter how long or complex, whether it was indeed such, provided only that it is what we have called 'theoretically predicative'. There is textual evidence that this is the kind of requirement that Dummett had in mind for the *anti-realist*:[21]

> a grasp of the meaning of a statement consists in a capacity to recognize a proof of it when one is presented to us, and a grasp of the meaning of any expression smaller than a sentence must consist in a knowledge of the way in which its presence in a sentence contributes to determining what is to count as a proof of that sentence.

Dummett had here moved from the possibility that grasp of meaning could consist in mastery of a decision procedure (a procedure whereby the speaker will himself produce a proof, should there be one) to the weaker requirement that such grasp should consist, rather, in the speaker's capacity to check given constructions for proofhood (constructions that have been supplied to him by the tester of his competence, and not necessarily discovered by the speaker himself). The demand is weaker now because we are requiring less of the speaker epistemically than we would be if we were to insist that he actually *be* master of some decision procedure. We are not requiring him to be able, in general, to take the given sentence and by himself decide its truth-value (that is, we are not imposing (saM)); rather, we are asking of him only

---

[21] loc. cit., pp. 225–26.

that he be able to tell, of any purported basis for such a decision, supplied by someone else, whether the decision has been made correctly (that is, we are imposing only (wpM)). The speaker is allowed to be epistemically passive rather than required to be epistemically active. He is asked only to appraise the fruits of other people's theoretical labours rather than undertake those labours himself. We could still, as noted above, be idealizing even when imposing this weaker requirement that allows the speaker to be passive, and simply confronted by constructions supplied by others. For we are saying still that he should be able, *in principle*, to exercise his recognitional capacities successfully with regard to all constructions, no matter how long or complex. Those who think that this is to idealize too far away from actual competence will complain that we are demanding too much here; that there should be some reasonable limits imposed on the length and complexity of the gobbets of would-be proof that we are requiring the speaker to be able to stomach and digest correctly. We should not, says this objector, ask the understander to bite off more than one can reasonably require him to chew.

We are still exploring how the *realist* might plausibly formulate a more precise version of something in the general spirit of the manifestation requirement loosely expressed as (MR) above. In the previous chapter we discussed a plausible way in which one might sustain the 'in principle' form of the manifestation requirement while still acknowledging the special problems posed by the sheer length and complexity of the constructions that might be presented to the speaker. We suggested a shift to a factorizable, aspectual test of grasp with respect to overly long and complex constructions. No longer would we require that the speaker simply take the sentence ϕ and the construction Π and eventually deliver a verdict as to whether Π was a proof or a disproof (or neither) of ϕ. Instead, we would require, more weakly, only that, with regard to any local aspect α of the construction Π, the speaker be able to check whether the aspect α were in order. This would mean that, in effect, a potentially unbounded flock of counterfactual conditionals would be grounding the speaker's attributed competence, even if the speaker himself suffered the limitation of such extreme finitude (in comparison with ϕ and Π) that there would not be any reasonable chance of his finishing checking the status of Π during his own lifetime. The suggestion now would be that such a proposal would be equally available to the realist, provided only that in checking whether local aspects were in order, their being *classically* in order would suffice.

Setting aside the niceties of the 'in principle' reading, and the solution offered to the difficulties that lie in its way by invoking aspectual, factorizable grasp, we turn now to face another objection to the recognitional criterion of Dummett's just formulated. The objection is that such proofs and disproofs as are normally vetted by a competent user of, say, arithmetical language, vastly underdetermine the full range of sentences of which we would unhesitatingly say he had an adequate grasp. We credit a speaker with a grasp of many a sentence ϕ without ever dreaming of testing his recognitional capacities with regard to particular would-be proofs or disproofs of ϕ itself. No doubt, this objector concedes, we *could* test the speaker on such constructions if we so wished, and the attribution of grasp would in principle remain hostage to the outcome of such a test; but the fact is that we somehow attribute to him a grasp of the meaning of ϕ on the basis of a much narrower — albeit perhaps more judiciously selective—range of 'manifestations' on the speaker's part. We do not so much as entertain the counterfactual question as to how we think the speaker would perform were we to confront him with some construction and ask him to determine (even if only aspectually, rather than 'as a whole') whether or not it was a proof or a disproof of ϕ. In recognition of this very phenomenology involved in the default attribution of grasp of meaning, it behoves us to inquire whether we might indeed loosen the manifestation requirement even further, so as to put it more in tune with what we actually and normally require of a speaker, by way of manifestation in his past behaviour, before we are happy to credit him with the appropriate grasp. We are still seeking to forge a path to a plausible version of the manifestation requirement (MR) along which the realist could follow. Let us remind ourselves what that requirement is:

> (MR) Any speaker should be able fully to manifest his grasp of the meaning of any sentence ϕ that he understands, by a suitable exercise of salient recognitional capacities in connection with ϕ.

Here, then, is a yet weaker way in which a speaker could try to be equal to the manifestation requirement (MR). It has already been hinted at above. Why should not the speaker be able to appeal to the principle of compositionality in order to buttress his claim to have grasped the meaning of a sentence? The suggestion is that it should suffice if the speaker could show that he understood *how the sentence was composed out of its constituent expressions*, and in turn understood *each of those expressions*. Given any (primitive) constituent expression E of a complex sentence ϕ, the speaker need only demonstrate to our satisfaction that he had mastered a sufficient range of *canonical contexts* in which E occurs.

By a 'canonical context' we mean something that is sense-conferring,[22] or criterial for the meaning of the expression. Such would be the case with the logical schema of $\wedge$-introduction:

$$\frac{A \qquad B}{A \wedge B}$$

or with the recursion equations for $+$:

$$t + 0 = t$$
$$t + s(u) = s(t + u).$$

It may be thought that we are hereby calling for what Dummett calls an *atomistic* theory of meaning, rather than a *molecular* one. But such an impression would be mistaken. Dummett defines these two kinds of theory of meaning as follows:[23]

> If a theory correlates a specific practical capacity with the knowledge of each axiom governing an individual word, that is, if it represents the possession of that capacity as constituting a knowledge of the meaning of that word, I shall call it *atomistic*; if it correlates such a capacity only with the theorems which relate to whole sentences, I shall call it *molecular*.

But Dummett means, by an 'axiom governing an individual word', something like a *metalinguistic* Tarskian axiom. The Tarskian axioms could deal either with extra-logical vocabulary or with logical vocabulary. Those of the former kind would be concerned with specifying the condition for satisfaction of a primitive predicate of the object-language; or specifying the denotation condition for a name; or specifying the operation represented by a function symbol. Those of the latter kind would be concerned with specifying the way in which the satisfaction conditions of an open formula formed by means of a certain logical operator depend on the satisfaction conditions

---

[22] Each context might be only partially sense-conferring, requiring certain others in order to clinch a sense for the expression. The idea is that each primitive expression should have its sense conferred on it by at least one finite range of canonical contexts. If these involve yet other primitive expressions, the same will hold for the latter; and so on, but well-foundedly. Ultimately there will be primitive expressions whose canonical contexts deal exclusively with them and them alone.

[23] 'What is a Theory of Meaning? (II)', in G. Evans and J. McDowell (eds.), *Truth and Meaning*, Clarendon Press, Oxford, 1976, pp. 67–137; at p. 72.

of its immediate subformulae. These axioms of a Tarskian theory of satisfaction and truth are *our theoretical representations* of speakers' knowledge of their language. As such, according to Dummett, the knowledge in question must correspond to practical abilities, abilities that can be made manifest in observable behaviour.

Now it is not exactly *this* sort of 'atomicity' that is required of the theory of meaning that is here being proposed on the part of the realist. Rather, the suggestion is that we should indeed be focusing much more on individual words of the speaker's language, when testing his grasp; but one need not insist that we do so by looking for exercises of practical abilities that can be correlated neatly with the *Tarskian* 'axioms governing individual words'. Rather, what is recommended is that the sorts of tests that really count are ones that enable us to focus on a speaker's grasp of particular words by seeing whether he is aware of, say, the crucial axioms or fundamental principles that involve them at the level of the *object* language—that is, *his* language. We would still be looking at his grasp of whole *sentences*, but they would be sentences judiciously chosen as especially relevant for proper grasp of certain of their constituent words. So the theory being proposed is somewhere between an atomistic one and a molecular one. It might therefore deserve the label 'radical'!

Here we are opting, on the realist's behalf, for a much more relaxed reading of the phrase 'in connection with ϕ' in the loose statement (MR) of the manifestation requirement given above. We are allowing now that there might be various foci other than the sentence ϕ itself, for the several acts of recognition on the part of the speaker. Moreover, those foci will be tractable, in the sense just explained. The speaker will be directing his attention (at our behest) towards the various constituent expressions of ϕ as they occur in the canonical contexts with which we require him to display familiarity. He will also be directing his attention to ϕ when displaying his knowledge of how ϕ is composed from its constituent expressions; and, ironically, ϕ will be *fragmented* in this exercise. We could, of course, maintain that it remains 'whole', as it were, as the second argument in the two-place relation 'E is a sub-expression of ϕ''; but in so doing we are tacitly admitting that we are having to liberalize our conception of what is to count as being 'in connection with' ϕ.

In a similar fashion the notion of *salience* in (MR) is hereby being relaxed or stretched; it will be unnecessary to elaborate or labour this point here. And we are widening also our conception of what counts as a *suitable* recognitional capacity. We are not, on the realist's behalf, narrowly insisting on the speaker's being able to recognize what the truth-value of ϕ happens to be (that is, being able to recognize that ϕ's truth-condition obtains, if it does obtain, and being able to recognize that it does not obtain, if it does not). Instead, we are allowing now (as justifying attribution of grasp of meaning) the speaker's manifest ability to recognize simple and short (that is, tractable) 'predicative' proofs if he is presented with them; and/or to recognize as cogent various canonical inferential or computational contexts in which the primitive constituent expressions of ϕ are conspicuously (and tractably) embedded.

We have been countenancing, then, a progressive loosening of the grip of decidability on the realist in his acquiescing construal of (MR), by:

1. first, making mastery of a decision procedure applied to ϕ *both necessary and* sufficient for full manifestation of grasp of the meaning of ϕ—(saM);

2. next, allowing grasp of meaning of ϕ to be fully manifested simply by recognising (or being able, in principle, to recognize) given constructions as proofs (or disproofs)[24] of ϕ when one is presented with them (however long or 'theoretically impredicative'—that is, however intractable—they might be)—(wpM);

3. then, allowing grasp of meaning of ϕ to be fully manifested simply by being able to recognize, of any local aspect of a given construction (no matter how long or complex) whether it was in order as needed for such a construction ultimately to count as a (classical) proof or a disproof of ϕ; and

4. finally, allowing grasp of meaning to be fully manifested by such exercise of recognitional capacities as would suffice to justify one in attributing to the speaker

   • a knowledge of how ϕ is constructed from its constituent expressions;

   • a knowledge of what canonical inferential and/or computational contexts govern those constituent expressions; and

   • a knowledge of what would count as a proof or a disproof[25] of ϕ (if it is relatively short and uncomplicated), or of various tractable

---

[24] These proofs and disproofs may, of course, be classical.

[25] Again, we emphasize that these proofs and disproofs could be strictly classical ones.

sub-sentences of ϕ or of various other tractable sentences that could be constructed from the constituent expressions occurring in ϕ

Let us call these four construals of (MR), respectively, *hawkish, conservative, moderate* and *radical*. In the *diminuendo* that would continue from the four positions already outlined, there must be room for the truly *anarchist* position occupied by the holist, according to whom just about anything and everything that the speaker might actually do with the sentence ϕ could count as evidence of 'correct' grasp of an uncritically accepted, unreconstructed meaning of ϕ. This would be the least constrained version of classical meaning, conferred on the sentence only by virtue of the totality of its inferential liaisons within our whole body of theorizing. That totality could include all the classical inferential connections, such as the alleged equivalence of $\neg \forall x P(x)$ with $\exists x \neg P(x)$, even for undecidable predicates $P(\ )$.

7.8   The central inference revisited; reconstruals rejected

It is important to distinguish these various readings of (MR) if we wish to assess how cogent is the argument first (albeit fallaciously) outlined by Dummett, but reshaped in greater detail above, to the effect that the manifestation requirement makes it impossible for bivalent truth-conditions to constitute the meanings of the sentences of our language—a language that is learned by observable example, and by means of which communication takes places solely by virtue of the observable behaviour of its users.

We saw above that the argument exploits the crucial inference

$$(wpM), (cBiv_D) \vdash (Dec_D).$$

The astute realist opponent will have noticed that, once we begin on his behalf to countenance a realist notion of truth (as possibly transcending the constructive existence of a truth-maker), the proof given above of our central inference is compromised anyway. Truth no longer being constructive, the first part of the tandem decision method—determination of a truth-maker or of a falsity-maker to present to the would-be manifester of understanding for his effective recognition—is no longer effective. Provided it is a classical, nonconstructive notion of truth embedded within $(nBiv_D)$, only the hawkish reading of (MR) would yield (Dec_D); while all the weaker readings of (MR)—(wpM) or weaker—fail to sustain the central inference:

$(saM), (nBiv_D) \vdash (Dec_D);$

$(wpM), (nBiv_D) \not\vdash (Dec_D).$

But the hawkish reading (saM) of (MR), we have agreed, is far too strong to be independently plausible as a requirement on the manifestation of grasp of meaning. The rueful conclusion, for the anti-realist, is that there is as yet no *inconsistency* on the part of the realist, within a provably undecidable discourse, in maintaining both (wpM) and $(nBiv_D)$, where in the latter the embedded notion of truth is non-constructive. At best the central inference only shows how, *for the anti-realist*, Bivalence must fall victim to undecidability in a discourse—because for the anti-realist the embedded notion of truth is constructive.

The realist, though, is threatening to eat both the anti-realist's manifestationist cake (wpM) and his own bivalence cake $(nBiv_D)$. He claims to be able consistently to

1. assert (wpM) (for *every D*);

2. assert neutral Biv_D for *every D*; and yet

3. reject (Dec_{D^*}) for particular D^* (such as arithmetic).

The 'weak, passive' manifestation principle (wpM), says the realist, is still strong enough in 'behaviourist manifestationist' spirit to do justice to the idea that every ingredient of meaning should be communicable in speakers' observable behaviour; yet weak enough to ensure that

$$(wpM), (nBiv_{D^*}) \not\vdash (Dec_{D^*}).$$

for discourses D^* such as that of arithmetic, for which decidability is known not to hold.

We have already agreed that the hawkish reading of the manifestation requirement is ruled out.

The next three readings—conservative, moderate and radical—all suffer from another drawback.[26] This is that they *underdetermine* the realist's imagined right to assert bivalence across the board, even if they are not provably inconsistent with it. These three readings of (MR) do not provide rich enough meanings for our sentences to guarantee their bivalence. Even though they are framed in terms of (recognition of) *classical* proofs and

---

[26] Bear in mind that the conservative reading (wpM) is what the realist has just cheekily advertised as his preferred form of manifestationism.

disproofs, this is not enough. For we know that even the realist has to concede the incompleteness of every formal system of *classical* proof for, say, arithmetic. To hang on to bivalence in the teeth of these results the realist would have to be some kind of Gödelian Optimist. That is, he would have to espouse, as an article of faith, that any sentence of arithmetic that happens to be true in the intended model of the natural numbers will be able to be shown to be so (even if only by means of a strictly classical proof) within some future formal system all of whose fundamental principles will have been recognized as certain and compelling. That has the realist saying that classical, bivalent truth does at least have to consist in the *non-constructive* existence of something effectively checkable—albeit only a *classical* proof using principles yet to be excogitated and acknowledged as compelling.

But now we encounter the same problem discussed earlier in connection with the Gödelian Optimist. Those future theoretical extensions cannot be allowed to modify the *present* meanings of our sentences. For the extensions are being invoked to justify the Gödelian realist's claim that our sentences, with their *present* meanings, are bivalent *now*. But are not the *present* meanings of our sentences exhaustively determined by all the principles that *at present* govern them? Whence, how can it be that some as yet unavailable principles not derivable from those we have now could not be meaning-affecting? For the classical holist they would *have* to be; whence the Gödelian Optimist's way out would only enmire the holist further. But the Gödelian Optimist who stops short of holism, and thereby avoids this difficulty, would still bear a heavy explanatory burden in response to the last of the questions just posed.

Finally, the *anarchist* reading of the manifestation requirement—that of the extreme holist—fails altogether to face up to the fact that there is a problem concerning the justification of our canons of inference. If we make every canon of classical inference, as the holist does, partially constitutive of the meanings of the logical operators involved, the problem of the justi-fication of deduction will simply have been defined away. It will follow for the holist—but trivially!—that the meanings of the logical operators that are disclosed by the use made of them justify that use.

The opposing positions, then, are crystallizing out as follows. The anti-realist insists on a constructive notion of truth, and espouses a plausibly weak form of manifestationism ((wpM) or something even weaker). In re-sponse to the undecidability of certain discourses, he is prepared to give up bivalence. This is because of the central inference from bivalence and manifestationism to decidability. The jettisoned principle of bivalence, however, has embedded within it a constructive notion of truth. The realist, on the other hand, insists on a non-constructive notion of truth. (Even the Gödelian Optimist, who believes that every truth admits of (classical) effectively checkable proof in some system, at least hedges by saying that he uses a non-constructive reading of the existential quantifier when claiming that truth consists in the existence of such a proof.) With this non-constructive notion of truth embedded in the principle of bivalence, both the Orthodox Realist and the Gödelian Optimist espouse both bivalence and the same plausibly weak form of manifestationism. Yet now they are unmoved by the undecidability results, since with their notion of non-constructive truth bivalence can no longer do its joint work with manifestationism in the would-be central inference. That inference, namely

$$\text{weak } (wpM), \text{ neutral } (nBiv_D) \ ?\text{-} \ (Dec_D)$$

fails. The realists (Orthodox and Gödelian Optimist) are left apparently entitled to maintain the joint consistency, for any discourse, of bivalence for (non-constructive) truth, manifestationism and undecidability.

The question left now for the anti-realist to press is whether the realist (be he Orthodox or a Gödelian Optimist) is entitled to that non-constructive notion of truth.

7.9 Rubbing out the wrong pictures

Let us return now to the possibilities pictured early in Chapter 6, and let us consider how the rivals to Moderate Anti-Realism are to be ruled out.

The manifestation argument that we have given above leads to the denial of Bivalence only when the latter principle is construed as embedding a constructive notion of truth. This suffices, for one already convinced that the notion of truth must be constructive, to rule out the pictures on offer from the Gödelian Optimist and from the Orthodox Realist. Both these pictures err, according to this view, by having $T = T^+$, when instead we should have $T \subset T^+$. Moreover, we saw that the Gödelian Optimist has the insuperable difficulty of explaining how the *present* meanings of our sentences justify maintaining Bivalence for them *now*. Nor would we be able to find an acceptable reading for the realist of the manifestation requirement (MR), which could be used instead of (wpM) so as to avoid implying (Dec_D) in the presence of constructive $(cBiv_D)$.

The original manifestation challenge tells strongly against the two realist positions that endorse the possibility of recognition-transcendence: namely, Orthodox Realism and M-realism.

7.9.1   Arguing against M-Realism

The main contentious feature of the M-Realist's picture is his coupling of the claim of Knowledge-Transcendence—that (at the very least)

$$\mathcal{K} \sqsubset \mathcal{T} \text{ (option (3) above)}$$

and even, perhaps,

$$\mathcal{K} \subset \mathcal{T} \text{(option (2) above)} —$$

with opposition to Bivalence—holding (at the very least)

$$\mathcal{T} \sqsubset \mathcal{T}^+ \text{ (option(3) above)}$$

and even, perhaps,

$$\mathcal{T} \subset \mathcal{T}^+ \text{ (option (2) above)},$$

depending on how strongly he endorses the line of argument that we gave above for the rejection (that is, denial) of Bivalence. There are instabilities, however, in the M-Realist's position. His denial of Bivalence (or even mere refusal to assert it) sits unhappily with his claim of Knowledge-Transcendence. The version of the argument we gave above, based on the constructively provable fact that arithmetic is undecidable, that would justify the denial of *neutral* Bivalence, appeals to the *strong* manifestation requirement (*saM*). That requirement in turn embodies a conception of the truth as knowable— that is, as recognizable via the exercise of our cognitive capacities. Without this commitment to $\mathcal{K} = \mathcal{T}$, it is difficult to see how the M-Realist can be motivated *by that argument* nevertheless to hold even the weak form $\mathcal{T} \sqsubset \mathcal{T}^+$ (option(3) above) of anti-Bivalence.

Prescinding from the question of how potent the original manifestation challenge is to M-realism, whether or not M-realism is a coherent position depends crucially on the truth of the following characterization of it by McDowell, which the traditional intuitionist would be able to dispute powerfully:

In the context of intuitionistic logic, to say, on the one hand, that the truth-condition of a sentence may obtain even if we cannot tell that it does, and may not obtain even if we cannot tell that it does not, is not to say, on the other, that the truth-condition of any sentence either does obtain or does not, even if we cannot tell either that it does or does not. For the position outlined [M-realism] combines, coherently if intuitionistic logic is coherent, refusing to say the latter with continuing to say the former.[27]

To understand why the intuitionist would dispute this, let us abbreviate as $\exists\phi U(\phi)$ the claim that

the truth-condition of a sentence [ϕ] may obtain even if we cannot tell that it does, and may not obtain even if we cannot tell that it does not

Our abbreviation $\exists\phi U(\phi)$ represents the logical form of this claim as 'For some sentence ϕ, the truth-condition of ϕ may obtain even if we cannot tell that it does, and may not obtain even if we cannot tell that it does not.' This existential reading is the only one permitted if we are to make consistent sense of the applicative 'any' in the context of the quotation from McDowell; for to have the universal quantifier in its stead would be far too strong, given the presence of decidable sentences. Let us abbreviate as $\forall\phi B(\phi)$ the claim that

the truth-condition of any sentence ϕ either does obtain or does not, even if we cannot tell either that it does or does not.

Here it is the universal quantifier that is appropriate, since, for his philosophical purposes, McDowell needs the claim here abbreviated to be the principle of bivalence, holding for all sentences (and not just the claim that a particular sentence ϕ is determinately truth-valued). $\forall\phi B(\phi)$ is none other than Bivalence. So McDowell is claiming that

In the context of intuitionistic logic, to say, on the one hand, that $\exists\phi U(\phi)$, is not to say, on the other, that $\forall\phi B(\phi)$. For the position outlined [M-realism] combines, coherently if intuitionistic logic is coherent, refusing to assert $\forall\phi B(\phi)$ with continuing to say $\exists\phi U(\phi)$.

---

[27]loc. cit., p. 55.

For McDowell to succeed in thus carving out for himself a stable niche (M-realism) between full-blown realism and standard anti-realism, he needs two logical features. First, $\exists\phi U(\phi)$ must be consistent in the context of intuitionistic logic.[28] Secondly, $\exists\phi U(\phi)$ must not entail $\forall\phi B(\phi)$ (Bivalence); more precisely, $\exists\phi U(\phi)$ must not intuitionistically entail Bivalence. The trouble is, however, that both these logical features are absent. Unfortunately for the would-be M-Realist, $\exists\phi U(\phi)$ is intuitionistically inconsistent, and therefore (by standard intuitionist lights) does entail Bivalence! To see the inconsistency, suppose that we have some particular sentence ϕ such that $U(\phi)$, that is, such that

> the truth-condition of ϕ may obtain even if we cannot tell that
> it does, and may not obtain even if we cannot tell that it does
> not.

Each envisaged possibility is in fact incoherent, even though we need the incoherence of only one of them to establish the incoherence of their conjunction. Take first the supposed possibility that

> the truth-condition of ϕ may obtain even if we cannot tell that
> it does.

For the intuitionist, the obtaining of the truth-condition of ϕ consists in the (constructive) existence of a proof of ϕ. Thus we would be able to tell that the truth-condition obtains. (McDowell is not, of course, relying on all such proofs being too long for us to recognize them as proofs; the 'can' in the phrase 'cannot' is a 'can in principle', in which one abstracts away from the limitations of our (actual) finitude.) Likewise, the supposed possibility that

> the truth-condition of ϕ may not obtain even if we cannot tell
> that it does not

is incoherent. For the intuitionist, the truth-condition's not obtaining consists in the existence of a refutation of the assumption that it does obtain. This refutation (a proof of absurdity) is likewise in principle recognizable as such.

The M-Realist therefore has no refuge in the logical space occupied by the proponent of intuitionistic logic. The logic itself imposes certain demands on

---

[28] Remember that it is the M-Realist who is opting for intuitionistic logic. And as we shall presently see, those who live by the sword but who do not wield it properly, die by the very same sword.

the meanings we can take our logical operators to have. One cannot simply give up the classical rules and carry on thinking like a realist. McDowell has failed to appreciate just what is involved, by way of semantic and philosophical foundations, in being an intuitionistic logician. Intuitionistic logic provides no home for the closet realist who wishes to think of himself as logically hobbled but still attuned to the transcendent.

7.9.2   Arguing against the Gödelian Optimist

How, then, is the anti-realist to dispose of the Gödelian Optimist? The anti-realist should reply as follows:

(i) at the very best, Gödelian Optimism is a merely *consistent* position that has no independently convincing credentials; and, moreover, when considered on its overall merits as a systematic theory that is intended to explain our intuitions and make sense of our practice, and explain how it is that we acquire mastery of language and of concepts such as truth, Gödelian Optimism does not fare well in comparison with the rival account afforded by the anti-realist; or

(ii) at worst, Gödelian Optimism is ultimately incoherent.

The burden of proof is on the Gödelian Optimist

The anti-realist advancing claim (i) is saying that in this last-ditch attempt to salvage bivalence, the burden of proof is borne by the Gödelian Optimist. Indeed, from the anti-realist's point of view the Optimist is saying that he believes that the world will always co-operate with him in his epistemic endeavours. With regard to any as yet undecided sentence ϕ from a discourse known to be effectively undecidable, he has no way of justifying in advance his belief that either ϕ will turn out true or $\neg\phi$ will turn out true. He simply believes that it is happily so, for any such sentence ϕ. This frame of mind reveals how bivalence (or the law of excluded middle) functions, for the realist, as a synthetic *a priori* principle. In essence, it expresses his metaphysical belief that reality is determinate in all articulable respects. As a synthetic principle, it lacks any justification solely in terms of *meaning*. Indeed, it succeeds in expressing the view that reality is determinate precisely because the only licit meanings for its constituent logical terms are the anti-realistically acceptable ones: the meanings that are captured by the rules for their use.[29]

What if this realist complains that one of these rules is the law of excluded middle itself (or any of its equivalents: double-negation elimination, classical *reductio*, or dilemma)? At that point the dialectic broaches the topics of separability, harmony and systematicity, where it is still the anti-realist who has the upper hand.[30]

More tantalizing than (i), however (for the anti-realist), is the prospect of establishing something as strong as (ii). For in every philosophical debate one yearns to provide a knock-down *refutation* of one's opponent's position. The mildest kind of refutation is one where the opponent's main principles are shown to be in tension with independent, intuitively grounded claims, which are accepted by both parties to the dispute and which can therefore arbitrate between the opposing philosophical viewpoints. The harshest kind of refutation is one which reveals an *internal inconsistency* among the principles advanced by one's opponent.

In the remainder of this chapter we shall explore the prospects for outcome (ii) against the Gödelian Optimist. The considerations to be set out in this regard are tentative and inconclusive; but they will show how intuitively close to incoherence the Gödelian Optimist ventures if and when he seeks to justify his position by alleging any deficiency in anti-realism.

A Quasi-Gödelian Refutation of Gödelian Optimism?

P is the set of axioms of Peano–Dedekind arithmetic. Our discussion throughout this subsection will be exclusively about arithmetic, and whether classical logic is justified for reasoning in arithmetic. The main classical logical principle is the law of excluded middle (*LEM*). *LEM* would be justified if the principle of bivalence held for arithmetical truth. The Gödelian Optimist seeks to justify the principle of bivalence by appeal to the principle of resolubility:

$$(R) \qquad \forall\phi \, \exists S(S \text{ is a consistent extension of } P \wedge (S \vdash \phi \vee S \vdash \neg\phi))$$

But this claim can be made trivially true simply by allowing, for any sentence

---

[29]For a fuller development of this view of bivalence as a metaphysical axiom, see my paper 'The Law of Excluded Middle is Synthetic A Priori, if Valid', *Philosophical Topics*, forthcoming.

[30]We shall not repeat here the arguments put forward in *AR&L*.

ϕ, that ϕ (or $\neg\phi$) is to be an axiom of S. We need some further constraint on the kind of system S that will be permissible. So let us say that a system S of axioms is *decent* $=_{df}$ S is a correct extension of $\mathcal{P}$, by axioms that have intuitive plausibility, or that arise by adopting new instances of induction upon extending the language.

$$\mathcal{D}(S) =_{df} S \text{ is decent}$$

Question: is there a Π_2 characterization (that is, one in $\forall\exists$-form) of $\mathcal{D}(\ )$? We shall be assuming below that the following principle holds:

(†) $\mathcal{D}(S) \rightarrow (S \vdash_C \phi \rightarrow \phi)$

The Gödelian Optimist's principle of resolubility will now read

(R) $\forall\phi\, \exists S(\mathcal{D}(S) \wedge (S \vdash \phi \vee S \vdash \neg\phi))$

We have not yet, however, formulated a sufficiently precise version of this principle. The debate is, essentially, over the status of the law of excluded middle, and its various equivalents (the so-called classical negation principles). The principle of resolubility therefore comes in one of two possible versions, intuitionistic or classical:

(R_I) $\forall\phi\, \exists S(\mathcal{D}(S) \wedge (S \vdash_I \phi \vee S \vdash_I \neg\phi))$

(R_C) $\forall\phi\, \exists S(\mathcal{D}(S) \wedge (S \vdash_C \phi \vee S \vdash_C \neg\phi))$

The Gödelian Optimist cannot rest his case for *LEM* solely on (R_I), since (R_I) itself tells us that the intuitionist does not need *LEM* in order to resolve any sentence. If (R_I) is the only claim on offer, then *LEM* can be seen, in its light, as no more than an expedient short cut. It would have no place in one's *logic*, in so far as logic is a canon of principles justified by their meanings alone.

The Gödelian Optimist cannot further his case by asserting only (R_C), for that would be to commit a *petitio principii*. He would then be claiming only that the resolubility of all sentences by means of *LEM* justifies the principle of bivalence in the metalanguage, which in turns licenses the use of *LEM* in the object language. This would be clearly circular.

So the Gödelian Optimist has to make a stronger claim: he has to assert

(R_C) and *deny* (R_I). The latter denial is:

$\neg(R_I)$ $\neg\, \forall\phi\, \exists S(\mathcal{D}(S) \wedge (S \vdash_I \phi \vee S \vdash_I \neg\phi))$

We shall show that this denial would turn out to be incoherent, if certain assumptions, to be identified below, were to hold. $\neg(R_I)$, by the Gödelian Optimist's own classical lights, entails

$$\exists\phi\, \neg\exists S(\mathcal{D}(S) \wedge (S \vdash_I \phi \vee S \vdash_I \neg\phi)),$$

so the Gödelian Optimist is himself committed to the truth of the latter existential claim. Let us then suppose that the sentence ψ is a witness thereto:

$$\neg\exists S(\mathcal{D}(S) \wedge (S \vdash_I \psi \vee S \vdash_I \neg\psi))$$

It follows (intuitionistically)[31] that the following two claims hold:

(α) $\forall S(\mathcal{D}(S) \to \neg(S \vdash_I \psi))$

(β) $\forall S(\mathcal{D}(S) \to \neg(S \vdash_I \neg\psi))$

The Gödelian Optimist claims that both (α) and (β) are true. Let us focus on (α). By (R_C) applied to α,

$$\exists S(\mathcal{D}(S) \wedge (S \vdash_C \alpha \vee S \vdash_C \neg\alpha))$$

Let S^* be such a system:

$$\mathcal{D}(S^*) \wedge (S^* \vdash_C \alpha \vee S^* \vdash_C \neg\alpha)$$

Since S^* is decent, and (α), according to the Gödelian Optimist, is *true*, we now have, by the principle (†),

(γ) $\mathcal{D}(S^*) \wedge S^* \vdash_C \alpha$

---

[31] Note that it is actually immaterial to the dialectic at this point whether the implications are intuitionistic or strictly classical. All that matters is that we should secure the Gödelian Optimist's assent to (α) and to (β).

Now consider the following metatheorem about Peano-Dedekind arithmetic $\mathcal{P}$, due to Harvey Friedman:[32]

$$\phi \text{ is } \Pi_2 \to (\mathcal{P} \vdash_C \phi \to \mathcal{P} \vdash_I \phi)$$

If this could generalize to all decent systems, we would have:

$$(\Phi) \qquad \phi \text{ is } \Pi_2 \to (\mathcal{D}(\mathcal{S}) \to (\mathcal{S} \vdash_C \phi \to \mathcal{S} \vdash_I \phi))$$

Suppose that we do indeed have this generalization. Then we could reason further as follows:

If (α) is Π_2, it will follow from (γ) and (Φ) that

$$\mathcal{S}^* \vdash_I \alpha,$$

that is,

$$\mathcal{S}^* \vdash_I [\forall \mathcal{S}(\mathcal{D}(\mathcal{S}) \to \neg(\mathcal{S} \vdash_I \psi))]$$

Now, by the intuitionist's understanding of negation, this justifies the claim that

$$\mathcal{S}^* \vdash_I \neg\psi$$

But, since $\mathcal{S}^*$ is decent, this would contradict (β).

The question, then, is whether there is a syntactically modest enough characterization of decency (Π_2 perhaps?) that would put the claim (α) within the scope of an appropriate generalization Φ of the Friedman result.

Unfortunately, however, there is no prospect of any arithmetical characterization of decency. But the most obvious reason for such pessimism invites very close scrutiny. The immediate objection would be that *if* there were an arithmetical characterization of decency, then '$\exists \mathcal{S}(\mathcal{D}(\mathcal{S}) \wedge \mathcal{S} \vdash \ldots)$' would be an arithmetically definable truth-predicate for arithmetic—which, by a celebrated result of Tarski, is impossible.[33] But wait a moment!—a truth-predicate for *whom*? Remember that the Gödelian Optimist is *denying* the intuitionistic resolubility principle (R_I); therefore *he* is unable to allege that '$\exists \mathcal{S}(\mathcal{D}(\mathcal{S}) \wedge \mathcal{S} \vdash_I \ldots)$' would be an arithmetically definable truth-predicate for (classical) arithmetic! Nor, since the intuitionist is not himself committed even to (R_C), would he (the intuitionist) be committed

<hr />

[32] The Π_1 form of this result was due to Gödel.

[33] Roy Cook made this observation too.

to conceding that '$\exists S(\mathcal{D}(S) \wedge \; S \vdash_C \ldots)$' would be (*per impossibile*) an arithmetical truth-predicate for (classical) arithmetic! It is not at all clear that an arithmetical characterization of decency would be impossible. But even if it were, the boot would be, as it were, on the other foot; for then the Gödelian Optimist himself would be deprived of any prospect of ever conclusively establishing both (R_C) and $\neg(R_I)$. Our inability to refute his position would have resulted, ironically, from his own inability to express it in any way that might lend itself to proof.

Having given the manifestation argument earlier for the denial of Bivalence, it remains now to buttress that argument by defending the even deeper principle on which we have seen it rests—the principle that truth is constructive, or, equivalently, that all truths are knowable. If we can protect this principle against the realist's assault on it, the Moderate Anti-Realist's picture will emerge as the one with the best overall credentials. To the defence of the principle of knowability we now turn.

Chapter 8

Truth as Knowable

8.1 Introduction

The moderate anti-realist, as we saw earlier, comes under fire from the strict finitist. It was shown, however, that moderate anti-realism, properly understood, can be prevented from supposedly sliding into strict finitism. But the anti-realist principle that every truth is knowable has also been threatened by an alleged slide in the other direction: to the very realism that flatly denies the principle. With the principle of knowability as a premiss, realists have constructed an argument for the arresting conclusion that every truth is known. The argument will be given in due course, in a very simple form, as a natural deduction. (It is called Σ below.)[1] The untoward conclusion of Σ, to be more precise, states that every truth is known by someone at some time, not that every truth is already known. On the assumption that even the anti-realist will not be able to bite this bullet, the search is on for ways of getting the anti-realist out of this second line of fire.

There are basically three strategies open to the anti-realist who is unwilling to bite the bullet:

(i) reconstrue the principle of knowability, so that the argument

---

[1] The argument Σ is due, in its essentials, to F. B. Fitch, 'A Logical Analysis of Some Value Concepts', *Journal of Symbolic Logic*, 28, 1963, pp. 135–42. See his Theorem 1, p. 138. W. D. Hart calls Fitch's result 'an unjustly neglected logical gem', in 'Access and Inference', *Proceedings of the Aristotelian Society*, Supp. Vol. LIII, pp. 153–65; at p. 164. It was cited by W. D. Hart and C. McGinn, 'Knowledge and Necessity', *Journal of Philosophical Logic* 5, 1976, pp. 205–8. Hart and McGinn concluded that $[\phi \rightarrow \Diamond K\phi]$ is false: 'there are truths which absolutely cannot be known.' The problem for the anti-realist is to reveal how Fitch's logical gem is flawed.

mentioned gains no purchase on it as a premiss;

(ii) restrict the principle in a principled way, so that the argument cannot make use of the principle in the way it needs to; or

(iii) criticize, especially on intuitionistic grounds, either the argument's structure, or its allegedly untoward consequences for the anti-realist position.

What about the anti-realist who is willing to bite the bullet? He will have to

(iv) provide a far-reaching overhaul of some of our central philosophical concepts (knowledge, truth, possibility and logical implication), so as to accommodate the rather arresting conclusion that every truth is known.

This chapter will motivate and defend the restriction strategy (ii). This line of defence for the anti-realist appears to be new. In order to be able to embark right away on the proposed line of defence, we defer to section 7 a discussion of the reasons why the rival or alternative reconstrual strategy (i)—which is, to date, the most widely canvassed strategy—will not work. This will involve close scrutiny of the recent literature on the topic. The matter is complicated; but the literature appears thus far to decide against the reconstrual strategy. That, at least, will be the upshot of the discussion in section 7. In developing the restriction strategy (ii), there will be occasion to make detailed criticisms of certain proposals from Williamson, which were in the spirit of strategy (iii), as to how the intuitionist anti-realist might accommodate the argument that gives rise to the original problem. In the course of the discussion comment will be called for on strategy (iv). It is worth enquiring whether $\phi \rightarrow K\phi$ is such an 'obviously silly form of verificationism' as Williamson alleges.[2] A closer look reveals that it is not obvious that it is obviously silly. Therefore, it may not be obviously silly. It may not be silly either, even if ultimately unacceptable.

The discussion below will at least furnish a way for the anti-realist to avoid being committed by the Fitch argument to $\phi \rightarrow K\phi$ on the basis of the knowability principle $\phi \rightarrow \Diamond K\phi$. In order to motivate the restriction strategy in the case of knowledge, we shall first motivate it in the analogous cases of belief and of wondering whether. We shall discover here that absurdities ensue if we do not place appropriate restrictions on what it is possible to

---

[2]T. Williamson, 'On the Paradox of Knowability', *Mind* 96, 1987, pp. 256–61, at p. 256.

believe and what it is possible rationally to wonder about. The obvious restrictions in these cases will then provide a guide to the restriction needed in
the case of knowledge. And the proposed restriction in the case of knowledge
will thereby be seen to be independently principled, and not *ad hoc*.

8.2   Rational thinkers

A rational thinker is one who grasps, in the logically specious present, all
the simple entailments among his attitudes and assertions; and is not caught
in any internal contradictions either within or between his attitude schemes.
An example of an internal contradiction *within* an attitude scheme would be
believing some proposition ϕ and believing its negation $\neg\phi$. An example of
a contradiction *between* two attitude schemes would be knowing that ϕ but
wondering whether ϕ. If a rational thinker is rationally committed, given
his having or lacking the attitudes that he does, to his having the attitude
A towards the proposition ϕ, then he does have attitude A towards ϕ.[3] This
will be called the *rule of rational commitment* (RC). The general form of
this rule when the attitude B of belief is taken as the attitude A would be

$$(RC) \qquad \frac{(i)\underline{\qquad} \quad \underline{\qquad}(i)}{\underbrace{\phi_1,\ldots,\phi_n}}$$

$$\vdots$$

$$\frac{B\phi_1\ldots B\phi_n \qquad\qquad \psi}{B\psi}{}_{(i)}$$

where $\phi_1,\ldots,\phi_n$ are the only assumptions in the subproof on
which ψ depends; and are discharged by applying the rule.

Examples of derived rules using applications of (RC) in the case of belief are:

$B\phi, B\psi \vdash B(\phi \wedge \psi);$

---

[3]This is especially plausible in the case where the commitment arises by simple logical
moves. In what follows, we shall be making only relatively simple logical moves in exploring
attitudinal commitments. Hence we shall not be exploiting much of the force of the
principle here enunciated.

$B(\phi \wedge \psi) \vdash B\phi$; and

$B(\phi \wedge \psi) \vdash B\psi$.

These will be used below. In fact, they will be the only consequences of (RC) to which we shall make any appeal.

If a belief claim is consistent, then it should be consistent with the truth of what is claimed to be believed. That is, if $B\phi$ is consistent, then $B\phi$ is consistent with ϕ. Conversely, if $B\phi$ is inconsistent with ϕ then $B\phi$ itself is inconsistent. This will be called the *rule of credibility* (C):

$$(C) \qquad \underbrace{B\phi \;,\; \phi}_{}{}^{\displaystyle{-(i)}}$$
$$\vdots$$
$$\frac{\perp}{\perp}{}_{(i)}$$

It may also be assumed that a rational thinker is one whose attitudes are *self-intimating* to the thinker himself. That is, if he has attitude A towards proposition ϕ, then he believes that he does: if $A\phi$ then $BA\phi$; and if he lacks attitude A towards ϕ, then he likewise believes that he does: if $\neg A\phi$ then $B\neg A\phi$. These will be called the rules of self-intimation (SI):

$$(SI) \qquad \frac{A\phi}{BA\phi} \qquad\qquad \frac{\neg A\phi}{B\neg A\phi}$$

One need not be concerned by the objection that as a matter of empirical, psychological fact, people's attitudes are not closed under logical consequence, and/or are not self-intimating. For explicit idealization is involved here. It is at least logically consistent, or conceptually coherent, to postulate a rational thinker whose attitudes are 'logically closed', and whose attitudes are self-intimating. It would even be coherent to assume, further, that for any attitude claim $A\phi$, exactly one of $A\phi$, $\neg A\phi$ is true. That is, attitudinal claims are bivalent. It would follow by (SI) that such a thinker would also have a correct belief as to whether $A\phi$. Thus we would have $(A\phi \wedge BA\phi) \vee (\neg A\phi \wedge B\neg A\phi)$ for any attitude A and any proposition ϕ.

One reservation someone might have over (SI) as part of an idealization of the intellectual powers of a rational agent is the following. The rational commitment condition (RC) already has the ideal rational agent believing all the logical consequences of what he believes. Thus, if he believes the axioms of some undecidable mathematical theory, he believes all the logical consequences of those axioms. That is, for any such consequence ϕ, we have $B\phi$. But by (SI) it will follow that $BB\phi$. Likewise, for any non-consequence ψ of what the rational agent believes, (SI) will allow us to infer $B\neg B\psi$. Thus, if we think of B as sustaining the reading 'occurrently believes', the rational agent would (apparently *per impossibile*) be able to decide of an arbitrary sentence of the mathematical language whether it was a theorem of the (undecidable) theory in question. The way to decide the matter would be to introspect to discover the self-intimated belief or disbelief. Surely, the objector will insist, this is too idealize too far.[4] The objector's point is well-taken, but there are two responses to it.

First, one could, if one so wished (for the purposes of the argumentation to be pursued below) restrict the conception of self-intimation of attitudes so that only reasonably obvious and decidable consequences of occurrent beliefs were required to be self-intimating (*qua* beliefs) to the agent. All the reasoning to be exploited below appeals to uses of (SI) only within the context of a simple propositional logic, and in pursuit of rather obvious consequences of a few salient propositions which one could well imagine occurrently entertained by a reasonable intelligence.

Secondly, the objection to the non-recursive (hence non-constructive) character of (SI), given (RC), cannot properly be directed against the anti-realist, given the dialectic of the present discussion as it will emerge in due course. For as the reader will presently see, (SI) is to be used to show only that the realist would have reasons for thinking that knowing and wondering whether, as propositional attitudes, have a certain 'reflexiveness problem' in common. This will be enough to motivate a principled restriction on the knowability principle; for such a restriction is manifestly required on the corresponding principle concerning wondering whether in place of knowing. So, given that the 'non-constructiveness' of the ideal rational agent's supposed abilities serves in making a point for the realist and by the realist's own lights, and given that one could, if one wished, get by with much less than the full scope of (SI) as stated above, one need have no qualms in proceeding with (SI), qualified in this way, in one's explorations of what is conceptually and logically possible concerning the attitudes of an ideal rational agent.

Note that in the idealization it is not being assumed that the rational thinker is highly or even correctly opinionated on matters of contingent

---

[4] Stewart Shapiro raised this objection.

fact. His rationality consists only in his logical ability instantaneously, as it were (in the 'logically specious present'), to close his attitudes under logical consequence, and in his introspective infallibility concerning the contents of his own mind. But as for whether he believes or knows such mundane matters as whether or not it is raining, or whether or not grass is green—that much will vary from thinker to thinker. Rational thinkers are smart, but they are not necessarily factually informed, nor even very opinionated. And, as already mentioned, they can be wrong (though not inconsistent) in their beliefs about factual matters.

Note also that, despite the idealization, one is dealing (in the logically specious present) with occurrent attitudes. That is, one is not assuming that a rational thinker, as here characterized, is at all times mindful of every proposition. All that is required is that, if he be mindful of such-and-such propositions, then he should also, at that time, be mindful of whatever other propositions are required for rational closure (RC) and correct introspection of his own attitudes (SI). There may of course be an infinity of these, but they will at least be able to form a proper subclass of the class of all propositions. In particular, a rational thinker could be totally uninterested in expanding his meagre (logically closed) stock of contingent beliefs. There may be contingent propositions on which he is undecided (propositions ϕ such that he neither believes that ϕ nor believes that $\neg\phi$); and he may lack any interest whatsoever in which of these, if any, are true. A very weak form of this claim is that there could be a (contingent) proposition ϕ such that the thinker, right now, neither believes nor disbelieves ϕ, and is not now wondering whether ϕ. A strong form of this claim is that for all (contingent) propositions ϕ that the thinker, right now, neither believes nor disbelieves, it might be the case that right now he is not wondering whether ϕ (not wondering, that is, about any of them).

Sincere declaratives betoken belief. If a rational thinker sincerely asserts a declarative sentence ϕ ($\alpha\phi$), then he is rationally committed to (the consequences of) our taking him to believe that ϕ, that is, to the consequences of $B\phi$. In particular, we have the following rule:

(αB) If $B\phi$ is inconsistent, then so is $\alpha\phi$ (his assertion of ϕ);

or, stated more formally as a rule of natural deduction:

$$(\alpha B) \qquad \begin{array}{c} \dfrac{}{B\phi}{}^{(i)} \\[4pt] \vdots \\[4pt] \dfrac{\alpha\phi \qquad \perp}{\perp}{}^{(i)} \end{array}$$

We can now resolve Moore's paradox. It is not consistent for a rational thinker of the kind just described to assert

'ϕ but I do not believe that ϕ'.

That is, $\alpha(\phi \wedge \neg B\phi)$ commits the speaker to absurdity.

> *Proof*: The assertion of $(\phi \wedge \neg B\phi)$ expresses the speaker's belief that $(\phi \wedge \neg B\phi)$. Furthermore, by conjunction elimination on the left, this belief logically implies ϕ. So if the speaker is a rational thinker, then by (RC) he believes that ϕ $(B\phi)$. But by conjunction elimination on the right, $(\phi \wedge \neg B\phi)$ also logically implies that $\neg B\phi$. Thus what the speaker believes (namely, $\phi \wedge \neg B\phi)$ is inconsistent with his rationally believing it (that is, with $B(\phi \wedge \neg B\phi)$). Hence the belief claim $B(\phi \wedge \neg B\phi)$ itself is inconsistent, in so far as it concerns the speaker as a rational thinker. So his assertion of $(\phi \wedge \neg B\phi)$ leads to contradiction. In summary: it is not consistent for me as a rational thinker to believe (ϕ and I do not believe that ϕ). That is, $B(\phi \wedge \neg B\phi)$ is inconsistent, where 'B' means 'I believe that'.

Note that in reaching this conclusion about belief, we have made no use at all of the rule (SI) of self-intimation.[5] The only rules used here that specifically concern belief are (RC), (C) and (αB). The regimentation of the foregoing informal proof, using our formal rules, is as follows:

---

[5]Thanks are owed to Diana Raffman for comments which resulted in the present statement of the foregoing argument, which is an improvement on that in an earlier draft. In particular, her comments made clear the need to emphasize that the argument presented here makes no use of the principle $B\phi \rightarrow BB\phi$ nor any use of the rule (SI) of self-intimation. The former principle is of course a special case of the latter rule, when the self-intimated attitude is that of belief.

$$\frac{\qquad}{\phi \wedge \neg B\phi}(1)$$

$$(RC)\ \frac{(3)\underline{\qquad}\qquad \dfrac{\overline{\phi \wedge \neg B\phi}^{(1)}}{\phi}}{B(\phi \wedge \neg B\phi)}$$

It is easy to see that our resolution of Moore's paradox does not involve commitment to the principle that if one believes that ϕ, then one believes that one believes that ϕ. The principle $B\phi \to BB\phi$ is a consequence only of our rule (SI), when the attitude A is taken to be B. In what follows, however, we use (SI) only for the case where the attitude A is that of wondering whether. Thus our treatment both of Moore's paradox and of all these other problems, overall, need not commit us to the truth of the principle $B\phi \to BB\phi$.[6]

So much for belief. The same would hold for knowledge. But one should not be misled into thinking that it is only the 'truth-representing' attitudes for which this sort of result holds. There are other, much more neutral attitudes, which give rise to inconsistencies of exactly similar form. It tells us something important about the rationality of attitudes and their iterations in the propositional contents involved. Let us turn now to the case of the attitude '(rationally) wondering whether'.

8.3   On wondering whether

Under what conditions is it rational for me to wonder whether ϕ? Wondering whether is an attitude properly directed to propositions about which one is undecided.[7] But what sort of attitude counts as deciding any particular matter? Certainly, if one knows that ϕ, then one has decided ϕ; likewise,

---

[6] In this respect our approach to Moore's paradox agrees with that of Hintikka (in *Knowledge and Belief: An Introduction to the Logic of the Two Notions*, Cornell University Press, 1962, at pp. 64–71). But by using the rule (C) of credibility in natural deduction we are able to give a simpler treatment of Moore's paradox than Hintikka accomplished by means of his model systems.

[7] In the case of analytical disagreement here, let us simply define the concept *schmondering whether* so that if one either believes or disbelieves that ϕ, then one cannot (logically) schmonder whether ϕ. In all other respects the newly defined concept will be like the objector's concept of wondering whether. The result that will be proved below would be just as alarming were it to be taken as a result about schmondering whether.

if one knows that $\neg\phi$. In either of these circumstances it would not be rational for one to wonder whether ϕ. One may also insist that if I believe (or disbelieve) that ϕ, then it is not rational for me to wonder whether ϕ; not, anyway, while I am in the grip of that belief (or disbelief). Belief is wonder-excluding. It would of course be a different matter if evidence were to crop up that put ϕ in a new light, and demanded its reassessment. But until such time as such evidence crops up, and while I am in the continuing grip of the belief that ϕ (or of the disbelief that ϕ), it is not rational for me to wonder whether ϕ. The wondering whether ϕ, if ever it did arise, would have to supplant the belief (or disbelief) that ϕ. The wondering whether cannot cohabit in my mind with either the belief or the disbelief—not, anyway, if I am a rational thinker as defined above.

This principle will be formulated as the rule

(WB) $W\phi$ is inconsistent with $B\phi$;

or, as a formal rule,

$$(WB) \quad \frac{W\phi \quad B\phi}{\bot}$$

In what follows, it is not crucial for the reader to acquiese with this rule for belief (B); it will suffice to accept the correponding rule for knowledge (K), or conviction. If one chooses knowledge, then the principle of self-intimation (SI) would have to be strengthened so as to involve K instead of B. There is nothing incoherent about assuming the existence of a rational thinker who obeys both (RC) and (SI) when the latter is in this stronger form. But the argument will be presented in terms of belief anyway. If necessary, the reader may simply substitute 'knows that' for 'believes that' throughout, and accordingly use the stronger form of (SI).

Suppose I am sitting outside at noon on a cloudless day, well aware that the sky is blue. Let ϕ be the proposition that the sky is (now) blue. So I believe that ϕ $(B\phi)$. Let ψ be any other proposition about which I am undecided—that the Dow-Jones index is above 6,000 say. Then I can rationally wonder whether $(\phi \wedge \psi)$. This wondering whether just translates into wondering whether ψ, for it is ψ, not ϕ, that is undecided, and on which a decision will decide the conjunction for me. I cannot, in these circumstances, rationally wonder whether ϕ, since, as the case has been described, I have already made my mind up about ϕ. So, even though $(\phi \wedge \psi)$ logically implies ϕ, my being able rationally to wonder whether $(\phi \wedge \psi)$ in these cirumstances (namely, where I believe ϕ) does not entail that, in those circumstances, I am able rationally to wonder whether ϕ. In this case, the only conjunct of $(\phi \wedge \psi)$ about which I can rationally wonder is ψ, for only ψ is as yet undecided in my mind. Moreover, I am able rationally to wonder whether $(\phi \wedge \psi)$—hence, in these circumstances, be committed to wondering whether ψ—only because I already believe that ϕ rather than disbelieve that ϕ. If I were instead to disbelieve that ϕ then I would not be able rationally to wonder whether $(\phi \wedge \psi)$, whatever the proposition ψ may be. This is because disbelief in ϕ would entail disbelief in $(\phi \wedge \psi)$, which in turn would exclude my rationally wondering whether $(\phi \wedge \psi)$. The same holds if I were to disbelieve that ψ. This principle will be expressed by the rules of inference

$(WB\neg)$ $B\neg\psi$ is inconsistent with $W(\phi \wedge \psi)$

$B\psi$ is inconsistent with $W(\phi \wedge \neg\psi)$;

or, as formal rules:

$$(WB\neg) \quad \frac{B\neg\psi \quad W(\phi \wedge \psi)}{\bot} \qquad \frac{B\psi \quad W(\phi \wedge \neg\psi)}{\bot}$$

Finally, if I rationally wonder whether $(\phi \wedge \psi)$ (hence, do not disbelieve that ϕ), and do not believe that ϕ, then I am committed to wondering whether ϕ, regardless of whether I believe ψ or am undecided whether ψ. This is because in these circumstances I might, for all I know or believe, have to decide ϕ in order to decide the conjunction $(\phi \wedge \psi)$. This principle may be expressed by the rule of inference

$(W\neg B)$ $\neg B\phi$, $W(\phi \wedge \psi)$; *ergo* $W\phi$;

or, as a formal rule:

$$(W\neg B) \quad \frac{\neg B\phi \quad W(\phi \wedge \psi)}{W\phi}$$

Now let us enquire into the consistency of $W(\phi \wedge \neg W\phi)$. Am I able rationally to wonder whether (both ϕ and it is not the case that I am rationally wondering whether ϕ)? It will emerge that I am not so able.

THEOREM: $W(\phi \wedge \neg W\phi)$ is logically inconsistent.

Proof: Assume for *reductio* that $W(\phi \wedge \neg W\phi)$. Assume also $B\phi$ for the sake of argument. By (WB), $W\phi$ is inconsistent with $B\phi$. So $B\phi$ implies $\neg W\phi$, whence, by (SI), implies $B\neg W\phi$. Thus by (RC) we have $B(\phi \wedge \neg W\phi)$. By (WB) this is inconsistent with our main assumption for *reductio*, namely, $W(\phi \wedge \neg W\phi)$. We now give up the assumption $B\phi$ and conclude $\neg B\phi$. The conclusion $\neg B\phi$ now rests only on the main assumption $W(\phi \wedge \neg W\phi)$. But by $(W\neg B)$, $\neg B\phi$ and $W(\phi \wedge \neg W\phi)$ together imply $W\phi$ which, by (SI), implies $BW\phi$. But now by $(WB\neg)$, $BW\phi$ is inconsistent with our main assumption $W(\phi \wedge \neg W\phi)$. The latter has accordingly been reduced to absurdity.

This informal proof can be regimented as a natural deduction using our formal rules, as follows:

Ω

$$
(WB)\frac{\overline{}(1)\quad \overline{}(2)}{W\phi \qquad B\phi}
$$

$$
(SI)\frac{\dfrac{\bot}{\neg W\phi}(1)}{(RC)\dfrac{B\neg W\phi \qquad \overline{}(2) \qquad \phi, \neg W\phi \vdash \phi \wedge \neg W\phi}{(WB)\dfrac{B(\phi \wedge \neg W\phi)}{}}}
$$

with $W(\phi \wedge \neg W\phi)$ on the right, leading to:

$$
(W\neg B)\dfrac{\dfrac{\bot}{\neg B\phi}(2) \qquad W(\phi \wedge \neg W\phi)}{(SI)\dfrac{W\phi}{(WB\neg)\dfrac{BW\phi \qquad W(\phi \wedge \neg W\phi)}{\bot}}}
$$

This is an extremely interesting result. It has the form of the theorem proved by Fitch, which was referred to above, but makes no appeal to his central assumption of closure under conjunction of the attitude involved. Indeed, Fitch did not even list 'wondering whether' as one of his 'value concepts'; and appears not to have been aware that his first theorem would hold for W, even without closure of W with respect to conjunction elimination. Fitch proved $\neg(\phi \wedge \neg A\phi)$ only for attitudes A for which the following closure condition obtains:

if $A(\phi \wedge \psi)$ then $A\phi$; and

if $A(\phi \wedge \psi)$ then $A\psi$.

What was shown above is that the same sort of result $[\neg W(\phi \wedge \neg W\phi)]$ holds in the case of rationally wondering whether, even though there is no version of this conjunctive closure condition for W. The foregoing discussion, however, yielded certain more complicated constraints on W in relation to B. We were able then to exploit three of these constraints—(WB), $(WB\neg)$ and $(W\neg B)$—along with both the assumption (RC) that the thinker was rational in his beliefs and in his wonderings whether, and the assumption (SI) that the thinker's attitudes were self-intimating, so as to reduce $W(\phi \wedge \neg W\phi)$ to absurdity. Note, however, that our uses of (RC) and of (SI) hardly impute outlandish intellectual abilities to our ideal rational agent. So the whole exercise could now be trimmed, if need be, so that the ideal rational agent is credited only with such abilities as permit the prosecution of the reasoning given above. Thus he could be made a little more logically myopic (via restrictions on (RC)), and a little less aware of all his own attitudes (via restrictions on (SI)).

Consider now the rule

$(\Diamond W)$ ϕ; *ergo* $\Diamond W\phi$ where ϕ is contingent;

or, as a formal rule:

$$(\Diamond W) \quad \frac{\phi}{\Diamond W\phi} \quad \text{where } \phi \text{ is contingent}$$

This rule gives expression to the principle that every contingent proposition ϕ is such that it is possible for me rationally to wonder whether ϕ. (If my rationally wondering whether ϕ happens to be ruled out in the actual situation by my having decided ϕ one way or the other, then the principle just enunciated allows us to make appeal to a possible situation in which I am undecided whether ϕ; and claims that in at least one such situation I would be able rationally to wonder whether ϕ.) It seems that this principle has to be right, whether one is a realist or an anti-realist about knowledge and truth. It deals uncontroversially with propositional contents that could be true and could be false, and with open-minded curiosity about them. The principle does not invoke any tendentious claims concerning the central notions involved—content, rationality and understanding—and so is neutral with regard to realist or anti-realist allegiances, whether these be in the theory of meaning, metaphysics, or epistemology.

Yet, for all that, the principle we have just stated has a catastrophic consequence. Given the unimpeachable modal principle

($\Diamond\bot$) Absurd propositions are impossible

— regimented as the formal rule

$$\frac{\qquad}{\phi}(i)$$

($\Diamond\bot$)
$$\vdots$$
$$\frac{\Diamond\phi \qquad \bot}{\bot}(i)$$

where the subproof has ϕ as its only assumption —

we can now prove the following theorem.

THEOREM: If ϕ is not logically true, then ϕ is logically inconsistent with $\neg W\phi$.

>*Proof*: We have the following trilemma:
>
>(i) the conjunction $\phi \wedge \neg W\phi$ is logically true
>
>(ii) the conjunction $\phi \wedge \neg W\phi$ is contingent
>
>(iii) the conjunction $\phi \wedge \neg W\phi$ is logically inconsistent.
>
>In case (i) we would have that ϕ is logically true, contrary to the assumption of the theorem. In case (iii) we would already have the desired result. It therefore suffices to consider case (ii).
>
>So assume now both ϕ and $\neg W\phi$. Then $\phi \wedge \neg W\phi$ —and, since we are dealing with case (ii), this conjunction is contingent. Hence by ($\Diamond W$) we have $\Diamond W(\phi \wedge \neg W\phi)$. But we have already seen, by means of proof Ω, that $W(\phi \wedge \neg W\phi)$ is inconsistent. Hence by ($\Diamond\bot$) $\Diamond W(\phi \wedge \neg W\phi)$ is inconsistent also. Since $\Diamond W(\phi \wedge \neg W\phi)$ follows from ϕ and $\neg W\phi$, we have reduced ϕ and $\neg W\phi$ jointly to absurdity. The result follows.

The reasoning in case (ii) of this informal proof (the case where $\phi \wedge \neg W\phi$ is contingent) can be regimented as a natural deduction using our formal rules, as follows:

$$\Gamma \qquad (\wedge I)\ \dfrac{\phi \qquad \neg W\phi}{} \qquad \dfrac{\overline{\qquad\qquad\qquad}^{(1)}}{W(\phi \wedge \neg W\phi)}$$

$$(\Diamond W)\ \dfrac{\phi \wedge \neg W\phi}{} \qquad\qquad \Omega$$

$$(\Diamond \bot)\ \dfrac{\Diamond W(\phi \wedge \neg W\phi) \qquad\qquad\qquad \bot}{\bot}{}_{(1)}$$

(for Ω, see above)

Let us now assume that the question whether I am rationally wondering whether ϕ is introspectively decidable. So the assumption $\neg W\phi$ in the argument just given can be discharged by making a terminal application of classical *reductio*. The argument thus extended would then show, for arbitrary contingent propositions ϕ, that if ϕ, then I am rationally wondering whether ϕ!—an incredible result.

My mind would have to be full of occurrent wonderings, concerning every single (contingent) proposition on which I have no opinion. Also, given that I cannot rationally wonder about anything on which I do have an opinion, this result would condemn me to a total lack of opinions on contingent matters! For any contingent truth ϕ, I would neither believe nor disbelieve that ϕ. That is, all I could believe would be logical truths; and all I could disbelieve would be logical falsehoods. Thus: I would be condemned to be wondering, at every instant, about every contingent proposition, but also debarred from ever forming an opinion about any of them. Philosophers may like this state of affairs; but something has to be wrong with the reasoning that got us here. It is fair to say that we are in the presence of paradox.

We do not have to look too far to find out what is wrong. It must be the principle $(\Diamond W)$ that is at fault. We simply have to restrict its scope to (contingent) propositions ϕ such that $W\phi$ is consistent. For we have seen above that the very logical structure of the rational attitudes of belief and of wondering whether exclude the possibility, for any (contingent) proposition ϕ, of my wondering whether

[ϕ and it is not the case that I am rationally wondering whether ϕ].

A rational thinker is neither conceptually nor epistemically deficient, for being logically unable to wonder whether this holds. Logic can give us some nasty shocks. In recognition of the logical limits on that towards which we can rationally hold our various attitudes, we should simply restrict the principle $(\Diamond W)$ as suggested. That is, it should now read

$(\Diamond W)\ \phi$; *ergo* $\Diamond W\phi$, where ϕ is contingent and $W\phi$ is consistent.

But then so too should we restrict the principles

$(\lozenge B)$ ϕ; *ergo* $\lozenge B\phi$.

$(\lozenge K)$ ϕ; *ergo* $\lozenge K\phi$.

In their restricted forms, these would become

$(\lozenge B)$ ϕ; *ergo* $\lozenge B\phi$, where $B\phi$ is consistent.

$(\lozenge K)$ ϕ; *ergo* $\lozenge K\phi$, where $K\phi$ is consistent.

It is no objection to the modified rules that the restrictions just formulated may in general be undecidable. For these are rules for philosophical argumentation only. They will be applied only where we do happen to know that the condition in question is met, or not, as the case may be. We have no interest in applying them beyond the scope of a few isolated philosophical arguments. They are not rules for the pursuit of first-order (or 'ontic')[8] knowledge in mathematics and science. Only in the latter case is it important that our canons of inference be decidably correct in their applications.

8.4   On knowing every truth

So far, we have been reading 'K' as 'I know (now) that'. Let us now reinterpret K in order to gain entry into the debate between realists and anti-realists over the principle that every truth is knowable. From now on, $K\phi$ will be short for $\exists t K_t \phi$ (that ϕ is known at some time) which in turn is short for $\exists t \exists x (x K_t \phi)$ (that someone at some time knows that ϕ). Let Δ be any set of propositions.

Consider the following general principle of inconsistency for knowledge:

(I) If ϕ is logically inconsistent with Δ, then so is $K\phi$

regimented as the natural deduction rule

$$
(I) \qquad
\begin{array}{c}
\overline{}^{(i)} \\
\underbrace{\Delta\,,\,\phi} \\
\vdots \\
\dfrac{K\phi \qquad \bot}{\bot}{}^{(i)}
\end{array}
$$

---

[8]The term 'ontic' was introduced by Shapiro for sentences of epistemic arithmetic that are free of epistemic operators. See his 'Epistemic and Intuitionistic Arithmetic', in S.Shapiro (ed.), *Intensional Mathematics*, North-Holland, 1985, pp. 11–46.

Consider now the following further rules:

$(\Diamond K)$ ϕ; *ergo* $\Diamond K\phi$.

$(K\wedge)$ $K(\phi \wedge \psi)$; *ergo* $K\phi$.

$(\Diamond K)$ expresses the anti-realist principle that all truths are knowable. $(K\wedge)$ is an unimpeachable rule of epistemic logic. It holds good even for non-factive interpretations of 'K', such as 'There is good evidence for ...'. (Non-factive interpretations do not validate the rule '$K\phi$; *ergo* ϕ'.)

The rules $(K\wedge)$ and (I) suffice to show that $K(\phi \wedge \neg K\phi)$ is inconsistent.

LEMMA: $K(\phi \wedge \neg K\phi)$ is inconsistent.

> *Proof* (call it Ξ):[9] Assume $K(\phi \wedge \neg K\phi)$ for *reductio*. We intend to use rule (I); so we aim to show that $K(\phi \wedge \neg K\phi)$ is inconsistent with $\phi \wedge \neg K\phi$. It will then follow by (I) that $K(\phi \wedge \neg K\phi)$ is inconsistent. So assume both $K(\phi \wedge \neg K\phi)$ and $\phi \wedge \neg K\phi$. By $(K\wedge)$ applied to the former we have $K\phi$; and by $\wedge$-E applied to the latter we have $\neg K\phi$. The *reductio* is therefore complete.

We can regiment this informal argument Ξ by using our formal rules as follows:

$$\Xi \qquad \cfrac{\cfrac{\overline{\phi \wedge \neg K\phi}^{(1)}}{\neg K\phi} \qquad (K\wedge)\cfrac{K(\phi \wedge \neg K\phi)}{K\phi}}{} $$

$$(I)\cfrac{K(\phi \wedge \neg K\phi) \qquad\qquad\qquad \bot }{\bot}{}^{(1)}$$

The proof Ξ establishes a very simple conceptual point: one cannot come to know $\phi \wedge \neg K\phi$. For in doing so one would have to come to know the first conjunct, thereby falsifying the second conjunct. (Note, however, that this is not a result that holds only for K. We saw earlier that it holds for W as well, albeit by a more complicated proof.)

Trouble for the anti-realist now comes from the following theorem, which is an analogue, for knowledge, of our earlier result for wondering whether.

THEOREM: ϕ is logically inconsistent with $\neg K\phi$.

---

[9]Our argument Ξ is slightly different from that of Fitch. He uses $(K\wedge)$ twice, along with the rule that knowledge implies truth.

Proof (call it Σ):[10] Assume ϕ and $\neg K\phi$. Their conjunction $\phi \wedge \neg K\phi$ follows. By $(\Diamond K)$ we have $\Diamond K(\phi \wedge \neg K\phi)$. But we have seen, by means of the argument Ξ, that $K(\phi \wedge \neg K\phi)$ is inconsistent. Thus by $(\Diamond\bot)$ we have that $\Diamond K(\phi \wedge \neg K\phi)$ is inconsistent. Hence ϕ is inconsistent with $\neg K\phi$.

This proof Σ can be regimented as follows:

$$
\Sigma \qquad (\wedge I)\ \dfrac{\phi \qquad \neg\, K\phi}{\phi \wedge \neg K\phi} \qquad \dfrac{\overline{\rule{3cm}{0pt}}^{(1)}}{K(\phi \wedge \neg K\phi)}
$$

$$
(\Diamond K)\ \dfrac{\phi \wedge \neg K\phi}{\qquad} \qquad \Xi
$$

$$
(\Diamond\bot)\ \dfrac{\Diamond K(\phi \wedge\ \neg K\phi) \qquad\qquad \bot}{\bot}{}_{(1)}
$$

(for Ξ, see above)

Realists will now permit themselves classical *reductio ad absurdum* at the end of Σ, and conclude that ϕ logically implies $K\phi$: all truths are known. But for the realist, many a truth may not be known; indeed, may not even be knowable. The obvious realist response, then, is to reject the rule $(\Diamond K)$.

If an anti-realist does not accept that ϕ is inconsistent with $\neg K\phi$, then he is what will be called a soft anti-realist. He will have to side with the realist in the debate on this issue. Both the realist and the soft anti-realist will have to find fault with Σ, and with any other purported proof of the same result.

The hard anti-realist is one who thinks (on independent grounds, to be given below) that ϕ is inconsistent with $\neg K\phi$. For him it is irrelevant whether or not Σ itself is regarded, in the end, as a compelling proof of this result. Even if the hard anti-realist were to agree on some diagnosed fault in the proof Σ, or in any other purported proof of the same result, he would still be willing to maintain that result (on the independent grounds to be given below). Anyone who agrees that ϕ is inconsistent with $\neg K\phi$ is forced to concede that

ϕ logically implies $\neg\neg K\phi$

and that

---

[10]This proof appears, essentially, in Fitch, loc. cit.; see Theorem 4, pp. 138–9. He gives the credit for it to an anonymous referee.

$\neg K\phi$ logically implies $\neg\phi$.

Each of these follows by negation introduction from what he accepts. One could also enquire whether he should concede further that

ϕ logically implies $K\phi$.

For the anti-realist, the role of logical inference is to preserve warranted assertibility.[11] Let us therefore test these three inferences with this in mind.

First, consider 'ϕ; *ergo* $\neg\neg K\phi$'. Suppose there is warrant to assert ϕ. Then it would be absurd to suppose that a contradiction could be derived from the assumption that ϕ were known. So anti-realism seems to be unruffled.

Secondly, consider '$\neg K\phi$; *ergo*, $\neg\phi$'. This too is in order. Remember that the anti-realist uses a strong interpretation of negation. $\neg K\phi$ means that the assumption that ϕ is known (by someone, at some time) leads to absurdity.[12] Surely this could only be so because ϕ itself leads to absurdity?

Thirdly, consider 'ϕ; *ergo* $K\phi$'. This will certainly follow from 'ϕ is logically inconsistent with $\neg K\phi$' whenever $K\phi$ is a decidable proposition. Is this so difficult to achieve? It is not—for $K\phi$ is decidable if and only if ϕ is decidable.

Let us prove this biconditional claim. Suppose that ϕ is decidable. Then here is a decision method for $K\phi$: apply the given decision method for ϕ. If you thereby determine that ϕ is true, then you know that ϕ. So you have determined that $K\phi$ is true. If, on the other hand, you determine that ϕ is false, then you have determined that $K\phi$ is false, because no one could ever know a falsehood. So if ϕ is decidable, then so is $K\phi$.[13] Now, for the converse,

---

[11]For the explanatory argument behind this claim, the reader should consult *AR&L*. Note, however, that in the present dialectical situation all that one has to accept is that 'For the anti-realist, ... ', not the embedded claim '... ' itself. This is because we are examining ways in which the anti-realist can draw the sting of the realist's Fitchian *reductio*, and can thereby keep his own point of view logically intact. Arguing *au fond* for that point of view, especially as it concerns the role of logical inference, would be another matter entirely.

[12]This point is made also by Williamson, in 'Knowability and Constructivism', *The Philosophical Quarterly*, 38, 1988, pp. 422–32; at p. 429.

[13]This confutes Williamson's claim (loc. cit., p. 428) that if $K\phi$ means $\exists t K_t\phi$, then it is not effectively decidable. He appears to neglect the possibility that ϕ itself might be decidable. Since he was partial (at p. 423) to Gray's 'Full many a flower is born to blush unseen' as providing a whole field of counter-examples to 'ϕ; *ergo* $K\phi$', this is rather embarrassing. For that a particular flower is in bloom, or that it has such-and-such a colour, strikes me as an eminently decidable proposition. All of Williamson's examples

suppose that $K\phi$ is decidable. Then here is a decision method for ϕ: apply the given decision method for $K\phi$. If you thereby determine that $K\phi$ is true, then you will have determined that ϕ is true, for knowledge implies truth. If, on the other hand, you determine that $K\phi$ is false, you have reduced to absurdity the supposition that someone, at some time, knows that ϕ. But as already remarked above, this (for the anti-realist) would surely warrant the denial of ϕ. Thus anyone who accepts that ϕ is inconsistent with $\neg K\phi$ will, for decidable propositions ϕ, have to accept also that ϕ logically implies $K\phi$.

That completes our demonstration that $K\phi$ is decidable just in case ϕ is decidable. By (Σ) above, ϕ is in general logically inconsistent with $\neg K\phi$. For *decidable* ϕ it now follows that 'ϕ implies $K\phi$'. Now hard anti-realism claims to be able to absorb the impact of 'ϕ; *ergo* $K\phi$' even when ϕ is undecidable. Moreover, the hard anti-realist will give independent grounds for accepting this inference, grounds which do not require him first to accept the inconsistency of ϕ with $\neg K\phi$. This inconsistency will, rather, follow from the validity of the inference 'ϕ; *ergo* $K\phi$', independently established. What, then, are these independent grounds for accepting the general inference 'ϕ; *ergo* $K\phi$'?[14]

Suppose the premiss ϕ is warrantedly assertible. This means that some-one has been ingenious enough to find (an effective method for determining) a canonical proof for ϕ. So ϕ is thereby known—whence the conclusion $K\phi$ is warranted too. Note that this holds also for hypothetical contexts, where one is assuming the truth of ϕ (assuming that ϕ) for the sake of argument. The hard anti-realist content of such an assumption (regardless of our actual knowledge) is that, in such a context, one has a proof of ϕ; from which, naturally, it would follow (in that context) that ϕ were known. Nothing, to his mind, could be simpler or more obvious. It therefore follows at a stroke that the hard anti-realist will also accept the inferences

ϕ; *ergo* $\neg\neg K\phi$

$\neg K\phi$; *ergo* $\neg\phi$

ϕ; *ergo* $K\phi$ (for decidable ϕ)

---

in support of the 'truism' that there are unknown truths were in fact of this variety— undecided decidable propositions! But if you give the anti-realist an arbitrary undecided decidable proposition, he does not yet have any guarantee that he has an unknown truth.

[14]The following line of argument was first suggested by W. D. Hart, 'Access and Inference', *Proceedings of the Aristotelian Society*, Supp. Vol. 53, 1979. Wright appears to endorse what follows. Cf. Wright, loc. cit., p. 430.

that anyone else would be committed to accepting once they accept that ϕ is inconsistent with $\neg K\phi$.

Williamson, however, raises an objection to the argument just given in support of the inference 'ϕ; *ergo* $K\phi$'.[15] He insists that the constructive content of the premiss is not that someone has found a proof of ϕ, but rather that a proof-type with conclusion ϕ (timelessly, albeit constructively) exists. Thus it would be illicit to perform the 'reflection' required (once one reaches the conclusion ϕ of the supposed token π of the proof-type Π) to turn π into a proof-token π^* of the sought conclusion that ϕ is known (on the basis of that proof-token π). ϕ can be a proposition eligible to be shared by different minds, and eligible to be asserted on the basis of a (timelessly existing) proof-type Π, without anyone ever occurrently grasping ϕ as the conclusion of any token of that proof-type Π. Of course, it is possible that someone sometime occurrently grasp ϕ as the conclusion of some token of the proof-type Π. That much is guaranteed by the principle of knowability. But that is all that is guaranteed. We cannot construe the premiss of the inference 'ϕ; *ergo* $K\phi$' as saying more than that. For, to say more than that is to help oneself to the very inference whose validity is in question.

This response of Williamson's is compelling; it seems to clinch the case in favour of the soft anti-realist as against the hard anti-realist. But it is the soft anti-realist who is in a difficult predicament over the proof Σ, and who would be in such a predicament over any other purported proof of the same result. Williamson's attempt, on behalf of the intuitionist anti-realist, to accommodate Σ faces insuperable difficulties, as will be argued below. So it is crucial that Σ be defused. It will be so, provided one follows the restriction strategy mentioned earlier.

The prime bone of contention is whether indeed there is any proposition ϕ such that 'ϕ is consistent with $\neg K\phi$' could be true. The realist says 'Most decidedly so!' The hard anti-realist says 'Most decidedly not!' The soft anti-realist is caught in the middle, but inclined to side with the realist on this issue.[16] Let us allow, then, for propositions that happen to be true but which are not (actually) known to be true. The soft anti-realist will still

---

[15] Cf. 'Intuitionism Disproved?', at pp. 206–7; and 'Knowability and Constructivism', at pp. 429–31.

[16] The matter is rather subtle, as far as the soft anti-realist is concerned. Refusing to assert that for every ϕ, ϕ is inconsistent with $\neg K\phi$ does not commit one to denying it. And denying that for every ϕ, ϕ is inconsistent with $\neg K\phi$ does not intuitionistically entail that for some ϕ, ϕ is consistent with $\neg K\phi$. Of these three respective positions, the first would be his safest demurral against his hard anti-realist colleague.

want to deny that there could be any proposition that happens to be true but which could not possibly be known to be true. That is, he will still want to maintain that all truths are knowable, even if not actually known. That, after all, is what makes him an anti-realist.

Anyone who refuses to accept the result that ϕ is inconsistent with $\neg K\phi$ must make a case that at least one of the rules $(\Diamond\bot)$, $(\Diamond K)$ or $(K\wedge)$ is objectionable at its application in the proof Σ. It is hopeless to attempt to assail either the modal rule $(\Diamond\bot)$ or the epistemic rule $(K\wedge)$. Let us try, therefore, to object directly to the knowability rule $(\Diamond K)$ at its application in Σ:

$$(\Diamond K)\ \phi \wedge \neg K\phi;\ ergo\ \Diamond K(\phi \wedge \neg K\phi)$$

'But isn't this just obviously invalid?' the realist will ask. In the conjunction $(\phi \wedge \neg K\phi)$ we have a proposition which, if true, cannot be known to be true (as our earlier argument showed). Such a proposition, for the realist, would be, if true, a perfect example of a knowledge-transcendent truth. Its very logical structure ensures that it is impossible to know it. So, if it is true, then it is impossible to know it. Moreover, for the realist, for a great many ϕ, the proposition $(\phi \wedge \neg K\phi)$ is consistent; hence possibly true, that is, true in some possible world, even if not in this one.

Note that the argument given above for the inconsistency of $K(\phi \wedge \neg K\phi)$ is acceptable to both the realist and the anti-realist. So the anti-realist agrees also that $(\phi \wedge \neg K\phi)$ is a proposition which, if true—a very big 'if'!—cannot be known to be true. But the hard anti-realist will not be impressed by the realist's claim that we have here a schema for generating knowledge-transcendent truths. From the hard anti-realist's point of view, there is no truth of the form $(\phi \wedge \neg K\phi)$ to be had! Moreover, he maintains this, as we saw above, on independent grounds, regardless of whether the proof Σ is correct. (And even the soft anti-realist should be wondering what examples of truths of the form $(\phi \wedge \neg K\phi)$ might be given.)

On the one hand, $(\phi \wedge \neg K\phi)$ is maintained, by the realist, to be consistent, hence possibly true. As such, he says, it provides a counter-example to rule $(\Diamond K)$; and it is to this very counter-example $(\phi \wedge \neg K\phi)$ that rule $(\Diamond K)$ needs to be applied in the proof Σ above. For this reason, says the realist, the rule $(\Diamond K)$ has been shown by the proof Σ to be incorrect. But so far (it can quickly be retorted on the anti-realist's behalf) no other counter-examples worth considering have been offered to rule $(\Diamond K)$. On the other hand, $(\phi \wedge \neg K\phi)$ is maintained, by the hard anti-realist, to be inconsistent, hence not possibly true. As such, it provides no counter-example at all to rule $(\Diamond K)$.

The hard anti-realist concurs with each step within the argument (which we called Ξ) for the inconsistency of $K(\phi \wedge \neg K\phi)$, but this is ultimately to no avail. Showing him, by means of that argument Ξ, that $(\phi \wedge \neg K\phi)$ cannot be known is just fanning the flames. He claims to be able to corroborate this result later on, since the proof Σ (with Ξ as a subproof) shows that $(\phi \wedge \neg K\phi)$ could not possibly be true—hence, could not possibly be known! And here the realist has the temerity to present him with this utterly toothless would-be counter-example to the application of $(\Diamond K)$ within Σ ...!

We have reached an impasse. Are there any true propositions of the form $(\phi \wedge \neg K\phi)$? All the realist can do is claim (in realist spirit) that there are such propositions, or at least that there could, for all we know, be such propositions. In his claim the existential quantifier (and the modal operator for possibility) would have to be interpreted non-constructively. For, in the nature of the case, the realist is prevented (by the proof Ξ) from showing, for any particular ϕ, that $(\phi \wedge \neg K\phi)$ is true (but unknowable). For this would be to know that $(\phi \wedge \neg K\phi)$ —but the proof Ξ shows that $K(\phi \wedge \neg K\phi)$ is impossible! He might be able to give particular examples of (what for him are) consistent but unknowable propositions of the form $(\phi \wedge \neg K\phi)$; but he cannot go further and provide conclusive backing for any claim to the effect that such a consistent proposition is true. One is hard put, as an anti-realist, to think of a more tenuous existence claim.

8.5   Diagnosis of the underlying problem

We have been considering purported counter-examples to the anti-realist principle that all truths are knowable. The principle in its present form is unrestricted: it concerns all propositions, of any logical form, and regarding any areas of discourse. The strategy of purported counter-exemplification that we have been considering here has a familiar feel and form. It involves a reflexive trick: constructing a proposition(al compound) $(\phi \wedge \neg K\phi)$ containing a negation of a proposition that itself involves the key notion in the consequent of the principle under attack. We saw the effects of the same trick earlier, in our discussion in section 3 , where we used the proposition $(\phi \wedge \neg W\phi)$. This was a counter-example to the general claim that every contingent proposition ψ is such that I am able rationally to wonder whether ψ. In the same way, the Liar sentence 'This sentence is not true' undermines the naïve principle that every sentence not involving a repetition of non-logical terms can be made true; and the undecidable Gödel sentence for Peano arithmetic (which says, via the Gödel coding, 'I am not provable in Peano arithmetic') undermines the claim that every arithmetical truth is provable in Peano arithmetic. This observation will become salient when we consider, below, the possibility of restricting the principle of knowability.[17] The suggested restriction will be along the lines motivated quite innocently earlier, in connection with the '(wondering whether)-ability' principle ($\Diamond W$). The restriction is intended to rule out these trickily reflexive counter-examples, and other problematic cases, but in a principled way. The restricted principle will still, however, be a substantive epistemological claim that can be a genuine point of contention between the realist and the anti-realist. But more on this in due course.

Concerning the anti-realist principle (in its present unrestricted form) that all truths are knowable, then, the realist should simply refuse to assert it, rather than go so far as to deny it; for he cannot provide any definitive counter-examples. This is rather amusing; it is not unlike the anti-realist being unable to give any particular counter-examples to the realist's principle of bivalence, on pain of self-contradiction. Each must play the game of merely refusing to assert the other's favourite principle; while avoiding being lured into citing putative counter-examples, on pain of self-contradiction. It is interesting how analogous their respective predicaments are. The realist may, however, be able to do a little better by his own lights. He may strengthen his refusal to assert the anti-realist principle that all truths are knowable, to an assertion that there are counter-examples to it. But then he must have his audience understand the existence claim non-constructively, on pain of self-contradiction! And it is precisely this understanding which the anti-realist is not willing to profess.

Williamson makes a related analogy,[18] but more care is needed with it. He writes

> the intuitionist status of $[\phi \to K\phi]$ is like that of the law of excluded middle. For $[\neg(\phi \lor \neg\phi)]$ contradicts itself in intuitionistic logic.

For his analogy to hold, clearly $\neg(\phi \to K\phi)$ has to contradict itself in intuitionistic logic. But of course it cannot do this, unless (i) the logic is supplemented with the knowability principle $\phi \to \Diamond K\phi$, and (ii) $\neg(\phi \to K\phi)$ is taken to imply both ϕ and $\neg K\phi$. But while $\neg(\phi \to K\phi)$ intuitionistically

---

[17]It is this possibility that Williamson (loc. cit.) crucially fails to explore.

[18]See 'Intuitionism Disproved?', at p. 206.

implies $\neg K\phi$, it does not intuitionistically imply ϕ. It does, however, intuitionistically imply $\neg\neg\phi$. So if ϕ is decidable, $\neg(\phi \to K\phi)$ will intuitionistically imply ϕ, and Williamson's analogy will appear to be in order; until we realize that when ϕ is decidable, $\phi \lor \neg\phi$ is also intuitionistically acceptable. Certainly, $\neg(\phi \lor \neg\phi)$ will in this case still contradict itself in intuitionistic logic; but for a more straightforward reason than the one Williamson was trying to exploit to make the analogy with $\neg(\phi \to K\phi)$ useful.

It is also necessary to be careful with the scopes of the propositional quantifiers when considering assertions and denials of these logical laws. Williamson does at least note[19] that $\neg\forall\phi(\phi \to K\phi)$ does not intuitionistically imply $\exists\phi(\phi \land \neg K\phi)$, but fails to note that the implication will hold if ϕ is decidable and the proof Σ is accepted. For then $\neg\forall\phi(\phi \to K\phi)$ will be inconsistent:

$$
\frac{(1)\underline{\qquad}\quad\underline{\qquad}(2)}{\neg K\phi \;,\;\; \phi}
$$
$$
\Sigma
$$
$$
\frac{\underline{\;\bot\;}(1)}{K\phi}(2)
$$
$$
\frac{\phi \to K\phi}{\forall\phi(\phi \to K\phi) \quad \neg\forall\phi(\phi \to K\phi)}
$$
$$
\bot
$$

(For the justification of the step marked (1), remember that $K\phi$ is decidable, since ϕ is decidable.)

This is a crucial oversight, given that all the counter-examples that Williamson urged against $\forall\phi(\phi \to K\phi)$ involved decidable sentences ϕ. It is only the claim $\exists\phi(\phi \land \neg K\phi)$, and not (in general) the claim $\neg\forall\phi(\phi \to K\phi)$, that is reduced to absurdity by our proof Σ (which exploits the anti-realist's principle of knowability). But for decidable ϕ both these sentences are intuitionistically absurd, given our proof Σ. For undecidable ϕ, the intuitionist anti-realist can either refuse to assert $\forall\phi(\phi \to K\phi)$, or deny it (that is, assert $\neg\forall\phi(\phi \to K\phi)$) without thereby being committed to asserting the claim $\exists\phi(\phi \land \neg K\phi)$, and being caught in consequent difficulties via the proof Σ, which reduces the latter to absurdity. When ϕ is decidable, however, this ploy is to no avail.

The comfortable space that Williamson has tried to mark out for the soft anti-realist therefore does not exist. Williamson wanted the anti-realist

---

[19] In his later paper 'Knowability and Constructivism', at p. 423.

to be able to refuse to assert $\forall \phi (\phi \rightarrow K \phi)$, or be able to deny it, and be untouched (for any ϕ) by the Fitchian *reductio* of $\exists \phi (\phi \wedge \neg K \phi)$. It was an ingenious idea, but it does not withstand closer scrutiny. It would appear that something different is needed if we are to be able to cut the Gordian knot of truth, possible knowledge and actual knowledge.

There are two interpretations of 'K', which have not yet been distinguished in the discussion of knowability, since the distinction would not have affected anything said so far.[20] On the weak interpretation, '$K \phi$' asserts that ϕ is known 'timelessly': someone, at some time, knows that ϕ. Thus on the weak interpretation the negation $\neg K \phi$ can be read as 'ϕ will never be known'. On the strong interpretation, '$K \phi$' asserts success by the time of its assertion. Where 'now' refers to the time of assertion, any assertion of '$K \phi$' is to be taken as meaning 'Someone by now knows (or has known) that ϕ.' Thus on the strong interpretation the negation $\neg K \phi$ can be read as 'ϕ is not yet known.'

When the hard anti-realist considers the warrant-preserving nature of the inference

ϕ; *ergo* $K \phi$

he can have either interpretation of 'K' in mind.[21] On either interpretation of 'K', the epistemic success claimed in the conclusion is not alleged to antedate the time of the assertion of the premiss. That is what makes the inference constructively acceptable to the hard anti-realist.

We have not yet considered, however, occurrences of 'K' within the principles involving it, that might enjoy an arbitrary subscript t for a time that may differ from the time of assertion ('now'). Even the hard anti-realist,

---

[20]The sole exception is the demonstration above that if $K \phi$ is decidable, then ϕ is decidable. This demonstration requires the weak interpretation of K.

[21]When Williamson rhetorically asks (loc. cit., p. 429) why an anti-realist should not bite the bullet, as it were, and accept the inference 'ϕ; *ergo* $K \phi$' as intuitionistically compelling, he has only the weak interpretation of K in mind. He does not consider the strong interpretation of K, and so fails to suggest (albeit if only rhetorically) the even stronger position that the inference could be maintained even on the strong interpretation! Williamson's complaint was that if the anti-realist were to accept the inference (even if only on the weak interpretation) then he 'would still seem to lack any way of acknowledging the truism that not all truths are ever known'. But for the hard anti-realist, this 'truism' is refutable!—whereas that other touted 'truism', that every proposition is true or false, is merely not to be accepted. Hard anti-realism comes into the philosopher's life like a sword. Not only logical reform is needed for the evils of realism; metaphysical and epistemological reform is needed as well.

for example, might wish to assert now that Goldbach's Conjecture was not known on 1 January 1900: $\neg K_{1/1/1900}(GB)$. In general, let $K_t\phi$ mean that ϕ is known at or by time t. The strong interpretation of 'K' makes $K\phi$ mean $K_{now}\phi$. The weak interpretation of 'K' makes $K\phi$ mean $\exists t K_t\phi$.

As far as one can determine, no pattern of temporal subscriptings and quantifications over times will cajole the proof Σ into a correct form for the more radical conclusion that

$\neg K_t\phi$ is logically inconsistent with ϕ,

no matter what modified versions of our rules we consider.[22] Every obvious modification of Σ involves a fallacious move from the claim that a conjunction is known at some time or other to the claim that one or other of its conjuncts is known at time t.[23] Moreover, one has to be careful not to use too demanding a reading of 'K' in the knowability principle, lest the anti-realist disavow it. There is independent interest, however, in the fact that if we allow the strong interpretation of 'K' in the knowability principle—so that it maintains of every truth that it is logically possible that it be known now—the proof Σ still serves up the result that ϕ is logically inconsistent with $\neg K\phi$.

There is a limit, then, to the epistemic success that even the hard anti-realist will claim. It would appear to be impossible to construct an argument, using time-indexing of knowledge, that would justify the claim that from the truth of Goldbach's Conjecture it follows that it was known on, say, 1 January 1900. Such a result would be so preposterous, anyway, that we would be bound to find fault with one or more of the steps within any purported proof of it.

According to the hard anti-realist, however, it does follow from the presumed truth of Goldbach's Conjecture that there is a time at which it is known. For its truth would have to consist in there being some recognizable truth-maker, i.e. a canonical proof. If we can assert that there is such

---

[22] Williamson (loc. cit.) appears not to have anticipated the possibility of a further alarming slide of this kind, in the form of a formal proof even more devastating than Fitch's—a proof obtained, perhaps, by modifying the Fitch proof appropriately. Williamson introduced temporal subscripts only to have them always bound by quantifiers, and then concerned himself only with investigating different combinations of scope distinctions. But once temporal subscripting is available, then the operator K_t (for particular times t, such as *now*) is eligible for consideration too.

[23] Williamson notes the same problem in his 'Intuitionism Disproved?', *Analysis* 42, 1982, pp. 203–7; at p. 205.

a thing, we must be able to provide a way of finding it, a way which is, moreover, recognizably what it is claimed to be. Given (at time t) such a canonical proof (or a recognizable way of providing, in due course, a canonical proof), the truth of the Conjecture is known at time t. The knowledge in question is not deferred and unclaimable until such time as someone might have travelled the whole way in question to the canonical proof itself. Once convinced that there is indeed a method for determining a canonical proof of ϕ, the anti-realist can claim right away to know that ϕ without having first to apply the method in question so as actually to produce the canonical proof itself. Provided that we understand the anti-realist's knowledge-claims as justified in this appropriately liberal way, there is no cogent objection, says the hard anti-realist, to the inference 'ϕ; ergo $K\phi$', whichever of the following ways it is rendered:

'ϕ; ergo $K_{now}\ \phi$' (strong reading of K);

'ϕ; ergo $\exists t K_t \phi$' (weak reading of K).

There is an anti-realist objection to

'ϕ; ergo $K_t \phi$'

where t is a time antedating our earliest warranted assertion of the premiss ϕ; but, as we have already remarked, there appears to be no convincing argument for this untoward time-indexed conclusion.

Although an attempt has just been made to reconcile him to it, the soft anti-realist will wish to avoid the overly actualist consequence of his principle of knowability, which seems to be foisted on him by the proof Σ. The nub of his complaint will be that the proof is just too 'tricky'. (Note that the same complaint was made above against the realist's attempt to counter-exemplify the unrestricted principle of knowability!) The proof Σ, the soft anti-realist complains, uses the special compound propositional schema $(\phi \wedge \neg K\phi)$ as a parametric instance of the principle of knowability, and yields as a result an extremely general (and unacceptable) inconsistency claim, concerning all propositions ϕ. The suggestion now from the soft anti-realist is that we should avoid the overly actualist conclusion (despite the hard anti-realist's earlier attempts to reconcile him to it) by blocking the application of $(\Diamond K)$ within Σ in a non-*ad hoc*, principled way. And the soft anti-realist is not just wriggling on the epistemic hook here. For the whole thrust of our earlier discussion of the attitude of 'rationally wondering whether' was that we ought to recognize logical limits on the kind of propositions towards which we can have various attitudes. This was because of the logic of the attitudes themselves, not because of any inherent epistemic limitations on thinkers themselves, whether they be human or ideally rational.

Let us now develop this line of thought. One can thereby remove the felt need for any distinction between soft and hard anti-realists in so far as a response to the proof Σ is called for. For Σ will no longer be correct; it will no longer persuade even the hard anti-realist of its result. Two responses will therefore be open to the anti-realists. They can unite in relief over not having to respond to the divisive 'proof' Σ. Or the hard anti-realist could still go his own way, pressing the independent arguments above that stressed the constructive content, and consequent validity, for him, of the inferences

$$\phi;\ ergo\ \neg\neg K\phi$$

$$\neg K\phi;\ ergo\ \neg\phi$$

and indeed even

$$\phi;\ ergo\ K\phi.$$

What is interesting, though, is that this line would now be an optional extra serving to define hard anti-realism, an extra that is no longer called for, on the part of the moderate anti-realist, in response to the conceptual emergency presented by the result established by the 'proof' Σ. For Σ will be no more. Let us now see why.

8.6   Cartesian contents, and our proposed solution

The proposition (or content) 'No thinkers exist' is consistent, but could not (in any world in which it were true) be known to be true. We owe this insight to Descartes. Let us call *anti-Cartesian* any proposition ϕ such that the proposition that ϕ is known is inconsistent. There are three broad kinds of anti-Cartesian proposition ϕ, corresponding to the kind of reason why knowledge that ϕ is impossible.

First, the proposition ϕ itself may be inconsistent; whence the proposition that ϕ is known will be inconsistent. So, for example, any compound proposition of the form $(\phi \wedge \neg\phi)$ is anti-Cartesian.

Secondly, knowledge of a (consistent) proposition ϕ may be impossible because the very act of considering or judging (falsely) that ϕ requires the falsity of (some consequence of) ϕ. *A fortiori* the proposition that ϕ is known is inconsistent. It is in this way that the proposition that no thinkers exist is anti-Cartesian.

Thirdly, the proposition that ϕ is known may be logically inconsistent because of its own overall logical structure, involving iterations of K (and perhaps of other attitudes).[24] Thus for any ϕ the proposition $(\phi \wedge \neg K\phi)$ is such that *that $(\phi \wedge \neg K\phi)$ is known* turns out to be logically inconsistent (as we saw via the proof Ξ above). That is, $(\phi \wedge \neg K\phi)$ is anti-Cartesian.

Propositions whose corresponding knowledge claims are *consistent*, by contrast, will be called *Cartesian*.[25]

ϕ is Cartesian $=_{df}$ not$(K\phi \vdash \bot)$.

Note that on this definition of Cartesian propositions, it is not analytic that they are true only if they could be known. It is a substantive epistemological claim that every true Cartesian proposition could be known. The anti-realist would want to make this claim; the realist would want to deny it.

Note that the anti-realist principle that every truth is knowable has, prima facie, an actualist and a necessitarian reading. On the actualist reading, all that is maintained is that every truth in the actual world is knowable. Thus a proposition such as 'No thinkers exist' affords no counter-example to the knowability principle; for, in the actual world, it is false that no thinkers exist. In general: no actual falsehood can furnish a counter-example to the actualist principle that every truth (in the actual world) is knowable herein.

On the necessitarian reading, by contrast, we have to be more careful with examples such as 'No thinkers exist.'[26] On this reading the principle

---

[24] The word 'logical' is used here to apply to inferences within modal and epistemic logic as well as standard logic. Hence the notion of consistency generalizes in the same way.

[25] Note that a Cartesian proposition is not being defined to be any of the following:

(i) one whose truth follows from its being thought;

(ii) one whose truth follows from any proposition's being thought;

(iii) one whose truth requires that there be thinking; or

(iv) one whose truth is inconsistent with its not being known.

A simple label is needed for the notion that has been defined, and 'Cartesian' has been chosen for convenience.

[26] Williamson is therefore in error when he remarks in passing ('Knowability and Constructivism', p. 422, n. 4) that 'it would not materially affect the argument' if we were to adopt a necessitarian rather than an actualist formulation of the principle of knowability. It might not have affected his argument, in so far as it went; but then he did not see fit to challenge the application of the principle of knowability to the reflexively tricky case of $(\phi \wedge \neg K\phi)$.

claims that in every possible world, every truth in that world would be knowable therein. But presumably there is a possible world in which there are no thinkers, and, as Descartes made us aware, the truth in such a world of the proposition that there are no thinkers would be unknowable therein.

One's immediate intuition is that one would not wish the anti-realist's principle of knowability to be deprived of its necessitarian import just because of tricky examples like 'No thinkers exist.' One's reaction would therefore be to restrict the principle of knowability, but in a principled way, without depriving it of its philosophical bite.[27] One would look for some general property $\mathcal{F}$ of propositions such as 'No thinkers exist', a property $\mathcal{F}$ whose possession by any proposition ϕ would make it abundantly clear why ϕ should be exempted from the intended scope of the anti-realist principle of knowability. The latter principle could then take the restricted form that, necessarily, all true propositions lacking property $\mathcal{F}$ are knowable.

It is clear that the anti-realist with necessitarian aspirations already has good reason, in the form of propositions such as 'No thinkers exist', to restrict the scope of his principle of knowability. Such reason can very well precede those afforded by yet further troublesome examples for the unrestricted principle, such as (for any ϕ) the compound proposition $(\phi \wedge \neg K\phi)$. What the anti-realist should try to provide, therefore, is some uniform characterization $\mathcal{F}$ that will cover at least propositions of both these kinds; and then use $\mathcal{F}$ to restrict his principle in the way just indicated.

The following is a good choice for $\mathcal{F}$: $\mathcal{F}(\phi)$ just in case the proposition that ϕ is known is inconsistent. Thus 'not-$\mathcal{F}$' means 'Cartesian'. Hence the restricted anti-realist principle of knowability becomes: *necessarily, all true Cartesian propositions are knowable.*

The suggestion, then, is that rule $(\Diamond K)$ should be stated with an extra condition as follows:

$(\Diamond KC)$ ϕ; *ergo* $\Diamond K\phi$, where ϕ is Cartesian.

The application of $(\Diamond K)$ within Σ cannot be regarded as an application of $(\Diamond KC)$. For $(\phi \wedge \neg K\phi)$ is not Cartesian. Whether or not we think $(\phi \wedge \neg K\phi)$ is consistent, the corresponding knowledge claim $K(\phi \wedge \neg K\phi)$ is inconsistent (as we have already seen, via the proof Ξ given above). Hence, if the anti-realist's principle of knowability is expressed more modestly as the rule $(\Diamond KC)$, the anti-realist ceases to have to accept the conclusion that

---

[27]It is this reaction that Williamson (loc. cit.) failed to explore.

ϕ is logically inconsistent with $\neg K\phi$. For the 'proof' Σ will now contain an incorrect application of $(\Diamond KC)$, in which the Cartesian condition is violated.

Does our restriction of $(\Diamond K)$ to $(\Diamond KC)$ render the knowability principle thereby expressed toothless? Does the restriction to Cartesian truths secure the truth of the knowability principle by sheer stipulation? Does it amount to claiming that the principle holds except where it doesn't? Not at all. Think of all the Cartesian propositions of mathematics and empirical science, propositions that involve no mention, within them, of epistemic notions. To claim that every such truth is in principle knowable is still to forswear metaphysical realism.

Note that the restricted rule $(\Diamond KC)$ comes in progressively more secure forms, in a sequence of reflections on the deducibility relation in the condition that $\text{not}(K\phi \vdash \bot)$.[28] Let us call the progressively more secure forms $(\Diamond KC)_0$, $(\Diamond KC)_1$, $(\Diamond KC)_2$, ... The first version $(\Diamond KC)_0$ of the rule in this 'reflection sequence' appeals to the notion of '$\vdash$' constituted without the use of that rule itself. Thus '$\vdash$' here means deducibility within the modal and epistemic extension of the logic of the area of discourse in question. The next version, $(\Diamond KC)_1$, of the rule allows the deducibility relation in the condition that $\text{not}(K\phi \vdash \bot)$ to be defined with respect to the use of $(\Diamond KC)_0$. In general, $(\Diamond KC)_{n+1}$ allows the deducibility relation in the condition '$\text{not}(K\phi \vdash \bot)$' to be defined with respect to the use of $(\Diamond KC)_n$. As we go down the sequence, the Cartesian condition becomes harder to satisfy, so the rule is more secure. But even the first rule in the sequence, namely, $(\Diamond KC)_0$, has a sufficiently demanding Cartesian condition to block the construction of Σ and so avert the result that ϕ is inconsistent with $\neg K\phi$, where ϕ involves no epistemic or modal operators (as in straightforward mathematics and natural science).

With the unrestricted knowability principle $(\Diamond K)$ the hard anti-realist would have to insist on a highly constructive interpretation of the existential quantifier and on highly constructive contents of assertions, generally, in order to reconcile himself to the result established by Σ: that every proposition ϕ is inconsistent with $\neg K\phi$. But with the restricted principle $(\Diamond KC)$, one is deprived of that proof (and, it would appear, of any proof) of that result, and the threat of this uncomfortable actualism recedes. The anti-realist can maintain that every (Cartesian) truth is knowable, without thereby being committed to saying that every (Cartesian) truth is known. The soft anti-realist can also decline the hard anti-realist's overly constructive construal of

---

[28] Discussion with Stewart Shapiro has been helpful here.

the existential quantifier and of contents of assertions generally. There will, then, be no route that the soft anti-realist is obliged to acknowledge, even for decidable propositions, to the conclusion that every true proposition is known.

8.7   The failure of the reconstrual strategy

In section 1 we deferred a discussion of what was called the reconstrual strategy (i). In the interests of completeness we must now see why it is unsatisfactory. Note, however, that it is not necessary, so far as the overall case is concerned, to establish that the reconstrual strategy is defective. For the concern has been to show that the anti-realist has, in the restriction strategy, a way out of the Fitchian difficulties posed for the knowability principle. And two ways—reconstrual *and* restriction—would of course be better than one. The fact remains, however, that a new solution to a vexing problem merits greater interest the more likely it is to turn out to be the sole solution to that problem.[29] So if further discussion undermines the credentials of the reconstrual strategy, then (at least on this score) the restriction strategy developed above can lay more urgent claim upon the anti-realist's attention.

The reconstrual strategy was first pursued by Edgington.[30] She quantifies over possible situations, and allows knowledge in one situation to have as its object the truth of a proposition in *another* situation. Thus in her hands the knowability principle says that for every proposition ϕ true in a given situation there is another situation in which ϕ's truth in the former situation is known. But this analysis of the modal form of the principle of knowability faces formidable difficulties, well laid out by Williamson[31] and Wright.[32]

Williamson argues that Edgington's analysis forces one to accept one or other of these unpalatable alternatives: either the analysis so limits the anti-realist principle of knowability that the knowledge it claims to be possible can

---

[29] Our dialectical situation here is therefore similar to the one we faced earlier when opposing content irrealism. There we had two possible avenues: either refute content irrealism quickly and directly, with the kind of transcendental argument put forward by Boghossian; or make a more detailed case by subverting each and every step of the content irrealist's own argument for scepticism about meaning. The first possibility, as we saw, unfortunately came to naught; so we had to explore the second possibility, taking on Kripkenstein point by point.

[30] D. Edgington, 'The Paradox of Knowability', *Mind* 94, 1985, pp. 557–68.

[31] T. Williamson, 'On the Paradox of Knowability', *Mind* 96, 1987, pp. 256–61.

[32] C. Wright, *Realism, Meaning and Truth*, 2nd edition, Blackwell, 1993, pp. 426–32.

be knowledge only of necessary truths; or one is required to have a conception of non-actual thought about the actual, of which no causal account could be given, even when the propositions involved have to do with bodies and events in space and time.

Wright, for his part, does not wholly dismiss Edgington's analysis, but does point to further difficulties that it faces. Of these, the most serious is that the proposed analysis over-liberalizes the anti-realist's evidential requirements on true propositions. Originally the demand was that there should be actual evidence for truth. Edgington requires only that evidence be possibly available, and invokes counterfactual circumstances in explicating the latter notion. But if that is permitted, Wright complains, it is hard to see how for many of the sentences for which, the anti-realist maintains, bivalence does not hold (such as Dummett's example 'Jones was brave'), it would continue to be the case that bivalence did not hold.

Wright also raised two independent problems.[33] These were Skorupski's example 'Thatcher is a master criminal' (whose truth would prevent there being evidence for it), and a new one of Wright's own making, which will be called the disjunction problem. The disjunction problem is that the anti-realist claims that it is possible to know a disjunction only if it is possible to know one or other of the disjuncts; but also claims to know that $\phi \lor \neg\phi$, for decidable ϕ, without necessarily having applied the available decision procedure to determine which disjunct is true. In response to these problems, Wright borrowed Edgington's analysis of the knowability principle to conclude that it yielded 'at least the shape of a satisfactory anti-realist response to these problems';[34] then he went on to set out his misgivings about Edgington's over-liberalization of the anti-realist's evidential requirements for truth!

Williamson, in a later paper[35] in effect solves Wright's disjunction problem by introducing quantification over temporal variables subscripted to the 'knows that' operator. Williamson does not appeal to possible situations at all. The irony is that Edgington had motivated her proposed modal analysis, involving quantification over situations plus an indexical operator 'actually', by appealing to the analogous analysis of temporal discourse, where one has quantification over times plus the indexical operator 'now'. Williamson shows that the latter, temporal analysis provides sufficiently discriminating

---

[33]loc. cit., pp. 425–7.
[34]loc. cit., p. 429.
[35]'Knowability and Constructivism', *Philosophical Quarterly*, 38, 1988, pp. 422–32.

materials to draw the sting of Wright's disjunction problem. And earlier,[36] Williamson had given very telling objections to Edgington's modal analysis.

The upshot, then, is that (a) Edgington's modal analysis (in pursuit of a reconstrual strategy) does not succeed; (b) Wright's disjunction problem is not a problem for the anti-realist who is fastidious with temporal subscripts to his knowledge claims; (c) the problem posed by Skorupski's example 'Thatcher is a master criminal' remains; and (d) the original problem for the knowability principle $\phi \rightarrow \Diamond K\phi$ would remain. Problem (c) has been set to one side in this chapter. The proper setting for its solution is a new anti-realist account of constructive falsifiability, rather than verifiability, for empirical discourse. But that is beyond the scope of the present chapter. Here the concern has been only with proposing, in the restriction strategy, a new and finally satisfactory solution to the original problem for the knowability principle $\phi \rightarrow \Diamond K\phi$.

8.8   Taking stock

It is time now to pause to take stock of what we have accomplished so far. We have surveyed the issues involved in the realism debate, and have articulated the main tenets of anti-realism. These are the manifestation requirement and the principle that all truths are in principle knowable. We have averted the slide to strict finitism that would be threatened by too exigent a sense of 'knowable' and 'manifestable'. We have defended the principle of knowability in a novel way against the most concerted (and, many have hitherto believed, conclusive) realist objection to it. We have also countered non-factualist scepticism about the objectivity of meaning discourse, pointing out systematic dialectical deficiencies on the part of Kripkenstein. We have applied the manifestation requirement so as to make it clear how, in the presence of the provable undecidability of truth in a discourse, the anti-realist must reject bivalence. We have examined, in the light of metamathematical results, the various philosophical positions one might occupy concerning the relationships among the decidable, the knowable and the true; and we have found good reasons to exclude all possible competitors to moderate anti-realism.

That completes our defence of moderate anti-realism against attacks on all its flanks. In the remainder of this work we draw out what is constructively original and arresting in anti-realism, especially as it concerns

---

[36] Cf. 'On the Paradox of Knowability', loc. cit.

analyticity, choice of correct logic, cognitive significance and the proper construal of defeasible empirical discourse. What follows will in all likelihood be anathema to the Quinean. For we are about to:

1. resuscitate the analytic-synthetic distinction, and, in particular, allow analytic truths to carry existential commitments to necessary existents;

2. trim our canons of deductive inference to those of intuitionistic relevant logic, the correct kernel within classical logic;

3. rejuvenate the notion of cognitive significance, showing how scientific good sense is constrained by human sensibility; and

4. give a new lease of life to hypothetico-deductivism and falsificationism in an account of the logic of scientific explanation and prediction.

The remaining chapters take up these agenda in the order just given.

Chapter 9

Analyticity and Syntheticity

9.1   Logic and analyticity

Three features of deductive logic are stressed to the beginner. First, logic is said to be the study of valid arguments: arguments that preserve truth from their premisses to their conclusions. (The premisses and conclusions can, of course, be mathematically but not logically true, or be contingent statements about the external world.) Secondly, validity is said to be a matter of form, not content. Thirdly, logic is said to have no 'subject-matter'; it is ontologically neutral and non-committal. This is so even though (perhaps: only because?) it effects inferential transitions among sentences that are far from being ontologically neutral and non-committal themselves.

It will be argued here that standard ways of developing these claims have led us astray in our understanding of parts of logical and mathematical knowledge as analytic or synthetic, and as *a priori* or *a posteriori*. It may be that the two distinctions were brought into disrepute by unresolved confusions over the precise nature of logic. One needs to clear up these confusions and shed some light on the ill-starred distinctions. It will emerge that the question of the necessary existence of mathematical entities such as the natural numbers is crucial for a satisfactory classification of truths according to the rehabilitated distinctions. This classification answers both to analytic intuitions and to epistemological concerns.

9.2   A brief history of the two distinctions

The analytic-synthetic distinction has suffered ever since the failure, beginning in the late nineteenth century, of attempts to show that mathematics[1]
was wholly analytic, or that it was wholly synthetic. In inventing the
analytic-synthetic distinction in the first place, Kant had wanted to show
that mathematics was (wholly) synthetic *a priori*, arising out of the pure
forms of intuition of space and time.[2] Arithmetic arose out of the pure form
of intuition of time; Euclidean geometry out of the pure form of intuition of
space. Knowledge was therefore boxed as follows. The crossing-out indicates
that the box in question is empty. For the sake of clarity, we omit examples of synthetic *a posteriori* truths, leaving that box blank—which does not
mean that it is empty.

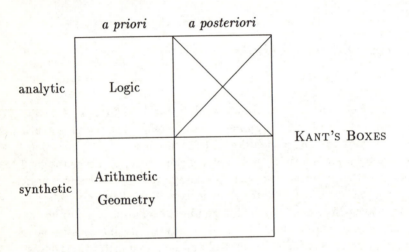

KANT'S BOXES

Throughout this discussion we shall make no mention of the (usually synthetic and *a posteriori*) status of empirical laws or of those among them (such
as the law of causation) that Kant reckoned to the synthetic *a priori*. We
want to show the variety of views on offer regarding only the status of mathematics and logic. We shall also avoid examining in any detail the possible
variations in technical sense from author to author of the term 'analytic'
itself. One of the well-known objections to Quine's attack in 'Two Dogmas of Empiricism' on the analytic-synthetic distinction is that he showed

---

[1] More specifically: arithmetic, real analysis and geometry.
[2] Cf. *Critique of Pure Reason*, tr. N. Kemp-Smith.

at best only that the narrower notion of 'Frege-analyticity' resisted non-circular explication. This narrower notion of analyticity encompasses only those truths that can be obtained by substituting synonyms within logical truths. Thus it does not even apply to an analytic claim such as 'All red things are coloured.' We shall assume, for the purposes of the following survey of positions, that whatever such variations in sense there may be across authors does not detract from the interest of the classificatory vacillations to be outlined below.

Frege, while agreeing with Kant that geometry was synthetic, nevertheless sought to argue that arithmetic, on the contrary, was wholly analytic (hence still *a priori*), by virtue of reductive definitions to, and derivations within, pure logic.[3]

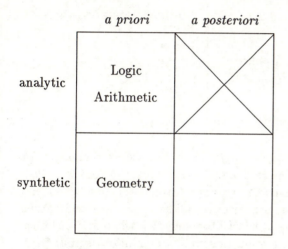

FREGE'S BOXES

The founding father of Logical Positivism, Schlick, agreed with Frege's views on arithmetic, as developed further by Russell and Whitehead in *Principia Mathematica*. But he dealt with geometry somewhat differently, given the success of Hilbert's axiomatizations of Euclidean and various non-Euclidean geometries, and the use of non-Euclidean geometries in Einstein's theory of general relativity. He distinguished between pure (or formal) geometry, and applied (or physical) geometry. On Schlick's view, the geometry of physical space (that is, applied geometry) was indeed synthetic, as both Kant and Frege had maintained; but, moreover, was *a posteriori*. Pure geometry, by contrast, followed logically (hence: analytically) from axioms that

---

[3] Cf. *Foundations of Arithmetic*, tr. J. L. Austin, Blackwell, Oxford, 1950.

were conventions, or implicit definitions of the concepts involved in them. Thus the *a priori* status of pure geometry is compromised by its being analytic. Either way, geometry is not both synthetic and *a priori*.[4] These were some of the most important considerations that resulted in Logical Positivism's famous evacuation of the synthetic *a priori*:

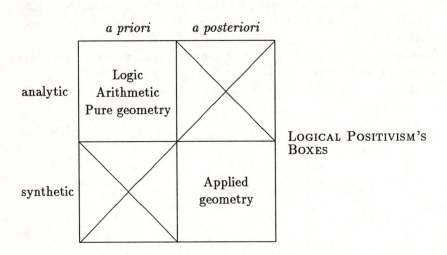

LOGICAL POSITIVISM'S BOXES

Carnap wrote his *Habilitationsschrift* under Schlick's direction in Vienna, after studying with Frege in Jena. In this work[5] he took a slightly different line from Schlick on geometry. For Carnap the *topological* core of applied geometry (common to projective, affine, Euclidean and various non-Euclidean geometries) was *a priori*. Topology was the only part of the science of space that was still a transcendental precondition for our being able to think about things in space at all.[6] Only the metrical part of applied geometry was *a posteriori*. The correct choice of axioms for the geometry for physical space, in so far as the measurement of distances and angles was concerned, could only be made *a posteriori*.

---

[4]Cf. M. Schlick, *Allgemeine Erkenntnislehre*, Springer, Berlin, 1918; revised edn. of 1925 translated (by A. E. Blumberg) as *General Theory of Knowledge*, Open Court, La Salle, 1985. See especially §II.C.38: 'Is there a Pure Intuition?', pp. 348–58.

[5]Published as *Der Raum*, a *Kantstudien Ergänzungsheft*, 1921.

[6]This view is echoed by Onora O'Neill in 'Space and Objects', *Journal of Philosophy*, 73, 1976, pp. 29–45; but she makes no mention of Carnap.

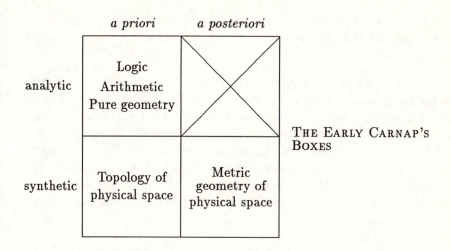

THE EARLY CARNAP'S
BOXES

Later, with Gödel's proof of the incompleteness of arithmetic,[7] it was thought that the logicist reduction of arithmetic must fail, and that arithmetic was after all synthetic:

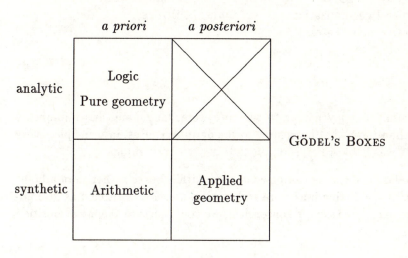

GÖDEL'S BOXES

Behind the classification of arithmetic as synthetic is Gödel's Platonism. He regarded arithmetical knowledge as knowledge of facts concerning an abstract structure, the progression of natural numbers, to which we had

---

[7] 'Über formal unentscheidbare Sätze der Principia Mathematica und verwandter Systeme I.', *Monatshefte für Mathematik und Physik*, 37, 1931, pp. 173–98.

intellectual access by means of a faculty of intuition akin to perception. So our arithmetical statements were about an aspect of our world, albeit a wholly abstract one.

It should come as no surprise, then, that a distinction that had led to such chopping and changing of the status of so important an area of human knowledge should eventually come under attack. After all, if one couldn't classify major areas of human knowledge uncontentiously by using the distinction, it must be at best unclear and at worst useless. So, according to Quine, we should dismantle both distinctions (analytic-synthetic and *a priori/a posteriori*)[8] and think at best in terms of the degrees of entrenchment of our knowledge claims in their collective confrontation with sensory experience:

Sensory experience
　—Periphery —
Observation sentences
Standing sentences
Low-level generalizations　　　QUINE'S BOLUS
Scientific hypotheses
Mathematics
Logic
　—Core —

Those claims that lay nearer to the core were, for Quine, less immune to revision than those that lay nearer to the periphery. But, in principle, every statement was liable to revision, including even laws of logic.

These last two claims can be construed within boxes rather than a bolus if we like. If the distinctions were still in play, and not jettisoned as groundless, or hopelessly vague, or nonsensical, we could picture the latest position as follows:

---

[8]It was Putnam who pointed out that Quine's attack on the analytic-synthetic distinction was just as much an attack on the *a priori/a posteriori* distinction. See his "Two Dogmas' Revisited' in *Realism and Reason, Philosophical Papers Vol.3*, Cambridge University Press, 1983, pp. 87–97.

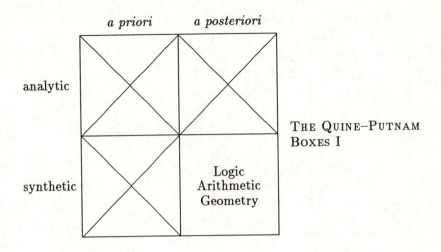

THE QUINE–PUTNAM
BOXES I

One begins to appreciate, however, the futility of maintaining the two distinctions when the boxes look like *that*.

One well-known criticism of the Quinean position of radical revisability is that there still have to be some constraints on how truth-values are to be reassigned to statements in the light of sensory experience.[9] And these constraints must surely belong to logic, and be *a priori*. Moreover, the only explanation for their being *a priori* is that they are legitimated by the very meanings of the logical operators involved. Thus they (that is, their sentential renderings)[10] are also analytic. Hence the boxes should really look like this:

---

[9] Cf. Graham Priest, 'Two Dogmas of Quineanism', *Philosophical Quarterly*, 29, 1979, pp. 289–301.

[10] Ideally one would wish to treat inferences on a par with statements, and apply the distinctions in play to inferences as well. But the weight of convention limits discussion to the status of statements, or sentences, thereby excluding transitions among sentences.

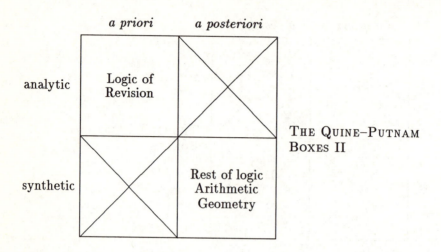

THE QUINE–PUTNAM
BOXES II

Yet another variation has been proposed for the status of logic. In the early 1970s, Hintikka suggested that some logical truths were 'more synthetic' than others, because of the constructions involved in their proofs. Propositional logic may well be analytic. But in first-order logic existential eliminations, or moves involving *ecthesis*, were responsible for varying degrees of syntheticity. The degree of syntheticity of a first-order theorem was a reflection of how many (types of) individuals one had to think about in their relation to each other in the course of proving it.[11] Presumably even pure geometry, on this reckoning, counts as synthetic. Indeed, the feature of geometric reasoning that Kant took as definitive of the synthetic status of geometric truths—the 'construction' of 'concepts', or of what might also be called arbitrary objects, such as perpendiculars or parallels—is here being diagnosed by Hintikka as pervading logical reasoning in varying degrees quite generally.

---

[11] See *Logic, Language Games and Information*, Oxford University Press 1973. For Hintikka, the proofs in question were tree proofs, really like Beth tableaux. A tree proof of Q from $P_1, \ldots, P_n$ is a branching structure of sentences rooted in $P_1, \ldots, P_n, \neg Q$. It is closed just in case every branch contains a contradiction. As branches grow, in accordance with the rules of permissible branchings, they preserve satisfiability. Hence a closed tree for $P_1, \ldots, P_n, \neg Q$ shows that these are not jointly satisfiable; hence that $P_1, \ldots, P_n$ logically imply Q. In the construction of a closed tree one instantiates existential quantifiers with new 'witnesses'. Every such witness is then in the scope of every universal quantifier. By pursuing relevant facts about the witnesses one eventually obtains a contradiction on every branch.

	a priori	*a posteriori*
analytic	Some logic	
synthetic	Rest of logic Arithmetic (?) Pure geometry	Applied geometry

HINTIKKA'S BOXES

The last variation that deserves mention is Martin-Löf's suggestion, venturing even further than Hintikka's, that *all* of logic is synthetic, since all proofs are constructions, and we can only know that a sentence is logically true by constructing a proof of it.[12] In doing so, it is not the proof-token that is important, but rather the abstract proof-type of which it is a token. The process of construction is to be understood as *a priori*.[13] Note that the constructivity supposedly giving rise to syntheticity is at the level of whole proofs, not just at the level of parametric instantiations for existential quantifier eliminations (that is, 'constructions' of 'arbitrary objects') within those proofs.

---

[12]See his paper 'Analytic and synthetic judgements in type theory', in P. Parrini (ed.), *Kant and Contemporary Epistemology*, Kluwer, 1994, pp. 87–99.

[13]Some care is needed in representing Martin-Löf's view in this way. Although he makes it clear that every synthetic judgement is grounded on an analytic judgement, the latter have a more liberal constitution, or syntax, than the former. An ordinary sentence A in the language of arithmetic, say, when asserted, becomes the judgement

   A is true

which, on Martin-Löf's account, is the existential judgement in type theory

   proof(A) exists

to the effect that there is a proof of A. The latter, being existential, is synthetic.

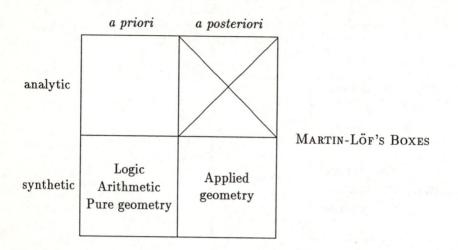

MARTIN-LÖF'S BOXES

Against the background of such a variety of competing classifications of logic, arithmetic and geometry based on the two distinctions, and of Quine's attack on the distinctions themselves, it might seem futile

(1) to invoke or rely upon the distinctions, and
(2) to offer a classification of logical and mathematical knowledge using them.

This is nevertheless what we propose to do.

9.3   The impact of Gödel's first incompleteness theorem

Before elaborating on this position, however, it is appropriate to comment at this stage on the received view that, in the light of Gödel's first incompleteness theorem, one should be drawn away from the belief that at least some arithmetical truths are analytic, and towards the belief that they are all, albeit still *a priori*, nevertheless synthetic. There is compelling reason to hold, to the contrary, that a significant part of arithmetical truth is analytic, even if at least some part of it (namely, the rest of it) has to be regarded as synthetic. Good candidates for syntheticity would be those sentences that have been shown to be independent of Peano–Dedekind arithmetic. These truths could be the independent Gödel sentences constructed for any given formal system via the coding of arithmetical syntax; or they could be the more 'natural' independent claims such as the Ramsey-type combinatorial statements formulated by Paris, Harrington and Friedman.[14]

On the received view, the incompleteness phenomena allegedly show that logic alone (thought of as a system of finitary, formal deduction) is not enough to get one from the second-order Peano–Dedekind axioms (supposed by the analyticity theorist to be exhaustive of the content of the arithmetical notions involved) to all the truths of arithmetic. But it would be a mistake to conclude from this that all true statements of arithmetic depend, for their truth, on non-logical, non-analytic 'facts of the matter' as to how the members of the totality of natural numbers are disposed to one another in the familiar arithmetical relationships of addition and multiplication. The right view, one could contend, is that there are indeed 'facts of the matter', but some of these are of a purely logical kind, constituted by proofs that do no more than exploit the meanings of expressions involved in their conclusions. The states of affairs in question involve objects, but only eternal logical objects, whose existence is necessary. Here we are opposing that reading of Kant (carried to an extreme by Martin-Löf) according to which the need for a construction of (proofs or) concepts is enough to make a judgement synthetic. The view on offer here is that, provided such construction can be accomplished on the basis of a mastery of the language alone, then the judgement in question qualifies as analytic.

We should therefore avoid a misguided rush to the supposed syntheticity of (all of) arithmetic.[15] We have axioms (be these first- or second-order) that are justifiable by analytic reflection on the content of the arithmetical notions. But what the incompleteness theorem tells us is that we should not, as analyticity theorists or logicists, expect (by means of finitary rules of inference) to wring from these axioms even so much as the full set of first-order truths about the natural numbers. There is a tension between deductive power of the logic and the expressive power of the language involved. At first order, we have an axiomatizable logic; but only because we have limited the expressive power of the language. Indeed, this limitation is enough to secure the compactness of logical consequence. (By 'axiomatizable' here one means that the set of logical truths is recursively enumerable.) Similarly, at second-order the classical logician, with a much more expressively

---

[14]Cf. J. Paris and L. Harrington, 'A Mathematical Incompleteness in Peano Arithmetic', in J. Barwise (ed.), *Handbook of Mathematical Logic*, Amsterdam, North-Holland, 1977, pp. 1133–42.

[15]This word of caution is called for even when one is not assuming, with the Gödelian or classicist, that arithmetical truth is bivalent.

powerful language—a language capable of specifiying categorically what the structure of the natural numbers is, and therefore suffering from the non-compactness of its logical consequence relation—has to resign himself to the non-axiomatizability even of the logical truths of the language.[16] These considerations, however, show that Gödel's incompleteness theorem does not yet deal a fatal blow to the logicist and the analyticity theorist as far as arithmetical truths are concerned. For they can still maintain that the truth of statements of arithmetic in an extensive and important fragment is logically immanent in the content of the (second-order) Peano–Dedekind axioms; and the non-axiomatizability of classical second-order logic is only a limitation on our epistemic access to those logical validities. If, however, the analyticity theorist is an intuitionist, there will be no 'incompleteness' at second order that needs to be accommodated in these realist terms. One will not countenance any supposed second-order logical 'truths' that transcend one's means of proving them.

Secondly, even if we restrict ourselves to first-order logic (hence also to the first-order language of arithmetic), the analyticity theorist can rescue a significant part of arithmetic as analytic. For note that the first-order arithmetic of successor and addition is not only complete, but also decidable.[17] So too is the first-order arithmetic of successor and multiplication.[18] Why not, on the original terms of the debate joined, maintain that at least this much need not be regarded as synthetic? Why not reserve syntheticity just for that portion of arithmetic truth that lies beyond the reach of any decision procedure, even if it does not escape the deductive net, when multiplication and addition interact? For the classicist, moreover, that part of (complete) $Th(N)$ that escapes some favoured deductive net, such as Peano–Dedekind arithmetic, could be synthetic as well.

There are indeed further variations on this line of accommodation, if

---

[16] For an exposition of these results, see my *Natural Logic*. See also S. Shapiro, *Foundations without Foundationalism: A Case for Second-order Logic*, Clarendon Press, Oxford, 1991.

[17] M. Presburger, 'Über die Vollständigkeit eines gewissen Systems der Arithmetik ganzer Zahlen, in welchem die Addition als einzige Operation hervortritt', *Comptes-rendus du I Congrès des Mathématiciens des Pays Slaves*, Warsaw 1930, pp. 92–101, 395. Note that we are taking decidability and completeness of a theory as *jointly sufficient* for the view that theoremhood in that theory is analytic. But neither completeness nor decidability is *necessary* by way of justification for such a view.

[18] T. Skolem, 'Über einige Satzfunktionen in der Arithmetik', *Skrifter utgitt av Det Norske Videnskaps-Akademi i Oslo, I. Matematisk-naturvidenskapelig klass 1930*, no. 7, 28 pp. I am grateful to Alex Oliver for drawing this reference to my attention.

we are accepting the restriction to first-order logical analysis and axiomatization. The analyticity theorist might be prepared to back off just to the language of zero and successor (and perhaps also the predicate $N(x)$, for 'x is a natural number'), and call all the truths in that fragment analytic, leaving the others, that involve either addition or multiplication or both, to the syntheticity theorist. Or, alternatively, why not restrict in some way the logical complexity of the statements themselves, maintaining, say, that all singular statements of arithmetic are analytic, while those involving quantification over all natural numbers might be conceded as synthetic? Or that statements with bounded quantifiers are analytic?

Greater sophistication in the division of arithmetic spoils (given the restrictive, first-order perspective) between the analyticity theorist and the syntheticity theorist could well lead to peaceful coexistence between them. Since the second-order induction principle can be justified as analytic (by being derived, logically, from rules that offer genuine analyses of the arithmetical notions involved), there is no need for the analyticity theorist to give up her claim too readily to a considerable part of quantified arithmetic truth. We can certainly claim the first-order closure of the Peano–Dedekind axioms as analytic; and, if denied appeal to second-order notions, leave the rest of first-order arithmetic (shown, by Gödel's incompleteness theorem, to be non-trivial) to the syntheticity theorist.

This is the thrust also of the arguments put forward by Isaacson.[19] This proposal means that there is no straightforward division of spoils along lines of logical complexity. For Gödel's unprovable sentence is Π_1—that is, a universal quantification of a primitive recursive matrix. And we know also from Matijasevič's theorem that this matrix could be chosen to be a polynomial.[20] Moreover, Friedman's recent (unpublished) independence results concern even simpler Π_1 sentences, and indeed show them to be independent of extraordinarily strong systems of set theory. So there are relatively simple sentences that could defy classification as analytic. On the other hand, arbitrarily complex ones are analytic, or at least could be maintained to be so by the analyticity theorist—for there are theorems of Peano–Dedekind arithmetic of arbitrary (unbounded) quantificational complexity.

There is actually a principled reason why the epistemic analyticity theorist should claim analyticity for first-order Peano–Dedekind arithmetic, but

---

[19] Cf. 'Some considerations on arithmetical truth and the ω-rule', in *Logic Colloquium '85*, edited by the Paris Logic Group, Elsevier Science Publishers B.V. (North-Holland), 1987, pp. 147–69.

[20] I owe this observation to Matt Foreman.

concede syntheticity to, say, any true Gödel sentence that is unprovable in that system. Such a sentence has the form $\forall n G(n)$. We can prove (in the metatheory) that $\vdash G(0), \vdash G(s0), \vdash G(ss0), \ldots$ Thus, so we wish to conclude, each of these instances is *true*; whence, the universal quantification $\forall n G(n)$ is true. With each numerical instance, we make a move from provability (in the system we start with) to truth; and then infer the truth of the unprovable sentence by mathematical induction in the metatheory. We can formalize this reasoning by extending the vocabulary of the original theory so as to include a primitive truth-predicate. This yields an extended system, for it allows one to form new instances, in the extended language, of the axiom scheme of mathematical induction. So the reasoning for the truth of the formerly unprovable Gödel sentence can now go through in the extended system. But this means that the proof of the Gödel sentence thereby obtained is 'theoretically impredicative': its proof has to contain occurrences of items of non-logical vocabulary (namely, the truth-predicate in question) that are not involved in the sentence itself. Thus, grasp of the meaning of the sentence itself is not sufficient for one to be warranted in asserting it; that is, the sentence is not epistemically analytic, even though its truth has been established *a priori*.[21]

Alternatively, one might distinguish between *direct* and *indirect* analyticity—or even make analyticity stratified by levels, with the directly analytic sentences being analytic at level 0, and with the indirectly analytic sentences generated inductively at each level in a straightforward way. This would parallel the treatment to be given, in the next chapter, of cognitive significance. A *directly* analytic sentence would be one that could be proved using only rules governing expressions occurring within the sentence. An *indirectly* analytic sentence would be one that could be proved *a priori*, and indeed by means of a proof all of whose steps involve only meaning-determining rules; but not by means only of rules governing only such expressions as occur within the sentence itself. Besides the independent Gödel sentences in arithmetic (which involve recourse to a truth-predicate not occurring in the sentence), there are perhaps simpler examples.[22] Take the sentence 'There are at least two objects'. On our account (to be developed below), this sentence is analytic, because it follows from the existence of 0 and of 1. Each of these can be proved to exist, and to be distinct. The proof (in our 'constructive logicist' arithmetic) involves the rules for 0 and the successor

---

[21] I have benefited from discussion with Stewart Shapiro here.
[22] I owe these to Stewart Shapiro.

function $s(\ )$. But these expressions do not occur in the sentence 'There are at least two objects'. Nor, for familiar reasons, can there be any proof of that sentence using only the rules that govern expressions occurring within it.

To the objection that one would not be able to tell, by looking at a sentence, whether it was analytic or not (since the Peano–Dedekind theory is undecidable), the reply would be that that was indeed an interesting fact about analyticity; and why should one maintain analytic truth should be decidable? (After all, even first-order logical truth, like first-order consequence from the Peano–Dedekind axioms, is undecidable.) Decidability is a red herring, as far as analyticity is concerned. One's grasp of the meaning alone of a sentence ϕ could suffice for one's being warranted in asserting ϕ (namely, whenever one was possessed of a proof of ϕ that used only rules for expressions occurring in ϕ) *without* one's being able to apply an effective method capable of yielding an answer in general to the question whether any given sentence's meaning (and in particular, that of ϕ) was indeed such that grasp of it would so suffice.

9.4 An alternative view

Here are three conventionally alleged features of logic and mathematics, especially arithmetic:

(A) The logical validity of an argument depends only on the meanings of the logical expressions involved, and the pattern of occurrences of these and of the non-logical expressions.

(B) Logic should not, and does not, carry any existential commitments. That is, logic should be neutral not only as to how the world might be, but also as to what it might contain. Logic should not commit one to the existence of any particular thing; nor should it commit one to there being things of any particular kind.[23]

(C) The truth of mathematical axioms and the validity of mathematical reasoning depends only on features of the mathematical structures that we

---

[23] As Alex Oliver has pointed out, second-order logic is committed to the existence of the empty set (or concept). Hence its unpopularity as logic on this conventional view, set out here as (A), (B) and (C).

intend to describe. Mathematical expressions have the meanings that they do solely in virtue of their roles in describing these structures. They have no other source of meaning; hence the truth of mathematical axioms and the validity of mathematical reasoning does not arise from the meanings of mathematical expressions. One might say here: the meanings of mathematical expressions arise solely from their representational power concerning these structures. (It is not the other way round, which would be to have the structures that are represented, and the expressions' power to represent them, arise from the meanings of mathematical expressions, where these meanings had an independent source.)

The position we hold, by contrast, is that we should accept (A), when properly construed; but, on compelling grounds, reject (B) and reject (C). In brief, the position we hold is as follows:

(A*) The logical validity of an argument depends only on the meanings of the logical expressions involved, and the pattern of occurrences of these and of the non-logical expressions. Similarly, the mathematical validity of an argument depends only on the meanings of the logico-mathematical expressions involved, and the pattern of occurrences of these and of the non-logico-mathematical expressions. Moreover, one should not be too conventional when classifying an expression as logical or as mathematical. Closer analysis may reveal that expressions usually thought of as mathematical are in fact logical.[24] In brief: erstwhile 'mathematical' expressions for which we can furnish suitable introduction and elimination rules will thereby have

---

[24]The problem of demarcating the logical constants is well known. Whether or not there is a principled way of doing so, most modern writers take the sentential connectives (negation, conjunction, disjunction and the conditional) and the universal and existential quantifiers as logical; and some also go so far as to include the identity predicate as a logical expression. It then follows from their choice of a class of logical expressions that all other 'constant' expressions in the formulation of a mathematical theory are mathematical expressions. The view favoured here is that an expression counts as logical by virtue of being governed by a harmoniously balanced pair of introduction and elimination rules. Those that are not so governed, or that are governed by yet further rules not derivable from such an harmoniously balanced pair, would count as non-logical (or, in a mathematical theory, as mathematical). This characterization has as a consequence that expressions conventionally regarded as mathematical may turn out to be logical. This will be the case when a formerly 'mathematical' expression is discovered to be governed (precisely) by some harmoniously balanced pair of introduction and elimination rules. Moreover, it opens the way for an account of a significant part of that mathematical theory as analytic rather than synthetic.

been revealed as logical.[25]

(B*) Logic can, should and does carry existential commitment, both to particular things and to particular kinds of thing. These are what one might call the necessary existents and the indispensable categories for thought about the world.[26]

(C*) The truth of mathematical axioms and the validity of mathematical reasoning depends not only on features of the mathematical structure(s) that we intend to describe, but also on the meanings of the mathematical expressions involved. Mathematical expressions have the meanings that they do not just in virtue of their roles in describing abstract mathematical structures (note the contrast here with (A) above), but also by virtue of the way they organize, integrate and extend our thought about the external world. They therefore have another important source of meaning, namely, the conceptual constraints[27] that they provide on our spatial, temporal and categorical thinking, constraints that make various mathematical operations (such as counting) 'make contact' with the world as we conceive it to be. The 'representational' powers of mathematical expressions, whereby they are taken to describe abstract structures, indeed arise from these conceptual constraints, not the other way round.

9.5   The wider logic of number

An important conceptual constraint in the case of the natural numbers is that for each natural number n, we should be able to derive as an analytic principle the corresponding instance of our earlier Schema C:

---

[25]This is the case, for example, in unpublished work by the author on a natural foundation for projective geometry. It turns out that the incidence operators can be furnished with harmoniously balanced introduction and elimination rules, thereby rendering projective geometry *analytic*.

[26]In 'The Necessary Existence of Numbers', *Noûs*, forthcoming, I argue that the natural numbers are necessary existents, and that fundamental arithmetical principles remain analytic despite the fact that, in an appropriately free logic, they commit us to the existence of numbers.

[27]We saw in Chapter 4 how important such constraints are for an effective critique of Kripkean scepticism. The constraint expressed by our Schema C will feature again in the next section.

there are n F's

   if and only if

the number of F's $= \underline{n}$.

To refresh the reader's memory: the left-hand side can be expanded as a quantified sentence in which there is no occurrence of n as a singular term. In the right-hand side, the phrase 'the number of...' is regimented as a variable binding term-forming operator '$\#x(\ldots x \ldots)$', so that 'the number of F's' is formalized as the singular term '$\#xF(x)$'. $\underline{n}$ is the numeral for the natural number n; that is, '$s(\ldots s(0)\ldots)$', in which the successor function $s(\ )$ enjoys exactly n occurrences.

The requirement that Schema C be fulfilled is unique to the theory of constructive logicism developed in *AR&L*. Moreover, it is weaker than Hume's Principle, on which Wright bases his Fregean logicism.[28] Humes's Principle is the stronger second-order schematic claim that

$$\#xF(x) = \#xG(x)$$
   if and only if
   there is a 1–1 correspondence between the F's and the G's,

regardless of the numerosity of F (and of G). Thus Hume's Principle commits one to the existence of unconstrainedly infinite numbers. Schema C, by contrast, commits one, constructively, to the existence only of *finite* numbers. Wright uses Hume's Principle as an axiomatic starting-point. By contrast, we lay down only very simple analytic principles governing 0, $s(\ )$ and $N(\ )$, and from these principles we *derive* not only the Peano–Dedekind axioms but also every instance of Schema C. Thus on our account Schema C features in an adequacy condition on a theory of number, in a manner exactly analogous to that in which Tarski's Schema (T) features in his adequacy condition on a theory of truth.[29]

---

[28] Cf. *Frege's Conception of Numbers as Objects*, Aberdeen University Press, 1983.

[29] That adequacy condition, the reader will recall, is that in the metalinguistic truth theory one should be able to derive every instance of Schema (T):

   S is true if and only if p

where an instance is obtained by replacing 'S' by a metalinguistic designation of some sentence of the object-language, and replacing 'p' by a metalinguistic translation of the object-language sentence designated by 'S'. See Tarski, 'The Concept of Truth in Formalized Languages', in *Logic, Semantics, Metamathematics*, Clarendon Press, Oxford, 1956; at pp. 187–8.

The outcome of theses (A*), (B*) and (C*) can be illustrated with a new set of boxes (see below) for the classification of the important truths in which we are interested. The major addition to the diagram will be that of a new explicit distinction: the distinction between sentences (theories) that have no existential commitments, and those that do have existential commitments. We recognize an important new category of truths: analytic truths with existential commitments. We are prepared to say that it is part of the very meaning of certain expressions (say, term-forming operators) that there must exist referents for the terms constructed by means of them.

9.6 Necessary existents

These referents are always abstract, necessary existents. They are abstract because they are not located in the spatio-temporal order and they are causally inert.[30] They are necessary because they must be in any world that admits of conceptualization and of thought about it (or at least about states of affairs within it). That is to say, they must be in any world. This is not to say that thinkers in these worlds automatically incur commitment to (better: attain recognition of) the existence of these necessary existents. Rather, what is being said is that thinkers in these worlds would have to

---

[30] In 'Der Gedanke', *Beiträge zur Philosophie des deutschen Idealismus*, 1918, Frege sought to invest abstract thoughts with causal powers. According to him, these abstract objects could indirectly influence the motions of masses because of things we thinkers are sometimes moved to do in grasping them and holding them to be true. The view advocated here, however, is opposed to Frege on this point. We would not seek in Frege's manner to invest any abstract objects with causal powers, even if there were some unproblematic sense in which our minds grasped, or 'made contact' with them.

'Der Gedanke' is translated by P. T. Geach and R. H. Stoothoff as 'Thoughts' in *Logical Investigations*, ed. by P. T. Geach, Blackwell, Oxford, 1977, pp. 1–30. The crucial passage is at pp. 28–9. But beware of the mistranslation on p. 29, repeating the earlier mistake of A. M. and Marcelle Quinton's translation in *Mind*, 65, 1956, pp. 289–311, at p. 310. The Quintons' translation reads 'And so thought can have an indirect influence on the motion of masses.' The Geach–Stoothoff translation reads 'And so thought may indirectly influence the motion of masses.' Both these translations are in error. They proceed as though the German subject term were *das Denken*, standing for the act or process of thinking, rather than the plural term in Frege's text—*Gedanken*—which is a grammatical substantive that Frege clearly intended to be taken as standing for thoughts as abstract entities. The mistranslated sentence (at p. 77 of the original) is 'Und so können Gedanken auf Massenbewegungen mittelbar Einfluß haben.' The opening line of the paragraph in which this mistranslation occurs is 'Wie wirkt ein Gedanke?' This was a question not after the causal powers of an episode of thinking, or of the *having of* thoughts, but rather after the causal powers of an abstract object that is there to be grasped by thinkers.

allow such consistent extension of their conceptual repertoires and systems
of belief as would suffice to secure the commitments-through-thought-and-
language in question.

Examples would be the empty set and the number zero. In Carnapian
spirit, one might say that adopting the language in which the set-term form-
ing operator $\{x|\Phi(x)\}$ ('the set of all Φ's') or the number-term forming
operator $\#x\Phi(x)$ ('the number of Φ's') occur already involves commitment,
on grounds of their meaning alone, to the existence of referents for certain of
these terms. As soon as such a language were adopted, particular abstract
objects would be taken (by the speakers and thinkers) to exist. It is even
tempting to say that these objects indeed must have already existed, even
before any language of the appropriate kind might have been adopted; and
that they would exist even if no language of the appropriate kind were ever
in fact adopted. This is because of the abiding possibility that such a language be adopted. Thus the abstract objects already exist, and necessarily,
on grounds of meaning alone; albeit meaning that had not as yet been borne
by sentences-in-use.

On a Carnapian view numbers would be necessary existents only in the
qualified sense of 'having to be acknowledged within the linguistic framework
adopted'.[31] We should now go one further than that. The empty set and the
number zero exist necessarily. They exist in every possible world, whether
or not the world in question contains beings possessed of an appropriate
linguistic framework that gives intellectual access to the existents in question.
A cosmos that started (as perhaps ours did) with a big bang, and then
bubbled with inorganic soups that never gave rise to intelligent creatures
able to communicate and think, would nevertheless contain the number zero.
In such a world, 0 would happen to be the number of intelligent creatures.
It would also, as in every other world, be the number of things not identical
to themselves.

Here, then, are the new boxes promised:

ANTI-REALISM'S BOXES

---

[31]Cf. 'Empiricism, Semantics and Ontology', *Revue Internationale de Philosophie*, 4,
1950.

	a priori	*a posteriori*	
Without existential commitment	Some logic, inc. parts of logic of numbers and logic of sets		analytic
Existential commitment to *logically* nec$^{\underline{y}}$ objects	Rest of logic, inc. Dedekind arithmetic; Theory of hereditarily finite pure sets		analytic
Existential commitment to *metaphysically* nec$^{\underline{y}}$ objects	Projective geometry		analytic
Existential commitment to *metaphysically contingent* objects	Topology of physical space; large cardinals?	Physical metric geometry	synthetic

Some notes of explanation for this diagram:

1. An example of a principle that would belong to what we have called the 'logic of numbers' is that half of the Frege axiom to the effect that the number of F's is identical to the number of G's *only if* there are exactly as many F's as there are G's.[32]

2. An example of a principle that would belong to what we have called the 'logic of sets' is that half of Church's conversion schema to the effect that if t is a member of the set of all F's, then $F(t)$. The logic of sets is generated by the introduction and elimination rules for the set term-forming operator $\{x \mid \ldots x \ldots\}$.[33]

3. What we have called 'Dedekind arithmetic' consists of the (deductive closure of) the basic axioms governing 0, $s(\ )$ and $N(\ )$, including mathematical induction.

---

[32] See *AR&L*, ch. 25, for a full account of what is here called the logic of numbers.
[33] See *Natural Logic*, ch. 7, for a full account of what is here called the logic of sets.

4. The constructive logicist is reluctant to regard ω (the set of all finite ordinals) as a necessary existent. Thus he cannot help himself, via the power set axiom, to the existence of any sets other than the hereditarily finite pure sets. A classically-minded analyticity theorist, however, could do so.

5. By 'pure' set one means here a set that does not involve any non-logical objects. (Remember that on our account the natural numbers are logical objects.)

6. We have distinguished between 'metaphysically necessary' and 'logically necessary' existents, though not much rests on this. The logically necessary existents would be those to which commitment is incurred by discourse obeying conceptual controls linking it with ordinary discourse about (possibly only contingent) ordinary things. We have in mind here statements such as '0 is the number of F's' and '$\emptyset$ is the set of all F's', where F is any predicate that can be shown to be empty. F may express an ordinary, contingently possessed property, such as being red or occupying a spherical region; or it may express an impossible property, such as non-self-identity. The point is that even with F of the former type, one can incur commitment to the existence of 0 as the number of F's; and with F of the latter type, one appreciates that this commitment is commitment to a necessary existent. Because it is not at this stage clear that spatial points would play the same kind of role here as natural numbers, we have taken them to be only metaphysically necessary existents, not logically necessary ones. Commitment to numbers is immanent in any conceptual scheme allowing for the discrimination of particulars; whereas it is not at all clear that one would be committed to, say, points in three-dimensional space by any conceptual scheme adequate to any range of possible experience whatsoever. We are assuming that space has to have at least two dimensions for empirical knowledge or experience as of an external world to be possible; and this will yield spatial points (of projective incidence of lines) as metaphysically necessary. But for them to be logically necessary, one would have to be forced to acknowledge them within any discourse about particulars whatever. This, however, does not seem plausible; for the discourse of pure arithmetic in an otherwise empty, non-spatial world (apart, perhaps, from non-embodied thinkers) would provide a counter-example. Here, 0 is the number of physical, non-

thinking things; 1 is the number of things identical to 0; ... and so on. There is individuation, there are relations among individuals, and we can quantify over them; but there is no need for spatial points.

9.7 The dogma of existence

One of the main obstacles in the past to clear and confident assignment of certain logico-mathematical truths to 'boxes' was the unsettling effect of the existential commitments they appeared to carry. The theory of the analytic and the synthetic was too crude to allow for analytic truths carrying existential commitment. It had always been thought, and mistakenly so, that

having existential commitments entails syntheticity.[34]

Let us call this the *dogma of existence*; it deserves to be regarded as the fourth dogma of empiricism, alongside the other three well-known dogmas:

1. that there is a distinction between analytic and synthetic;

2. that natural science can be reduced to a phenomenological basis; and

3. that there is a distinction between scheme and content.

But the fourth dogma should be challenged, along with the second and third. Having existential commitments does not entail syntheticity. It depends entirely on what sort of thing one is committing oneself to. If, by the use of certain expressions in one's language, one commits oneself to (better: accommodates oneself to, or acknowledges) the existence of certain entities that exist necessarily anyway, one is not going beyond the meanings of the expressions involved if one says, by means of those expressions, that those entities exist. Indeed, the wrong meanings would have been attached to these expressions, or their meanings would be defective, if those meanings failed to provide a route to referents that necessarily existed! If we know that the entity e exists necessarily,[35] and that it is to be the function of an

---

[34] Just as it had long been thought that all metaphysical necessities were *a priori*, until Kripke pointed out such counter-examples as 'Water is H_2O'. See his *Naming and Necessity*, Harvard University Press, Cambridge, Mass., 1980, at p. 128.

[35] Not just: 'If we know that, if the entity e exists at all then it exists necessarily...'; for one wishes to distinguish between the case of God and the case of the number zero.

expression 'E' to pick out e, then the statement 'E exists' will be true solely in virtue of its meaning—that is, it will be analytic.[36]

Our new account of the analytic-synthetic distinction keeps logic squarely within the analytic *a priori*. The principles of logic depend, for their correctness, on meanings alone. The meanings in question are those of the logical words involved in those principles. We are maintaining that we have to be able to justify our choice of logic. This means that we have to show how the basic logical principles that generate the rest arise from the very meanings of the logical words occurring in them. This in turn obliges us to examine carefully what counts as a licit source of such meanings. It cannot be the whole usage of the language (even on the assumption that no one makes what others would regard as performance errors), on pain of being forced to abandon the justificatory task. In the next chapter we seek to isolate the licit sources of logical meanings, and answer the question as to which logical system is justified by what flows from them. Even if the recalcitrant realist/classicist refuses to go along with every step of the argument we shall be advancing, we shall at least have presented a case for a logic that is to be commended on the grounds both of its internal simplicity and of the overall simplicity of the scheme that provides its philosophical justification.

---

[36] In 'The Necessary Existence of Numbers', loc. cit., this claim is defended against the view, held by Field, that mathematical objects enjoy at best contingent existence, if indeed they can exist at all. See Field's paper 'The Conceptual Contingency of Mathematical Objects', *Mind*, 102, 1993, pp. 285–99.

Chapter 10

Finding the right logic

10.1 On rational advocacy of reform

In *The Logical Basis of Metaphysics*,[1] Dummett writes of a 'pernicious' tendency in recent years to insist that the metalanguage should obey the same logic as the object language. He holds that so to insist makes it impossible to persuade the classical logician and realist that one's reformist position is correct. The dispute could not be rationally resolved, Dummett thinks, unless it were conducted in some sort of neutral medium, or on neutral territory. His suggestion takes the form of an approving observation: semantic theories such as those of Kripke and Beth for an intuitionistic object language can be developed in both intuitionistic and classical metalanguages. Dummett seems to think that this is some kind of virtue on the part of these semantic theories. But it is difficult to see how this amounts to the sought neutrality. After all, if the theory can be developed intuitionistically then it can be developed classically also. This follows from the simple fact that the intuitionistic deducibility relation is a sub-relation of the classical one. So if the insistence is met—if, that is, the metalanguage is intuitionistic—then the semantic theory developed within it is surely available to the would-be classicist.

The point Dummett is insisting on is a double-edged sword. For some time one of the classicist's favourite criticisms of the intuitionist was that the completeness theorem for intuitionistic first-order logic had only a classical proof in the metalanguage. This situation was an embarrassment for the intuitionist. His dialectical position was weakened against the classicist. For

---

[1] Harvard University Press, 1991; at pp. 54–5.

he was urging logical reform, and putting forward a semantical account of the meanings of the logical operators. Yet (at that time) he had to resort to classical logic to show that that semantical account 'picked out' intuitionistic logic as the correct logic for the object language. This was not just theft over honest toil, but theft of the dentures to bite the hand that fed one! Fortunately the situation was remedied by Veldman and de Swart's discoveries of intuitionistic completeness proofs for intuitionistic first-order logic.[2] Now the intuitionist need not be embarrassed any more by the erstwhile objection from the classicist. He had attained what, it was complained, he needed: an account that was philosophically stable, in the sense that the justification given for one's choice of logic did not have to exploit logical resources (in the metalanguage) that lay outside the chosen system. Having recovered his composure on this score, the intuitionist then tried to turn it to fuller advantage. He did so by insisting that disputed logical principles should not be justified, by the classicist, in any question-begging way. That is, it would be unacceptable to attempt to justify the law of excluded middle, for example, by appeal to that very principle in the metalanguage, or to any of its equivalents.

Dummett now complains, in magnanimous accommodation of the classicist, that the classicist would be 'bewildered' by this insistence, and simply not understand the basis on which the intuitionist who so insists would be rejecting the justification offered of the disputed principle. Is Dummett here suggesting that pointing out a *petitio principii* is no longer a good move in this argumentative game? If Dummett is so suggesting, why is it not a good move?

Suppose that there really is only one correct logic, and that it is a proper sub-logic of classical logic. Such, after all, is the reformist's contention. So let us just suppose, for the sake of argument about how one might argue, that the reformist is right. Then it would be a virtue of the correct logic (indeed, part of its being the correct logic) that it could be used in the metalanguage to develop the semantics of the object language, all the way up to and including a completeness theorem for the logic in question. It would also be the case that the arguments offered by the classical logician in support of the disputed (and, by supposition, incorrect) classical principles would be defective. For, if they were not defective, then those disputed principles

---

[2]Cf. W. Feldman, 'An Intuitionistic Completeness Theorem for Intuitionistic Predicate Logic', *Journal of Symbolic Logic*, 41, 1976, pp. 159–66; and H. de Swart, 'Another Intuitionistic Completeness Proof', *ibid.*, 41, 1976, pp. 644–62. See also de Swart, 'An Intuitionistically Plausible Interpretation of Intuitionistic Logic', *ibid.*, 42, 1977, pp. 564–78.

would be justified, contrary to our assumption above. Now there are only two ways in which an argument intended to establish a conclusion can be defective. One way is to invoke a false or unjustified premiss. The other way is to apply an unacceptable rule of inference, or to apply an acceptable one incorrectly. Surely, now, a glaring way in which the classicist might give a defective argument for his disputed principles (which, remember, we are assuming to be incorrect and unjustifiable) would be to use those very principles in the course of his argument. Simply pointing out to him, therefore, that he is doing so (as indeed, he would have to, in order to 'reach' his conclusion at all) is perfectly in order as far as the reformist is concerned.

What the reformist has to watch out for (relaxing for a moment our assumption that his logic is indeed the correct logic) is any argument advanced by the classicist that invoked only principles that the reformist himself would accept, and that issued in a conclusion to the effect that some principle that the reformist disputes was, after all, sound. It is in order to protect himself against this 'possibility' that the reformist is, understandably, eager to point out, if he can, the question-begging character of any attempt by the classicist to justify the disputed logical principles. There is nothing 'pernicious' at all in this tendency. If it's classical turtles all the way down, there is nothing wrong at all in pointing this out to the classicist. It should make him go away and think harder about the nature of the problem.

The source of the dialectical problem here is the asymmetry involved: the reformist's logic is a proper sub-logic of classical logic, not the other way round. If the reformist takes up the gauntlet to provide a philosophically stable account of his logic, then by the same token the classicist may only seek to persuade him of the soundness of the disputed classical principles by providing an argument based somehow only on principles which the reformist can accept. If the latter turns out to be impossible (as it would be if the reformist were right!), then so much the worse for polite attempts to accommodate the classical disputant. There just will not be any neutral point from which to adjudicate the dispute. And why not simply accept that? We are after all engaged in a dispute about the most fundamental principles governing thought itself. It would be a logical miracle if, should the right logic be a sub-logic of classical logic, the incorrectness of attempts to justify the incorrect classical principles could consist in anything other than their invoking the incorrect principles themselves. Once the classicist's bewilderment at having this pointed out to him has passed, he may fall to reflecting on the consequences.

The anti-realist has, then, an agenda for logical reform. In this chapter we lay the logical foundations for much of what is to follow. We develop a new way of doing logic, centred on an epistemically constrained characterization of logical consequence or deducibility. The new logic will be applied in developing our theories of cognitive significance and of constructive falsifiability. We shall set forth epistemological and computational considerations that determine the best way to 'relevantize' a logic. These considerations concern epistemic gain in logical proofs, and algorithmic efficiency in the search for proofs in decidable propositional logics. They determine the system *IR* (intuitionistic relevant logic) as the right system of intuitionistic logic, and the system *CR* (classical relevant logic) as the right system of classical logic. The motivation can be summarized, in the sequent calculus setting, as the requirement that we should be able to prove a Dilution Elimination Theorem in addition to the well-known Cut Elimination Theorem. The motivating considerations determine not only the form of the rules for the logical operators, but also some very general restrictions on their applications in proofs. These restrictions are imposed in order to avoid dilutions.

IR is *epistemically constrained*, then, in two senses of that phrase: it embodies epistemic constraint on truth, and epistemic constraint on logical consequence. Just as importantly, it is *epistemologically adequate*. It suffices for intuitionistic mathematics[3] and for the hypothetico-deductive method in science.[4]

10.2 Systematicity, immediacy, separability and harmony

There are several strands to the justification of intuitionistic logic—or at least, something in the region of intuitionistic logic—as the correct logic. They will emerge and be highlighted as the discussion unfolds below.

The intuitionist inquires after the nature of our grasp of the meanings of logical operators. For the correct choice of a logic is to be justified by appeal to those meanings. Its rules of inference should exactly exploit them. The rules should make the most of those meanings, but no more. Correct

---

[3] Cf. my 'Intuitionistic Mathematics Does Not Need 'Ex Falso Quodlibet'', *Topoi*, 13, 1994, pp. 127–33.

[4] Cf. *AR&L*. The corresponding result for minimal logic had been proved in my paper 'Minimal logic is adequate for Popperian science', *British Journal for Philosophy of Science*, 36, 1985, pp. 325–9.

rules should not involve one's having to 'read into' the operators any illicit ingredients of content whose grasp could not be made manifest in our ability to employ certain (finitely many) basic rules that suffice to generate the rest.

In speaking thus of meanings and/or contents one is not committing oneself to reifying them. It is not so much that they have to be taken as objects, but rather that we have to acknowledge the objectivity of meaning-facts (facts 'about' meaning(s)) and can do so without committing ourselves to there having to be such things as meanings for them to be about. The intuitionist is therefore assuming Meaning Objectivity, without committing herself to any picture involving Meanings as Objects.

Our logical competence involves being able to generate potentially infinitely many valid arguments, and being able to check potentially infinitely many would-be arguments for validity. For familiar reasons such competence on the part of finite creatures must be reducible to, or generable from, a finite stock of basic competences. One could not imagine, for example, that every single valid argument in a logical system should have to be mastered in its own right before one could claim the competence represented by the system. The requirement of systematicity in our system of proof is not simply for epistemological convenience. It reflects the fact that we have to codify our own logical competence finitely and schematically in order to exhibit the very possibility of our understanding what it is upon which validity of argument in general rests. Certainly it would be repugnant to offer a picture of infinitely many valid arguments' validity having to be separately and irreducibly grasped before competence could be conceded to any reasoner. Such a rampant, infinitary holism can be summarily dismissed. This might be called the analytic postulate of anti-realism. Those who think that logic is empirical could opt out of the discussion here. Our empiricism is not pragmatic empiricism; it is analytic empiricism.

There is a very obvious objection to this brief account as it stands. It comes from the moderate holist, who accepts the task of finitary distillation of competence, but who thinks that the finitary distillation found in classical logic is perfectly in order. This classical opponent of intuitionistic logic could complain that a contested rule of inference (such as the rule of double-negation elimination) could simply be taken as one of the (finitely many) key basic rules with respect to which our very competence is to be assessed. She could complain that in acquiring her grasp of the meanings of the logical operators, she had it drummed into her that double-negation elimination was a correct move:

$$\frac{\neg\neg\phi}{\phi}$$

It had community-wide approval, except among some Dutch mathematicians, and some philosophical eccentrics at Oxford. Thus her applications of the rule of double-negation elimination do not reveal her as a logical deviant, appealing to illicit ingredients of meaning for the negation operator. Rather, with the seal of communal approval, and in confirmation of all their confident expectations on her behalf, she eliminates double negations in her own arguments and acquiesces in their elimination by others in theirs.

One could elaborate a long response to this objection, to show why it is misguided.[5] This response can be stated only briefly here. It involves setting aside the contentious rules such as double-negation elimination. The latter is contentious as a basic rule because it involves two occurrences of the logical operator in question. Why should we have to deal with two occurrences simultaneously? (When an intuitionist searches for systematicity, the search is in earnest.) Surely, the intuitionist maintains, whatever disagreement there may be about the very meaning of negation should be able to be brought into the open in the context of differing (schematizable) logical practices with regard to single occurrences of the logical operator concerned? After all, if meaning is compositional, and an operator makes the same systematic contribution to sentence meaning at each of its occurrences therein, surely any difference in the meanings imputed by, say, the classicist and the intuitionist, should make themselves manifest in single occurrences of the operator in question?

The intuitionist will accordingly ask the opposition to agree to look closely at the rule which most crucially determines the meaning of an operator: namely, its introduction rule. This is the rule that spells out the conditions under which one canonically justifies an assertion with a single occurrence of that operator dominant. Thus the canonical justification of a denial (that is, a sentence of the form $\neg\phi$, with the negation operator dominant) consists in a canonical *reductio ad absurdum* of the hypothetical assumption ϕ. The thought is that an assertion of $\neg\phi$ would be justified if and only if the conditions spelled out by the introduction rule were to hold: namely, that the hypothesized assertion of ϕ would be absurd. That serves to pin down the exact meaning of the negation operator. That meaning, combined with the meaning of ϕ (assumed to be antecedently accessible or graspable), yields the total graspable meaning of $\neg\phi$. What goes into a jus-

---

[5] See *AR&L* for details.

tified assertion of $\neg\phi$, uniformly and generally for all sentences ϕ, then, is all that counts in determining the meaning of $\neg$. We say that the introduction rule schematically fixes the meaning of the operator that is dominant in its conclusion. Each introduction rule sums up what goes into a speaker's being justified in making an assertion with its operator dominant.

Now what goes in should be able to come out; and that is precisely what the elimination rules rely on. An elimination rule serves to draw out or explicate the sense already conferred on its operator by its introduction rule. The introduction rule for $\neg$ spells out the conditions that have to be met by anyone seeking to justify the conclusion $\neg\phi$. Correlatively, the elimination rule spells out what the hearer can take the speaker as having committed himself to by any sincere assertion of $\neg\phi$ assumed to be thus justified. The elimination rule is framed by asking oneself the following question:

> Given that my interlocutor has sincerely asserted $\neg\phi$, so that, trusting him as I do, I now have the information that $\neg\phi$ to rely on, what inference may I immediately make, given $\neg\phi$ as a premiss? What move of mine, in reliance on what he has told me, would my interlocutor be forced to acknowledge as immediately justified if he was correct in making his assertion of $\neg\phi$ in the first place?

The answer, of course, is that if the hearer ever finds reason to believe that ϕ, she will *ipso facto* and immediately have reason to believe that the ultimate grounds for such a belief are defective. That is, such putative grounds ought to lead to absurdity ($\perp$), if her interlocutor had got matters right. The situation can be summarized by the so-called reduction procedure for negation. The way this reduction procedure is to be understood is revealed by the following logical narrative.

> The canonical justification Π moves the speaker sincerely to assert $\neg\phi$. The way this happens is as follows. Π consists in a canonical *reductio ad absurdum* of the assumption ϕ:

$$\phi$$
$$\Pi$$
$$\perp$$

> The speaker then takes a step of $\neg$-introduction to conclude $\neg\phi$, with this conclusion now independent of the assumption ϕ:

$$\neg I \; \frac{\begin{array}{c} [\phi] \\ \Pi \\ \bot \end{array}}{\neg \phi}$$

Relying on his assertion, the hearer infers that any 'reason' Σ that she may have, or might be offered, to believe ϕ will be defective. She does this by means of the elimination rule for $\neg$:

$$\neg E \; \frac{\neg \phi \qquad \overset{\Sigma}{\phi}}{\bot}$$

But why precisely, we may ask, is she justified in thinking this? Because, the answer goes, her use of the elimination rule exactly balances his use of the introduction rule. They are in harmony with each other. The fact of harmony is brought out by the following reduction procedure:

$$\neg E \; \frac{\neg I \; \dfrac{\begin{array}{c} [\phi] \\ \Pi \\ \bot \end{array}}{\neg \phi} \qquad \overset{\Sigma}{\phi}}{\bot} \qquad \rightarrow \qquad \frac{\begin{array}{c} \Sigma \\ (\phi) \\ \Pi \end{array}}{\bot}$$

Note that in the proof schema on the left, the elimination step comes immediately after the introduction step. No sooner does an asserter put the finishing touch on an assertion than the hearer can start to unravel its implications. Any conclusion can be used as a premiss. That is how we make deductive progress, especially in mathematics. Conclusions used as premisses are called lemmata. Indeed, many of the statements within a proof taking us from some axioms to a theorem can be regarded as so many lemmata: intermediate stages at which one arrives and from which one may then depart.[6] Just as one buys one's ticket before travelling, and then presents it as proof of entitlement to the ride, so too one pays one's dues with the introduction rule before one (or one's audience) enjoys the inferential benefits

---

[6]Some of them, of course, may rest on assumptions 'for the sake of argument' which are subsequently discharged. But what mathematicians describe as lemmata usually rest on no more than the axioms of the theory within which they are working.

via the elimination rule. The final steps towards, and first steps away from, sentences of our language are all that count for the validity of arguments. For the arguments boil down, ultimately, to properly arranged constellations of such steps. In Aristotle's terminology, proofs are 'perfected' arguments, each of whose steps is immediately compelling on grounds of the first layer of logical form, and meaning.

The first layer of logical form is revealed by observations such as: 'That sentence is a negation', or 'That sentence is a conjunction.' That is, it involves identifying only the dominant logical operator of the sentence in question, closing one's eyes to the exact logico-grammatical make-up of its immediate constituents and treating them schematically instead. Thus the first layer of logical form of the sentence $(A \wedge B) \vee (B \supset \neg C)$ is simply $\phi \vee \psi$, where ϕ and ψ are schematic letters blurring the exact make-up of $(A \wedge B)$ and $(B \supset \neg C)$ respectively. We may therefore speak of a requirement of immediacy on any system of rules of inference that is claimed to provide, or embody the principal results of, a complete meaning analysis for the logical operators.

We now appreciate that what seemed like a rather technical feature of proof theory has a deep philosophical basis. Let us pinpoint and summarize the various principles that have guided the intuitionist's account thus far.

1. Logic is analytic: its rules are to be justified by appeal to the meanings of the logical operators. Indeed, certain of these rules are so basic as to be meaning-constituting; they afford a complete analysis of the meanings of the logical operators. They show what immediate moves in reasoning may be taken as irreducibly justified on grounds of the 'first layer of logical form' and meaning alone. The remaining rules can then be justified by appeal to those meaning-constituting rules. Some of the latter may even share that same feature of showing what immediate moves in reasoning may be taken as irreducibly justified on grounds of the 'first layer of logical form' and meaning alone.

   The justification of these latter rules by appeal to the former rules would have to be well-founded or recursive, giving the meaning-constituting rules priority or pride of place. This in fact is what happens in the intuitionist's account of canonical justifications, which are definable recursively with an asymmetric dependence on the introduction rules as meaning-constituting.

2. The meanings of the logical operators are graspable, and one's grasp of them can be made fully manifest in one's inferential behaviour. Moreover, one's grasp can only be acquired by observing others' inferential behaviour, and responding to corrections of one's own inferential behaviour.

3. There are privileged rules —the introduction rules—that fix the meanings of the logical operators. These rules state canonical conditions for the justified assertion of a sentence with a single, dominant occurrence of the logical operator in question. Thus the operator occurs dominant in the conclusion of the introduction rule.

4. Matching the meaning-fixing introduction rules are the elimination rules, which serve to explicate the meanings of the logical operators. These rules state what inferences one would be licensed to draw from a sentence with a single, dominant occurrence of the logical operator in question. Thus the operator occurs dominant in the major premiss of the elimination rule.

5. That this match between introduction and elimination rules does indeed obtain—that they are in harmony with each other—is brought out by the existence of a reduction procedure. This procedure shows one how to avoid having any sentence in a proof stand as the conclusion of an introduction and as the major premiss of a corresponding elimination.

As a technical corollary to (5) we have the normalizability requirement: that all proofs should be able to be converted into normal form, that is, a form in which there are no sentences standing as the conclusion of an introduction and as the major premiss of a corresponding elimination.

There are some further, ancillary observations to be made at this point.

Ad (3), (4): In our statements (3) and (4) we should also emphasize that the introduction and elimination rules are, and should be, formulated in such a way that the only occurrence of a logical operator mentioned in them is precisely the dominant occurrence within the conclusion of the introduction rule or the dominant occurrence within the major premiss of the elimination rule. The rules have to be thus focused. Otherwise they are not isolating sufficiently the logical operator whose meaning is in question. This is not to say that there are not valid inferences which depend for their validity on multiple occurrences of different operators, and their resulting 'interaction'. Naturally there are such valid inferences!—to maintain otherwise would be to deprive logic of most of its scope. Rather, the contention here is that the analytic project must take the operators one-by-one. The basic rules that determine logical competence must specify the unique contribution that each operator can make to the meanings of complex sentences in which it occurs, and, derivatively, to the validity of arguments in which such sentences occur. This is a requirement of separability.

It follows from separability that one would be able to master various fragments of the language in isolation, or one at a time. It should not matter in what order one learns (acquires grasp of) the logical operators. It should not matter if indeed some operators are not yet within one's grasp. All that matters is that one's grasp of any operator should be total simply on the basis of schematic rules governing inferences involving it. With mastery thus decomposable into various logical co-ordinates, we see validity of argument, and our competent appreciation of it, as a sort of vector sum of our co-ordinated grasps of the various distinct and separable operators.

Ad (5): The statement of (5) as it stands assumes that we are allowing for proofs that indeed can contain sentences standing within them as conclusions of introductions and as the major premisses of the corresponding eliminations. But suppose that one demurred at having such 'proofs' altogether. Suppose that one insisted that any arrangement of sentences that is to count as a proof must indeed not involve such maximal sentence occurrences. In the terminology of proof theory: suppose one said that to be a proof is to be a proof in normal form. How then could the point expressed by (5) still be made? The answer is staightforward: if Π is a proof of ϕ from Δ and if Σ is a proof of ψ from Γ,ϕ then there is some proof Θ of ψ from Δ,Γ. The existence of the former two proofs ensures the existence of the latter proof:

$$
\left.\begin{array}{c}
\Delta \\
\Pi \\
\phi \\
\\
\Gamma, \phi \\
\Sigma \\
\psi
\end{array}\right\} \quad \text{ensure} \quad
\begin{array}{c}
\Delta, \Gamma \\
\Theta \\
\psi
\end{array}
$$

Thus one can perform a logical cut 'externally' to the system, so to speak. Whatever logical passages should ultimately be navigable turn out to be so. The point is simply that such an externalist reading of harmony will do. In order to be able to state harmony, it is not required that we commit ourselves to a system of proofs within which abnormal proofs may be constructed. The orthodoxy happens to tolerate abnormal proofs; but the point here is that it needn't.

So far we have the requirements

1. of *analytic systematicity*:

    • that there be basic rules for each logical operator;
    • that these be finite in number;

2. of *separability*: that these rules

    • deal with one dominant occurrence of a logical operator at a time, and
    • accordingly be purely schematic 'everywhere else';

3. of *immediacy*: that these rules consequently take the form of:

    • the basic rule for an operator dominant in a conclusion (call it the introduction rule);
    • the basic rule for an operator dominant in a premiss (call it the elimination rule; and call that premiss the major premiss); and

4. of *harmony*: that the introduction rule and elimination rule for any given operator should balance one another—and that they should suffice for the proof of this fact (*vide infra*).

We are now in a position at last to parry an objection that might have been in the reader's mind a little earlier, at the point where we asked rhetorically on behalf of the intuitionist:

> Surely ... whatever disagreement there may be about the very
> meaning of negation could be brought into the open in the con-
> text of differing (schematizable) logical practices with regard to
> single occurrences of the logical operator concerned?

The objection is that it is not just the rule of double-negation elimination,
with its two occurrences of the negation operator, to which the classicist
could resort when urging that the disputed rule in question had been learned
at her parents' knees. There are also the rules of classical *reductio*, excluded
middle and dilemma:

$$
\begin{array}{ccc}
[\neg\phi] & & \\
\Pi & \quad LEM\underline{\qquad} & \\
\underline{\bot}\ CR & \phi \vee \neg\phi & \\
\phi & &
\end{array}
\qquad
\begin{array}{cc}
[\phi] & [\neg\phi] \\
\Pi & \Sigma \\
\underline{\psi} & \underline{\psi}\ Dilemma \\
& \psi
\end{array}
$$

Any one of these rules would yield classical logic if appended to the rules of
intuitionistic logic. How, then, to exclude them?

Each of them falls foul of one of our requirements so far. Classical *reductio*, though it confines itself to a single occurrence of the negation operator,
and is schematic elsewhere, nevertheless has that occurrence in the wrong
place: neither in the conclusion, nor in a major premiss, but rather in an hypothetical assumption for discharge within the subordinate proof. The rule
of dilemma is objectionable for the same reason. Finally, the law of excluded
middle sins by joining negation and disjunction inseparably. Such a marriage
is bound to be unstable, given that each of them is going to have to consort
separately with other operators in order to produce valid arguments. In
his desperation to register a further 'basic' and meaning-constituting rule,
the classicist has either to proliferate occurrences (as in Double-Negation
Elimination) or mislocate them (as in Classical *Reductio* and Dilemma) or
force them into shoddy marriages of convenience (as in the Law of Excluded
Middle).

One possible extension (that we have not yet mentioned) of the requirement of compositionality and analytic correctness of logical reasoning is that
the validity of any argument should turn only on the syntactic (hence semantic) ingredients of the sentences involved, namely, the premisses and the
conclusion. Thus, if one is to argue validly from $P_1, \ldots, P_n$ to Q, then every
intermediate sentence serving to mediate the suasive passage (on grounds of
meaning alone) from $P_1, \ldots, P_n$ to Q should already 'be there', available as
a constituent of one of the premisses $P_1, \ldots, P_n$ or of the conclusion Q. One

should be able to 'unpack' the premisses so as to expose or get at all such constituents, and be able then to 'repackage' them in the form required for the conclusion.

As our first technical corollary giving precise expression to the foregoing, we have the so-called subformula requirement: that every sentence featuring in a normal proof of Q from $P_1, \ldots, P_n$ should be a sub-sentence of Q or of one of $P_1, \ldots, P_n$. As our second technical corollary we have the conservative extension requirement: that the rules for the operators actually occurring in the argument '$P_1, \ldots, P_n$, so Q' should suffice for its proof, should the argument be valid.

The subformula requirement might appear to be violated by proofs of formerly independent Gödel sentences Q in arithmetic, which finally admit of proof when we extend the language with a new truth predicate, thereby creating new instances of the rule of mathematical induction. But if the rule of induction is thought of sententially (as it usually is), then the 'newly available' instance of induction used in the proof of Q in the extended language is an axiom involving an occurrence of the truth-predicate. Hence, if this new axiom is reckoned among the premisses $P_1, \ldots, P_n$ of the proof, the subformula principle might be said to be intact. More problematic would be the case of the sentence 'There are at least two objects', which we discussed in Chapter 9. On our account, this sentence comes out as a logical truth, even though its proof involves appeal to rules governing expressions not contained in the sentence itself. One possible way to meet this objection, which we shall not explore in detail here, would be to insist that all quantifications should be 'explicitly sortal', or typed. Then, instead of having quantification over objects *tout court*, one would need to be more specific in the sentence saying that there are at least two of them: 'two of *what* type of object?' would be the legitimate response. When the answer 'natural numbers' is provided, then this licenses appeal to the rules governing the predicate $N(\ )$; for that predicate now occurs explicitly in the claim of twoness. Thus, it is suggested, we would regain conformity with the subformula principle. This stratagem echoes a doctrine of Geach, according to which statements of identity should never be as underspecific as 'a is the same as b'. Geach is adamant that one should always provide explicitly the sortal information that would forestall the question 'Same *what*?' It is interesting that we have here certain proof-theoretic reflections leading us to similar philosophical conclusions.

We now have the following main requirements on the board, related to further, implied and subsidiary, requirements as follows:

1. Analytic systematicity

   ($\Rightarrow$ finitely many schematic rules)

2. Separability

   ($\Rightarrow$ single dominant occurrences of operators)

3. Immediacy

   ($\Rightarrow$ introduction and elimination rules)

4. Harmony of introduction and elimination rules

   ($\Rightarrow$ reduction procedures, normalizability)[7]

5. Compositionality

   ($\Rightarrow$ subformula requirement; conservative extension)

How does classical logic fare against these requirements? In its standard formulation as a system of (single conclusion) natural deduction it involves the rules for intuitionstic logic plus one of the four classical negation rules already stated above. We have seen that each of these four rules sins against at least one of Separability and Immediacy. Moreover, their use inevitably leads to further sinning against the subformula requirement and the requirement of conservative extension. Both requirements are breached by the classical theorem $(\phi \supset \psi) \vee (\psi \supset \phi)$. This theorem cannot be proved by means of the natural deduction rules for $\supset$ and $\vee$ alone, so the requirement of conservative extension is violated. And any proof of it in a standard classical system (regardless of which classical negation rule is adopted) violates the subformula requirement. The same holds for Peirce's Law $((\phi \supset \psi) \supset \phi) \supset \phi$. This theorem cannot be proved by means of the natural deduction rules for $\supset$ alone, and any standard classical proof of it violates the subformula requirement.

We have been careful to stipulate that these classical theorems cannot be proved by means of the *natural deduction* rules. An objector may point out that if we adopt the rules of a sequent system, we can prove these strictly classical results by means of just the logical rules for introducing their operators on the left (in the antecedent) and on the right (in the succedent)

---

[7]We set aside the distinction between weak and strong normalizability here. Cf. Prawitz, 'Towards a Foundation for General Proof Theory', in *Logic, Methodology and Philosophy of Science IV*, edited by L. Henkin, P. Suppes, A. Joja and G. Moisil, North-Holland, Amsterdam, pp. 225–50.

of a conclusion sequent. This objection is not well-taken; for it suppresses the fact that such sequent proofs are available only when we allow multiple membership of succedents. That is, the classical logician has to treat of sequents of the form $X:Y$ where the succedent Y may in general contain more than one sentence. In general, this smuggles in non-constructivity through the back door. For provable sequents are supposed to represent acceptable arguments. In normal practice, arguments take one from premisses to a single conclusion. There is no acceptable interpretation of the 'validity' of a sequent $X:Q_1, \ldots, Q_n$ in terms of preservation of warrant to assert when X contains only sentences involving no disjunctions. If one is told that $X:Q_1, \ldots, Q_n$ is 'valid' in the extended sense for multiple-conclusion arguments just in case $X:Q_1 \vee \ldots \vee Q_n$ is valid in the usual sense for single-conclusion arguments, the intuitionist can demand to know precisely which disjunct Q_i, then, proves to be derivable from X. No answer to such a question can be provided in general with the multiple-conclusion sequent calculus of the classical logician. It behoves us, then, to stay with a natural deduction system, and to present it in sequent form only if we observe the requirement that sequents should not have multiple conclusions.

Let us prescind for a moment from the question of the exact form of rules chosen to present a case for classical logic. Let us focus instead on what we know about classical deducibility, regardless of how the deductions are articulated. We see clearly from the account laid out above that harmony and separability are but necessary conditions on any adequate meaning analysis that is to provide a foundation for logic. Neither requirement is claimed to be sufficient. Nor are they even jointly sufficient, unless one can provide an argument from just the requirements of harmony and separability to each and every one of the other requirements listed above. The intuitionist's adversions to harmony, then, have to be understood within this wider context of why harmony is both appealing and important to him. It is no argument against the combined weight of requirements (1)–(5) that some form of 'harmony' might be shown to be displayed by a set of rules that happens to yield classical logic. One will want to know whether the rules in question meet the more exacting form of harmony to be described presently. One will also want to know whether they satisfy the other requirements as well. As we have shown, the requirements of separability and immediacy are conceptually prior to the requirement of harmony itself. The statement of the requirement of harmony itself only makes sense as a constraint on our meaning analysis if it is understood in the context of the earlier requirements of separability and immediacy. Fall foul of these two requirements, and any serious debate over the adequacy of a proposed classical analysis of the logical operators is called off, as far as the intuitionist is concerned. It is with the harmony of very specific sorts of rules that the intuitionist is concerned: rules already satisfying the requirements of separability and immediacy. If one grossly disfigures them so as to violate these two requirements, it will be a harmony in name only that they might satisfy.

The Principle of Harmony is as follows:

> The conclusion of λ-introduction should be the strongest sentence that can so feature; moreover one need only appeal to λ-elimination to show this; but in so showing this, one needs to make use of all the forms of λ-elimination that are provided

> The major premiss for λ-elimination should be the weakest sentence that can so feature; moreover one need only appeal to λ-introduction to show this; but in so showing this, one needs to make use of all the forms of λ-introduction that are provided

The strongest sentence with property P is that sentence θ with property P such that any sentence σ with property P is deducible from θ; while the weakest sentence with property P is that sentence θ with property P that can be deduced from any sentence σ with property P.

The following two proof schemata show that the usual introduction and elimination rules for $\supset$ are in harmony:

$$
\frac{\displaystyle \overset{-(1)}{\phi} \qquad \phi \supset \psi}{\underset{\sigma}{\dfrac{\psi}{}}(1)} \supset E
\qquad\qquad
\frac{\displaystyle \overset{-(1)}{\phi} \qquad \sigma}{\dfrac{\psi}{\phi \supset \psi}(1)} \supset I
$$

The proof on the left uses only $\supset E$ to show that if σ features like the conclusion $\phi \supset \psi$ of $\supset I$ then σ can be deduced from $\phi \supset \psi$. Thus $\phi \supset \psi$ is the strongest sentence that can feature as the conclusion of $\supset I$. The proof on the right uses only $\supset I$ to show that if σ features like the major premiss $\phi \supset \psi$ of $\supset E$ then $\phi \supset \psi$ can be deduced from σ. Thus $\phi \supset \psi$ is the weakest sentence that can feature as the major premiss of $\supset E$.

By way of further example, the following two proof schemata show that the usual introduction and elimination rules for $\vee$ are in harmony:

$$
\vee E \; \dfrac{\phi \vee \psi \qquad \overset{-(1)}{\dfrac{\phi}{\sigma}} \qquad \overset{-(1)}{\dfrac{\psi}{\sigma}}}{\sigma}(1)
\qquad\qquad
\dfrac{\sigma \qquad \vee I \dfrac{\overset{-(1)}{\phi}}{\phi \vee \psi} \qquad \vee I \dfrac{\overset{-(1)}{\psi}}{\phi \vee \psi}}{\phi \vee \psi}(1)
$$

Note how in the second proof schema we need to employ both forms of $\vee I$ in order to construct the proof schema; the reader should consider once again the precise statement of the Principle of Harmony given above.

10.3   Epistemic gain in logic

Suppose one has a logical system for which the existence of proofs is indicated by $\vdash$, a relation of exact deducibility holding between a set of premises on the left and a conclusion on the right. The intuitive meaning of '$X \vdash A$' is that there is a proof whose conclusion is A and whose undischarged assumptions (premises) form the set X. Any premiss P is reckoned to X 'just once', no matter how often P may have been 'used' as an assumption in the proof. There are two extreme cases:

(i) X is empty. Then '$\vdash A$' means that A is a theorem. That is, there is a proof of A 'from no assumptions'. Any assumptions used for the sake of argument within the proof will have been discharged by the stage at which we reach A as the conclusion. Example: The one-step proof

$$\frac{\overline{}^{(1)}}{ B}^{(1)}$$
$$B \supset B$$

justifies the claim $\vdash B \supset B$.

(ii) A is 'empty'. Then '$X \vdash$' means that there is a proof that X is inconsistent. Example: The one-step proof

$$\frac{\neg B \quad\quad B}{\bot}$$

justifies the claim $B, \neg B \vdash$.

In a single-conclusion natural deduction calculus one usually uses a special symbol, $\bot$ say, to mark this, and one writes '$X \vdash \bot$' instead of '$X \vdash$'. Thus: $B, \neg B \vdash \bot$. It is the sequent calculus which prompts the use of the turnstile with nothing to the right, because in the sequent calculus we prove the inconsistency of X by deriving the sequent $X :$ with the empty succedent.

Thus the last proof, recast in the sequent calculus, would be

$$\frac{B : B}{B, \neg B :}$$

$\perp$ is very much like the symbol 0 in arithmetic. Rather than writing nothing, we indicate that it's nothing that we intend by writing something in particular, which is to stand for the nothing that we intend. Thus the rule of negation elimination in a system of natural deduction is usually written as

$$\frac{\neg A \qquad A}{\perp}$$

instead of

$$\frac{\neg A \qquad A}{}$$

where the absence of anything below the inference stroke would explicitly represent a logical dead-end. Likewise, the rule of negation introduction is usually written as

$$\underbrace{\Delta \; , \; \overset{\rule{1em}{0.4pt}{}^{(i)}}{A}}_{}$$

$$\vdots$$

$$\frac{\perp}{\neg A}{}^{(i)}$$

instead of

$$\underbrace{\Delta \; , \; \overset{\rule{1em}{0.4pt}{}^{(i)}}{A}}_{}$$

$$\vdots$$

$$\frac{\rule{1em}{0.4pt}}{\neg A}{}^{(i)}$$

where the absence of anything between the lower two inference strokes would explicitly represent a logical dead-end. It is a pity that we have no convention of using empty spaces in natural deductions to represent emptiness. For it would be nice to be able to say that a proof 'of $\perp$' is just a proof of the empty conclusion; and to say that, for example, the sequent $X : \perp$ is a sub-sequent of $X : A$.

Let us pretend that this notational quirk of natural deduction does not prevent us from saying such things. Thus, when Y is a subset of X, one can say that both $Y:A$ and $Y:\perp$ are sub-sequents of $X:A$. And one can speak of proper sub-sequents whenever Y is a proper subset of X or $\perp$ is involved in place of A. When S^* is a proper sub-sequent of S, we shall also say that S is a *dilution* of S^*. The proper sub-sequent relation is well-founded, so it will make sense to speak, given any sequent $X:Y$ with property F, of minimal sub-sequents of $X:Y$ enjoying the property F. The notation $[X]:[A]$ will indicate a sub-sequent of $X:A$. Likewise, the notation $[X]\vdash[A]$ will mean that there is a proof of some sub-sequent of $X:A$.

Suppose we know that

(I) $X \vdash A$

and subsequently learn that

(II) $Y \vdash A$

where Y is a proper subset of X. Which is the better result (I) or (II)?[8] Obviously, (II) is. We have used fewer of the original premises to secure the conclusion A. We have discovered a logically stronger result. We have made *epistemic gain*.

Now suppose that we learn

(IIIa) $Y \vdash \perp$

Which is the best result, (I), (II) or (IIIa)? Obviously, (IIIa) is. We now know that lurking in our original set X of premises was an inconsistency.[9] Indeed, the inconsistency is revealed in the proper subset Y of X. It is much better to know this than to know that anything purportedly follows from X, or indeed even from Y. Once again, we have made epistemic gain.

---

[8] In posing this question, we are assuming that one has access to proofs that justify the deducibility statements in question.

[9] If A itself had been of the form $B \wedge \neg B$, an objector might complain that $Y \vdash B \wedge \neg B$ is *more* informative than $Y \vdash \perp$, since the former gives us information as to some particular contradiction entailed by Y. There is not really any loss of information in this regard, however; for the particular contradiction in question will be recoverable from any proof justifying the deducibility claim $Y \vdash \perp$.

Suppose, finally, that we learn, not (IIIa) but

(IIIb) $\vdash A$

Then this is the best result possible for the case where X itself is not inconsistent.

In general: our knowledge that $X \vdash A$ (that the sequent $X : A$ has a proof) is always improved when we learn that a *proper sub-sequent* of $X:A$ has a proof—whether by making do with fewer premises, or by showing their inconsistency, or by showing the logical truth of the sought conclusion. We make epistemic gains by paring down on what is to the left or to the right of the turnstile. One can propose, then, the following epistemic constraint on logical consequence:

Pare down as much as possible on both sides of the turnstile.

10.4   The maxim of narrow analysis

This observation prompts the following maxim:

> MAXIM OF NARROW ANALYSIS
> When given a deductive problem $X?\text{-}Y$ that admits of proof, always seek a proof of a minimal sub-sequent of $X:Y$ that admits of proof.[10]

If an investor can get a higher return on bond X^* than on bond X, and with no greater risk, then it always pays him to substitute bond X^* for bond X throughout his portfolio. If X is collateral for a loan, then X^* can serve as collateral instead; and may even secure a better interest rate on the loan. If X is to be liquidated soon, then X^* can be liquidated instead; and will probably realize a better price than X would have.

Analogous considerations should hold for any investment of intellectual effort that yields an epistemic gain with no attendant risk (for we are dealing here with deduction). One should be able to substitute the result of that investment (the new proof Π^* of the proper sub-sequent $X^*:Y^*$) throughout one's knowledge-portfolio for the weaker result of earlier investment of

---

[10]The proof-finding algorithms in *Autologic* are designed with this in mind.

intellectual effort (the old proof Π of the original sequent $X:Y$). And one should expect higher epistemic returns across the board as a result.

It sounds obvious, and one feels it ought to be true. But for many a deductive system of logic it is false: one can be thwarted when trying to follow the maxim of narrow analysis as vigorously as one would like. In these systems of logic, if one substitutes in all one's proofs Σ the better subproof Π^* (of the stronger result) for the worse subproof Π (of the weaker result), then one does not in general preserve proofhood. Nor is one in general able to recover or restore the situation, by producing new proofs in the light of that substitution.

A case in point would be the following introduction rule for a 'relevant' conditional $\rightarrow$:

$$
\begin{array}{c}
\overline{}^{(i)} \\
\underbrace{\Delta \, , \, A} \\
\vdots \\
\dfrac{B}{A \rightarrow B}^{(i)}
\end{array}
$$

where A must be among the assumptions on which B depends;

or the corresponding 'right' rule of the sequent calculus, namely,

$$
\dfrac{X, A : B}{X : A \rightarrow B}
$$

where A is not in X

The trouble with this form of $\rightarrow$-introduction (or, in the sequent version, $\rightarrow$R) is that we cannot always substitute logical strengthenings of the subordinate proof without sacrificing proofhood. For example, if we had an application

$$
\begin{array}{c}
\overline{}^{(i)} \\
\underbrace{X \, , \, A} \\
\Pi \\
\dfrac{B}{A \rightarrow B}^{(i)}
\end{array}
$$

of $\rightarrow$-introduction, and then discovered a proof Π^* of B from (some subset Y of) X alone, we would not be able to substitute Π^* for Π. For then we would get

$$
\underbrace{Y \ , \ \overline{??}^{(i)}}_{\Pi^*}
$$
$$
\frac{B}{A \to B}^{(i)}
$$

incorrect application of →-introduction, since
there is no assumption A to be discharged

Likewise, if we discovered a proof Π^* of $\perp$ from (some subset Y of) X and
the assumption A, the attempted substitution of Π^* for Π would produce

$$
\underbrace{Y \ , \ \overline{A}^{(i)}}_{\Pi^*}
$$
$$
\frac{\perp}{A \to B}^{(i)}
$$

incorrect application of → -introduction, since
B is not the same as $\perp$

In each case we would fail to produce a proof of (any sub-sequent of)
$X : A \to B$. Nor would there be any guaranteed way of transforming the
resulting non-proofs into a proof of (any sub-sequent of) $X : A \to B$.[11]

We see, then, that some systems can be unreasonably finickity about
the use one may make of assumptions for the sake of argument, especially
with a rule like the rule of conditional proof. In a new would-be subordinate
proof Π^* of a stronger result, some of those assumptions may be eschewed,
or the subordinate conclusion may be of the wrong form ($\perp$ instead of the
'sought' conclusion B). When such Π^* is substituted to replace the subproof
Π (of the weaker result) within some larger proof Σ, the result $\Sigma(\Pi/\Pi^*)$
may fail to be a proof, because the 'lost assumptions' or the changed form of
the subordinate conclusion make some rule-application in the wider proof-

---

[11]It was this problem that motivated a change in the treatment of the conditional ventured in $AR\&L$ to that which was preferred in *Autologic* and in 'Intuitionistic Mathematics
Does Not Need *Ex Falso Quodlibet*', *Topoi*, 1994, pp. 127–33. The preferred treatment is
given below.

context Σ illicit. And there might not be any way, in general, of capitalizing on the epistemic gain represented by the new subproof Π^*, and distributing its potential returns within the wider proof Σ.

10.5   Non-forfeiture of epistemic gain

This complaint cannot be levelled, however, against the relevance systems that we call intuitionistic relevant logic (IR)[12] and classical relevant logic (CR).[13] These systems, unlike other systems of relevance logic, are devoted to the non-forfeiture and potentially wider distribution of epistemic gains. IR, for example, satisfies the following principle:

> PRINCIPLE OF NON-FORFEITURE OF EPISTEMIC GAIN
> Let Π be a proof of the sequent $X:A$, occurring as a subproof of the proof Σ of the sequent $Y:B$. Let Π^* be a proof of some proper sub-sequent of $X:A$. Then $\Sigma(\Pi/\Pi^*)$—the result of substituting Π^* for Π in Σ—can be effectively transformed into a proof of some sub-sequent of $Y:B$. Indeed, the transformation can be effected in polynomial time.

Note that I am not saying that a strict gain via Π^* with respect to some subproof Π will always turn into a strict gain with respect to the overall proof Σ. In many cases it will; but in some cases the result established by (the transform of) $\Sigma(\Pi/\Pi^*)$ will be the original result $Y:B$. An example of mere non-forfeiture without overall strict gain would be where we passed from

$$
\cfrac{A \vee B \qquad \cfrac{\overset{\overline{\quad}^{(i)}}{X,Y,A}}{\underset{C}{\Pi}} \qquad \cfrac{\overset{\overline{\quad}^{(i)}}{Z,Y,B}}{\underset{C}{\Theta}}_{(i)}}{C}
$$

to

---

[12]The philosophical and metamathematical arguments in favour of IR were given in *AR&L*. The neatest presentation of the system in its present form is in *Autologic*, where the computational considerations in favour of IR were given.

[13]The system CR was first introduced in 'Perfect validity, entailment and paraconsistency', *Studia Logica*, 43, 1984, pp. 179–98.

$$\frac{\stackrel{\displaystyle -(i)}{X,A} \quad \stackrel{\displaystyle -(i)}{Z,Y,B}}{\cfrac{\cfrac{\Pi^*}{A \vee B \quad C} \quad \cfrac{\Theta}{C}_{(i)}}{C}}$$

The latter, like the former, is a proof of C from $X, Y, Z, A \vee B$ even though its subordinate proof Π^* establishes the result $X, A : C$, which is stronger than the result $X, Y, A : C$ established by the subordinate proof Π of the former.

Still, non-forfeiture of epistemic gain would be very good news. For we would never lose any of our erstwhile deductive knowledge by forgetting Π and remembering Π^* instead. And this cannot be said for many a rival system of relevance logic.

10.5.1 The Sub-sequent Constraint

Our principle of beneficial substitution can take the form of a new constraint on the formulation of rules in a sequent calculus. (A principle to the same effect can be formulated for a system of natural deduction.)

THE SUB-SEQUENT CONSTRAINT

For any sequent rule

$$\frac{S_0 \ldots S_n}{T}$$

the following should hold for any of its correct applications: if any premiss sequent S_i is replaced by a proper sub-sequent S_i^* of S_i, the resulting application of the rule is incorrect only if S_i^* is a proper sub-sequent of T.

Since we are dealing with finitely many finite sequents, and since it is decidable whether the rule has been correctly applied, it is decidable whether the rule satisfies the Sub-sequent Constraint. When this constraint is satisfied, it does not matter if a rule 'application' becomes incorrect upon substitution of a stronger subordinate proof. For in this case we have a stronger overall result (S_i^* is a proper sub-sequent of the final sequent T itself), and we can therefore dispense with the final rule-application in question. We would already be 'one step ahead', as it were, in following the maxim of narrow analysis. On the other hand, even if the rule-application remained correct upon substitution of the stronger subordinate proof, the resulting overall proof might still have a stronger result in the form of some proper sub-sequent of T. In general, this much is certain: we will never 'lose' by making the substitution, when our rules satisfy the Sub-sequent Constraint. And we will be following the maxim of narrow analysis by using such rules.[14]

10.5.2 Truth-preservation is not enough

The requirement that logical rules of inference be truth-preserving helps us to narrow down considerably the range of forms that our rules for the logical operators may take. A natural deduction establishes a conclusion A from a set X of undischarged assumptions. Such a deduction is truth-preserving just in case whenever all the sentences of X are true, the sentence A is true also. With rules of natural deduction, we require that applications of rules to truth-preserving subdeductions should create only truth-preserving deductions. The 'initial rule' is that

A is a natural deduction of A from $\{A\}$.

This clearly creates only truth-preserving deductions. The rules for the introduction of a dominant logical operator in the conclusion A, and for the elimination of a dominant logical operator in a premiss drawn from X, are

---

[14]The Sub-sequent Constraint is a loose converse of the following constraint put forward in 'On Maintaining Concentration', *Analysis*, 1994, pp. 143–52, which is rephrased here so as to apply to the sequent calculus:

(γ_1) In any application of a sequent rule

$$\frac{S_0 \ldots S_n}{T}$$

we must ensure that no premiss sequent S_i is a sub-sequent of the conclusion sequent T

This injunction (γ_1) was intended to prevent dilutions creeping into proofs. It was an attempt to formulate the maxim of narrow analysis. In the paper just cited the attempt was made to secure its intended effect by imposing restrictions on the orderings of $\wedge I$ and $\wedge E$ so as to prevent dilutions from ever arising. But there was no suggestion that the rules themselves ('locally', as it were) should be changed—that their conditions of application should be made more exigent, by simply incorporating (γ_1) as a precondition. But of course that alternative is still open to us. Since (γ_1) is a decidable condition, we could make it a 'local' precondition for rule-applications. Then we would not need to worry about formulating restrictions on the global ordering of different rules within a proof in the hope that such restrictions would ensure satisfaction of the 'local' precondition itself.

designed with the truth-preservation requirement uppermost in our minds. Thus the natural deduction rules for ∧ are usually stated as follows:

$$\wedge I \; \frac{A \qquad B}{A \wedge B} \qquad \wedge E \; \frac{A \wedge B}{A} \qquad \wedge E \; \frac{A \wedge B}{B}$$

The introduction rule stated this way is, however, somewhat underspecific. In some systems one might count applications of the form

$$\frac{\begin{array}{cc} X & Y \\ \Pi & \Theta \\ A & B \end{array}}{A \wedge B}$$

as correct, where the subordinate proofs Π and Θ are allowed to have different sets (X and Y respectively) of undischarged assumptions, and the overall proof establishes the conclusion $A \wedge B$ from the set $X \cup Y$ (the union of X with Y) of undischarged assumptions. In other, stricter systems, only the form of application

$$\frac{\begin{array}{cc} X & X \\ \Pi & \Theta \\ A & B \end{array}}{A \wedge B}$$

would be correct, establishing the conclusion $A \wedge B$ from the set of undischarged assumptions X which now has to be common to both Π and Θ. Neither the stricter nor the more liberal form of ∧-introduction can be favoured on grounds of truth-preservation alone. Something more would be needed in order to be able to say, for example, that the stricter form is overly demanding.

What holds for systems of natural deduction holds also for systems of sequent proof. Here we infer sequents $X : A$ from other sequents. A sequent is truth-preserving just in case whenever all the sentences of X are true, the sentence A is true also. The rule of initial sequents is $A : A$, which is clearly truth-preserving. And the sequent rules for the introduction of a logical operator on the left (in some member of the premiss set) or on the right (in the conclusion) are designed to ensure that from truth-preserving sequents only truth-preserving sequents may be inferred. To continue with the example of ∧, the sequent rule for ∧ on the right (corresponding to the introduction rule in natural deduction) might be in either of the following two forms, the first more liberal and the second stricter:

$$\frac{X:A \quad Y:B}{X,Y:A \wedge B} \quad \text{(different premiss sets, or antecedents)}$$

or

$$\frac{X:A \quad X:B}{X:A \wedge B} \quad \text{(same premiss sets, or antecedents)}$$

and the sequent rule for $\wedge$ on the left (corresponding to the elimination rule in natural deduction) might take either one of the following two forms:

$$\frac{X,A:C}{X,A \wedge B:C} \qquad \frac{X,B:C}{X,A \wedge B:C} \qquad \text{(only one conjunct of } A \wedge B \text{ 'used')}$$

or

$$\frac{X,A,B:C}{X,A \wedge B:C} \qquad \text{(both conjuncts of } A \wedge B \text{ 'used')}$$

Again, considerations of truth-preservation are not enough to favour a particular form for $\wedge$ on the right or on the left over the others; something else is needed in order to make that decision. The contention here is that the extra considerations needed here are those of narrow analysis, as realized in the Sub-sequent Constraint.

10.6   The Principle of Harmony

A considerable amount of attention has been paid in recent years to another principle or constraint governing the formulation of rules for the logical operators: the principle of harmony[15] between introduction and elimination rules. This was discussed above, and for convenience will be restated here:

THE PRINCIPLE OF HARMONY

The introduction and elimination rules for any logical operator λ should be framed in such a way that:
(i) in the statement of the introduction rule for λ, the conclusion (with λ dominant) should be the strongest that can be inferred under the conditions specified; and

---

[15] See *Natural Logic*, pp. 74–7.

(ii) in the statement of the corresponding elimination rule, the
major premiss (with λ dominant) should be the weakest that can
be used in the way specified.

This principle serves to tailor the elimination rule to a previously chosen
introduction rule, or vice versa. In proving (i), we appeal to the elimination
rule; in proving (ii), we appeal to the introduction rule. The principle of
harmony is used as a surrogate for the truth-preservation requirement when
one tries to eschew the usual notion of truth, and make do instead with
a more proof-based notion of warranted assertibility. Proofs must preserve
warranted assertibility from their undischarged assumptions to their conclusions. Warranted assertibility is to be based on a special kind of proof, called
canonical proof, in which introduction rules feature prominently. Proofs in
general are composed of applications of rules, including elimination rules.
So it turns out that proofs in general will preserve warranted assertibility if
and only if the introduction and elimination rules display the appropriate
kind of harmony.[16]

Note that harmony places great value on the logical strength of one's
inferred compound conclusions, and on the logical weakness of any compound
premisses on which one wishes to base a conclusion. That is, it seeks to make
our inferences as strong as possible, and thereby also our proofs. So it is very
much like the principle of narrow analysis: try to get as strong a conclusion
as you can by using as little as you can in the way of premisses.

Introduction-elimination pairs displaying this harmony allow one to perform certain reductions or transformations on proofs $\Sigma(P/\Pi)$ that result
from supplying a canonical proof Π for a premiss P that is undischarged in
a proof Σ of A:

$$
\begin{array}{ccc}
Y & & \\
\Pi & & Z \;\; (\subseteq X \cup Y) \\
X, [P] & \rightarrow & \Xi \\
\Sigma & & A \\
A & &
\end{array}
$$

These transformations will produce a proof Ξ of A in 'normal form' that
might not even proceed via P, but will secure the conclusion A more directly from premisses that are among those available in the proof on the
left, namely, $\Sigma(P/\Pi)$. And one beneficial side-effect can be that one gets
by, in the transformed proof Ξ on the right, without having to use all the

---

[16] For the philosophical consequences of harmony, see *AR&L*.

premisses available in $\Sigma(P/\Pi)$. (So Z might be a *proper* subset of $X \cup Y$.) One may say: normalization of proofs can allow one to pare down on the premisses. Normalization can help us follow the maxim of narrow analysis; but normalization alone cannot always ensure that this maxim will be prosecuted as vigorously as it might be.

It is not our purpose here to argue for a proof-based approach to the theory of meaning for the logical operators, or to advance any new formulation of the harmony principle mentioned earlier, or any new argument for that principle. The harmony principle has been mentioned only in order to illustrate the point that wider considerations about the form of proofs, and about how proofs of one form can be transformed into proofs of another form, have already helped us to focus on a narrower range of possible forms for the rules of inference themselves—and hence, ultimately, on the correct logic.

10.7   The Principle of Extraction for natural deduction systems

What is sought (in the natural deduction setting) is an even more radical kind of transformation on natural deductions than normalization: a process that can allow one to 'subset down' on the conclusion as well as on the premisses. Thus, given even a natural deduction

$$X$$
$$\Sigma$$
$$A$$

in normal form in intuitionistic logic, with conclusion A and premisses X, we want to be able to extract from it a natural deduction

$$[X]$$
$$\Sigma^*$$
$$[A]$$

(perforce in normal form) in intuitionistic logic, whose premisses are drawn from X and whose conclusion, if not A, is absurdity.[17] Moreover, we want

---

[17]Such an extraction theorem was first proved in 'Entailment and Proofs', *Proceedings of the Aristotelian Society*, 79, 1979, pp. 167–89. In 'A Proof-theoretic approach to entailment', *Journal of Philosophical Logic*, 9, 1980, pp. 185–209, I proposed that this furnishes a basis for relevant logic.

$[X]:[A]$ to be as minimal as possible. We are seeking, that is, to adhere to the following:

> THE PRINCIPLE OF EXTRACTION
> FOR NATURAL DEDUCTION SYSTEMS
>
> Every natural deduction Σ in normal form of a conclusion A from a set X of undischarged assumptions should be able to be transformed into a natural deduction Σ^* of either A or $\bot$ from some subset of X, where Σ^* will contain as little 'dilution' as possible.

What is meant when one says that Σ^* will contain as little 'dilution' as possible? In particular, we can expect Σ^* not to contain any applications of *ex falso quodlibet*, which is a prime case of dilution. Nor should Σ^* make frivolous use of assumptions that are not really needed, or apply 'discharge' rules without any assumptions of the required form being available for discharge. Σ^*, that is, should be as tight as possible. All these cautionary provisions are subject, of course, to the overriding need for a form of rules for the logical operators that will allow one to prove an Extraction Theorem modelled on the principle just stated. (The form in which it has just been stated applies equally to intuitionistic logic and classical logic, since both these logics involve only single conclusions in the natural deduction setting.) The Principle of Extraction requires, then, at least the truth of the following metatheorem. In order to secure its truth, the natural deduction system must define proofs in such a way as to ensure that extraction is always possible.

> EXTRACTION THEOREM FOR NATURAL DEDUCTION
>
> Every natural deduction Σ in normal form of a conclusion A from a set X of undischarged assumptions can be transformed into a natural deduction Σ^* of either A or $\bot$ from some subset of X, where Σ^* has no applications of the absurdity rule.

10.8   The Anti-Dilution Principle for sequent systems

So far we have motivated the Principle of Extraction (and its partial realization, the Extraction Theorem) for the setting of natural deduction. Similar considerations apply in the sequent calculus setting. But in the sequent calculus setting the corresponding principle should be called the Anti-Dilution Principle. In order to secure its truth, the system of sequent proof must be so defined as to make the required dilution eliminations possible.

ANTI-DILUTION PRINCIPLE

Any cut-free proof of $X:Y$ can be turned into a cut-free dilution-free proof of some sub-sequent of $X : Y$ that is as minimal as possible.

Here, what one is looking for (in the sequent calculus setting) is an even more radical kind of transformation on sequent proofs than cut-elimination: a process that will allow one, if possible, to 'subset down' on the succedent of the final sequent as well as on its antecedent. Thus, given even a cut-free sequent proof

$$\Sigma$$
$$X:A$$

in intuitionistic logic, with conclusion A and premisses X, we want to be able to transform it into a sequent proof

$$\Sigma^*$$
$$[X]:[A]$$

(perforce cut-free) in intuitionistic logic, the antecedent of whose final sequent is a subset of X and the consequent of whose final sequent, if not $\{A\}$, is empty. Moreover, $[X]:[A]$ should be as minimal as possible. This means that Σ^* will contain as little 'dilution' as possible. In particular, we can expect Σ^* not to contain any applications of the rule of dilution itself (since we are observing the Sub-sequent Constraint). Σ^* should be as tight as possible. This cautionary provision is subject, of course, to the overriding need for a form of rules for the logical operators that will allow one to prove the result sought. The Anti-Dilution Principle requires, then, at least the truth of the following.

DILUTION-ELIMINATION THEOREM
FOR SEQUENT CALCULUS

Any cut-free proof of $X:Y$ can be turned into a cut-free dilution-free proof of some sub-sequent of $X:Y$.

We see, then, that we have parallel concerns in both the natural deduction setting and the sequent setting. In order to prove the Extraction Theorem for the natural deduction setting, or its analogue the Dilution-Elimination Theorem in the sequent setting, we need to find the right forms, respectively, for the rules governing the logical operators. We shall defer, for the time being, the question of the extent to which the Extraction and Dilution-Elimination Theorems embody the full force of the requirements of the Principle of Extraction and the Anti-Dilution Principle, respectively.

10.9 Relevance

Harmony considerations tend to favour some form of intuitionistic logic over classical logic. That is: harmony *constructivizes*. Likewise, non-forfeiture of epistemic gain *relevantizes*. The aim here is to supplement the considerations of harmony so as to narrow even further the range of possible forms for the rules of inference governing the logical operators. Such supplementation comes from the Principle of Extraction (for natural deduction) and the Anti-Dilution Principle (for sequent calculus). Both these principles are the realizations, for those respective systematic settings, of the Principle of Non-Forfeiture of Epistemic Gain:

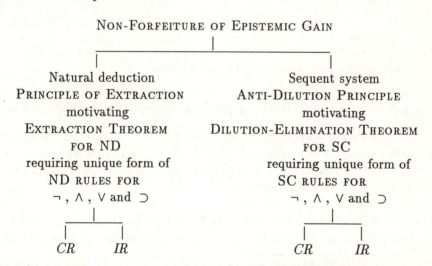

Adding the consideration of non-forfeiture of epistemic gain leads one from intuitionistic logic (I) to intuitionistic relevant logic (IR); and from classical logic (C) to classical relevant logic (CR). Even if one is unconvinced by the considerations of harmony, and therefore in favour of a classical logic, one could still be moved by the consideration of non-forfeiture of epistemic gain, and thereby end up with the system *CR* of classical relevant logic rather than the system *IR* of intuitionistic relevant logic.

We shall, in what follows, stay in the context of intuitionistic logic when illustrating how non-forfeiture of epistemic gain helps one to fashion more exactly an acceptable set of rules for the logical operators. We shall conduct the following discussion also within the framework of the sequent calculus and its Anti-Dilution Principle; but everything we say can be translated with ease into the framework of natural deduction, with its Principle of Extraction.[18] The result of our investigation will be that *IR* is uniquely determined as the correct system of constructive reasoning. A similar result, for *CR*, would be available to the classicist.

We are seeking separable rules of inference, then, for ¬, ∧, ∨ and ⊃; rules which will at least enable a proof of Dilution-Elimination to go through in the intuitionistic case as desired. We want to show how sentences with these respective operators dominant can come to feature to the left or to the right of the colon in a conclusion sequent. We are interested, that is, in logical rules, not in structural rules. Indeed, one of the main benefits of this investigation will be to show that the only structural rule needed is the rule of initial sequents

$A : A$

by means of which sequent proofs get started.

10.9.1   Uniquely determining rules for the logical operators

We wish to demonstrate what precise form the sequent rules for logical operators should take for intuitionistic logic, when it is subjected to the requirement of non-forfeiture of epistemic gain. Our demonstration proceeds against two background requirements:

(1) provable sequents have the form $X : A$, for a finite set X of sentences and a sentence A, or the form $X :$, for a non-empty finite set X of sentences; and

---

[18] For the method of transforming natural deductions in *IR* (which have to be in normal form) into sequent proofs in *IR* (which must eschew applications of Cut and Dilution), and vice versa, see 'Natural Deduction and Sequent Calculus for Intuitionistic Relevant Logic', *Journal of Symbolic Logic*, 52, 1987, pp. 665–90.

(2) the rules are, prima facie, as strong as they can be; in particular, they will never, in any application, allow conclusion sequents that properly dilute any premiss sequent.

(1) is the argument-form principle. (2) is the anti-dilution principle. As it stands, (2) at present bans proper dilution locally, at any one rule-application. One could also impose a global form of (2): banning any rule-application that would result in a proper dilution of any sequent already available within the proof, somewhere above that rule-application. Our investigation, however, can make do for the time being with just the local form of the anti-dilution principle (2).

The logical rules have to be truth-preserving, in the sense that if their premiss sequents are truth-preserving, then so are their conclusion sequents. This narrows down the range of possibilities for rules for ¬, ∧, ∨ and ⊃ on the right and on the left; but still, as we have seen, there is some slack. The precise form of each rule is not yet uniquely determined, although we are somewhere in the right neighbourhood. We have now to decide further between various alternative forms that the rules may take, compatibly with the constraint of truth-preservation. We have to decide, for example, whether to allow, in rules with more than one premiss sequent, for distinct antecedents (the 'liberal' form) or only for identical antecedents (the 'strict' form). And we have to decide on our discharge conventions: what components of a compound principal formula have to appear in premiss sequents, and how?; and how might they disappear in the conclusion sequent, in which the principal sentence makes its first appearance? These remaining aspects of 'slack' in the determination of the forms of our logical rules are to be taken up by the Sub-sequent Constraint, which is the realization, focusing on rules for the logical operators, of our principle of non-forfeiture of epistemic gain (or: maxim of narrow analysis).

Consider, then, the rules for ¬. We want to allow for *reductio ad absurdum*: establishing ¬A by assuming A and deriving absurdity therefrom. So ¬R must have as a special case

$$\frac{A:}{:\neg A}$$

In general, though, requirement (1) says that we want to be able to get ¬A from certain assumptions X. So the form of the rule should encompass

$$\frac{X, A:}{X:\neg A}$$

Now if A were a member of X, we would sin against the anti-dilution principle (2). Thus the form of $\neg R$ is

$$\frac{X, A:}{X:\neg A} \quad \text{where } A \text{ is not a member of } X$$

That is unique for the intuitionistic case, where a sequent may have at most one sentence in its succedent.

What about $\neg L$? Here we want to derive a sequent of the form $X, \neg A:B$ where we may assume that $\neg A$ is not in X. The premiss sequent(s) cannot involve $\neg$, whence, by the requirement of truth-preservation, A will have to occur on the right of the colon in a premiss sequent, if at all. But of course A must make such an appearance, on pain of violating the anti-dilution principle (2). So, since we are countenancing only single-conclusion sequents, the rule must take the form

$$\frac{X:A}{X, \neg A:}$$

We have therefore specified our negation rules uniquely.

What about $\wedge R$? Should it have the liberal or the strict form? The Sub-sequent Constraint counsels the liberal form. For one of the subordinate proofs might admit of strengthening by doing away with some of the premisses used, and the other subordinate proof not. The first (strengthened) proof might still establish A, and the second proof establish B. In such a situation, substitution of the stronger proof of A should leave us with a licit application of $\wedge R$. This will be the case only if $\wedge R$ has the liberal form:

$$\frac{X:A \quad Y:B}{X, Y:A \wedge B}$$

allowing for distinct antecedents in the premiss sequents.

For $\wedge L$, the choice is between insisting that both conjuncts A and B be used in the subordinate proof, or not. Of course, at least one of A and B must be so used, on pain of violating the anti-dilution principle (2). Again, the requirement of joint use of A and B would subvert the Sub-sequent Constraint. We might find a better subordinate proof that gets by without one of the premisses A, B but does still use the other one. We would want the substitution of the stronger proof not to debar the application of $\wedge L$ immediately below it. Thus $\wedge L$ should have the form

$$\frac{X:C}{X\backslash\{A,B\}, A\wedge B:C} \quad \text{where } X\cap\{A,B\} \text{ is non-empty}$$

Similar considerations apply to $\vee$. $\vee L$ should have at least the liberal form

$$\frac{X, A:C \quad Y, B:C}{X, Y, A\vee B:C}$$

because this is required by the anti-dilution principle (2) in view of the prospect of subsetting down on the premisses.

But there is another prospect in the context of proof by cases: that of 'subsetting down on the conclusion'. One of the premiss sequents (representing a 'case-proof') might admit of a stronger proof that has the empty set (absurdity) instead of C as its conclusion. If either one does, but the other doesn't, we still want C as an overall conclusion. If both do, we want absurdity as the overall conclusion. (We are assuming that the first case-proof still uses A as a premiss, and the second case-proof still uses B as a premiss.) The correct form of $\vee L$ is therefore the very liberal rule

$$\frac{X, A:[C] \quad Y, B:[C]}{X, Y, A\vee B:[C]} \quad A \text{ not in } X \text{ nor in } Y, \; B \text{ not in } X \text{ nor in } Y$$

which is to be understood as follows: if C appears as the consequent of either one of the premiss sequents, then it is the consequent of the conclusion sequent; otherwise, all consequents are empty. Note also that the anti-dilution principle (2) ensures that A must occur in the antecedent of the first premiss sequent, and not be in X, Y; and that B must occur in the antecedent of the second premiss sequent, and not be in X, Y.

The rules $\vee R$ are the obvious ones:

$$\frac{X:A}{X:A\vee B} \quad \frac{X:B}{X:A\vee B}$$

What, finally, are the rules for $\supset$? We saw earlier how a strict 'use requirement' concerning the antecedent could subvert the Sub-sequent Constraint. How might we relax that requirement? And why would the result still deserve the title of 'relevant logic'? A first stab at $\supset R$, or conditional proof, would be

$$\frac{X, A : B}{X : A \supset B}$$

The Sub-sequent Constraint forces us to allow as a special case both

$$\frac{X : B}{X : A \supset B} \quad \text{where } A \text{ is not in } X$$

and

$$\frac{X, A :}{X : A \supset B} \quad \text{where } A \text{ is not in } X$$

The principle of truth-preservation requires us to allow

$$\frac{X, A : B}{X : A \supset B} \quad \text{where } A \text{ is not in } X$$

What about allowing A, in this last rule form, to be in X? (That is, what about allowing for applications of conditional proof that do not discharge all the assumption occurrences of A?) That would sin against the anti-dilution principle (2), which enjoins us to conclude to the strongest possible sequent in the circumstances. Discharge if you can!—the result of so doing is always stronger. We have therefore arrived at the following precise form of $\supset R$:

$$\frac{X, [A] : [B]}{X : A \supset B}$$

where A is not in X and either A or B
occurs in the premiss sequent

Why is the conditional thus characterized a relevant conditional?—because it is required that one or other, and possibly both, of its antecedent A and consequent B occur in the premiss-sequent for conditional proof. This gives just the right amount of relevance, and no more. To require more is potentially to forfeit epistemic gain. The form of $\supset L$ is the usual one:

$$\frac{X : A \quad Y, B : C}{X, Y, A \supset B : C} \quad \text{where } B \text{ is not in } Y$$

where X has to be allowed to be distinct from Y because of the anti-dilution principle (2).

10.9.2   Intuitionistic Relevant Logic

The rule of initial sequents, plus the rules that we have determined above for $\neg$, $\wedge$, $\vee$ and $\supset$, constitute the propositional part of intuitionistic relevant logic. They obey the Sub-sequent Constraint, and the anti-dilution principle. To summarize:

THE SEQUENT RULES FOR IR

RIGHT

$$\frac{X, A:}{X : \neg A}$$

A not in X

$$\frac{X:A \quad Y:B}{X, Y : A \wedge B}$$

$$\frac{X:A}{X : A \vee B} \qquad \frac{X:B}{X : A \vee B}$$

$$\frac{X, [A] : [B]}{X : A \supset B}$$

A not in X
and either A or B
occurs in the premiss sequent

LEFT

$$\frac{X:A}{X, \neg A :}$$

$$\frac{X:C}{X \backslash \{A, B\}, A \wedge B : C}$$

$X \cap \{A, B\}$ non-empty

$$\frac{X, A : [C] \quad Y, B : [C]}{X, Y, A \vee B : [C]}$$

A not in $X \cup Y$, B not in $X \cup Y$

$$\frac{X:A \quad Y, B:C}{X, Y, A \supset B : C}$$

B not in Y

The orthodox rule of unrestricted Cut has the form

   If $X, A \vdash B$ and $Y, B \vdash C$ then $X, Y \vdash C$.

The system IR, however, does not obey cut in this unrestricted form. For in IR we have

$$P \vdash P \vee Q \text{ and } \neg P, P \vee Q \vdash Q \text{ but } P, \neg P \not\vdash Q.$$

Nevertheless, the following metatheorem holds for IR:

$$\text{If } X, A \vdash B \text{ and } Y, B \vdash C \text{ then } [X, Y] \vdash [C].$$

Our metatheorem snatches victory from the jaws of defeat. If the failure of unrestricted transitivity of deduction causes pain, it is fully assuaged by the resulting epistemic gain.[19] In the last example, we have, in IR, $P \vdash P \vee Q$ and $\neg P, P \vee Q \vdash Q$. Hence by the Dilution-Elimination Theorem we should have $[P, \neg P] \vdash [Q]$. And indeed we do: $P, \neg P \vdash$.

The orthodox Deduction Theorem[20] for logical calculi states that

$$X \vdash B \text{ if and only if } X \setminus \{A\} \vdash A \supset B.$$

In IR, this holds from left to right. But the converse fails, for in IR we have $\neg A \vdash A \supset B$ but not: $\neg A, A \vdash B$. The lesson here is that we have to be careful to distinguish between asserting a conditional and making an inference. We have determined a conditional that is exactly what is needed in order to have the best possible system of relevant inference. The price of 'unpacking' a conditional is eternal vigilance with regard to the joint consistency of the new set of assumptions in play, and with regard to the possible logical truth of the new conclusion.

10.9.3   Classical Relevant Logic

So far we have illustrated how one determines the rules of IR as forming the right logic, given that one has opted for an intuitionistic logic to begin with. But what about the classicist who is unmoved by the need to

---

[19] For a fuller discussion of transitivity, substitutivity and various types of soundness and completeness for these 'not unrestrictedly transitive' logics, see 'Transmission of Truth and Transitivity of Proof', in D. Gabbay (ed.), *What is a Logical System?*, Studies in Logic and Computation Series, Vol. 4, Oxford University Press, pp. 161–77.

[20] For a full discussion of the various desiderata for logical systems, and how IR and CR fare in comparison with other well-known systems in these regards, see 'Delicate Proof Theory', in J. Copeland (ed.), *Logic and Reality: Essays on the Legacy of Arthur Prior*, Oxford University Press, 1996, pp. 351–85.

preserve warranted assertibility from premisses to conclusions, and who is therefore unimpressed by the requirement of harmony on the introduction and elimination rules of a natural deduction system? What set of classical rules would result just by pursuing our anti-dilution principle and our Sub-sequent Constraint? The answer is the one that would be expected by any logician familiar with how the intuitionistic sequent system results from the classical sequent system by restricting succedents to have at most one sentence:

THE SEQUENT RULES FOR CR

RIGHT

LEFT

$$\frac{X, A : Y}{X : \neg A, Y}$$

A not in X

$$\frac{X : A, Y}{X, \neg A : Y}$$

A not in Y

$$\frac{X : A, Z \quad Y : B, W}{X, Y : Z, W, A \wedge B}$$

A not in Z, B not in W

$$\frac{X : Y}{X \setminus \{A, B\}, A \wedge B : Y}$$

$X \cap \{A, B\}$ non-empty

$$\frac{X : Y, A}{X : Y, A \vee B} \qquad \frac{X : Y, B}{X : Y, A \vee B}$$

A not in Y B not in Y

$$\frac{X, A : Z \quad Y, B : W}{X, Y, A \vee B : Z, W}$$

A not in $X \cup Y$, B not in $X \cup Y$

$$\frac{X, [A] : Y, [B]}{X : Y, A \supset B}$$

A not in X, B not in Y

$$\frac{X : A, W \quad Y, B : Z}{X, Y, A \supset B : W, Z}$$

A not in W, B not in Y

Unrestricted cut fails for CR as it did for IR. But the same compensating metatheorem holds for CR as for IR:

If $X, A \vdash B, Z$ and $Y, B \vdash W$ then $[X, Y] \vdash [Z, W]$

where we now allow for more than one sentence in consequents. Likewise, the orthodox Deduction Theorem fails in one direction for CR as it does for IR; but once again we can reconcile ourselves to this failure, because of the compensation of epistemic gain.

10.9.4   Benefits for computational logic

It is their obedience to Dilution-Elimination that suits the sequent systems IR and CR so especially to efficient proof search (in the propositional fragment). Imagine that we are posed a deductive problem $X?\text{-}Y$. We set out in search of a proof of (some sub-sequent of) $X:Y$. Any such proof represents a positive solution. Failure to find any such proof represents a negative solution. We work 'bottom up' in building a sequent proof. We break $X:Y$ up into sub-problems, whose exact form depends on the rule tentatively applied at that 'final' stage. (Some sub-sequent of) $X:Y$ will be the conclusion of that 'final' rule-application; and this means that various premiss sequents are called for. The latter become the new deductive problems posed, and the process iterates. In successful proof-search, we eventually break sub-problems down into the form $\{\dots B \dots\}?\text{-}\{\text{- - -}\ B\ \text{- - -}\}$,[21] to which we have an immediate positive answer in the form of the initial sequent $B:B$.

When we gather together the fruits of our labours, however, it can often turn out that at some stage at which we were seeking a proof of (some sub-sequent of) $Z:W$, we find indeed that we have a proof of some *proper* sub-sequent of $Z:W$. What is so important about the Sub-sequent Constraint is that it guarantees that this will not be labour lost. The subproof of the stronger result can always be used for the construction of a proof of a possibly proper sub-sequent of the sequent $X:Y$ that we were originally posed. But even if we do not end up with a proof of a proper sub-sequent of $X:Y$, we will not have to discard the earlier subproof of the proper sub-sequent of $Z:W$. Instead, it can still be used in the construction of a proof of $X:Y$ itself. The tighter the logical sinews deep within, the stronger will be the body of the proof.

10.9.5   On choosing the right relevant logic: the method summarized

The epistemological and computational considerations set forth above make up a persuasive case for the system IR as the right system of intuitionistic logic, and for the system CR as the right system of classical logic. We

---

[21]In the intuitionistic case, the succedent will consist just of B.

have seen how epistemic gain relevantizes, and picks out a unique system in both the intuitionistic case and the classical case. That choice results from heeding just the following basic principles and injunctions:

1. sequents are made up from finite sets of sentences (the second of which, in the intuitionistic case, will have at most one member);

2. eschew all structural rules except the rule of initial sequents;

3. ensure that logical rules are truth-preserving;

4. ensure that logical rules deal with just one occurrence of a dominant operator at a time;

5. ensure that there is no local dilution in the application of rules; and

6. ensure that a proof of a proper sub-sequent of $Z:W$ can always be preferred to a proof of $Z:W$ itself, in so far as after substituting the former proof for the latter proof within any proof of $X:Y$ we will be able effectively to determine a proof of some sub-sequent of $X:Y$.

These motivating constraints, which determine IR from I and CR from C, can be neatly summarized. We shall give this summary for the case of IR. The case for CR is exactly analogous, and is obtained simply by allowing multiple conclusions in consequents of sequents as usual.

In the usual presentation of the sequent calculus, there are two structural rules besides the rule of initial sequents. These are the rules of Cut and Dilution (or Thinning):

CUT $$\frac{X:A \quad Y, A:B}{X, Y:B}$$

DILUTION $$\frac{X:A}{X, Y:A} \quad \frac{X:}{X:A}$$

When Dilution is available as a rule, we can give a very uniform presentation of the rules for the logical operators. They can be stated as follows:

THE SEQUENT RULES FOR I WHEN DILUTION IS AVAILABLE

RIGHT	LEFT

$$\frac{X, A :}{X : \neg A} \qquad\qquad \frac{X : A}{X, \neg A :}$$

$$\frac{X : A \quad X : B}{X : A \wedge B} \qquad\qquad \frac{X : C}{X \backslash \{A, B\}, A \wedge B : C}$$

$$\frac{X : A}{X : A \vee B} \quad \frac{X : B}{X : A \vee B} \qquad\qquad \frac{X, A : Z \quad X, B : Z}{X, A \vee B : Z}$$

Z at most a singleton

$$\frac{X : B}{X \backslash \{A\} : A \supset B} \qquad\qquad \frac{X : A \quad X \backslash \{A \supset B\}, B : C}{X, A \supset B : C}$$

Note how the antecedents of the premiss sequents of multi-premiss rules involve the same set X. We do not have to make explicit provision for possibly distinct antecedents for these premiss sequents, since distinct ones can always be topped up by applications of Dilution to their union, before we apply the logical rule in question.

It is well known that we need never make applications of Cut in any proof of any sequent $X : Y$ (Y at most a singleton, in the intuitionistic case). This is Gentzen's famous Cut-Elimination Theorem. It takes the form:

Any proof of $X : Y$ can be turned into a cut-free proof of $X : Y$

Two observations are in order. First, the proof of Cut-Elimination relies heavily on the presence of Dilution as a rule in the system. These dilutions are needed in order to 'top up' sequents into the right form for application of the logical rules, as one shuffles cuts up over applications of the latter.[22] Secondly, note that the cut-free proof is a proof of the original sequent $X : Y$.

---

[22] One spectacularly irrelevantist way of topping up would be to confine all the dilution necessary to initial sequents in proofs, by having the rule of initial sequents take the form 'infer $X : Y$ when X and Y share at least one sentence'.

A simple question to ask now is: what about a 'Dilution Eimination Theorem'? What happens if we try to eliminate all dilutions from the cut-free proof guaranteed by the Cut-Elimination Theorem? We certainly will not get a cut-free dilution-free proof of the original sequent of the cut-free proof with which we start. That much is clear from the cut-free proof of the first Lewis paradox:

$$\frac{\dfrac{A:A}{A, \neg A :} \quad \text{\footnotesize{\textit{dilution on right}}}}{A, \neg A : B}$$

By eliminating the dilution in this proof, all we shall obtain is the cut-free dilution-free proof

$$\frac{A:A}{A, \neg A :}$$

But at least this is a proof of a (proper) sub-sequent of the original sequent! Can we ensure such an outcome in general? That is, can we ensure that the elimination of dilutions, in so far as it fails to produce a proof of the original sequent, nevertheless always produces a proof of some (possibly proper) sub-sequent thereof? That is, how could (or should) one modify the forms of the logical rules to enable a proof of the following Dilution-Elimination Theorem?:

> Any cut-free proof of $X : Y$ can be turned into a cut-free dilution-free proof of (some sub-sequent of) $X : Y$.

The answer is that we cannot succeed in this attempt unless we modify the form of the logical rules involving more than one premiss sequent to make allowance for the fact that such premiss sequents might have distinct sets of side-formulae in the antecedent, or that they might disagree on the consequent (one having a single sentence, the other being empty). It turns out that there is one way to modify the logical rules so as to secure the Dilution-Elimination Theorem above, and it is the only one. Thus what could be done is what should be done, if we wish to have the above Dilution-Elimination Theorem. *IR* is the system that results when we use only the rules for the logical operators so modified, along with the rule of initial sequents to get proofs going. And *CR*, likewise, is the system that results in the same way, only allowing now for succedents containing more than one sentence.

Calling the 'non-relevant' parent system P, we have the following result for the relevant system PR determined in this way from P:

Every P-proof of $X : Y$ can be transformed into a PR-proof of some sub-sequent of $X : Y$.

which shows that relevantizing proofs in P always produces a result at least as good as, and possibly better than, the original one. There is everything to gain, and nothing to lose, by relevantizing the parent system in the manner we have explained. The paradoxes of relevance are of no value at all in scientific or mathematical reasoning.

Transitivity of relevant deduction holds wherever it ought to hold. For IR we have

Given any IR-proof of $X : A$ and any IR-proof of $Y, A : B$, we can effectively find an IR-proof of $[X, Y] : [B]$.

and for CR we have

Given any CR-proof of $X : A, Z$ and any CR-proof of $Y, A : W$, we can effectively find a CR-proof of $[X, Y] : [Z, W]$.

10.9.6   Prosecuting our principles further: a precondition on rule applications

At the end of section 8 we deferred the question of the extent to which the Extraction and Dilution-Elimination Theorems embody the full force of the requirements of the Principle of Extraction and the Anti-Dilution Principle, respectively. Our method has been to ensure that proofs of the Extraction Theorem (for natural deduction) and the Dilution-Elimination Theorem (for sequent calculus) would be forthcoming. This entailed casting the rules for logical operators into the right form (for natural deduction and sequent systems), and thereby determining what is claimed to be the right system of relevant proof (depending on whether one is an intuitionist or a classicist).

But does the Principle of Extraction (for natural deduction), or its correlate, the Anti-Dilution Principle (for sequent calculus) actually enjoin more than is ensured by the Extraction Theorem or the Dilution-Elimination Theorem, respectively? The answer is affirmative, as can be illustrated by the following proof in IR:[23]

---

[23]This example is due to Peter Milne; see his 'Intuitionistic Relevant Logic and Perfect Validity', *Analysis*, 54, 1994, pp. 140–2.

$$\frac{\dfrac{A:A \quad B:B}{A,B:A\wedge B} \quad \dfrac{A:A \quad B:B}{A,B:A\wedge B}}{A\vee B, A, B:A\wedge B}$$

Each rule-application is correct, as it stands; but the end-result is a sequent which, in some clear sense, dilutes what 'ought' to be a stronger result (namely, the non-diluted sequent $A, B : A \wedge B$). Nor is this end-result a substitution instance of such a non-diluted sequent.

Rather than adopt the precarious strategy of imposing restrictions on the relative orderings of rules such as $\wedge R$ and $\vee L$,[24] we shall here instead simply advocate making the Anti-Dilution Principle a precondition for any rule application. Thus, working downward with the sequent proof just given— in effect, following the inductive definition of proof—we would consider the contemplated final application of $\vee L$ and reject it, because we can see (for it is a decidable matter) that if we were to apply $\vee L$ there, the resulting conclusion sequent would be a dilution of a premiss sequent. In so doing, we are heeding the Principle of Non-Forfeiture of Epistemic Gain (or the maxim of narrow analysis) directly. Let us therefore demand that all the rules of IR and CR be subjected to the following decidable proviso, mentioned in section 4, on all their applications:

LOCAL ANTI-DILUTION PRECONDITION
ON RULE APPLICATIONS

In any application of a sequent rule

$$\frac{S_0 \ldots S_n}{T}$$

we must ensure that no premiss sequent S_i is a sub-sequent of the conclusion sequent T.

As it stands, this is a 'local' restriction, since it involves looking no higher within the proof than the immediate premiss sequents $S_0, \ldots, S_n$ from which T is to be inferred. The restriction, however, remains decidable even if we strengthen it so as to make it a 'global' one:

GLOBAL ANTI-DILUTION PRECONDITION
ON RULE APPLICATIONS

In any application of a sequent rule

---

[24]Or, at least, on their respective natural deduction counterparts $\wedge I$ and $\vee E$, as was proposed in 'On Maintaining Concentration', *Analysis*, 1994, pp. 143–52.

$$\frac{S_0 \ldots S_n}{T}$$

we must ensure that no sequent in the subproof of any premiss sequent S_i is a sub-sequent of the conclusion sequent T.

This would be entirely in keeping with the spirit of intelligent proof-search, when one is seeking to build a sequent proof 'bottom up' from the concluding sequent $V : U$. For, suppose one had constructed a nether proof-fragment and was working on a deductive sub-problem $X?\text{-}Y$ 'higher up' in the intended sequent proof of $V : U$. The situation would be:

$$X? \vdash Y$$
$$\vdots \quad \ldots$$
$$\overline{V : U}$$

Suppose that one found a solution Σ to $X?\text{-}Y$ in the form of a proof of some sub-sequent $Z : W$ of $X : Y$, and that $Z : W$ was itself a sub-sequent of $V : U$:

$$\Sigma$$
$$Z : W \subseteq X? \vdash Y$$
$$\vdots \quad \ldots$$
$$Z : W \subseteq \quad \overline{V : U}$$

Then Σ itself would immediately count as a solution to the overall deductive problem $V?\text{-}U$, in accordance with the Principle of Non-Forfeiture of Epistemic Gain. An intelligent search algorithm would 'ditch' the nether fragment of proof worked up so far, and simply yield Σ as a solution. In effect, it would be heeding the Global Anti-Dilution Precondition on Rule Applications.

Clearly, satisfaction of the Local Anti-Dilution Precondition is guaranteed by satisfaction of the Global Anti-Dilution Precondition. What about the converse? It would be welcome if satisfaction of the Global Anti-Dilution Precondition by any step in a proof were guaranteed by satisfaction of the Local Anti-Dilution Precondition by all earlier steps. This would cut down the time and space needed to check at each step whether the Global Anti-Dilution Precondition was satisfied.

Note that anti-dilutionism has to place an explicit ban on inferring dilutions of the form $X : A$ where A is in X but is not the only member of X (or, in the classical case, $X : Y$ where X and Y are distinct sets but have a sentence in common). Instances of $P:P$ (for compound P) can be inferred even when the Global Anti-Dilution Precondition is satisfied. For example, the proofs

$$\frac{A:A \quad B:B}{\frac{A,A\supset B:B}{A\supset B:A\supset B}} \quad \frac{A:A \quad B:B}{\frac{A,B:A\wedge B}{A\wedge B:A\wedge B}} \quad \frac{A:A \quad B:B}{\frac{A:A\vee B \quad B:A\vee B}{A\vee B:A\vee B}} \quad \frac{A:A}{\frac{A,\neg A:}{\neg A:\neg A}}$$

satisfy the Global Anti-Dilution Precondition. Obviously we can do without these proofs, since we could get each such $P:P$ directly by substitution in $A:A$ where A is atomic. So what about banning proofs of $P:P$ for compound P? Such a ban would not be enough to avoid dilutions:

$$\frac{\frac{A:A \quad B:B}{A,A\supset B:B} \quad \frac{B:B \quad A:A}{B,B\supset A:A}}{\frac{A,A\supset B,B,B\supset A:A\wedge B}{A\wedge B,A\supset B,B\supset A:A\wedge B}} \wedge R$$

In this proof every application of the rule of initial sequents involves only an atomic sentence, and each step satisfies the Global Anti-Dilution Precondition in its present form. But its conclusion is still of the form $X:P$ where P is a member of X (but not the only one). The rot really set in at the penultimate step, the application of $\wedge R$. There the first premiss sequent $A, A \supset B : B$ has its right-hand sentence, B, occurring on the left in the conclusion sequent $A, A \supset B, B, B \supset A : A \wedge B$ immediately below. Likewise, the second premiss sequent $B, B \supset A : A$ has its right-hand sentence, A, occurring on the left in that conclusion sequent. This application of $\wedge R$ could be ruled out if $\wedge R$ took the form

$$\frac{X:A \quad Y:B}{X,Y:A\wedge B}$$

where $\{A, B\}$ is not a proper subset of $X \cup Y$.

If we decided not to restrict $\wedge R$ in this way, then the proof above would have to be disabled at its final step. For this we would have to impose the following ban:

BAN ON INFERRING DILUTIONS AND COMPOUND TRIVIALITIES

No application of a logical rule is correct whose conclusion would have the form $X:P$ where P is a member of X.

Remember that the rule of initial sequents $A : A$ (for atomic A) does not count as a logical rule, since it does not concern any particular logical operator. The ban proposed here incorporates into proof theory itself some of the insights involved in bottom-up proof search in computational logic. For, when posed a deductive problem $X\,?\text{-}A$ where A is already in X, an intelligent proof-finder delivers the solution $A:A$. The first strategic step of a good proof-finding algorithm is always to look to see whether the sought conclusion is already among the available premisses. Thus it would not be reasonable to expect any proof-finder to produce any of the last five 'proofs'. Why not then make it likewise impossible for the proof system itself to legitimate the construction of any such proofs? Provided there is no loss of logical completeness involved, it seems that there is nothing to lose, and indeed something to be gained, by framing the inductive definition of proof in such a way that anomalies like the last five 'proofs' simply cannot be certified as proofs. Our Local and Global Anti-Dilution Precondition, and our Ban on Dilutions and Compound Trivialities, are steps in this direction. They make it harder for an application of a logical rule to count as correct; but their satisfaction is always a decidable matter.

That is as far as we can pursue these matters here; but we have come far enough. We turn now to a problem that has long needed, for its solution, an appropriately tight characterization of relevant deducibility: the problem of formulating a criterion of cognitive significance.

Chapter 11

Cognitive Significance Regained

11.1 Re-evaluating the problem of cognitive significance

The theory of meaning and theory of knowledge thrive on distinctions. We intuit them and motivate them. Then we formulate them and apply them. When we tire of that, or find our formulations defective, we turn to undermining them and discrediting them. Finally we discard them or (so we think) demolish them. Then we rediscover them, and start all over again.

In this chapter we take a fresh look at the problem of how one might formulate a criterion for cognitive significance: a criterion that will distinguish between, on the one hand, those sentences that depend, for their truth or falsity, on our understanding and experience; and, on the other hand, those sentences that would not so depend (even on the assumption that they had truth-values at all). I take heart in this endeavour from a recent concession by Quine. He writes:[1]

> Tennant writes: 'I believe there is still the prospect of fashioning
> a criterion that would correctly trace the lines of impregnation
> by empirical meaning from periphery inwards: a criterion that

---

[1] W. V. Quine, 'Comment', in W. Salmon and G. Wolters (eds.), *Logic, Language, and the Structure of Scientific Theories*, University of Pittsburgh Press, 1994, pp. 345–51; at pp. 349–50. The reference (Quine 1990) is *The Pursuit of Truth*, Harvard University Press. Quine's quotation is from 'Carnap and Quine', in W. Salmon and G. Wolters (eds.), *op. cit.*, pp. 305–44.

will mark out "the best of these sentences." ' In Quine (1990) I
remarked, 'It would be a Herculean labor, not to say Augean,
to sort out all the premisses and logical strands of implication
that ultimately link theory with observation if or insofar as linked
they be' (p. 17). I agree that we should elicit these hidden lines of
impregnation or strands of implication as best we can, and that
a more discriminating analysis of cognitive significance might be
hoped for than I have managed on the basis of 'critical semantic
mass'.

The task, though, might turn out to be not too Augean. We shall be as
hygienic as possible with logical notions in what follows.

Sentences that depend, for their truth or falsity, on our understanding
and experience are those that are apt for assertion or denial. We allow
for the possibility that some sentences counting as cognitively significant on
our account will be prime targets for projectivist (or expressivist) construal,
rather than descriptivist construal. That is, a modern irrealist may attempt
to carve out some of his irrealist territory within the domain of what we shall
be calling the cognitively significant. He may, for example, want to construe
causal claims, or statements about theoretical entities, or hypotheses about
a speaker's interpretation of an expression in his language, in an irrealist
way. Yet these statements will be cognitively significant on the account to
be offered here. This point is worth stressing, given that certain important
areas of discourse that in the early days of Logical Empiricism were counted
as not cognitively significant would be prime candidates for modern irrealist
reconstrual: among them, most importantly, ethical discourse. We need to
realize, however, that modern irrealists have ventured irrealist reconstruals
even for areas of discourse whose status as cognitively significant was quite
unproblematic for the early Logical Empiricists.

The distinction between sentences that are cognitively significant and
those that are not cuts across, or is presupposed by, each of the following
distinctions, should they be tenable:

- analytic/synthetic

- conceptual/empirical

- a priori/a posteriori

- (logically) necessary or impossible/contingent

- (metaphysically) necessary or impossible/contingent

- observational/theoretical

- decidable/undecidable

- reducible/irreducible (with respect to some favoured class of sentences)

- apt for descriptivist construal/apt for projectivist or expressivist (irrealist) construal

The reader will no doubt be familiar with the embarrassing failure of the most famous early attempt to explicate the notion of cognitive significance. It was Ayer's definition of 'indirectly verifiable' sentences, which he gave in the second edition of *Language, Truth and Logic*.[2] Church showed, in his *JSL* review,[3] that under very weak assumptions every sentence came out as indirectly verifiable on Ayer's definition. Later, Ullian sharpened and simplified Church's result.[4]

The inadequacy of Ayer's definition was about as distressing as it could be. It wasn't just that he located the distinction wrongly, with some sentences coming out on the wrong side of the dividing line, but with most of them correctly located. Rather, he got it spectacularly wrong. His criterion collapsed. It failed to drive a wedge between two non-empty classes of sentences; it just skidded right past the whole language. Every sentence was ruled in, and none ruled out.

Anyone who works now on the problem of cognitive significance does so with the spectre of such failure at their shoulder. It is with great trepidation, therefore, that a new criterion of cognitive significance is ventured here. We shall in due course be formulating some inductive definitions. One of our inductive definitions characterizes, for a sentence S and a theory Δ, and finite levels n, the notion 'S is in F_n with respect to Δ', where F_n will be the set of sentences falsifiable at level n with respect to a theory Δ.[5] Another

---

[2] A. J. Ayer, *Language, Truth and Logic*, Gollancz, London, 2nd edn., 1946. Isaiah Berlin had shown in pretty short measure that Ayer's simpler account in the first edition was inadequate. See his paper 'Verification', *Proceedings of the Aristotelian Society*, 39, 1938–9, pp. 225–48.

[3] A. Church, 'Review of Ayer's Language, Truth and Logic, 2nd Edition', *Journal of Symbolic Logic*, 14, pp. 52–3.

[4] J. Ullian, 'A Note on Scheffler on Nidditch', *Journal of Philosophy*, 62, 1965, pp. 274–75. We shall examine Ullian's result below, and shall show how to avoid it.

[5] In this chapter we shall depart from our earlier notational convention according to which the usual generic variable for a sentence is 'ϕ'. Here we shall use 'S' instead, since its sibilance reminds us of the word 'significant'.

characterizes, for a non-logical expression E and a theory Δ, and finite levels n, the notion 'E is in Λ_n w.r.t. Δ', where Λ_n will be the expressions legitimated as cognitively significant by level n with respect to Δ. Note that these notions are parametrized with respect to the theory Δ; although in our notation we suppress mention of Δ for easier reading.

We shall propose that:

> a sentence S is cognitively significant with respect to a given theory Θ
>
> if and only if
>
> if S is contingent then for some level n, S is a compound of expressions in Λ_n with respect to some subtheory of Θ.

It will follow that every non-contingent sentence will be cognitively significant with respect to every theory. But contingent sentences will be cognitively significant only with respect to theories that make them so. (They will do this by making those sentences beholden to basic sentences in a way to be spelled out in the formal theory below.) This new criterion, we submit, is faithful to the original intuitions of the logical empiricists, and reveals these intuitions to be coherent. It avoids collapse: the wrong sentences are ruled out. It avoids belittling: the right sentences are ruled in. It can be formulated simply and elegantly, as we shall see, with minimal logical materials, as a system of inductive definitions.

Cynicism about the prospects for a criterion of cognitive significance has become part of the contemporary philosophical tradition even among analytical philosophers. It is no exaggeration to say that the failure of past proposals, even in the absence of an impossibility proof, have led to a widely shared intellectual conviction that is now allowed to override strong intuitions (at least among the historically less informed) to the contrary. Now and again the central intuition will resurface even in the writings of a sophisticated philosopher of science and mathematics. An example is from Hartry Field's *Science Without Numbers* (at p. 14):

> there is a marked disanalogy between mathematical theories and physical theories about unobservable entities: physical theories about unobservables are certainly not conservative, they give rise to genuinely new conclusions about observables.

Precisely how physical theories do this, and, as a result, acquire their cognitive significance, is what we aim here (failed past attempts notwithstanding) to explicate. In his classic paper 'Empiricist Criteria of Cognitive Significance: Problems and Changes',[6] Hempel wrote

> I think that the general intent of the empiricist criterion of meaning is basically sound. ...I feel less confident, however, about the possibility of restating the general idea in the form of precise and general criteria which establish sharp dividing lines ...between those sentences which do have cognitive significance and those which do not.

Hempel's lack of confidence in such a possibility resulted from the demonstrable failure of the various criteria that had been put forward by the time of his writing. He did not claim to have any general impossibility proof. All he laid out was a record of piecemeal failure.[7]

Perhaps because Hempel gave such a pessimistic prognosis, the notion of cognitive significance fell from favour. No one appeared to be willing to devote any more intellectual effort to the task of clarifying it. Although Carnap himself never lost faith in the tenability of the notion, Quine's 'Two Dogmas of Empiricism' consummated the slide to pragmatic holism. Not only was the attempt to demarcate the cognitively significant sentences regarded as misguided and certainly fruitless; but also, the celebrated distinction within the class of cognitively significant sentences, between those that were analytic and those that were synthetic, was abandoned. One is tempted to wonder how the subsequent course of analytical philosophy of language and of science might have been altered had these two distinctions been rescued with adequate explications, and had their denial not become such widespread orthodoxy for decades. We shall not, however, enter into such counterfactual speculation here. Instead, we shall confine ourselves to picking up the pieces of the problem now that the dust has settled—all too heavily, unfortunately—on past attempts to formulate a criterion of cognitive significance. If the criterion that we are offering fails, it will, we imagine, fail miserably, just like its predecessors. Nevertheless, if it fails, but not miserably, it may be of some value. And subsequent improvements might lead one to embark on the counterfactual speculations that we must here defer.

---

[6]in *Aspects of Scientific Explanation and Other Essays in the Philosophy of Science*, Macmillan, New York, 1965, pp. 101–22. Note that Hempel's pessimistic conclusions were reached as early as 1950, in one of the original sources for the latter anthologized paper, 'Problems and Changes in the Empiricist Criterion of Meaning', *Revue Internationale de Philosophie*, 4, pp. 41–63.

[7]This assessment was confirmed by Professor Hempel in private discussion in Konstanz in May 1991.

11.2   Conditions of adequacy on a criterion of cognitive significance

11.2.1   Sentences are cognitively significant only within the context of a theory that makes them so

We owe to Hempel the insight that sentences are cognitively significant only within the context of a theory that makes them so. Certain sentences (usually: observation sentences) are obviously cognitively significant. These we shall call *basic*. The problem is to work out, in a principled way, which sentences involving non-basic expressions are cognitively significant, and which are not, with respect to a theory. (Non-basic expressions are usually called non-observational, or 'theoretical'.)

Consider modern physical theory with the theoretical terms 'electron' and 'quark'. The claim 'All electrons contain quarks' is cognitively significant because its constituent terms 'electron' and 'quark' have been 'legitimated' as the kind of expression that can be used to form a cognitively significant sentence. Each of these expressions has in turn been legitimated because it has been involved as a 'new' expression in some statement (within the theory) that has acquired the status of a cognitively significant sentence by some stage, by virtue of the special logical relationships it bears to sequents[8] that consist solely of sentences previously legitimated as cognitively significant.

The religious term 'angel' is not cognitively significant—at least, not by virtue of its having acquired that status within any current theory whose confirmation or disconfirmation derives from basic statements. It would be no counter to this remark about the term 'angel' to say that within current physical theory the term 'electron' could be uniformly replaced by the term 'angel' throughout, thereby conferring cognitive significance on talk about angels. This wouldn't be a case of cognitive significance being granted to talk about the kind of angels that current religious discourse is supposed by its participants to be about. The newly suggested talk about 'angels' (resulting from the proposed substitution of the term 'angel' for the term 'electron' in current physical theory) would serve only to make the term 'angel' render the same cognitively significant service that the term 'electron' currently does. If all our talk about angels had been the substituted talk all along, no one would have entertained any objection to the term 'angel' being cognitively significant. It would have been legitimated as such, and

---

[8]A sequent $X : Q$ is here thought of as a statement of an argument (not necessarily valid). It consists of a set X of premises and a conclusion Q.

for precisely the same reason that our current term 'electron' is cognitively significant—namely, that it features in a physical theory, beholden to basic statements, in the way that it does.

It is when we can forge no sensible empirical connection between our current physical theory and some other stretch of discourse about 'angels' that we refuse to grant cognitive significance to the term 'angel' in that other stretch of discourse, or to contingent sentences within it that use that term. If, on the other hand, some stretch of discourse involving what might initially be regarded as the uninterpreted term 'angel' were to be brought into fruitful theoretical liaison with current physical theory, then we would grant cognitive significance to the term 'angel', and to contingent sentences containing it. But the term 'angel' would in that case, by virtue of the very grounds on which we grant it cognitive significance, be functioning very differently indeed from the term 'angel' of current religious discourse. It would not be the same kind of angel-talk at all.

These reflections point to the need for a definition of cognitive significance that allows one to grant cognitive significance to terms only because of the way they function within statements of a particular theory. So the predicate '...is cognitively significant', when properly explicated, will be essentially relational, parametrized by theories. This point, as remarked above, we owe to Hempel.

11.2.2   Basic sentences

A point of terminological clarification is in order concerning the use we shall make of the words 'basic' and 'basically'. These are theoretical labels in our analysis that would, in its most obvious application, be replaced by the words 'observable' and 'observably'; or by the words 'empirical' and 'empirically'. The distinction basic/non-basic is meant to mark the fact that some sorts of terms in our language—individual constants and predicates, or just plain propositional variables—have some sort of priority over the rest, and are accordingly called 'basic'. The analysis or explication we have given rests only on the existence of such a distinction. Just what lies on each side of the distinction is irrelevant to the operation or application of the distinction itself. The logical virtue of our analysis is that it is neutral between competing choices of what is meant, substantively, by saying that certain items of vocabulary (or the things, properties or concepts for which they stand) are basic. The analysis serves only to give a clear sense to what it is for any given sentence of the language to be able to rest ultimately, for its own truth or falsity, on what is basically the case. It seeks to trace the lines of infection or impregnation, as it were, by one's preferred species of meaning. We want to analyse how it is that the truth-value of a sentence is grounded in a certain basic class of facts. Choice of basic class is another matter altogether. Thus the project should be of interest to any epistemologist or philosopher of language entertaining the prospect of any sort of evidential or conceptual foundationalism.

11.2.3   Metalogical neutrality

The treatment here enjoys a certain metalogical neutrality. We have no epistemological axe to grind in the choice of what sort of sentence counts as basic. All we are concerned to do is to show how, once one has chosen a class of basic sentences, the meanings of other sentences in the language can be appropriately conditioned by them, so that those sentences count as cognitively significant. Of course, the usual applications of a criterion of cognitive significance have in the past had observation sentences (or protocol sentences) as basic. But the emphasis on such perceptual primacy is unnecessary. All that matters is that the basic sentences should be interpreted, and that they should be accepted as cognitively significant.

It is not important to know which basic sentences a theory contains, in order to determine which sentences involving non-basic expressions will be cognitively significant within it. The role of cognitively significant sentences that involve non-basic expressions is, rather, to furnish inferential connections among basic sentences (in the first instance), regardless of which of these latter are held to be true, and which are held to be false. It is the provision of these inferential connections, prescinding from the question of what is basically the case, that allows higher-level theoretical laws to support counterfactuals. Indeed, high-level physical theories, even though evidentially constrained by observation sentences, avoid commitment to the truth or falsity of any particular observation sentences. The boundary conditions of experiments, and the observational findings they deliver, are of secondary importance in identifying the theory as a logical entity.

One need not be worried unduly by the fashionable contemporary insistence that we have no pre-theoretical grasp of what is to count as basic; and that certain 'theoretical' sentences are often used to make 'basic observational' reports within a developed scientific theory. First, this fashionable inclination to blur a commonsense distinction ignores the extent to which one really could retrench, if need be, to a region of pre-theoretic ordinary discourse in order to make theoretically unalloyed observation reports. Secondly, the invitation here is to entertain the basic/non-basic distinction as *tentative* and *revisable* in the context of seeking to reconstruct one's scientific theory so as to show that all of it is cognitively significant according to the criterion to be given below. Eventually *some* division of sentences into the basic and the non-basic ought to be found that will allow one to do this. Moreover, it would be reasonable to require that, once such a division has been tentatively effected, an ordinary English speaker who is not versed in the scientific theory in question should know, simply on the basis of his perceptual experience, how to apply or withhold the 'basic' terms on this tentative identification.

11.2.4 Inductive levels, new vocabulary and extension

One works out from the basic to the non-basic. The basic level can be embroidered upon. This metaphor is a useful one: it suggests colourful and sometimes intricate developments, using a network of threads, but threads that are always tightly rooted in the fabric of the basic. As we work out, we legitimate both constituent expressions and sentences involving them as significant, in so far as they are properly related to the basic. (Exactly how they ought to be so related will be defined in due course.) For the purposes of regimentation, we envisage this as involving finite levels (generically subscripted by n). With typical ambiguity, we shall call levels up to and including any given level n 'old', and levels from $n + 1$ onwards 'new'. If the historical development of a theory closely matched the logical reconstruction in terms of levels, the 'old' theory would include just those expressions legitimated by level n; and the 'new' theoretical hypotheses would venture to introduce as yet unlegitimated expressions, making them legitimate at level $n + 1$. They would do this by making possible the drawing of certain inferences among old sentences that could not be drawn before.[9]

These logical connections forged by new cognitively significant sentences involving new non-basic expressions eventually come to involve previously legitimated cognitively significant sentences other than the most basic ones, as these are recruited to a growing theory. The theory can grow not only by our adopting new statements within the current vocabulary. It can grow also because we adopt new hypotheses involving new vocabulary intended

---

[9]When talking thus of 'old' and 'new' theory, we of course have in mind theoretical *extension* rather than revolutionary theoretical *displacement*.

to refer to hidden mechanisms, unobservable entities, etc. This observation is what leads to our notion of theoretical extension defined below.

The main idea behind the notion of extension is that while a theory might be indifferent as to the truth-values of the sentences in various invalid sequents $X : Q$ whose invalidity is to be 'overcome', nevertheless the inferential gap between these Xs and Qs cannot be bridged using only the resources that are within the theory by that stage and that can be articulated within the language of the sequents concerned.[10] Certain (sets of) new sentences S will be needed to make sequents $S, X : Q$ valid, thereby overcoming the invalidity of $X : Q$. So it will follow not only that

(i) infinitely many sequents $X : Q$ have to be involved (as we shall see in Lemma 3 below); but also that

(ii) the extending sentence(s in) S will need to contain some 'new' term(s), not occurring in any of the sequents $X : Q$ (as we shall see in Lemma 2 below).

These extending sentences in S will feature in sequents $S, X : Q$ that are not only valid, but valid in a special way. It is the main burden of the investigations in this chapter to characterize the kind of validity involved here. We call it *constrained creative extension*; more on which below.

Both features (i) and (ii) are found in scientific theorizing. One introduces new theoretical terms in new hypotheses that are designed both to unify our understanding of disparate phenomena and to extend the range of predictions that can be made about phenomena yet to be observed. The unification and extension involves the postulation of inner or hidden mechanisms, or of micro-constituents, or of large-scale force fields, etc. These posits require new referential terms to be introduced in new hypotheses that 'extend', and thereby unify and widen our range of scientific explanations. Moreover these explanations concern types of phenomena whose possible instances are infinitely various. They can vary in respect to time and place; or in respect of the particular exemplars that might be chosen from any natural kind. It would run against the thrust for generality to limit those natural kinds so as to have only finitely many exemplars.

---

[10] Compare our quotation from Field above.

11.2.5 Verifiability and falsifiability

Since 'verifiable' derives from 'verify', which means establish as true, it is fair to say that Ayer's term 'criterion of verifiability' is a misnomer, even on the strength of its first part, which was concerned with direct verifiability. Recall that according to his definition a sentence S would be directly verifiable if there were observation sentences $O_1, \ldots, O_n$ that did not by themselves logically imply some observation sentence O, but would do so when combined with S as an extra premiss. Thus 'All swans are white' is directly verifiable on Ayer's account. For 'This is a swan' does not logically imply 'This is white'; but 'This is a swan', combined with the extra premiss 'All swans are white', does logically imply 'This is white'. Schematically:

$St \nvdash Wt$; but

$St, \forall x(Sx \supset Wx) \vdash Wt$

To say, however, that 'All swans are white' is directly verifiable seems to be an unhappy way of putting the matter. It would be better to say that the logical relations exhibited show rather that 'All swans are white' is directly *falsifiable*. For the observation of but a single non-white swan would establish it conclusively as false; while yet no number of observed swans, even be they all white, would establish it conclusively as true.

The term 'verifiability', then, in Ayer's own writings, should be taken to include falsifiability as part of its sense. As we tackle the problem, our interest in truth and falsity on the basis of observation could be made perfectly symmetric, by dealing with sequents of the form $X : Y$ (where X and Y are sets of sentences) and by having theories in the form $W|V$ (where one asserts all of W and denies all of V). We should be interested in identifying those sentences, very roughly, to the determination of whose truth-value the truth-values of observation sentences are relevant. The truth-value could be True, and it could equally be False. Positive answers are no more and no less informative than negative answers; observationally informed, however, both kinds of answer must be. Nevertheless, since such thoroughly symmetric metalogical treatments are unusual, we have decided, for ease of exposition, to limit ourselves to the more familiar, asymmetric approach. Thus we shall deal with sequents of the form $X : Q$ (where X is a set of sentences and Q is a sentence) and with theories as sets of assertions. Furthermore, all theoretical extensions will be effected 'on the left', by adding to the premisses. The result is an apparent pride of place for falsifiability of theoretical hypotheses. It should be borne in mind, however, that this asymmetry is only apparent, and a consequence only of our preference for a familiar mode of exposition.

Unlike Ayer's criterion, our criterion does not presuppose, in its for-mulation, any distinction between analytic and synthetic sentences. All it presupposes is the distinction between logically necessary (or impossible) and contingent sentences—surely congenial to a Quinean—and the distinc-tion between so-called basic and non-basic primitive sentences. Although the interpretation of 'basic' is left open (so that the account can enjoy a certain generality across kinds of discourse), the motivating application is of course the one where the basic sentences are the observation sentences of the language. This too is surely congenial to the Quinean.

11.2.6   The principle of composition, or molecularity

Sentences consisting of only non-basic expressions will be cognitively signifi-cant if all their constituent expressions are significant.[11] These constituents will have been 'legitimated' as cognitively significant, and therefore be eli-gible to help form cognitively significant sentences. This is in keeping with the principle of compositionality, or molecularity. This 'legitimation' of new expressions, however, occurs relative to a theory as it is extended to in-clude hypotheses involving those new expressions along with older, already legitimated expressions, in a legitimating way. The latter sentences that legitimate the new expressions are ones that have acquired their cognitive significance via the way they helped to forge new inferential links among statements already enjoying that status, and consisting of previously legiti-mated expressions.

11.2.7   Constrained extension: higher-level hypotheses

In the account given below, this forging of new inferential links whereby sen-tences involving new vocabulary become cognitively significant is called con-strained creative extension of (families of) sequents consisting of sentences that are already cognitively significant. It is intended to explicate the man-ner in which cognitively significant sentences with 'new' expressions can owe their newly acquired cognitive significance to the way they function within a particular theory whose confirmation or disconfirmation derives, ultimately, from basic statements. Thus the whole account of how expressions and sen-tences acquire their cognitive significance is relativized to a (growing) theory throughout. Constrained creative extension is a refinement of the kind of

---

[11]The reader who asks whether one should strengthen this to 'if *and only if*' should consult the discussion below of Hempel's compositionality condition.

creative theoretical extension that Ayer appealed to in his ill-fated definition of indirect verifiability. Ayer was on to something important, but failed to shape it into the right metalogical form. He also stressed verifiability at the expense of falsifiability (even though Ayer's 'verifiability' was really a misnomer!—he should, as pointed out above, have spoken of falsifiability).

We start with the logical empiricist intuition that first found expression in Ayer's own account. This intuition is that cognitively significant sentences should effect extensions of arguments whose premises and conclusions are already cognitively significant. This condition, however, is not enough— as the well-known collapses of Ayer's criterion make vivid. We therefore go one step further, by adding an extra constraint at the logical level so as to capture the logical empiricists' intuition more precisely. We require not just extension, but constrained creative extension, in the sense to be defined below. This extra condition embodies a plausible deepening of Ayer's motivating intuition. It also rules out the standard collapses of Ayer's revised criterion (for which, see section 5 below).

The original motivation behind the formulation of conditions for what Ayer called indirect verifiability (which, as we would also stress, was really indirect falsifiability) was to accommodate higher-level theoretical hypotheses. These were logically connected, within some theory, to observational and other directly verifiable (or directly falsifiable) sentences in a characteristic way. It is the way that we term extension ('on the left' for falsifiability). These high-level theoretical hypotheses made a difference to the class of theory-generated conclusions one could expect, given certain observational or otherwise significant sentences as premises.

To take a simple example, consider various significant sentences $V_1, \ldots, V_n$ that do not, collectively, imply the significant sentence F. (Whence, by orthodox 'non-relevantist' logic, $V_1, \ldots, V_n$ are mutually consistent and F is not logically true.) But suppose that the theoretical hypothesis H is consistent with $V_1, \ldots, V_n$ and, when combined with $V_1, \ldots, V_n$ as premises, yields F as a conclusion. (In other words, suppose $H, V_1, \ldots, V_n : F$ is perfectly valid.)[12] Then we have the prospect of bringing H into confrontation with observable facts, and having to appeal to the latter in falsifying H. For there will be some situation (world, model) making H and $V_1, \ldots, V_n$ all true, and the question will then be whether the actual world is such a world. Since $V_1, \ldots, V_n$ are significant, their truth in any world in which they are true will

---

[12] A sequent is perfectly valid just in case it is valid but has no valid proper sub-sequent. So with a perfectly valid sequent each of its sentences is needed for its validity.

rest on the observable (= basic) facts in that world. Since F is significant, it will, if false in a world, likewise be false by appeal perforce to some of the observable facts in that world. Thus H can in principle be tested by recourse to the observable facts. For $V_1, \ldots, V_n$ may well turn out to be true in the actual world, and F false; and this will be the case by virtue at least of some observable (= basic) facts. In such a case H will have been falsified, but only by making appeal to the observable facts. When we say '$V_1, \ldots, V_n$ may well turn out to be true in the actual world, and F false', we leave open the possibility that the epistemic situation may not be conclusive, especially with respect to $V_1, \ldots, V_n$. For, particularly in the first-order case, one may not have access to finitary truth makers for $V_1, \ldots, V_n$. Their truth-by-virtue-of-at-least-some-basic-facts may be beyond the reach of finitary proof. One may, however, entertain them confidently as lower-level, as-yet-unfalsified statements about the actual world, and test H modulo those lower-level statements in the way just described.

This was clearly the main idea behind Ayer's treatment, but he did not go far enough in explicating it logically. We shall impose this further condition on how an hypothesis like H makes its special contribution in allowing one to pass from $H, V_1, \ldots, V_n$ to F when one cannot pass from $V_1, \ldots, V_n$ alone to F:

> if H is helping to forge a logical connection between significant premisses and a significant conclusion that does not obtain between them on their own, it must be because of how the truth of H secures consequences at the level of basic facts in a way that the truth of $V_1, \ldots, V_n$ alone does not.

Now suppose that the actual world turns out (in a semantic, or logical sense, rather than necessarily an epistemic sense) to make $V_1, \ldots, V_n$ true but F false. Suppose, in other words, that the actual world @ is a counter-example to the inference $V_1, \ldots, V_n : F$. Then the way things are at the observable (= basic) level in @ must be involved in making H false. We explicate this extra requirement below by saying that

> every @-disproof of H must use at least some basic axioms.

That is, in every falsity-maker for H in @ at least some basic facts will be ultimately implicated. (The same holds for any other world in place of @. The notions of @-proof and @-disproof will be explained in due course.)

I have chosen to illustrate the leading idea behind our strengthening of Ayer's criterion by reference to a multiple premiss set and a single conclusion, with the hypothesis H reckoned to the premises (on the left) for testing. But one could generalize our definitions to multiple conclusion sets and dualize to allow 'hypotheses' on the right. This would effect a thorough-going symmetry while remaining faithful to the leading idea. As remarked earlier, however, we prefer a conventional approach for ease and clarity of exposition.

As we shall see below, our newly and more amply characterized notion of cognitive significance appears to be robust and to answer also to intuitions about grades of theoreticity. Our account does justice to Hempel's view that cognitive significance depends both on linguistic framework and theoretical context; but it does so without going the way of Quinean holism. The new criterion belongs to that species of criterion, which we owe to Carnap, that exploits logical relations among sentences, as well as their compositional semantics.

Despite the emphasis on basic expressions in our discussion above of H, $V_1, \ldots, V_n$ and F, we do not have to insist in general that the cognitive significance of new terms be transmitted directly from the basic expressions themselves. Such insistence is appropriate only when $V_1, \ldots, V_n$ and F involve only basic expressions (hence are significant 'at level 0'). In general, however, when $V_1, \ldots, V_n$ and F (and their constituent expressions) are significant only by higher levels $k > 0$, the cognitive significance of new terms at level $(k + 1)$ could be transmitted from those expressions already legitimated as significant by level k. That is why we shall use the slightly more liberal notion of a *legitimate* axiom when describing the constraint on theory extenders. This is more faithful to actual scientific practice; for high-level theoretical terms are usually introduced in order to secure new inferential links among sentences involving only theoretical terms already legitimated. The latter sentences are not, in general, required also to contain basic terms; though of course they are not excluded from doing so.

11.2.8   A remark on significance via compounding

The simple example 'All swans are white' is instructive because it illustrates how a sentence might be thought to be cognitively significant for two sorts of reason: namely, by compounding and by theoretical extension. But in fact 'All swans are white' can be licensed as significant only by virtue of compounding. The provision for extension will anyway require, by Lemma 2 below, that the extender contain new vocabulary not yet legitimated within the language of the invalid sequents to be extended. 'All swans are white',

however, is a logical compound of the basic atomic expressions ('...is a swan'
and '...is white'), which are already legitimated at level 0. The sentence
is therefore cognitively significant by compounding at level 1 (with respect
to any theory—for they all legitimate its constituent terms—whether or not
the theory contains the sentence itself).

Significance via compounding cannot, on the account we are proposing,
be subsumed under significance via constrained extension. Constrained extension is required in order to legitimate new expressions in the sentences
effecting such extension. Once those expressions have been legitimated, then
any compound of them becomes significant. Hence, in particular, the sentences effecting the constrained extension are significant.

11.2.9   Hempel's compositionality condition

Our criterion meets Hempel's own necessary condition of adequacy on any
proposed criterion of cognitive significance. Hempel's condition, however,
is not quite correct in its original formulation. As the reader will recall,
Hempel's condition was that the criterion should ensure that any sentence[13]
is cognitively significant only if all its constituent expressions are cognitively
significant. The converse of Hempel's condition certainly holds: any sentence
is cognitively significant if all its constituent expressions are cognitively significant. But the original condition cannot hold, and cannot be shown to
hold, until we have qualified it.

Hempel gave the following definition.

> Suppose S is a subsentence of S'. Then S occurs non-vacuously
> in S' if and only if there are distinct truth-value assignments,
> differing at most in what they assign to atoms in S, which assign
> different values to S and assign different values to S'.

Note that S can occur non-vacuously in S' only if S' is contingent. Hempel
then stated his necessary condition of adequacy as follows:

> (A) If under a given criterion of cognitive significance, a sentence
> N is non-significant, then so must be all truth-functional com-
> pound sentences in which N occurs non-vacuously as a compo-
> nent. For if N cannot be significantly assigned a truth-value, then

---

[13] Here, we assume, the sentences are well-formed in such a way that licit combination of
significant words will not produce gibberish. Thus, for example, we would have to say that
Chomsky's example 'Green ideas sleep furiously', if regarded as gibberish, is ill-formed.
(Perhaps it violates sortal restriction conditions in the underlying grammar of English.)

> it is impossible to assign truth-values to the compound sentences
> containing N [non-vacuously]; hence, they should be qualified as
> non-significant as well.

My insertion above of '[non-vacuously]' supplies a qualification that Hempel
obviously intended. Otherwise he would be committed to saying, for example, that a logical truth like $\neg(N \wedge \neg N)$ cannot be assigned a truth-value.
But this would be wrong, since the proof of $\neg(N \wedge \neg N)$ shows it to be true
regardless of the truth-value of N. For N to occur non-vacuously in a compound S it must be the case that a difference in the truth-value of N could
make a difference in the truth-value of S; that is, in order to work out the
truth-value of S (by any means whatever) we would have to work out the
truth-value of N.

These reflections show that Hempel is in error when drawing the following
'corollary' of his requirement (A):

> (A2) If under a given criterion of cognitive significance, a sentence
> N is non-significant, then so must be any conjunction $[N \wedge S]$
> and any disjunction $N \vee S$, no matter whether S is significant
> under the given criterion or not.

This 'corollary' does not follow. Even if N is non-significant, if S is logically
false, then so is $N \wedge S$; so $N \wedge S$ is cognitively significant. Likewise, even if N
is non-significant, if S is logically true then so is $N \vee S$; so $N \vee S$ is cognitively
significant.

It follows that Hempel's necessary condition of adequacy should be reformulated as follows:

> (A*) Any *contingent* sentence is cognitively significant only if all
> its constituent expressions are cognitively significant

Our compositionality theorem below secures this result.[14]

---

[14]Suppose that S is cognitively significant but that N is not. Then the compound
sentence $S \wedge (S \vee N)$, it might be objected, should still count as significant, since N occurs
vacuously within it. But (A*) would disallow $S \wedge (S \vee N)$ as significant, for contingent S.

This is not a telling objection. We do not see much being lost if $S \wedge (S \vee N)$ and its ilk
are disallowed as significant. But for one who insists on their being significant, (A*) could
be modified to

> (A**) Any contingent sentence is cognitively significant only if all its con-
> stituent expressions enjoying non-vacuous occurrences are cognitively signif-
> icant.

Similar minor modifications in the definition below of significance via compounding would
secure (A**) as a theorem.

Conventionally the logical empiricists counted all logical truths and logical falsehoods as cognitively significant. In this we follow them. For the truth-value of a logical truth or logical falsehood can in principle be determined 'am Symbol allein'. It is a matter of the form, not the content, of the sentence concerned. We therefore allow as cognitively significant even sentences containing some non-basic terms (indeed: even ones containing only non-basic terms), provided that they are logically true or logically false. Thus the sentence 'It is not the case that (the Absolute is perfect and it is not the case that the Absolute is perfect)' is cognitively significant. Because it has the form $\neg(P \wedge \neg P)$, we can determine it as true without concerning ourselves with what the sentence P itself means. Even if P has defective meaning, the defects do not hamper our determination of the truth-value of $\neg(P \wedge \neg P)$ on the basis of its logical form alone.

All that is important in the definition of cognitive significance is that it should exclude those *contingent* sentences whose defective meanings do obstruct our determination of their truth-values on the basis, ultimately, of the observable (or basic) facts and sentence meaning. It is precisely this task which our definition below is designed to accomplish.

11.2.10   The first-order case

Any workable account of cognitive significance must deal with the first-order case, and not be restricted merely to propositional languages. Historically, however, the collapses of proposed accounts have been effected at the propositional level. That might lead one to think that the level of propositional logic would be the most appropriate one for the initial exposition of the central ideas behind a new criterion. Even at the propositional level, it would seem, there is challenge enough to get the account right. We have resisted this temptation so to restrict the exposition of the main ideas behind the criterion we propose, for the following compelling reasons.

First, Lemma 4 below shows that after getting all contingent compounds of basic propositional atoms to be significant at level 1 with respect to any theory, we get no more significant sentences (in a propositional language) at all. For all $n > 1$, a sentence is significant at level n only if it is already significant at level 1. This should be no surprise. A finitary classical propositional language is hardly one in which to get a grip on regularities in the world that can manifest themselves in infinitely various ways. Whatever 'theoretical' sentence of a classical propositional language we may introduce into our theory (a sentence, that is, containing non-basic propositional atoms), the deductive links it effects among (compounds of) basic atomic sentences can be just as well effected by adopting as an hypothesis a compound of basic atomic sentences. But this is not so at first order!

Secondly, just as a criterion can fail through collapse, so too it can fail through belittling. A criterion of cognitive significance would be belittled if there were some obviously cognitively significant sentence (within some theory) that, according to the criterion, could not be seen to count as such. The danger, in restricting oneself to the propositional level for an exposition of a new criterion, is that critics of the new criterion will be entitled to conclude that it can be belittled. The serious theorist about scientific theories will want to work right away with examples of quantified sentences from the natural sciences, and (quite rightly) will be at a loss to see how they could be accommodated as cognitively significant by any proposed criterion that is limited to the propositional level.

11.2.11 The invariance of non-significance under reformulation

The cognitive non-significance of a theory should be invariant. 'Once nonsense, always nonsense' is what the logical empiricists wanted to be able to say about meaningless metaphysical discourse. It was important to Carnap to be able to show that bad theory could not insinuate or inveigle itself into a better status via any finagled mix of the good with the bad. A good, terminologically clean theory in the physical sciences, affording no respectability to the terms of Heideggerian metaphysics, cannot be reformulated in conjunction with Heideggerian metaphysics in such a way as to force one to concede cognitive legitimation for the terms of Heideggerian metaphysics. No matter how much the dodgy and caddish terms may be made to rub shoulders with the gentle and honest terms, they will remain, essentially, worlds apart. Holism provides no refuge for the shifty, footloose and phenomena-free language of the Heideggerian. We need to be able to show this. What we want is a theorem about linguistic class differences. Our Quarantine Theorem below improves on Carnap's result to this effect.[15] It shows that our criterion cannot be collapsed. That is, there can be no metatheorem to the effect that every sentence is (on the definition given) cognitively significant with

---

[15]Carnap's result was at p. 55 of 'The Methodological Character of Theoretical Concepts', in H. Feigl and M. Scriven (eds.), *The Foundations of Science and the Concepts of Psychology and Psychoanalysis*, Minnesota Studies in the Philosophy of Science, Vol. I, University of Minnesota Press, 1956, pp. 38–76.

respect to any given theory.

11.3   The formal theory

11.3.1   Extension

Let X be a (possibly empty) set of sentences and let Q be a sentence. We include the absurdity sign $\perp$ as a special case of Q. $X : Q$ is a sequent. Instead of $X : \perp$ we can also write $X : \emptyset$ where $\emptyset$ is the empty set. This enables us to think of $X : \perp$ as a proper sub-sequent of $X : Q$ when Q is $\perp$. Also, if Y is a proper subset of X then $Y : Q$ is a proper sub-sequent of $X : Q$.

DEFINITIONS

A *countermodel to $X : Q$* is a model that makes every sentence in X true, and Q false.

The sequent $X : Q$ is *valid* if and only if $X : Q$ has no countermodel.

$X : Q$ is *perfectly valid* if and only if it is valid and has no valid proper sub-sequent: that is, it ceases to be valid if any sentence is removed on the left or on the right.

$X : Q$ is *skeletally valid* if and only if it is perfectly valid and is not a proper substitution instance of a perfectly valid sequent: that is, not only does every sentence matter, but also every aspect of each sentence's logical structure.

We shall write $X \vdash Q$ when $X : Q$ is valid. Instead of $\emptyset \vdash Q$ we shall write simply $\vdash Q$. $\vdash Q$ means that Q is logically true. $X \vdash \perp$ means that X is not satisfiable. We shall write $X \nvdash Q$ when $X : Q$ is invalid (that is, has a countermodel). With this notation likewise we suppress mention of $\emptyset$ if it occurs on the left or on the right. $X \nvdash$ means that X is satisfiable; $\nvdash Q$ means that Q is falsifiable. '$X \nvdash Q$' can be made vivid as follows: the language can be partitioned (by some countermodel) so that on the left are all the true sentences, including all those in X, and on the right are all the false sentences, including Q.

Suppose $X : Q$ is non-empty, that is, either X is non-empty or Q is not absurdity. Suppose further that $P, X : Q$ is perfectly valid. Then the proper sub-sequent $X : Q$ is invalid, whence some model makes every sentence in X true, and Q false, and therefore makes P false (on pain of counter-exemplifying $P, X : Q$). Likewise, removing some member of X or replacing Q by absurdity leaves an invalid proper sub-sequent when P is on the left, whence there is a model that makes P true. Thus if $P, X : Q$ is perfectly valid, P can be made true and P can be made false; that is, P is contingent.

LEMMA 0: Suppose $X \nvdash Q$. Then for every sentence S, exactly one of the following holds:

(i) $\neg S, X \vdash Q$ and every countermodel to $X : Q$ makes $\neg S$ false
(ii) $S, X \vdash Q$ and every countermodel to $X : Q$ makes S false
(iii) $\neg S, X \nvdash Q$ and $S, X \nvdash Q$.

Proof: Consider the set of countermodels to $X : Q$. Then exactly one of the following holds:

(i′) every one of them makes S true

(ii′) every one of them makes S false

(iii′) some of them make S false and some of them make S true

These are respectively equivalent to (i), (ii) and (iii) above. So we know also that if $X \nvdash Q$ then

(iv) if $\neg S, X \vdash Q$ then every countermodel to $X : Q$ makes S true

(v) if $S, X \vdash Q$ then every countermodel to $X : Q$ makes S false. QED

We now need some definitions that will enable us to talk about extensions of scientific theories. These arise from a given theory by adding to it new hypotheses—in particular, hypotheses involving new theoretical vocabulary. We need to provide in general for infinite theories, which may or may not be logically closed.

DEFINITIONS (regarding theories)

We shall treat *theories* as sets of sentences. A *model for* a theory makes all its sentences true. A *satisfiable* theory is one that has a model. We shall always assume our theories to be satisfiable.

W is *logically closed* if and only if *W* contains every sentence (in the language of *W*) that is true in every model for *W*. We do not assume logical closure for theories. (In this respect we do not follow the conventions observed by most mathematical logicians. But our own usage is arguably more in keeping with how philosophers of science actually talk about scientific theories—as sets of sentences not necessarily containing all their logical consequences.) [*W*] will denote the logical closure of the theory *W*.

W is a *subtheory* of *X* if and only if [*W*] is a subset of [*X*]. (Note that it might be the case that *W* is a subtheory of *X* even though it not be the case that *W* is a subset of *X*! This is because *X* might not be logically closed.) When *W* is a subtheory of *X* we shall also say that *X* is an *extension* of *W*.

DEFINITIONS (regarding sequents)

$X : Q \succeq Z : R$ if and only if every countermodel to $Z : R$ is a countermodel to $X : Q$.

$X : Q \otimes Z : R$ if and only if not both $X : Q \succeq Z : R$ and $Z : R \succeq X : Q$

$\succeq$ could be read 'is logically as strong as', or 'is as easy to counter-exemplify as'. Clearly $\succeq$ is reflexive and transitive. $\otimes$ could be read as 'is not logically equivalent to'.

We can relativize these notions to a given theory. Thus:

$X : Q \succeq Z : R$ modulo *W* if and only if every model of the theory *W* that is a countermodel to $Z : R$ is a countermodel to $X : Q$

$X : Q \otimes Z : R$ modulo *W* if and only if not both $X : Q \succeq Z : R$ modulo *W* and $Z : R \succeq X : Q$ modulo *W*

If a sequent $X : Q$ is thought of as the claim $(\wedge X \supset Q)$, it is easier to appreciate why '$\succeq$' can be read as 'is logically as strong as'. For if $X : Q \succeq Z : R$ modulo *W*, then $(\wedge X \supset Q)$ logically implies $(\wedge Z \supset R)$ modulo *W*. The relation $\succeq$ among sequents modulo a given theory is a partial ordering of those sequents.

Note that if $X : Q \succeq Z : R$ modulo *W* and W^* is an extension of *W*, then $X : Q \succeq Z : R$ modulo W^*.

$\otimes$ is the relation of logical non-equivalence (modulo W) by means of which we shall distinguish sequents.

Validity of sequents can also be relativized to a given theory:

$X : Q$ is *valid modulo* W if and only if no model of W is a countermodel to $X : Q$—that is, $X, W \vdash Q$. Hence

$X : Q$ is *invalid modulo* W if and only if some model of W is a countermodel to $X : Q$—that is, $X, W : Q$ has a countermodel.

Note that if $X : Q$ is valid modulo W and W^* is an extension of W, then $X : Q$ is valid modulo W^*. Ordinary validity is validity modulo the empty theory.

Note also that if a sequent $X : Q$ is invalid modulo W then so is any sub-sequent of $X : Q$.

DEFINITION
Let $\mathcal{F}$ be a set of sequents. W *clinches* (each member of) $\mathcal{F}$ if and only if every sequent in $\mathcal{F}$ is valid modulo W—that is, for every $X : Q$ in $\mathcal{F}$ we have $X, W \vdash Q$.

DEFINITION
A *family* for W is a non-empty set of sequents in the language of W that are invalid modulo W.

The sequents in a family for a theory W are to be thought of as those inferences (in the language L of one's theory W) that one might wish to be clinched by some theoretical extension of W.[16] In general these will include both those sequents expressing law-like regularities that we wish to be able to explain, and other sequents expressing regularities of which we might not yet be apprised. By introducing new theoretical vocabulary, and new theoretical hypotheses involving both the old and the new vocabulary, we generate the former sequents as explanations; whereas the latter sequents may be generated as new predictions by means of which the extended theory can be tested. We should therefore bear in mind that when we undertake theoretical extensions we may not be motivated at the time by the full range of invalid sequents (modulo the unextended theory) that will form the family

---

[16]The clinching, however, will have to be effected in a very special way; see below.

involved in the extension. Indeed, it is usually required of theoretical extensions motivated by the desire to explain a given range of regularities that it
should also generate predictions concerning other regularities of which the
theory-builder may not yet be aware. The sequents expressing these latter
regularities can then be put to the test; hence also the extended theory that
generates them.

DEFINITION
Suppose $\mathcal{F}$ is a family for W and S is a finite set of sentences. *S extends W
for $\mathcal{F}$*
    if and only if
S, W is satisfiable and for each of the sequents $X : Q$ in $\mathcal{F}$, there is some
subset W_X of W and some (perforce non-empty) subset S^* of S such that
the extended sequent $X, S^*, W_X : Q$ is skeletally valid.

When S extends W for $\mathcal{F}$ we shall call S an *extender of W for $\mathcal{F}$*. Note
that an extender S is always finite. Note also that if S extends W for $\mathcal{F}$
then S is not a subtheory of W. For, if S were a subtheory of W, we would
have each sequent in $\mathcal{F}$ valid modulo W, contrary to the requirement that
$\mathcal{F}$ be a family for W.

LEMMA 1. If S extends W for $\mathcal{F}$, then every sequent in the family $\mathcal{F}$ is finite.

> *Proof*: Since for each such sequent $X : Q$, we have a skeletally
> valid sequent of the form $X, S^*, W_X : Q$, and validity is compact,
> X must be finite. QED

Even if W already clinches $\mathcal{F}$, some extender S might be theoretically
desirable, on grounds of simplicity and unifying explanatory power. If W
does not already clinch $\mathcal{F}$—and especially if $\mathcal{F}$ is a family for W—then an
extender S is called for in order to clinch $\mathcal{F}$. Note that S might be a theory
in the same language as W, even though it is not a subtheory of W. In
that case, if S extends W for a family $\mathcal{F}$ then it does so in a rather unin-
teresting way. S would, in effect, merely state (whatever extra is needed,
modulo W, to clinch) the regularities expressed by the sequents in $\mathcal{F}$, but
would not need to resort to linguistic expressions other than those already
used in (sequents in) $\mathcal{F}$. More interesting is the case where a finite extender

S extends W for a family $\mathcal{F}$, and does so by resorting to new vocabulary. And most interesting of all is the case where a finite extender S extends W for a family $\mathcal{F}$, and does so *by having to resort to new vocabulary*. In that case the theory W would have to have been $\mathcal{F}$-less in the following sense:

DEFINITION
Let $\mathcal{F}$ be a set of sequents in the language of W. The theory W *is $\mathcal{F}$-less* if and only if no satisfiable extension W, S obtained by adding only finitely many sentences (i.e. those in S) in the language of W, clinches $\mathcal{F}$

LEMMA 2. If S extends W for $\mathcal{F}$, and W is $\mathcal{F}$-less, then S must contain at least one new term not in the language of W.

Proof. Suppose that S extends W for $\mathcal{F}$, but that every term in S is in the language of W. Consider the extended theory $W^* = W, S$. *Ex hypothesi* W^* is satisfiable and is in the language of W. Moreover, for each sequent $X : Q$ in $\mathcal{F}$, since there is a skeletally valid sequent of the form $X, S^*, W_X : Q$, it follows by dilution that $X, W, S \vdash Q$, hence $X, W^* \vdash Q$, contrary to the assumption that W be $\mathcal{F}$-less. QED

LEMMA 3. Extension of an $\mathcal{F}$-less theory for a family $\mathcal{F}$ requires $\mathcal{F}$ to be infinite.

Proof. Suppose that S extends W for $\mathcal{F}$, and that W is $\mathcal{F}$-less. Suppose there are only finitely many sequents in $\mathcal{F}$. Call them $X_i : Q_i$ ($i = 1, \ldots, n$). Note that W, S is satisfiable, and for each sequent $X_i : Q_i$ ($i = 1, \ldots, n$) there is a (finite) subset W_i of W and a (non-empty, finite) subset S^* of S such that $X_i, S^*, W_i : Q_i$ is (skeletally) valid. Hence every model of S fails to be a countermodel to $X_i, W_i : Q_i$. Thus every model of W that is also a model of S fails to be a countermodel to $X_i : Q_i$ ($i = 1, \ldots, n$). Hence every model of W that is also a model of S fails to make $(\wedge X_i W_i) \supset Q_i$ false; hence, makes it true.[17] Consider now the sentence σ:

---

[17]The acute reader will have noticed that this step is non-constructive, like certain others in what is here perforce a more classical exposition of ideas than we would prefer. The reader may rest assured, however, that we are taking this more relaxed, 'classical semantical'-looking route only for ease of exposition. We do not want to compound difficulties of comprehension that might arise from a reader's unfamiliarity with constructivism with difficulties of comprehension arising from this new attempt to characterize cognitive significance. The main ideas that we are capturing here in this more classical vein—ideas

(σ) $(\wedge X_1 W_1 \supset Q_1) \wedge \ldots \wedge (\wedge X_n W_n \supset Q_n)$

Note that every model of W that is also a model of S makes σ true. Hence, since W, S is satisfiable, it follows that W, σ is satisfiable also. σ is in the language of W. Each sequent $X_i, W_i, \sigma : Q_i$, i.e.

$$X_i, W_i, (\wedge X_1 W_1 \supset Q_1) \wedge \ldots \wedge (\wedge X_n W_n \supset Q_n) : Q_i \; (i = 1, \ldots, n)$$

is valid. By dilution

$$X_i, W, \sigma \vdash Q_i$$

But consider the extended theory $W^* = W, \sigma$. This, as we have seen, is satisfiable. Moreover we now have, for each sequent $X_i : Q_i \; (i = 1, \ldots, n)$ in $\mathcal{F}$, that

$$X_i, W^* \vdash Q_i;$$

which is contrary to the requirement that W be $\mathcal{F}$-less. QED

LEMMA 4. For extension of an $\mathcal{F}$-less theory for a family $\mathcal{F}$ to be possible, the language used, if classical, has to be more powerful than a propositional language that has only finitely many propositional constants.

> *Proof*: Suppose we are dealing with a propositional language L that has only finitely many propositional constants. Suppose S extends the $\mathcal{F}$-less theory W for the family $\mathcal{F}$. By Lemma 3, $\mathcal{F}$ is infinite. Suppose its pairwise logically non-equivalent members modulo W are $X_i : Q_i \; (i = 1, 2, \ldots)$. For each such sequent $X_i : Q_i$ in $\mathcal{F}$ there is a (finite) subset W_i of W and a (non-empty, finite) subset S^* of S such that $X_i, S^*, W_i : Q_i$ is skeletally valid (hence also finite). So the conjunction of all the members of S logically implies (modulo W) each of the infinitely many sentences $(\wedge X_i) \supset Q_i \; (i = 1, 2, \ldots)$ which are pairwise logically non-equivalent modulo W. But this is impossible within a

---

about constrained creative extension, and of subformula occurrences having to 'do some work' within a proof—can be captured also within the more austere context of *IR*.

classical propositional language. QED

It is when S extends W for $\mathcal{F}$, and W is $\mathcal{F}$-less (hence $\mathcal{F}$ is an infinite family for W) that the extension deserves to be called *creative*. The *finite* extender S helps to clinch the *infinitely many* regularities (sequents) in $\mathcal{F}$ that *no* satisfiable extension of W, within the language of W, can clinch. And the finite extender S does this only by virtue of involving *new* theoretical vocabulary, and theoretical assertions involving that new vocabulary.

What we need to ensure, now, is that every member of S is involved in the clinching of at least infinitely many of the sequents in the family $\mathcal{F}$. We want to prevent the family $\mathcal{F}$ from containing finitely many 'rogue' sequents which alone are responsible for S's containing some of the sentences that it does. Every member of S has to be rendering an infinite amount of extending service, so to speak. In effect, therefore, in creative extension, there is a certain sort of *homogeneity* to the problematic sequents in $\mathcal{F}$, and a homogeneity of purpose in S's having all the (finitely many) member sentences that it does, in order to clinch these sequents.

Let us call a subset $\mathcal{F}^*$ of $\mathcal{F}$ a *cofinite* subset of $\mathcal{F}$ just in case it contains all but finitely many members of $\mathcal{F}$ (so $(\mathcal{F} \setminus \mathcal{F}^*)$ is finite). Note that if W is $\mathcal{F}$-less and $\mathcal{F}^*$ is a cofinite subset of $\mathcal{F}$ then W is $\mathcal{F}^*$-less. This is because, if some satisfiable extension W, S^* obtained by adding only finitely many sentences (i.e. those in S^*) in the language of W, were to clinch $\mathcal{F}^*$, then the adoption of only finitely many more sentences in the language of W would suffice to clinch in addition the finitely many remaining sentences in $(\mathcal{F} \setminus \mathcal{F}^*)$. For each of the finitely many sequents $X : Q$ in $(\mathcal{F} \setminus \mathcal{F}^*)$, the sentence $(\wedge X) \supset Q$ would do.

DEFINITION

S *creatively extends* W for $\mathcal{F}$
    if and only if
(i) S extends W for $\mathcal{F}$, and W is $\mathcal{F}$-less; and, moreover,
(ii) no proper subset of S extends W for any cofinite subset of $\mathcal{F}$.

Since $\mathcal{F}$ is a cofinite subset of itself, it follows from (ii) that if S creatively extends W for $\mathcal{F}$ then no proper subset of S extends W for $\mathcal{F}$. So each member of a creative extender S is needed just for the plain extending that S accomplishes. Indeed, (ii) secures more: each member of S is needed for an infinite amount of the plain extending that S accomplishes.

This notion of creative extension can be illustrated with a simple mathematical example.[18] Let E_n be a sentence of first-order logic with identity that says 'There are at least n individuals'. Consider the family of sequents $\{\emptyset : E_n | n > 2\}$. This is a family for the empty theory in the language of identity, since E_n is logically contingent for $n > 2$. Moreover, a corollary of the compactness theorem for first-order logic tells us that no finite satisfiable theory (hence, no finite satisfiable extension of the empty theory) in the language of identity can clinch this family. So the empty theory is $\{\emptyset : E_n | n > 2\}$-less. Now consider a finite 'theory of infinity' S—that is, a finite satisfiable theory S that has only infinite models. S could extend the empty theory for $\{\emptyset : E_n | n > 2\}$, since for each E_n there could be a subset S^* of S such that each sequent $S^* : E_n$ is skeletally valid. Examples of such finite theories of infinity are

{0 is not a successor, Everything has a successor, No two successors are identical}

and

'R is a dense linear ordering of at least two elements', i.e.
$\{\ \exists x \exists y\, Rxy,\ \forall x \forall y(Rxy \supset \neg Ryx),\ \forall x \forall y(Rxy \supset \forall z(Ryz \supset Rxz)),$
$\forall x \forall y(Rxy \supset \exists z(Rxz \wedge Rzy)),\ \forall x \forall y(y = x \vee Rxy \vee Ryx)\ \}$

The first of these involves the successor function symbol $s(\ )$; the second involves the two-place predicate R.

This example nicely confirms our general expectations about creative extension. We have seen (Lemma 2) that any extender has to involve at least one new term not in the language of the unextended theory (such as the successor function symbol s or the two-place predicate R). We have also seen (Lemma 3) that extension of an $\mathcal{F}$-less theory for a family $\mathcal{F}$ requires $\mathcal{F}$ to be infinite (such as $\{\emptyset : E_n | n > 2\}$).

11.3.2   How sentences depend on the atomic facts within a model for their truth or falsity

Partition the primitive extra-logical expressions of L into two classes. Call one the class of *basic* primitive expressions. Call the other the class of *non-*

---

[18]I am indebted here to Randy Dougherty.

basic primitive expressions. We are concerned to define a sense in which the truth-value of a given sentence rests on the basic facts rather than on the non-basic facts. (Note that 'non-basic' does not imply 'non-atomic'.)

Let M be a model that deals with both basic and non-basic primitive expressions, and suppose from now on that it deals with all the primitive expressions occurring in any sentence we mention. The identity predicate, if it occurs in the language, counts as basic. A *basic atomic sentence* is one made up entirely of basic primitive expressions. The adjectives 'basic' and 'non-basic' will transmit in the obvious way to assumptions, rule assumptions and axioms.

Consider a propositional language, based on $\neg$, $\vee$, $\wedge$ and $\supset$. Consider any truth-value assignment M dealing with the propositional variables. To any propositional variable, M assigns the value T or the value F. Let the *atomic diagram* corresponding to M be the set that results by taking each propositional variable that is assigned T by M, and taking the negation of each propositional variable that is assigned F by M. Let us call the atomic diagram obtained in this way $[M]$. Thus if $\{A, B\}$ is the set of propositional variables, and if M is the assignment

$$A \to T$$
$$B \to F$$

then the atomic diagram $[M]$ is the set $\{A, \neg B\}$. We can go one step further and form the inferential diagram $|M|$ corresponding to M by replacing each unnegated atom A in $[M]$ by the atomic axiom

$$\frac{\quad}{A}$$

and replacing each negated atom $\neg A$ in $[M]$ by the atomic rule of inference

$$\frac{A}{\bot}$$

Thus in our previous example the inferential diagram $|M|$ would be the set

$$\{ A, \frac{B}{\bot} \}$$

of atomic rules. For ease of layout we shall also write $\{|A, B|\bot\}$. The inferential diagram represents 'the way the world is' according to M. Given a truth-value assignment M, one uses truth tables in the familiar way to work out the truth-value of any sentence formed from atoms to which M assigns a truth-value. Now corresponding to any such evaluation of any sentence S as true under M, we can provide a proof of S from (i.e. by using axioms and rules in) $|M|$ (called an M-*proof* of S); and for any sentence S false under M we can provide a proof of $\perp$ from $|M|, S$ (which we may call an M-*disproof* of S).

Each M-proof (and M-disproof) is built up by means of logical rules and also, possibly, the atomic rules in the inferential diagram $|M|$ described above. The logical rules consist of the familiar introduction and elimination rules for each logical connective.

KALMÁR'S THEOREM[19] (inferential version)

For any sentence S and any truth-value assignment M dealing with the atoms of S,
(i) if S is true under M then there is a proof of S whose only undischarged assumptions are rule assumptions drawn from $|M|$; and
(ii) if S is false under M then there is a proof of $\perp$ whose only undischarged sentential assumption is S and whose undischarged rule assumptions are drawn from $|M|$.

The proof is by induction on S, and is easy enough to leave to the reader.

We now have a precise sense for the claim that a sentence's truth-value is based on certain atomic facts according to a given evaluation. Each way of 'working out' that a sentence is true under a given truth-value assignment corresponds to a distinct proof of that sentence using rules in the inferential diagram corresponding to the assignment. To take a very simple example, if M makes both A and B true, then there will be two ways of showing that the sentence $(A \lor B)$ is true:

$$\frac{\overline{A}}{A \lor B}$$

---

[19] The reader will recognize this as the core of a well-known completeness proof for classical propositional logic. Cf. L. Kalmár, 'Über die Axiomatisierbarkeit des Aussagenkalküls', *Acta Sci. Math.* (Szeged) 7, 1934–5, pp. 222–43.

$$\frac{\overline{B}}{A \vee B}$$

Likewise for disproofs of false sentences.

'Evaluation' proofs with respect to a truth-value assignment M have one of the two forms

$$\Sigma \ (\subseteq |M|)$$
$$\vdots$$
$$S$$

$$\underbrace{S, \Sigma} \ (\subseteq |M|)$$
$$\vdots$$
$$\bot$$

where Σ, the set of undischarged rule assumptions, is drawn from the inferential diagram $|M|$. Proofs of the first form are M-proofs, and those of the second form (ending with $\bot$) are M-disproofs. For brevity of subsequent definitions, we shall say that Σ is the set of axioms of a proof of either form. In the case of proofs of the first form, Σ summarizes the atomic 'facts' (according to M) on which the *truth* of S rests. In the case of proofs of the second form, Σ summarizes the atomic 'facts' (according to M) on which the *falsity* of S rests.

Note that the truth or falsity of S rests on Σ according, respectively, to the proof or disproof in question. To stress this point, consider a complex sentence S true under M. There will in general be more than one M-proof of the form

$$\Sigma \ (\subseteq |M|)$$
$$\vdots$$
$$S$$

and in general the various Σ could be distinct. Such cases represent over-determination of truth, as we saw in the simple case of $(A \vee B)$ when both A and B are true. Likewise with falsity.

So there are in general different ways of seeing that a given sentence is true in M (if it is true) and different ways of seeing that a sentence is false in M (if it is false). The existence of exactly one way of arriving at a truth-value for a given sentence will be the exception rather than the rule.

Thus different selections of 'atomic facts' in M can be responsible—that is, sufficient—for the determination of a sentence's truth-value in M.

Thus far we have dealt only with the propositional case, where M is a truth-value assignment to propositional variables. We have spoken of M-proofs and M-disproofs. It is time now to generalize to the first-order case.

Here instead of a truth-value assignment M we shall have a *model M* consisting of a domain of individuals and with extensions as usual for primitive extralogical terms such as predicates. We can still talk of M-proof and M-disproof. We just have to bear in mind that these proofs will have (at the quantifier steps $\exists$E and $\forall$I) a distinct subproof for each individual in the domain of M, in a way to be explained presently. Just as an M-disproof Π of the conjunction $A \wedge B$ might proceed:

$$\frac{A \wedge B}{\begin{array}{c} A \\ \Theta \\ \bot \end{array}} \wedge E$$

where Θ is an M-disproof of A, so too an M-disproof Π of $\forall x F(x)$ could proceed:

$$\frac{\forall x F(x)}{\begin{array}{c} F(t) \\ \Theta \\ \bot \end{array}} \forall E$$

where Θ is an M-disproof of $F(t)$, and t is (the name for) a member of the domain of M. Matters would be correspondingly simple for M-proofs of existential sentences of the form $\exists x F(x)$.

But what about an M-proof of $\forall x F(x)$? And an M-disproof of $\exists x F(x)$? An M-proof of $\forall x F(x)$ is going to be as wide, at its final step, as M is large. That is, it will have as many branches (subordinate M-proofs) at the point of 'universal introduction' as there are members of the domain of M. Indeed, for each member a of the domain of M there will have to be an M-proof Θ_a of $F(a)$ as a subordinate proof for 'universal introduction' in the final step of an evaluation-as-true-in-M of the universal sentence $\forall x F(x)$:

$$\frac{\ldots \Theta_a \ldots}{\ldots F(a) \ldots}{\forall x F(x)}$$

where the final step is 'M-relative universal introduction'.

Likewise an M-disproof of $\exists x F(x)$ is going to be as wide as M is large. That is, it will have at least as many branches (subordinate M-disproofs) at the point of 'existential elimination' as there are members of the domain of M. For each member a of the domain of M there will have to be an M-disproof Θ_a of $F(a)$ as a subordinate proof for existential elimination:

$$\frac{\exists x F(x) \qquad \dfrac{\overline{\quad}^{(i)}}{\begin{array}{c}\ldots F(a) \ldots \\ \ldots \Theta_a \ldots \\ \bot\end{array}}{}^{(i)}}{\bot}$$

where the final step is 'M-relative existential elimination'.

If the domain of M is finite, then these M-relative proofs and disproofs will of course be finitary objects. But if the domain of M is infinite, these proofs and disproofs will in general be infinitary. Nevertheless, they will be well-defined mathematical objects. (Compare Carnap's use of the ω-rule in arithmetic to ensure that every arithmetical sentence came out as L-determinate.)

It is clear then that we have a notion of M-relative proof and disproof for any model M. Intuitively, such proofs correspond to evaluations of their conclusions as true-in-M; and such disproofs correspond to evaluations of a sentence as false-in-M. The assumptions in the former case, and the side assumptions in the latter case, must come from the 'atomic diagram' of the model M. That is, they will be singular (atomic) sentences or negations of such sentences. (We shall allow individuals in M to occur in such sentences as their own names, if necessary.)

We are now in a position to formulate the notion of constrained creative extension. Let Λ be a set of terms. A Λ-*axiom* is an atomic axiom that involves at least one Λ-term.

DEFINITION

S effects a Λ-constrained extension of the theory W for the family $\mathcal{F}$
  if and only if

S creatively extends W for $\mathcal{F}$

    and (the Λ-constraint:)

for every sequent $X : Q$ in $\mathcal{F}$, for every countermodel M to $X, W : Q$ every M-disproof of any M-false member of S uses at least one Λ-axiom in the vocabulary of W.

When S effects a Λ-constrained extension we shall also speak of 'constrained extension via Λ' for grammatical ease in contexts below.

11.3.3   Some inductive definitions

We are now in a position to define, inductively, a relation that holds between sentences and theories, at finite levels, and a relation that holds between expressions and theories, at finite levels. The relation involving sentences is:

    'S is basically falsifiable at level n with respect to theory Θ'.

The relation involving expressions is:

    'E is legitimated at level n with respect to theory Θ'.

The set of all sentences that are basically falsifiable at level n with respect to theory Θ will be called 'F_n w.r.t. Θ'. We stipulate that if a sentence is basically falsifiable at a given level w.r.t. a theory, then it is basically falsifiable at that level w.r.t. any extension of that theory. We are also taking the levels to be cumulative. That is, once a sentence finds its way into F_n, with respect to a given theory, then it is automatically in F_{n+1} with respect to any extension of that theory.

The set of all expressions that are legitimated at level n with respect to theory Θ will be called '$\Lambda_n[\Theta]$'. We stipulate that if an expression is legitimated at a given level w.r.t. a theory, then it is legitimated at that level w.r.t. any extension of that theory. We are also taking the levels to be cumulative. That is, once an expression finds its way into Λ_n with respect to a given theory, then it is automatically in Λ_{n+1} with respect to any extension of that theory.

The set of cognitively significant sentences at level n w.r.t. Θ contains:

1. all logical truths;

2. all logical falsehoods; and

3. contingent sentences that are compounds of expressions in $\Lambda_n[\Theta]$.

We stipulate that if a sentence is cognitively significant at a given level w.r.t. a theory, then it is cognitively significant at that level w.r.t. any extension of that theory. And once a sentence is cognitively significant at level n w.r.t. a given theory, then it is cognitively significant at level $n + 1$ w.r.t. any extension of that theory.

Basis step
Every basic sentence is basically falsifiable at level 0 w.r.t. the empty theory. Every basic expression is legitimated at level 0 w.r.t. the empty theory.

Corollary of basis step:
All sentences compounded from basic expressions are cognitively significant at any level w.r.t. any theory.

Recall that a basic axiom was of the form 'infer A' or 'from A infer absurdity', where A was a basic atom (in the propositional case). A more liberal notion that can now be put in its place is that of a *legitimated* axiom. A legitimated axiom is one *all* of whose vocabulary has been legitimated within the theory with respect to which a constrained creative extension by S is to be made, as described by the following inductive subclause. Note how this subclause also keeps track of the set of terms that have been legitimated with respect to the growing theory. The subclause applies to (finite sets of) sentences S that contain arbitrarily but finitely many non-basic expressions not yet legitimated by the theory W at level n. These 'new' terms will be legitimated at level $n+1$, with respect to the theory that results by adopting S.

Inductive subclause 1 (for compounds containing expressions that are not yet legitimated, and for those expressions)

Suppose that S effects a constrained creative extension of W for the family $\mathcal{F}$ via $\Lambda_n[W]$ and that each sequent $X : Q$ in $\mathcal{F}$ involves only sentences that are significant at level n w.r.t. W. Then:

> S is included in F_{n+1} w.r.t. the extended theory W, S;
> and
> the result of adding the new terms of S to the already legitimated vocabulary $\Lambda_n[W]$ is the extended legitimated vocabulary $\Lambda_{n+1}[W, S]$.

Note here how the sentences in S get added to the theory in order to be in F_{n+1} with respect to the theory resulting from that addition. This respects the intuition that it is only within the context of the theory to which it belongs that a theoretical hypothesis (hence also: each of its terms) acquires its cognitive significance. As remarked earlier, these 'new' terms in S will be legitimated at level $n + 1$, with respect to the extended theory that results by adopting S.

Inductive subclause 2 (for compounds of already significant expressions)

Suppose E_i is in $\Lambda_n[W_i]$ $(i = 1, \ldots, k)$. Then any contingent compound of $E_1, \ldots, E_k$ is significant at level $n+1$ w.r.t. the 'union of theories' $W_1, \ldots, W_k$.

There are the usual closure clauses for these inductive definitions.

11.3.4   Main results

COMPOSITIONALITY THEOREM

For any contingent sentence P, for any theory Θ,
    for some n, P is significant at level n w.r.t. Θ
        if and only if
    there is some m such that each constituent
    expression of P is in $\Lambda_m[\Theta]$

> *Proof*: The 'if' part follows from inductive subclause 2 above, which provides for the compounding of legitimate expressions. For the 'only if' part, note that a sentence can come to be cognitively significant at level n w.r.t. Θ only by being a compound of expressions in $\Lambda_n[\Theta]$. QED

PERSISTENCE THEOREM

If P is in F_n w.r.t. Θ then P is cognitively significant at level $n + 1$ w.r.t. any extension of Θ.

> *Proof*: To get into F_n w.r.t. Θ, P (if not a compound of basic expressions) had to be in some finite S that effected a constrained creative extension of some subtheory of Θ. All the non-logical

expressions of P thereby got into $\Lambda_n[\Theta]$. Thus P would be cognitively significant at level $n+1$ w.r.t. any extension of Θ. QED

The following observation may be thought of as a principle of relevance. For the propositional case it is obvious. In the first-order case it is a version of Robinson's consistency theorem:[20]

> If the sequents $W_1 : V_1$ and $W_2 : V_2$ have no terms in common, then $W_1, W_2 \vdash V_1, V_2$ only if either $W_1 \vdash V_1$ or $W_2 \vdash V_2$.

It is plain that successive applications of the inductive clause above involving extenders generates a sequence of sets of legitimated terms with respect to the respective satisfiable theories thereby generated. These theories will form a chain by inclusion. Each of the sets of terms in the sequence contains the new terms of the extender at that point in the sequence.

QUARANTINE THEOREM

Let Θ_1 be a satisfiable theory legitimating all its terms. Let Θ_2 be a satisfiable theory all of whose terms are non-legitimated w.r.t. Θ_1. Let Θ_0 be any theory logically equivalent to Θ_1, Θ_2, assuming the latter to be satisfiable. Then no sequence of sets of legitimated terms w.r.t. any chain of subtheories of Θ_0 can ever reach a point at which, in order to achieve the next extension accomplished 'within Θ_0', it has no alternative but to involve a set of terms containing a term of Θ_2.

> *Proof*: Θ_1 and Θ_2 have no terms in common. Suppose for *reductio* that there is a sequence σ, say, of sets of legitimated terms w.r.t. respective members of a chain of subtheories of Θ_0, that reaches a point at which, in order to achieve the next extension accomplished 'within Θ_0', it has no alternative but to involve a set containing a term of Θ_2, and a constrained creative extension using that term. Suppose that $\{E_1, \ldots, E_k\}$ is the first set in σ containing a term of Θ_2. σ reaches $\{E_1, \ldots, E_k\}$ via the constrained creative extender S, say, involving $E_1, \ldots, E_k$ as 'new' terms. S is a (finite) subtheory of Θ_0. Let Δ_0 be the corresponding subtheory, in the chain, with respect to which S effects the constrained creative extension for the family $\mathcal{F}$, say. So we are supposing S extends Δ_0 in this way for $\mathcal{F}$.

---

[20] See *Natural Logic*, p. 120.

We shall now construct an alternative extender to S, not involving any terms of Θ_2, but still extending Δ_0 for the family $\mathcal{F}$. This will establish our result.

Δ_0 is a subtheory of Θ_0. All the expressions in S, apart from $E_1, \ldots, E_k$, are legitimate w.r.t. Δ_0—hence, by our assumption concerning $\{E_1, \ldots, E_k\}$ within σ, w.r.t. Θ_1. We shall define *cleanliness* of X to be the following property:

> X contains only such terms as precede $\{E_1, \ldots, E_k\}$ in the sequence σ, and so are legitimate w.r.t. Δ_0—hence, by our assumption concerning $\{E_1, \ldots, E_k\}$ within σ, w.r.t. Θ_1

Cleanliness of a sentence or sequent, or of a set of sentences or sequents, will be indicated from now on by prefixing it with the superscript °. We are assuming that S creatively extends Δ_0 for the family $\mathcal{F}$ (which we now call $°\mathcal{F}$) and hence that

> (α) Δ_0 is $°\mathcal{F}$-less.

It is clear from inductive subclause 1 above that the sequents in $°\mathcal{F}$ contain only such terms as precede $\{E_1, \ldots, E_k\}$ in the sequence σ, and so are legitimate w.r.t. Θ_1. For every sequent $°X : °Q$ in $°\mathcal{F}$ we have that for some subset Δ_{0X} of Δ_0 and for some non-empty subset S^* of S, the sequent $°X, S^*, \Delta_{0X} : °Q$ is skeletally valid. We have also that:

> (α) for no satisfiable extension Δ_0^* of Δ_0, obtained by adding only finitely many sentences in the language of Δ_0, do we have for each sequent $°X : °Q$ in $°\mathcal{F}$ that $°X, \Delta_0^* \vdash °Q$

Since S is a subtheory of Θ_0, and Θ_0 is logically equivalent to Θ_1, Θ_2, it follows that there are finite sets Z_1, Z_2 of sentences drawn from Θ_1, Θ_2 respectively, such that

$$Z_1, Z_2 : \wedge S \text{ is perfectly valid} \ldots (1)$$

where $\wedge S$ is the conjunction of all the members of S. This conjunction can be formed since S is finite. Remember that for each sequent $°X : °Q$ in $°\mathcal{F}$, there is some subset Δ_{0X} of Δ_0 and some subset S^* of S such that the extended sequent

$$^\circ X, S^*, \Delta_{0X} : {}^\circ Q \text{ is skeletally valid;}$$

whence

$$^\circ X, \wedge S, \Delta_{0X} : {}^\circ Q \text{ is valid } \ldots (2)$$

whence by cut on $\wedge S$ in (1) and (2) we have

$$^\circ X, \Delta_{0X}, Z_1, Z_2 \vdash {}^\circ Q$$

whence, since $^\circ X, \Delta_{0X}, Z_1 : {}^\circ Q$ and $Z_2 : \emptyset$ are vocabulary disjoint,

either $^\circ X, \Delta_{0X}, Z_1 \vdash {}^\circ Q$
or $Z_2 \vdash \emptyset$.

But $Z_2 \vdash \emptyset$ is contrary to (1).

So we have

for each sequent $^\circ X : {}^\circ Q$ in $^\circ \mathcal{F}$, there is some subset Δ_{0X} of Δ_0 such that $^\circ X, \Delta_{0X}, Z_1 \vdash {}^\circ Q$

hence

for each sequent $^\circ X : {}^\circ Q$ in $^\circ \mathcal{F}$, $^\circ X, \Delta_0, Z_1 \vdash {}^\circ Q$

Note that Z_1 is finite. But now, if Z_1 is clean, i.e. in the language of Δ_0, this will be contrary to (α), and we will have shown that the involvement of a term from Θ_2 was impossible. On the other hand, if Z_1 is not clean, it will at least not involve any term from Θ_2. And then the theory Z_1 will be a finite entender of the theory Δ_0 for the family $^\circ \mathcal{F}$. Since Z_1 is a subtheory of Θ_1 it is an alternative to S as the extender at that stage within Θ_0. One is not obliged to go the way of S into the territory of Θ_2-terms in order to forge the inferential connections one wants within Θ_0. Within Θ_0, no matter how it may be formulated, one may eschew all Θ_2-terms as illegitimate. QED

11.4   Comparison with Carnap's account

The best-known attempts to formulate a criterion of cognitive significance were all made in the shadow of the Carnapian doctrine, in *The Logical Syntax of Language*, according to which all interesting notions in the philosophy of science could be explicated by using only the notion of logical consequence—and a syntactically characterized one at that. It was only at the end of the heyday period of theorizing about cognitive significance that Carnap produced his most liberal formulation, in 'The Methodological Character of Theoretical Concepts'. Carnap's account is not without its problems, as we have seen; but it appears also to have been neglected by theorists who might have been able to improve upon it. In the exchange with Hempel in the Schilpp volume,[21] Carnap's proposal received scant attention. Hempel did not pursue its novel merits, and Carnap did not emphasize them as perhaps he should. The debate seemed to have lost steam, or become unfashionable. Admittedly, Carnap had not made his reader's work easy in his final foray on the topic.

Our new criterion is a much-mutated descendant of Carnap's. We have gone beyond Carnap, however, by incorporating extra safeguards against collapse (via the notion of constrained creative extensions), as well as some important liberalizations and refinements in the interests of faithful explication of scientists' theoretical practice. Despite these liberalizations, it is still possible to prove the theorem above, which we call the Quarantine Theorem. This theorem is crucial for showing that terms and sentences ruled non-significant by the criterion cannot defy that ruling by appearing in reformulations of the union of a significant theory with a non-significant one, and thereby forcing us to recognize them as legitimate.

It would be useful in conclusion to have a summary of points of contrast and points of affinity between Carnap's much neglected 1956 account and that put forward above. The following are the important similarities:

1. We both parametrize with respect to a theory.

2. We both subscribe to a compositionality principle: Carnap's D3 has the same effect as our inductive subclause 2.

The following are the important points of contrast between Carnap's approach and ours:

1. Carnap parametrizes with respect to just one theory, taken as fixed for the purposes of defining cognitive significance for terms and for

---

[21] C. G. Hempel, 'Implications of Carnap's work for the philosophy of science', in P. A. Schilpp (ed.), *The Philosophy of Rudolf Carnap*, Library of Living Philosophers, Vol. XI, Open Court, La Salle, 1963, pp. 685–709; R. Carnap, 'Carl G. Hempel on Scientific Theories', in P. A. Schilpp (ed.), *op. cit.*, pp. 958–66.

sentences; whereas we build up the theory in the process of inductive definition.

2. Carnap deals with only finitely axiomatized theories; whereas we deal with arbitrary ones. (We both, however, countenance only finite extenders.)

3. Carnap has only the following features of perfect validity: the premisses are consistent (and one of them is the whole theory); the implication fails if the new sentence (with the new term) is missing. Hence the conclusion is contingent. We insist by contrast on skeletal validity. Thus our account too envisages only some, not necessarily all, the sentences of the theory featuring as premisses of the extended sequents. The insistence on skeletal validity also blocks both Kaplan's 'definitional extension' problem and his 'deoccamization' problem, which arise for any account based on perfect, but not skeletal, validity.[22]

4. Carnap distinguishes the correspondence rules from the theoretical postulates. For our account the distinction is unnecessary.

5. Carnap has the basic sentences only on the right of extended sequents, appealing to the deduction theorem to justify this. We have basic sentences both on the left and on the right, which is perhaps a good idea in case the deduction theorem fails for the logic concerned.

6. Carnap requires basic sentences to be in the invalid sequent being extended; whereas we require only sentences whose terms have already been legitimated, even if these terms are not basic.

---

[22] See D. Kaplan, 'Significance and Analyticity: A Comment on Some Recent Proposals of Carnap', in J. Hintikka (ed.), *Rudolf Carnap, Logical Empiricist: Materials and Perspectives*, Reidel, Dordrecht, 1975, pp. 87–94; and R. Creath, 'On Kaplan on Carnap on significance', *Philosophical Studies*, 30, 1976, pp. 393–400. It is interesting to note that Creath resorted instead to legitimation of sequences of sets of terms, rather than just sequences of terms, in response to Kaplan's problem. But he need not have!—the notion of skeletal validity would have done the trick. Ironically, Creath's introduction of sequences of sets of terms is needed for an altogether different reason—namely, to capture holistically interdependent theoretical concepts. Nor did Creath observe that his liberalization to allow sets of terms in legitimation sequences would render Carnap's own proof of what we have called his 'Quarantine Theorem' incorrect. Note that Creath's elaborate requirement on each set in the sequence is furthermore rendered otiose by our requirement of constrained creative extensions.

7. Carnap's extender always has its new non-basic term as its sole descriptive term. In our extenders, by contrast, several new non-basic terms may be brought into play simultaneously. Hence we can account for the introduction of holistically interdependent theoretical concepts.

8. Carnap has no analogue to our constraint condition on extension, which is what renders his account vulnerable to Ullian's collapse proof. We shall see presently how our account parries the general thrust of such collapse proofs.

There are two strategies embodied in our response to Ullian-style collapses of the original criteria of Ayer and Carnap.

One is the *Hempelian strategy*: to insist that the theory must feature as an extra relational term in the analysis of cognitive significance. We must appreciate that the 'new' expressions are initially uninterpreted, but acquire their interpretations by being incorporated into theoretical conjectures (in the theory) that turn out to be extenders. On this strategy, the extension can be required to take place in a stricter or in a more liberal form. The stricter form insists on forging new inferential links among basic sentences. The more liberal form requires only that new inferential links be forged among already legitimated sentences (some or all of which might not be basic). The constraint we are imposing on these new inferential links, however, makes up for the liberalism just mentioned.

The Hempelian strategy was of course first explicitly adopted by Carnap. It allowed him at the same time to focus on theoretical terms instead of whole sentences, and to exploit compositionality to form significant sentences from legitimated terms. As Schlesinger has emphasized,[23] this was

> the special power of Carnap's new meaning criterion

and it

> truly represents a turning point in the history of the efforts to formalize empirical significance. For ... the earlier efforts of verificationalists were concentrated upon the devising of a criterion to test the meaning of whole sentences and not of terms. All the criteria suggested in the past however could be circumvented by devising meaningless sentences which complied with those criteria.

---

[23] G. Schlesinger, 'The formalization of empirical significance', *Philosophy of Science*, 31, 1964, pp. 65–7; at p. 66.

In the light of this remark it is worth noting that the recent attempt by Wright[24] to improve upon the Ayerian account did not follow Carnap in adopting the Hempelian strategy.

The other strategy in response to Ullian-type collapses of Ayerian accounts is what we shall call the *constraint strategy*. It insists on more stringent conditions on the kind of logical entailment that is involved when the new 'extender' sentences in S forge inferential connections not previously available among already significant sentences. This was, in effect, the only strategy employed by Wright,[25] with his requirement of what he called 'S-compact entailment'. On our account the strategic thought here in question shows up as the requirement of constrained creative extension.[26] The constraint strategy also comes in both a stricter and a more liberal form. The stricter form requires that one appeal, in the evaluation proof or disproof within any countermodel to the unextended sequent, to basic axioms. The weaker form requires appeal merely to already legitimated axioms.

There is an important, independent element of intuitive appeal about the constraint strategy, even though the Hempelian strategy—indeed, the Hempelian strategy in its more liberal form—suffices for the proof of what we have called the Quarantine Theorem. We incorporate the constraint strategy as well, even though only in its more liberal form. A beneficial and non-*ad hoc* result is that we acquire a prophylactic to Ullian-style collapse proofs. But—more importantly—we thereby acquire also a much-needed immunity to Kaplan's problem of definitional extension and his problem of deoccamization, which Kaplan raised for Carnap's account.

Carnap seems, in the account in 'The Methodological Character of Theoretical Concepts', to neglect to discuss the original criterion put forward by Ayer, and Church's collapse of it. He does not make enough expository appeal to the consideration leading to the Hempelian strategy, with its insistence on the theory as an extra relational term. He was also writing in

---

[24]C. Wright, 'Scientific Realism, Observation and the Verification Principle', in G. Macdonald and C. Wright (eds.), *Fact, Science and Morality*, Blackwell, Oxford, 1986, pp. 247–74. See D. Lewis, 'Statements Partly About Observation', *Philosophical Papers*, 1988, pp. 1–31 for criticism of Wright's proposal, and C. Wright, 'The Verification Principle: Another Puncture - Another Patch', *Mind*, 98, 1989, pp. 611–22 for an emendation still within the self-imposed limitation of the second strategy discussed next in the text.

[25]loc. cit.

[26]Constrained creative extension by S is distinct from Wright's S-compact entailment. We require (for extension) that a whole (infinite) family of logically distinct invalid sequents be involved in theory extension by S, whereas Wright requires only that some invalid sequent be so involved.

the wake of Quine's celebrated essay 'Two Dogmas of Empiricism', in which the slide to pragmatic holism was consummated, with not even jaded regard for the fortunes of the technically demanding approach that Carnap was still pursuing. Perhaps Carnap's difficult prose, at the end of a long and wearying tradition of previous failed attempts to formulate a technically adequate criterion, lost the day for logical empiricism over pragmatic holism.[27] Quine's striking metaphors had greater appeal.

Carnap's account is at a disadvantage with its insistence on the whole theory occupying a uniform argument place in the analysis. This is in contrast to the approach adopted above, in which the theory itself is built up as new 'extenders' are adopted as theoretical conjectures. We need to show that we can deal with non-finitely axiomatizable theories; but we must avoid giving an analysis that works for these only by having such theories as wholes in the relational analysis of significance.

For this would be to concede that the context principle had taken a striking turn for the worse. If non-finitely axiomatizable theories had to appear as wholes in the relational analysis of significance, then the context principle would have at best the following invidious formulation:

> Only in the context of a whole theory does a theoretical term get its meaning

On our analysis, by contrast, we are still able to maintain that

> Only in the context of a theoretical sentence does a theoretical term get its meaning

This important result is secured, on our analysis, by the compactness of consequence.

What we have called the Quarantine Theorem has been proved here, rather surprisingly, on a very liberal formulation of the criterion for cognitive significance, even though that liberalization has entailed more work in the proof than was involved for the corresponding but cruder result of Carnap's. Carnap's analysis insisted on the new expression being the sole descriptive

---

[27] The secondary literature on Carnap's proposal is rather limited and indecisive. The problems that were raised for it seem to have been dealt with reasonably adequately by Carnap's defenders. Thus W. Salmon, 'Barker's Theory of the Absolute', *Philosophical Studies*, 10, 1959, pp. 50–3 against S. Barker, *Induction and Hypothesis*, Cornell University Press, Ithaca, 1957, pp. 136–42; and Creath, loc. cit. 1976 against Kaplan, loc. cit. 1975. None of these critics, however, raised the problem of otiose conjuncts: the problem, namely, that in the extended sequent $S \wedge (A \supset B), A : B$ the conjunct S is 'doing no work'.

term within the extending theoretical sentence. Inspection reveals that his own proof of his related result makes essential use of this condition. On our analysis, by contrast, we allow for arbitrarily finitely many new terms all at once within the extending theoretical sentence. This surely improves the prospects for legitimating concepts that are holistically interdependent in a scheme of explanation, in the way, for example, that Peacocke has tried to explicate.[28] The other liberal feature of our account, which has not jeopardized proof of the Quarantine Theorem, is that extension is required only among legitimated sentences, not basic ones.

11.5   Blocking Church–Ullian collapses

Ayer's original criterion can be expressed as a set of rules that serve to define the notions involved. The reader will easily check that the rules below are faithful to Ayer's own formulation. We shall use 'O', with or without subscripts or superscripts, for observation sentences. Note that Ayer, notoriously, omitted reference to any theory with respect to which significance was to be conferred on sentences. The rules capturing Ayer's criterion are:

$$\frac{}{O \text{ is directly verifiable}}$$

$$\frac{O_1,\dots,O_n \nvdash O \\ S,O_1,\dots,O_n \vdash O}{S \text{ is directly verifiable}}$$

$$\frac{P_1,\dots,P_n \nvdash P \\ S,P_1,\dots,P_n \vdash P \\ P \text{ is directly verifiable} \\ \text{Each } P_i \text{ is analytic or directly verifiable or can be shown} \\ \text{to be indirectly verifiable without showing that } S \text{ is}}{S \text{ is indirectly verifiable}}$$

Instead of direct or indirect verifiability, let us talk instead of significance (at or by a certain level). Without changing the scope of what they license as

---

[28] See his *Holistic Explanation: Action, Space and Interpretation*, Clarendon Press, Oxford, 1979.

significant, the rules just given can be turned into a more clearly inductive form of definition as follows:

O is significant at level 0

$S, O_1, \ldots, O_n : O$ *is perfectly valid*
$\overline{\qquad\qquad\qquad\qquad\qquad\qquad\qquad}$
S is significant at level 1

$S, P_1, \ldots, P_n : P$ *is perfectly valid*
$P_1, \ldots, P_n$ *are significant at level* m
P *is significant at level* 1
$\overline{\qquad\qquad\qquad\qquad\qquad\qquad\qquad}$
S is significant at level $m + 1$

These rules of Ayer's succumb to the following collapse proof originally due in a different form to Ullian, and presented here in the notation developed above. The steps in the proof are justified either by Ayer's rules above or by obvious facts about logical deducibility:

$$
\cfrac{
\cfrac{}{S, O \vdash S \wedge (O \vee \neg O_1)} \quad
\cfrac{O \nvdash S}{O \nvdash S \wedge (O \vee \neg O_1)}
}{S, O : S \wedge (O \vee \neg O_1) \text{ is perfectly valid}} \qquad
\cfrac{
\cfrac{S \wedge (O \vee \neg O_1), O_1 \vdash O \quad S \nvdash \quad O_1 \nvdash O}{S \wedge (O \vee \neg O_1), O_1 : O \text{ is perfectly valid}}
}{S \wedge (O \vee \neg O_1) \text{ is significant at level } 1}\!\!{\scriptstyle(\dagger)}
$$

S is significant at level 2

The proof establishes that, if the observation sentence O_1 does not imply the observation sentence O, which in turn does not imply the contingent sentence S, then S is significant. These are extraordinarily weak conditions on S. We might as well say that any contingent sentence S comes out as significant (indeed, already at level 2) on Ayer's definition. This is a spectacular collapse indeed.

It is the step marked ($\dagger$), in our view, that has to be blocked at all costs. Note that even Carnap's 1956 account,[29] if it is taken to apply at the propositional level, allows the step marked ($\dagger$) to go through unchallenged, albeit only with the conclusion '$S \wedge (O \vee \neg O_1)$ is significant at level 1 with respect to any theory containing it'. But this is reason to be worried, even with such relativization with respect to a theory. For the intuition is that the embedded sentence S is not doing any work in securing the passage from the two premisses $S \wedge (O \vee \neg O_1)$ and O_1 to the conclusion O. S is theoretically idle. It should not be regarded as a significant sentence, despite the fact that it

---

[29] 'The Methodological Character of Theoretical Concepts', loc. cit.

would be significant—on Carnap's account—by virtue of being a constituent expression of the now supposedly significant compound $S \wedge (O \vee \neg O_1)$; and despite the fact that it would be significant—on Ayer's account—by virtue of the subsequent step in the proof above.

How, then, can we block the step (†)? We have suggested, in effect, a two-pronged defence. First, we are requiring the significance-conferring extensions to have to involve the new vocabulary in order to effect the extensions in question. In the Church–Ullian cases this requirement is violated. A simple truth-functional combination $O \vee \neg O_1$ of constituents already in the language will effect the sought extension of the sequent $O_1 : O$. The theory being extended is not, in our terminology, $\{O_1 : O\}$-less. We can clinch the family $\{O_1 : O\}$ by theoretical extension within the language already at hand. This first prong alone is enough to block the step (†).

The second prong of defence against the step (†) is to take seriously the idea that S is 'not doing any work' despite the perfect (indeed: skeletal) validity of the sequent $S \wedge (O \vee \neg O_1)$, $O_1 : O$. This second line of defence will be needed even when dealing with genuine creative extension for some family $\mathcal{F}$, where the unextended theory is indeed $\mathcal{F}$-less. For one has to avoid otiose conjuncts from piggy-backing on the theoretical assertions that effect the creative extension, and from thereby acquiring the status of cognitive significance without doing any proper work. In the Ullian example above, the otiose conjunct S is not doing any work because it fails to 'join forces with' O_1 and O in making the sequent $S \wedge (O \vee \neg O_1), O_1 : O$ valid. In other words, $S \wedge (O \vee \neg O_1)$ is not a *constrained* extender of the invalid sequent $O_1 : O$. There is a counter-example M to $O_1 : O$—namely, the one in which S is false—in which the evaluation, as false, of the compound sentence $S \wedge (O \vee \neg O_1)$ need not exploit the truth of O_1 or the falsity of O. The M-disproof

$$\frac{S \wedge (O \vee \neg O_1)}{\frac{S}{\bot}}$$

uses only the non-basic axiom (rule) $S|\bot$. It makes no use of the basic axioms $|O_1$ or $O|\bot$. This is what explicates the intuition that S 'does no work' in making the sequent $S \wedge (O \vee \neg O_1), O_1 : O$ skeletally valid.

The requirement of constrained creative extension also serves to dispose of Foster's problem,[30] whereby $Pa \wedge \neg Pb$ serves to secure $\neg a = b$, no matter

---

[30] J. Foster, *A. J. Ayer*, Routledge & Kegan Paul, 1985, pp. 19–20.

how 'metaphysical' the predicate P may be. First, the example cannot even get off the ground since no theory is $\{a = b : \emptyset\}$-less. So we would never have to resort to $Pa \wedge \neg Pb$ as a creative extender for the family $\{a = b : \emptyset\}$. But even if we did, the extended sequent $Pa \wedge \neg Pb : \neg a = b$ violates our constraint. Any countermodel M to the unextended sequent $\emptyset : \neg a = b$ makes $Pa \wedge \neg Pb$ false, and any M-disproof of $Pa \wedge \neg Pb$ uses only non-legitimated axioms. Once again, we have a two-pronged defence against an attempted counter-example, with each prong sufficient.

It is in order to avoid a simple but decisive problem for both Ayer's and Carnap's accounts that we have made use of the notion of constrained creative extension. All we have done is give formal expression to an intuition which, we are convinced, was guiding their thinking without coming explicitly to the surface. Ayer thought only in terms of sentences, not terms; he stayed at the propositional level; and he neglected the Hempelian 'theory parameter'. Carnap advanced the thinking on this topic at the time so as to cover terms as well as sentences; he ventured to first-order, and adopted a uniform theory parameter. We have followed Carnap in treating terms as well as sentences. But we have tried to show also that we not only may, but must venture to first-order. Furthermore, we have allowed the theory-parameter to vary (by 'growing monotonically') in a way that is faithful to the development of scientific theories as they extend their explanatory and predictive reaches in between incidents of refutation and revolutionary theory change. And we have tightened the logical linkages exploited to confer significance, by insisting on constrained creative extensions.

The result is an account of cognitive significance that, so far as we are able to determine, avoids extant problems for previous accounts; and provably avoids collapse. It is also formulated liberally enough, we believe, to find application in suitably regimented reconstructions of scientific theories. It is entirely in harmony, also, with the anti-realist outlook in semantics, epistemology and ontology. Our account of cognitive significance roots humanly graspable scientific contents in the humanly sensible. It pictures those contents as compositional. With its emphasis on the truth as in principle knowable (or at least, in the empirical case: on falsity as in principle knowable!) it motivates the search for a criterion to rule out metaphysical gobble-degook of the more pernicious varieties. Modern anti-realism, by insisting on compositionality, and insisting that the cognitively meaningful must be systematically graspable, averts the slide to pragmatic holism and emerges, albeit belatedly, as the proper heir to the tradition of Logical Empiricism.

Chapter 12

Defeasibility and Constructive Falsifiability

12.1 Rationalism and relativism

Here is a naïvely rationalist view of theories, the world, and scientific method. Our theories consist of representations that we make of the world, to which all speakers have, in principle, access by understanding, and which all speakers can, in principle, put to the test. These representations come in levels: at the lowest level are observation sentences, and at the highest level are very general hypotheses about the ultimate constituents of the world. The representations at the lowest level serve uniformly for competing theories. The representations measure up against the world, and are made true or false by it.

The naïvely rationalist view continues as follows. The world is independent of our means of making those representations and of the methods by means of which we arrive at them. Good inductive methods are ones that reliably lead us from true representations at a lower level to true representations at a higher level, as we construct our theories. Good deductive methods are ones that are guaranteed to lead us from true representations to true representations, as we test our theories. The deductive methods form a stable canon of forms of inference. The same methods apply uniformly across all theories. Our application of method, and our appraisal of our representations, is objective. Our guiding interests are explanatory scope and the truth. We can expect our theories to improve over time, and to approximate more and more closely to the truth. When we replace one theory by another, it will always be for good reasons, having to do with explaining the data so far, and giving a simple and unified account of disparate phenomena.

We have, then, on the naïvely rationalist view:

- the statement view of theories, with semantic objectivity and community of criticism

- the observational/theoretical dichotomy

- commensurability of theories and non-theory-ladenness of observation sentences

- the correspondence theory of truth

- realism via independence of concepts

- realism via independence of method

- reliance on induction

- reliance on deduction, and monism about deductive logic

- the unity of scientific method

- a principle of objectivity

- belief in scientific progress

- rationality of scientific change; respect for total evidence, simplicity and scope

Let us contrast this now with a crudely constructivist and relativist view of theories, the world, and scientific method. Our theories consist not just of representations that we make of the world, but also a hodge-podge of techniques based on available instrumentation. Many of these are so specialized and abstruse that only small élites can understand them. They can control and manipulate their 'data', restrict access to it for competitors, and develop proprietary tests and instruments that they can monopolize.

The representations, when they are made clear (if they ever are) come in levels: at the lowest level are observation sentences, and at the highest level are very general hypotheses about the ultimate constituents of the world. But the representations at the lowest level cannot serve uniformly for competing theories, for they derive much of their content from the theories to which they belong. The representations do not measure up against the world; we choose among them for reasons to do with our prejudices, biases, interests and needs. The world is not independent of our means of making those representations, nor of the methods by means of which we arrive at them. Good inductive methods are not to be had. Good deductive methods are ones that lead us from true representations to true representations, as we test our theories; but we will always be confronted with the problem of which representations to give up or adjust when they fail a test collectively. Moreover, even deductive logic can be disputed, and the phenomena themselves may dictate a change of logic.

The crude constructivist and relativist view continues as follows. No methods apply uniformly across all theories; theories help to form the very methods by means of which they are tested and even replaced. Our application of method, and our appraisal of our representations, is not at all objective. Our guiding interests are not just explanatory scope and the truth; they include also political agenda, concerns about power and authority, careerist ambitions and commercial advantage. We cannot expect our theories to improve over time, and approximate more and more closely to the truth. When we replace one theory by another, it will sometimes be for bad reasons, not having to do with explaining the data so far, and giving a simple and unified account of disparate phenomena, but having rather to do with political agenda, concerns about power and authority, careerist ambitions, and commercial advantage. As time goes by, we lose track of earlier evidence, through deterioration of records, neglect, lack of scholarliness, and failure to appreciate its relevance. In fact, our theories are not independently constrained by the world, for there is no 'reality' independent of the representations we make of it. The world is socially constructed, through our theories 'about it', and we choose the theories we do more as a result of arational social forces than as a result of having appraised competing theoretical claims objectively against an 'independent tribunal' of experience.

According to the crude constructivist and relativist view, then, we have:

- a hybrid account of theories

- the observational/theoretical dichotomy blurred or non-existent

- non-commensurability of theories because of theory-ladenness of observation sentences

- a projectivist theory of truth

- anti-realism via dependence on concepts

- anti-realism via dependence on method

- distrust of induction

- reliance on deduction, but wary and provisional

- the Poincaré–Duhem–Quine problem

- fragmentation of scientific method

- no claim to objectivity

- scepticism about scientific progress

- scepticism about rationality of scientific change

- no guarantee that our theories take into account the total accumulated evidence from human experience

- the social construction of reality

The correct view, as always, must lie somewhere in the middle. It will be helpful to bear these two extremes in mind throughout the theorizing in which we engage below about defeasibility and constructive falsifiability.

12.2 On defeasible empirical claims

As intimated earlier, there is a crucial difference between logico-mathematical assertions based on proof, and empirical claims based on the evidence of our senses. For the former, truth is eternal; for the latter, not. The latter are what are known as *defeasible* claims. They can be defeated as more evidence accrues. This is true for simple psychological reports such as 'Jones is in pain', as much as for high-level scientific hypotheses such as Newton's Law of Gravitation. Whether we are talking about wincing and writhing bodies, or about falling and orbiting bodies, when we advance strictly beyond what is observed we are open to future refutation. This is none other than Hume's problem.

The defeat can be weak or strong. Weak defeat merely involves retraction. The claim P is retracted in the light of new evidence that undermines its earlier 'warrant'. In the case of weak defeat the old and new evidence, together, do not yet justify one in denying P, that is, in asserting $\neg P$. Strong defeat, by contrast, involves not only retraction, but revision. When P is strongly defeated, the new evidence affords justification for its denial $\neg P$.

The defeat can be temporary or permanent. Even strong defeat might be only temporary. Suppose we have seen Jones writhing, and have formed the belief P that Jones is in pain. Then we learn that Jones had been bribed to sham pain, so that we change our minds from 'Jones is in pain' to 'Jones is not in pain'. P has been strongly defeated, leading us to assert $\neg P$. But the claim $\neg P$ can turn out to be just as defeasible as was the former claim P. When we learn that Jones's bribers have beaten him up for not having been convincing enough for them in the shamming practice rounds, we revert to our earlier judgement that Jones is in pain. We shall examine below rather carefully the kinds of 'intra-theoretic' explanatory contexts in which this sort of 'flip-flopping' on a conjecture P can occur. These intra-theoretic contexts are to be distinguished, however, from crucial experiments that refute a claim once and for all, flipping it in such a way that it will never flop back. (How and why will become clearer in due course.) This would be a case of strong and permanent defeat. If we carry on using the theoretical concepts involved in the defeated claim P, we shall be committed to its denial $\neg P$. But the defeat of a theoretical conjecture may be so strong and permanent that we are led to abandon the conceptual apparatus implicated in the claim P and its cognates. In that event we do not insist that strong defeat should involve allegiance to $\neg P$; for we may not regard ourselves as entitled, any longer, to the use of the concepts in P.

Let us return to our quest for correct conjectures as to how it is internally with Jones. Suppose that we find out that, shortly before the assault by his bribers, Jones (who is a medical student) administered to himself a highly effective anaesthetic that ensures that one feels no pain even after physical trauma. He did this in anticipation of the chastising assault. In the light of this new information, we would revert to the judgement that Jones is not in pain, despite his writhing.

We would then have to address the question of why he was writhing after the assault, given that (presumably, because of the anaesthetic) he was not in pain. We could imagine evidence coming to light to support the contention that Jones thought, despite the assault, that his bribers would nevertheless 'honour' their bribe if he were to go out and perform convincingly, as though he were in pain. Given this idiosyncratic belief about his bribers' and assaulters' 'honourable' intentions, his writhing is intelligible, and not evidence of his being in pain.

Alternatively, we might learn that the bribers, when beating him up, told him that they intended him never to be able to move again, so that writhing would be impossible for him, and he would not be able to perform his end of the 'bargain' (being now, so they suppose, genuinely in pain) and collect on the bribe. And Jones is intent simply on showing them that they have failed in their intentions. He is made of sterner stuff; he wants to cock a snook at them by turning in the performance of a lifetime, and to demonstrate that, despite the beating, they have not succeeded in crippling him. He may also think that their superiors will honour the 'bribe'. Funnily enough, given the anaesthetic, Jones's performance really is the performance of a lifetime, both because it is a sham (he feels no pain) and because it involves calling on great reserves of strength (for they really did all but cripple him).

What is going on here, as far as our conjectures about Jones's internal states are concerned? Let us try to characterize, with sketchy logical detail, the explanations that we opt for in the different evidential situations just described. The details are instructive, because they will show us whether we have genuine refutations of theories, and consequent revision of those theories, in these cases. The answer, perhaps surprisingly, will be negative; and we shall have occasion to reflect on the methodological implications of this conclusion below.

In the first evidential situation (call it S_0) we see Jones writhing and moaning etc. (E). We immediately adduce a mini-theory to explain what we see. This theory consists of a general law H_0 about the usual manifestation of pain in observable behaviour, and the singular conjecture P concerning Jones's internal state. The interpretation of the implication connective $\Rightarrow$ in our statement of the general law H_0 (and of various H_i subsequently) is of course subject to various *ceteris paribus* clauses, or so-called *default conditions*, that are suppressed here:

H_0 $\forall x(x$ is in pain $\Rightarrow x$ writhes etc.$)$
P Jones is in pain
E Jones writhes etc.

In the next situation, S_1, there is some extra information that we can use in our attempted explanation of Jones's observed writhing. This is the information B_1, that Jones had been offered a large bribe to writhe. We now think, in the light of this information B_1, that Jones is shamming being in pain. The presence of B_1 prompts us to invoke, as an important general law, H_1 below. Jones's writhing is now seen, accordingly, as merely a performance motivated by the bribe. Our explanation now takes the form

H_1 $\forall x(x$ is offered a large enough bribe to $\phi \Rightarrow x$ ϕ's$)$
B_1 Jones has been offered a very large bribe to writhe
E Jones writhes

Note that we still subscribe to

H_0 $\forall x(x$ is in pain $\Rightarrow x$ writhes etc.$)$

as a general law of human nature. But we do not at this stage have to invoke P (that Jones is in pain), our earlier conjecture about Jones's internal state, as a premiss for the explanation of the observational evidence E, that Jones is writhing. The new evidence B_1 suffices, with a different general law H_1, to explain the evidence E. B_1 makes it unnecessary for us to have to postulate P; whence H_0, though still held to be true, is not used as a stepping-stone to the explanandum E.

In the next situation, S_2, the claim P (that Jones is in pain) enters the picture again, but this time not as an explanatory premiss. This is because we have now acquired the information B_2, that Jones has been beaten up by his bribers. The presence of B_2 prompts us to invoke, as an important general law, H_2:

H_2 $\forall x(x$ is beaten up $\Rightarrow x$ is in pain$)$
H_0 $\forall x(x$ is in pain $\Rightarrow x$ writhes etc.$)$
B_2 Jones has been beaten up by his bribers
E Jones writhes

Interestingly, our focal claim P (that Jones is in pain) is not one of the explicit premisses here, but is a consequence of two of them, namely, H_2 and B_2.

In the next explanatory situation, S_3, we are no longer committed to the truth of P. Here we have learned that Jones had administered the powerful anaesthetic α to himself (B_3) and we conjecture (Q) that Jones thinks his bribers (despite their assault on him) will honour their bribe if he performs as required. The presence of B_3 prompts us to invoke, as an important general law, H_3:

$[H_3$ $\forall x(x$ is administered $\alpha \Rightarrow x$ cannot feel pain$)]$
H_2 $\forall x(x$ is offered a large enough bribe to $\phi \Rightarrow x$ ϕ's$)$
B_1 Jones has been offered a very large bribe to writhe
$[B_2$ Jones has been beaten up by his bribers$]$
$[B_3$ Jones has administered α to himself$]$

Q Jones thinks his bribers will honour their bribe
E Jones writhes

Here it is really only H_2, B_1 and Q that are doing the explanatory work. H_3 and B_3 are at work as well, but 'backgrounded' (as indicated by the brackets). In the background they ward off any alternative explanatory thrust that would involve passing commitment to Jones's being in pain. Our conjecture (Q) is really to the effect that an important *ceteris paribus* clause of H_2 is not violated. This *ceteris paribus* clause of H_2 is that the person offered the bribe believes that, if he performs as demanded, the reward will be his. Q tells us that this default condition is fulfilled, despite the potential evidence B_2 to the contrary (whence B_2 also is bracketed). In the situation envisaged here, we are committed, by the 'backgrounded' premisses H_3 and B_3, to $\neg P$: Jones is not in pain.

We shall not consider in detail the alternative explanation alluded to above, involving Jones's perverse desire to cock a snook at his assailants even when he thinks the bribe is off. Suffice it to say that this explanation would involve a conjecture about Jones's internal states that would link with yet another general law about the social behaviour of human characters of a certain (if idiosyncratic) kind.

What we see here is a selection of different hypotheses H_i, each subject to *ceteris paribus* clauses or 'default' conditions, with different conjectures at times concerning Jones's internal states, and different pieces of information B_i about various influences on Jones. We tend to select the most salient or overriding influence—one which is the antecedent of the generalized conditional whose default conditions are, arguably, intact—and we cite that influence, along with that conditional, to get the explanation going. In so doing, we may explicitly conjecture that Jones is in pain (situation S_0), or be implicitly committed to that claim (situation S_2), or be implicitly committed to its denial (situations S_1 and S_3).

Note that our 'flip-flopping' on the singular claim P concerning Jones's internal states, as we acquire the successive pieces of evidence B_i, arises because we are hanging on to our more general background theory of human psychology and behaviour, while making different choices among these hypotheses H_i in response to different pieces of salient information B_i (in our examples, as it happens: the most recent one). We think of people as liable to be influenced in certain ways by large enough bribes, or by being physically assaulted, or by being administered anaesthetics. We tend to hold these conjectures constant, and then, in the light of information initially about Jones's pain behaviour, then about the earlier offering of bribes, then about the immediately preceding assault, and finally about the self-administered anaesthetic, we change our judgements as to Jones's internal states—as to his beliefs and desires, and as to whether he is, on the occasion when we observe him, genuinely in pain, or just shamming. The point to note here, however, is that the claim 'Jones is in pain' is just one conjecture among many. The others may be more general (such as the various H_i concerning all human subjects), but 'Jones is in pain' is conjectural nevertheless, since it can only be 'asserted'—that is, hypothesized—on the basis of indirect evidence. We do not observe Jones's pain, we observe only his pain behaviour. Since the claim is singular and conjectural, however, it is more likely to be given up than the more general and explanatorily well-entrenched conjectures we hold about human nature, in the event that all these conjectures, collectively, turn out to sit unhappily with the observable evidence concerning Jones that is available at any time. Likewise with the negative claim 'Jones is not in pain'. The endemic defeasibility of singular conjectures about human subjects' psychological states is a reflection of their being less 'entrenched' than are our interpretive canons of folk psychology. If we were to give up the latter, we would be at a loss as to how to attribute any internal states at all to individual subjects. For they derive their explanatory and predictive utility only in the context of the reasonably stable, even if occasionally revisable and extendible, folk psychological theory in whose general canons they appear.[1]

But another important feature to note in all this is that the flip-flopping on the conjecture P (that Jones is in pain) occurs in the continuing context of *seeking to find, within an established theoretical background, the best explanation for a particular evidential situation.* The theory of human nature itself is hardly being adjusted at all. We are only adjusting on various psychological 'boundary conditions' concerning the agent Jones. We are, throughout, addressing only one explanandum: Jones's observed pain-behaviour. As more and more ancillary information comes our way, concerning earlier causal influences on Jones, our marshalling of our explanatory hypotheses is adjusted accordingly. Our passing commitment to P or to $\neg P$ is a repeated casualty to this ongoing process. We have not at any stage decisively refuted a collection of hypotheses, along with statements of boundary conditions. We are rather seeking the most appropriate explanation of Jones's pain behaviour

---

[1] We find ourselves, therefore, in broad agreement with Fodor in Chapter 1 of his book *Psychosemantics*, MIT Press, Cambridge, Mass., 1987.

within a given theoretical framework. That framework is a whole constellation of hypotheses involving more or less theoretical terms. Our ongoing collection of evidence at no point constitutes a problem for the framework as a whole.

Now this feature of what one might call 'intra-theoretic juggling' is not confined to theories of human nature. It has nothing to do with the quirkiness of human intentionality, or with any supposed special problems about *Verstehen* as opposed to *Wissen*. Exactly the same sort of intra-theoretic juggling could be seen to be at work with regard to explananda in 'harder' sciences, as a stream of sufficiently varied evidence comes in. Take, for example, the explanandum 'Smith has such-and-such pathological symptoms of disease'. The explanation is to be provided by a medical diagnosis of the underlying condition responsible for Smith's symptoms; for only then can an effective and safe therapy be prescribed for his condition. One could imagine a sequence of more and more salient information invoking various conditionals about human physiology, with some of the information arranged so as to indicate that their default conditions are met, and with other parts of the information providing the needed antecedents of those conditionals. One could well imagine a conjecture such as 'Smith has a virus' flip-flopping in response to newer and more salient pieces of information, that cause us to prefer some conditionals over others because of the light thrown on their default conditions.

Indeed, even in ordinary physics, let alone physiology or psychology, we can have intra-theoretic juggling, and attendant flip-flopping judgements, as more evidence comes to hand. Suppose we observe from a distance a wooden ball falling from a height. At first we suppose it to be an uncomplicated wooden sphere, and to be falling under the influence of the Earth's gravitational field alone. But then we take a closer look at it, through binoculars, say. It is seen to be falling in a rather peculiar way. Its downward trajectory oscillates slightly from side to side, in a planar fashion, about the vertical line that we would have expected to be its trajectory had it been falling under the influence of gravity alone. We suppose there must be strong gusts of wind in the vicinity, alternating in direction, and that the ball is light enough to be blown from side to side. But then we look at the nearby trees and grass and see no evidence of such wind. Still thinking it is only a wooden ball, we imagine that it perhaps has something other than a perfectly smooth surface. Perhaps it is smooth on one side and roughened (or 'slatted') on the other, and is rotating ever so slowly, in such a way that the differential forces of air turbulence on smooth and rough side, respectively, cause the ball to swing from side to side as it descends. But when, finally, it hits the ground and bounces over to us, we find that it is perfectly smooth and hard; and, oddly, rather heavier than we would have thought. Aha! Perhaps it has a metal core, and had been passing through an oscillating magnetic field as it fell?

As the evidence comes in, we adjust our conjectures both about the object's constitution (internal states) and about the possible influences at work on it. We invoke general laws from a background theory of masses in motion to explain its observed behaviour, given the evidence and these conjectures about the object and the physical forces acting on it. Now compare:

As the evidence comes in, we adjust our conjectures both about the patient's constitution (internal physiological states) and about the possible pathogenic influences at work on it. We invoke general laws from a background theory to explain the observed symptoms, given the evidence and these conjectures about the patient and the pathogenic influences acting on him. And compare again:

As the evidence comes in, we adjust our conjectures both about the agent's constitution (internal psychological states) and about the possible social and physical influences at work on him. We invoke general laws from a background theory of human physiology and psychology to explain his observed behaviour, given the evidence and these conjectures about the agent and the social forces and physical influences acting on him.

In all three areas—physics of the motion of inanimate bodies, medical diagnosis of causes of symptoms in animate bodies, and the behaviour of psychological agents—our abductive explanations are pursued after a common pattern in the light of newly available evidence. In all three areas we have a background of relevant laws that are invoked with sensitive discrimination of default conditions. Even as we change our minds on any one conjecture about the falling body or indisposed patient or writhing subject, we recognize that this is because of our explanatory preferences *within a stable framework of general laws*. At most we are subscribing to different initial or 'boundary' conditions in order to target the explanandum (the observed trajectory; the observed symptoms; the observed pain-behaviour) as the conclusion of an explanatory argument invoking those initial conditions among its premises. The other premises—drawn from the general laws of our theoretical framework—are untouched by the incoming evidence. They are simply disregarded or backgrounded or explicitly invoked in response to the evidence we select and the other 'initial condition conjectures' that we make.

Thus our passing rejection of any particular conjecture (such as P: 'Jones is in pain' in the situation described above) is not to be likened at all to, say, the ultimate rejection of the Newton–Maxwell theory of motions of bodies and of instantaneous action at a distance of both gravitational and electromagnetic forces in absolute space-time, in the light of observable evidence that is nowadays taken to be to the contrary. When we passed from the Newtonian–Maxwellian theoretical framework to that of relativistic and quantum physics, it was in response to recalcitrant evidence of a suitable critical mass. This evidence undermined the very foundations of Newtonian–Maxwellian physics as a completely general account of matter, force and energy in space and time, even though that theory is still approximately applicable in many domains with reliably accurate results. The pieces of evidence B_i in my scenarios S_i above, whether taken singly or collectively, do nothing analogously to undermine our confidence in the overall theoretical framework afforded by the hypotheses H_i for the explanation of human behaviour. We are dealing here with *intra-theoretic juggling*, not with the refutation of any one theory in its full generality and a resulting transition to a new one.

12.3   Refutation of empirical theories

The Newton–Maxwell theory is decisively refuted in so far as it makes predictions about what will be observed in certain kinds of situation, predictions that turn out to be false when those situations are actually realized. Such refutation—and not the intra-theoretic juggling discussed at length above—is what we need to focus on when considering whether, for empirical discourse, there is any suitable and compelling analogue of the logico-mathematical slogan 'Once proved, always proved'.

And of course there is: 'Once empirically refuted, always empirically refuted'. When an explicitly formulated theory fails a well-defined and well-controlled experimental test, it is refuted. Moreover, *so long as we trust the evidence and the controls that applied to the experimental conditions*, it stays refuted. Note that by saying that it is the theory (that is, the collection of high-level hypotheses) that has failed the test, we are already supposing that the Poincaré–Duhem–Quine problem has been resolved. That is, we are agreed that the boundary condition statements were true (the experiment was properly controlled) and that the experimental observations were correct (we made no mistakes in reading our measuring apparatus, and it functioned correctly, etc.). Since what was observed conflicted with what was predicted (by flawless logical reasoning) from the theory and the boundary condition statements, we have concluded that it was the theory that was at fault:

Theory (hypotheses) +
Boundary condition statements +
Auxiliary assumptions about measuring apparatus
$$\underbrace{}$$

$$\vdots$$

Predictions , Observations
$$\underbrace{}$$

$$\vdots$$

$$\perp$$

Now, to the extent that we stick to our guns about our observations, our controlling of the boundary conditions, and the functioning of our measuring apparatus, we can say that the theory in question will stay refuted. No amount of extra evidence *consistent with that which we are holding firm* could possibly cause a 'flip-flop' on the theory itself. Note the stress on consistency here. We are *not* saying that we would never change our minds about particular evidential statements; for that can certainly happen. We are saying only that *if* we *don't* revise our evaluations of past evidential statements in the light of any new ones, then future consistent extensions of present evidence leave the refuted theory refuted. Even on this strict proviso, this situation is utterly disanalagous with that of intra-theoretic juggling against a stable background of general laws, as we seek the theory's best explanation of a particular observed episode.

The point of our restriction to 'extra evidence consistent with that which we are holding firm' is to forestall the objection that new evidence might prompt us to resolve the earlier Poincaré–Duhem–Quine problem differently, by placing the blame on some of those other 'evidential' statements that we had chosen to hold true. If this were to happen, then we might lose some premiss essential to the earlier refutation. Our restriction in effect says that no future evidence will come thus into conflict with what we take at present to be the settled evidence. The restriction, however, is entirely licit. Now why is this so?

Note first that the slogan 'Once proved, always proved' in mathematics can be explicitly restricted (without loss) so as to encompass only *consistent* extensions of our present axiomatic basis. That is to say, there is by default a consistency requirement on the axiomatic basis of mathematics. Secondly, note that there is by default a similar consistency requirement on whatever is supposed to constitute the 'total evidence' for or against any empirical theory. In every domain, consistency is a prerequisite for truth. The appropriate filling out of the slogan 'Once empirically refuted, always empirically refuted', then, is: if evidence E refutes theory T, then future evidence $(E+F)$—which of course we assume to be consistent—also refutes theory T. Similarly, in the logico-mathematical case: if axioms X enable us to prove theorem A, then future axioms $X+Y$—which of course we assume to be consistent—enable us to prove theorem A.

With a logico-mathematical assertion P there can be neither retraction nor revision, unless some mistake is revealed in what had been taken as a proof of P. 'Once proved, always proved' is the motto here. Knowledge (properly pedigreed) is strictly cumulative over time. And the deductive logic governing such assertions is *monotonic on its premisses*. That is, if X is a subset of Y, and X logically implies A, then Y logically implies A. In the logico-mathematical case, the subset X of premisses that consistently expands to become the set Y may be thought of as the foundational basis for one's assertions. Such sets provide the ultimate grounding or support for one's conclusions A. When X consists of mathematical axioms only, we say that A is a mathematical theorem. (When X is empty, we say that A is a logical theorem.) Our certainty in the mathematical axioms transmits, via logical deduction, to the theorems as well. Certainty transmits along lines of logical implication, from premisses to conclusions.

The deductive logic governing empirical claims based on empirical evidence is *also* monotonic, *despite* the fact that the history of scientific theorizing may reveal 'oscillations' in the fortunes of either an empirical hypothesis, or an evidential statement. The claim about monotonicity that we are making here is *not* to be interpreted as resting on a naïve epistemological analogy between mathematical axioms and evidential statements. *Of course* the former are far more certain than are the latter. Indeed, the former are often *self*-evident and necessary; whereas the latter are never so. The crucial difference between the two cases, however, is this. In the empirical case, unlike the mathematical case, the direction of logical implication (with respect to which such monotonicity holds) runs *counter to* the direction of evidential support. When we 'base' a (consistent) scientific theory X on empirical evidence E (consisting of true observation statements) we require (roughly)[2]

---

[2]Quine would prefer to say that we require X to yield 'pegged observational condition-

that X should logically imply E, not vice versa. This logical implication is, to be sure, monotonic on the premisses. But the premisses X (forming our scientific theory) are what, in this context, require the support! And it is the conclusion E that is supposed to provide it. The support that E affords X is not just a matter of X's logically implying E. The latter is necessary, but not sufficient, for the empirical evidence E to support the empirical theory X.

Another condition is that X should (perhaps in conjunction with further assumptions B) logically imply further observational conclusions E^*. The observation sentences E^* should be ones concerning which we have as yet no firm opinion. Such observational conclusions E^* logically inferred from X and B are the predictions of X (modulo B) that can be used to test X. The test will take place by arranging circumstances for which B holds, and then seeing whether E^* holds too. The conditions B are called *boundary conditions* for such experimental testing. When the experiment is conducted, there are, ideally, two outcomes: E^* is seen to hold, or E^* is seen not to hold. In the former case, the theory X is corroborated, for X's prediction (that E will hold in circumstances B) is borne out. Moreover, E will also have been *explained* by X in the circumstances B. In the latter case, where E is seen not to hold, X is refuted. We shall return presently to consider how decisive such refutation may be for any particular member of X. Just which members of X ought to be retracted in the light of such a refutation of X as a whole is in general a rather vexed question.

A third necessary condition for the empirical evidence E to support the empirical theory X is that the evidence within E should be gathered from various domains, and that the formulation of X should be economical and abstract enough not to reflect such diversity explicitly, but to do so only implicitly, by way of deductive application via the boundary conditions B. That is, X should provide *unifying explanations of disparate phenomena*. X should be of wide evidential scope. An example would be the way that Newtonian dynamics and the theory of gravitation (as such X) can be applied to provide explanations of such diverse phenomena as apples falling from trees, projectiles following roughly parabolic trajectories, spinning tops precessing, ocean tides correlating with the position of the Moon, the motions

---

als' of the form 'if O_1 and ... and O_n then O'. Some of the evidence E has to be accepted at face value, in the form of various O_i. The rest of E would then have to be covered via detachment using these conditionals. Obviously there will be a premium on minimizing the former and maximizing the latter. *Cf. The Pursuit of Truth*, Harvard University Press, Cambridge, Mass.,1990.

of pendula, the orbits of the planets, the efficacy of aerofoils, the vibrations
of a plucked string, the formation of sand-dunes, ripples on a pond, sonic
booms, and many other such phenomena.

A fourth necessary condition (which is related to the third) is that X
should be *simple*. This is a notoriously difficult virtue to analyse or explicate,
but scientists do have strong intuitions about whether particular theories are
simple. Theories can fail to be simple in various ways: they can be too *ad
hoc*; they can amount to little more than restatement of the evidence; they
can postulate too many kinds of hidden entity to perform the explanatory
job at hand; they can extrapolate from their data points in 'unsmooth' ways.
We shall not be too concerned here to detain the reader with any attempt to
explicate simplicity further. It is not important, for present purposes, that
one be able to do so.

We were considering the logic of scientific explanation, and how the direction of theoretical explanation runs counter to the direction of evidential
support. Theory X in circumstances B explains evidence E only if E provides evidential support, in circumstances B, for the theory X. And this
amounts to no more than E following logically from the conjunction of X
with B.[3] We do not intend to say anything about how the evidence mounts
up, or about how certain evidential statements can be more important than
others. We do not offer the prospect of any further metatheoretical development of the relation of support, either in the form 'E_1 would be better
evidence for X than would E_2' or in the form 'E would be better evidence for
X_1 than it would be for X_2'. Again, this is not needed for present purposes.
Nor do we intend to say anything about confirmation or probabilification of
hypotheses by evidence, and Bayesian conditionalization.

It is enough to confine our treatment to the strictly hypothetico-deductive
model of explanation. For it is clear that it is a workable model in so far
as it goes. The extent to which it does not accommodate all the intuitions
that scientists and methodologists may have about how theories relate to
the evidence does not concern us. All that is important is that one recognize
the fundamental features captured by the hypothetico-deductive model. It is

---

[3]Well, perhaps a *little* more: we would want to say that $X, B : E$ should be *skeletally*
valid. This requirement disposes, for example, of the standard objection to hypothetico-
deductivism to the effect that $X \wedge X', B : E \vee E'$ will be valid if $X, B : E$ is valid; whence
E' will 'support' X' in circumstances B if E is taken to support X in those circumstances.
For an account of this objection (and its mistaken acceptance), cf. P. Lipton, *Inference to
the Best Explanation*, Routledge, London, 1991; at pp. 99–100. Lipton, of course, is not
alone in thinking that hypothetico-deductivism is vulnerable in this way.

quite conceivable that there should be thinkers and reasoners who exploited and relied on those features and those features alone. Their thought about the external world and its deep regularities, and their quest for theoretical explanations of empirical phenomena, could be just as cogent and urgent as ours. Moreover, their scientific successes could be just as impressive as ours, and they could use their theories just as we do, as guides to life, as a means to anticipate courses of events, as considerations in choice of future actions, and as sources of technological innovation. That is to say (to invoke the philosopher's favourite outlandish being), there could well be Popperian *Martians*, even if there are only a handful of Popperian earthlings.

We are *not* trying in this chapter to provide a full account of human scientific rationality. That would be way beyond the scope of our concerns. Rather, we are isolating an essential logical core to our competence as empirical theorizers—a core which *could*, arguably, serve as the total competence of some species of rational agent (the aforementioned Popperian Martians), in so far as empirical theorizing is concerned, even if it falls short as an account of our own full competence in that regard.

Modest though our aim is, however, we should not underestimate the difficulty of the problem that nevertheless persists *even within* the pared-down framework with which we are concerned. That problem is how to give an account of constructive *falsifiability* (of sets of sentences) that would be appropriately complementary to the account we already have of constructive *verifiability* of individual sentences. The asymmetry between the two cases—namely, the concern with sets of sentences for falsifiability, but with individual sentences for verifiability—is a byproduct of the fact that constructive logic concerns itself with multi-premiss but only single-conclusion arguments. The asymmetry has nothing at all to do with the fact that, in general, mathematical axioms are more self-evident or certain than are empirical observation statements; nor does it have anything to do with the Poincaré–Duhem–Quine problem of how to react to empirical refutations—that is, how to apportion blame (i.e. falsity) among sentences (scientific hypotheses, boundary condition statements, observation statements, etc.) that have collectively led to absurdity. Our concern is even more foundational than that: it is to provide an account of precisely how the (constructive) Poincarés, Duhems and Quines among us could even reach the point where the problem *they* wish to pose could be seen *as* a problem!

Given this strictly limited and modest concern, we are accordingly under no obligation, just yet, to essay upon the abductive 'logic' of *discovery* or of scientific invention. We offer no account of how a scientific intellect, confronted with a range of evidence, would come up with a high-level theory that successfully explains it and that can be tested against the further predictions that it makes. We are content to leave that process mysterious and untouched. We are interested only in what happens, logically, after the theory has been formulated. We are interested only in the deductive logic of theory *testing*.

Similarly, we are content to deal only with a very regimented language, namely, the language of first-order logic. Even if this language should prove (*pace* Quine) to be inadequate for the expression of all our thought about the empirical world, it is nevertheless clear that there can be systematic thought, framed in a first-order language, about the empirical world, and that the essential features of the hypothetico-deductive model of explanation will be in place when the logical deducibility relation[4] in that language is taken as the relation involved in prediction and explanation.

By way of a final disclaimer: we do not intend to survey here the vast literature on the alleged inadequacies of hypothetico-deductivism as a full account of scientific theorizing in all its normative respects. This is not the place to argue that those inadequacies have been exaggerated, or that natural and modest (if ingenious) variations of standard hypothetico-deductivism can dispose of the main objections. We are concerned rather to assume hypothetico-deductivism as a 'stripped down' model of the core theoretical competence of an ideal cognizer; and to show that nothing stands in the way of extending anti-realism so as to cover the theoretical reasoning in which such a cognizer may engage on the basis of his empirical experience.

With this narrow focus and these limited materials, we have enough to bring out the central contrast between logico-mathematical discourse and empirical discourse: namely, that assertions in the former are not defeasible, whereas 'assertions' in the latter are. Why do we use scare quotes with 'assertions' in so far as empirical discourse is concerned? This question takes us to the heart of the matter. And the answer requires some finer discriminations than are usually offered.

In so far as there is a 'tribunal' of experience, represented by the observation sentences on which we can (as observers and theorists) communally agree, we would venture to concede that such sentences can be asserted without further ado, when the observable circumstances are right. Their warrants will involve some course of personal and shared experience in response to those circumstances, arranged in some orderly way, with various

---

[4] Or perhaps some suitably constrained subrelation thereof.

saliencies brought to one's attention. We need such sentences to be relatively theory-free in order that they be able to form an independent tribunal, even if it is for our theories taken as a whole. If we have any misgivings that our vocabulary for reporting certain kinds of evidence is too 'theory laden' or too 'infected with theoretical meaning' to play this anchoring role *vis-à-vis* our sensory experience, then our response ought to be to assert those sentences less full-heartedly, and to treat them as more conjectural; while seeking to find another more 'peripheral' level of more everyday vocabulary that is not so infected.

As soon as we move away from non-theory-laden observation sentences (and their truth-functional compounds) it is no longer appropriate to think of our observational warrants for assertion as non-defeasible. For every statement that ventures beyond the present observational evidence *is* vulnerable. We saw such an example above, which was even of singular form—'Jones is in pain'. Every such statement (and especially ones involving generality) is hostage to future evidence that is not yet available. Moreover, it is almost always so hostage in the company of yet other conjectural statements. This is an aspect of the well-known Poincaré–Duhem–Quine problem, already adverted to above. That problem is, in a nutshell, that when we have derived absurdity from a set of evidential statements in conjunction with a set of conjectural statements, we have many ways of proceeding from there. We may retract one or more of the evidential statements; and likewise with the conjectural statements. In general, we might be able to contract to any one of several consistent subsets of (evidence+conjectures). How we respond to refutations (proofs of absurdity) is, again, a matter more of the 'logic' of scientific discovery than it is a matter of the logic of testing. The refutation consummates the test; something has failed. Whether the failure is to be located among the conjectures venturing beyond the evidence, or in the so-called 'evidence' itself, is a matter that need not detain us. Let Δ contain all the premisses involved in the refutation. Thus Δ embraces conjectures (hypotheses) and evidential statements alike. The refutation of Δ is decisive, in the sense that any further evidence Γ leaves it untouched. If, now, we hold to the evidential statements in Δ, the hypotheses forming the rest of Δ stay jointly refuted, despite the accumulation of the new evidence Γ. So: as the tribunal of experience recruits more members (observation statements held true) and speaks with one voice (is logically consistent), we can say of the theories that founder on this evidence: once refuted, always refuted.

With the focus thus on refutation (hence on disproofs) in the logic of empirical discourse, we turn now to the question whether 'disproof' could be taken as the fundamental notion for an anti-realist theory of meaning for empirical discourse. This last foray into some proof-theoretic technicalities will bring these investigations to a close.

12.4   Normal forms for disproofs

A disproof is a proof with $\perp$ as its conclusion. Any disproof must end with an elimination. The major premiss of that terminal elimination will obviously be one of the undischarged assumptions of the disproof. An important but not immediately obvious fact is that this terminal major premiss for elimination (MPE) need not be a conditional or a negation if there is any other complex undischarged assumption that is not itself a conditional or a negation. A related, and deeper, fact is that every disproof can be reduced to a form in which not only is the final step an elimination (as it obviously has to be) but also any penultimate step ρ is a disproof-creating elimination, except where ρ is the terminal step of the minor proof for the final step, should the latter be a negation-elimination or conditional-elimination. In the excepted case ρ might well be an introduction:

$$
\begin{array}{cc}
\begin{array}{c}
\dfrac{\Theta}{} \; \rho \\[-2pt]
\dfrac{\neg A \qquad A}{\perp} \; \sigma
\end{array}
&
\begin{array}{c}
\qquad \qquad \dfrac{}{}\!\!\overline{}^{\,-(i)} \\[-10pt]
\dfrac{\Theta}{} \; \rho \quad C \\[-2pt]
\dfrac{B \supset C \qquad B \qquad \Sigma}{\perp} {}_{(i)}
\end{array}
\end{array}
$$

Another way of understanding this normal form result for disproofs is as follows. If one is addressing a problem of the form 'Find a disproof of the set Δ of assumptions', and tentatively tries a terminal elimination on a judiciously chosen major premiss among the assumptions available, then the major subproblems thereby generated will in general have the similar form 'Find a disproof of the set Γ of assumptions'; the sole kind of exception being a subproblem corresponding to the creation of a minor proof for the elimination of a negation or of a conditional.[5]

This normal form result is established by the existence of the following twelve transformations. These apply to disproofs, which, by virtue of our definition of proof in *IR*, are already in conventional normal form—that is, they have no sentence occurrence standing as the conclusion of an introduction and as the major premiss of a corresponding elimination. This is because the very forms of our elimination rules call for the major premiss

---

[5]Note that, as we are using the term 'minor', we do not call the case-(dis)proofs for disjunction elimination minor proofs.

to stand proud, and not to occur as the conclusion of any rule application, including an introduction. Possible forms of disproof lacking the desired stronger normal form just defined are on the left; and their transforms are on the right.

$$
\cfrac{\cfrac{B \supset C \quad \cfrac{\Theta \quad \Sigma}{\cfrac{B \quad A}{A}_{(1)}}}{\neg A}}{\bot} \qquad \xrightarrow{\qquad} \qquad \cfrac{\cfrac{B \supset C \quad B}{\Theta \quad \cfrac{\neg A \quad A}{\bot}_{(1)}}}{\bot}
$$

with $\cfrac{}{C}^{(1)}$ above.

$$
\cfrac{\cfrac{B \vee C \quad \cfrac{\Theta \quad \Sigma}{\cfrac{A \quad A}{A}_{(1)}}}{\neg A}}{\bot} \qquad \xrightarrow{\qquad} \qquad \cfrac{B \vee C \quad \cfrac{\Theta}{\cfrac{\neg A \quad A}{\bot}} \quad \cfrac{\Sigma}{\cfrac{\neg A \quad A}{\bot}_{(1)}}}{\bot}
$$

with $\cfrac{}{B}^{(1)} \ \cfrac{}{C}^{(1)}$ above.

$$
\cfrac{\cfrac{B \wedge C \quad \cfrac{\Sigma}{A}_{(1)}}{\neg A}}{\bot} \qquad \xrightarrow{\qquad} \qquad \cfrac{B \wedge C \quad \cfrac{\Sigma}{\cfrac{\neg A \quad A}{\bot}_{(1)}}}{\bot}
$$

with $\underbrace{\cfrac{}{B}^{(1)} \ , \ \cfrac{}{C}^{(1)}}$ above.

$$
\cfrac{\cfrac{B \supset C \quad \cfrac{\cfrac{D \vee E \quad \cfrac{\Sigma}{B} \quad \cfrac{\Theta}{B}_{(1)}}{ } \quad \cfrac{C}{\Xi}^{(2)}}{\bot}_{(2)}}{ }}{\bot} \qquad \xrightarrow{\qquad} \qquad \cfrac{D \vee E \quad \cfrac{B \supset C \quad \cfrac{\Sigma}{B} \quad \cfrac{\Xi}{\bot}}{\bot}_{(1)} \quad \cfrac{B \supset C \quad \cfrac{\Theta}{B} \quad \cfrac{\Xi}{\bot}}{\bot}_{(2)}}{\bot}
$$

$$
\cfrac{\cfrac{B \supset C \quad \cfrac{D \wedge E \quad \cfrac{\Sigma}{B}_{(1)} \quad \cfrac{\Theta}{C}}{\bot}_{(2)}}{B}}{\bot} \qquad \xrightarrow{\qquad} \qquad \cfrac{D \wedge E \quad \cfrac{B \supset C \quad \cfrac{\Sigma}{B} \quad \cfrac{\Theta}{\bot}_{(1)}}{\bot}_{(3)}}{\bot}
$$

$$
\begin{array}{c}
\quad\dfrac{}{E}{\scriptstyle(1)} \\[2pt]
\Sigma \quad \Theta \quad \dfrac{}{C}{\scriptstyle(2)} \\[2pt]
\dfrac{D\supset E \quad D \quad B}{B\supset C \qquad B}{\scriptstyle(1)} \quad \Xi \\[2pt]
\dfrac{}{\bot}{\scriptstyle(2)} \\[2pt]
\bot
\end{array}
\qquad\longrightarrow\qquad
\begin{array}{c}
\quad\dfrac{}{E}{\scriptstyle(2)}\ \dfrac{}{C}{\scriptstyle(1)} \\[2pt]
\Sigma \quad B\supset C \quad B \quad \Theta \quad \Xi \\[2pt]
\dfrac{D\supset E \quad D}{}\qquad \dfrac{}{\bot}{\scriptstyle(1)} \\[2pt]
\dfrac{}{\bot}{\scriptstyle(2)} \\[2pt]
\bot
\end{array}
$$

$$
\begin{array}{c}
\dfrac{}{Ba}{\scriptstyle(1)} \\[2pt]
\Sigma \\[2pt]
\dfrac{\exists x\,Bx \qquad A}{}{\scriptstyle(1)} \\[2pt]
\dfrac{\neg A \qquad\quad A}{}\\[2pt]
\bot
\end{array}
\qquad\longrightarrow\qquad
\begin{array}{c}
\dfrac{}{Ba}{\scriptstyle(1)} \\[2pt]
\Sigma \\[2pt]
\neg A \quad A \\[2pt]
\dfrac{\exists x\,Bx \qquad \bot}{}{\scriptstyle(1)} \\[2pt]
\bot
\end{array}
$$

$$
\begin{array}{c}
\underbrace{\dfrac{}{Bt_1,\dots,Bt_n}}{\scriptstyle(1)\quad(1)} \\[2pt]
\Sigma \\[2pt]
\dfrac{\forall x\,Bx \qquad A}{}{\scriptstyle(1)} \\[2pt]
\dfrac{\neg A \qquad\quad A}{}\\[2pt]
\bot
\end{array}
\qquad\longrightarrow\qquad
\begin{array}{c}
\underbrace{\dfrac{}{Bt_1,\dots,Bt_n}}{\scriptstyle(1)\quad(1)} \\[2pt]
\Sigma \\[2pt]
\neg A \quad A \\[2pt]
\dfrac{\forall x\,Bx \qquad \bot}{}{\scriptstyle(1)} \\[2pt]
\bot
\end{array}
$$

$$
\begin{array}{c}
\dfrac{}{Da}{\scriptstyle(1)} \\[2pt]
\Sigma \qquad \dfrac{}{C}{\scriptstyle(2)} \\[2pt]
\dfrac{\exists x\,Dx \quad B}{B\supset C \qquad B}{\scriptstyle(1)} \quad \Theta \\[2pt]
\dfrac{}{\bot}{\scriptstyle(2)} \\[2pt]
\bot
\end{array}
\qquad\longrightarrow\qquad
\begin{array}{c}
\dfrac{}{Da^{*}}{\scriptstyle(2)}\ \dfrac{}{C}{\scriptstyle(1)} \\[2pt]
\Sigma \quad \Theta \\[2pt]
\dfrac{B\supset C \qquad B}{\exists x\,Dx}\qquad \dfrac{}{\bot}{\scriptstyle(1)} \\[2pt]
\dfrac{}{\bot}{\scriptstyle(3)} \\[2pt]
\bot
\end{array}
$$

Note that by the usual restriction on $\exists E$, the parameter a in the preceding proof on the left does not occur in $\exists x\,Dx$, in B, or in any assumption other than Da on which the conclusion of Σ depends. In the transformed proof on the right a^{*} is chosen afresh, if necessary, so as to satisfy those restrictions and also so as not to occur in C —and *a fortiori* so as not to occur in $B\supset C$.

$$
\begin{array}{c}
\underbrace{\dfrac{}{Dt_1,\dots,Dt_n}}{\scriptstyle(1)\quad(1)} \quad \dfrac{}{C}{\scriptstyle(2)}\\[2pt]
\Sigma \qquad\qquad C \\[2pt]
\dfrac{\forall x\,Dx \quad B}{B\supset C \qquad B}{\scriptstyle(1)} \quad \Theta \\[2pt]
\dfrac{}{\bot}{\scriptstyle(2)} \\[2pt]
\bot
\end{array}
\qquad\longrightarrow\qquad
\begin{array}{c}
\underbrace{\dfrac{}{Dt_1,\dots,Dt_n}}{\scriptstyle(2)\quad(2)} \quad \dfrac{}{C}{\scriptstyle(1)}\\[2pt]
\Sigma \qquad\qquad \Theta \\[2pt]
\dfrac{B\supset C \qquad B}{\forall x\,Dx}\qquad \dfrac{}{\bot}{\scriptstyle(1)} \\[2pt]
\dfrac{}{\bot}{\scriptstyle(3)} \\[2pt]
\bot
\end{array}
$$

That completes the list of transformations needed. Although our normal form theorem for disproofs has taken the quantifiers into account, we shall in what follows confine ourselves just to the connectives in order to simplify the presentation.

12.5   Validity of arguments

A *basis* will consist of axioms and/or rules of inference involving only atomic sentences. Among these rules of inference may be ones to the effect that certain (atomic) sentences $A_1, \ldots, A_n$ are not mutually consistent. These will be called 'inconsistency rules':

$$\frac{A_1 \ldots A_n}{\perp}$$

There may also be rules allowing the outright assertion of atomic sentences:

$$\overline{A}$$

These will be called 'axioms'. If ever an axiom is used as an initial step in the construction of an argument, it does not count as an undischarged assumption of that argument. This much is indicated by the line placed over the axiom. There may also be rules of inference allowing one to conclude from atomic premises $A_1, \ldots, A_n$ (whether or not they are axioms) to an atomic conclusion A:

$$\frac{A_1 \ldots A_n}{A}$$

Finally, atomic rules in the basis can have the form of a multiple dilemma:

$$\frac{\overline{}^{(i)} \quad \overline{}^{(i)}}{\begin{array}{cc} A_1 & A_n \\ \vdots & \vdots \\ B \ldots B \end{array}}^{(i)}$$
$$B$$

according to which B may be the overall conclusion if it is the conclusion of any of the sub-arguments; whereas if every sub-argument is a disproof, then the result of applying the rule is a disproof also. Such a rule is really saying that $A_1, \ldots, A_n$ exhaust the possibilities.

A basis need not be assumed to be consistent;[6] and bases may in general admit of extension, consistent or otherwise.[7] It will turn out to be important, for what follows, to allow for the possibility of inconsistent bases in order to ground our definition of a *reductio* in the simplest possible case—that of an atomic disproof, that is, a disproof of some set of atomic assumptions, in which only atomic rules are applied. A simple example of an atomic disproof would be:

$$\frac{\text{This is red all over} \qquad \text{This is green all over}}{\bot}$$

In what follows we shall deal with arguments that allow for the assertion of a complex sentence conditionally upon others, or that establish the inconsistency of a set of assumptions, of which at least one will be complex. We shall speak of the conclusion, and the premisses, of the argument in question. When it is an inconsistency that is established, the conclusion will be said to be the empty conclusion. An argument with at least one undischarged premiss (assumption) will be called *open*. An argument with no complex undischarged assumptions will be called *closed*. Thus we allow for the possibility that, for example, the argument

$$\frac{R \qquad G}{\bot}$$

will count as closed provided that R and G are atomic, even if it is not the case that both R and G are themselves axioms in whatever basis may be in question.

The *initial* steps of a natural deduction are the single occurrences of sentences with which its branches begin. If such an occurrence of a sentence A is an axiom, then one can imagine a stroke placed over it, in order to indicate that that initial occurrence of A depends not on $\{A\}$ but on the empty set. If, on the other hand, A is not an axiom, then it is 'hypothetical' at that occurrence. It stands as an undischarged assumption. At that point A will depend on $\{A\}$. The *non-initial* steps of a proof are the steps that come after the initial sentence occurrences (be the latter axiomatic or hypothetical in status). Thus in the last example both the occurrence of R and the occurrence of G count as initial steps; whereas the transition to $\bot$ is a non-initial step.

---

[6] Here we depart from the definition of validity-in-a-basis given in *AR&L*.
[7] See *AR&L*, pp. 134–5.

Atomic arguments involve only atomic sentences. If all the non-initial steps of an atomic argument are in a basis $\mathcal{B}$, then that atomic argument is said to be in $\mathcal{B}$, even if its premisses are not axioms of $\mathcal{B}$. In particular, this means that any one-line atomic proof is in $\mathcal{B}$, even if the sentence concerned is not an axiom of $\mathcal{B}$. By definition atomic arguments are irreducible. An atomic argument that has a sentence as a conclusion is called an *atomic proof*. An atomic argument that ends with no sentence (i.e. that establishes an inconsistency) is called an *atomic disproof*.

Complex arguments involve at least one complex sentence, and are similarly of two kinds: proofs and disproofs, according to whether its conclusion is a sentence or $\perp$ (absurdity). A complex *proof* that ends with an application of an introduction rule will be called *canonical*. Likewise, a complex *disproof* whose final step, and all of whose non-minor penultimate steps,[8] are eliminations, will be called *canonical*.

A sentence occurrence in an argument standing as the conclusion of an introduction and as the major premiss of the corresponding elimination will be called a *maximal* sentence occurrence. A proof that has no maximal sentence occurrence is said to be in *normal form*. A disproof is in normal form if and only if it has no maximal sentence occurrence and, in addition, it has the structural features described above. Note that atomic proofs and disproofs are automatically in normal form.

The normalization theorem (which we shall not prove here) states that any logical argument[9] not in normal form reduces to one that is in normal form. The latter argument has the same conclusion, and its premisses are among those of the original. The normalization theorem in question here

---

[8]There will be more than one non-minor penultimate step in a disproof Π only when the final step of Π is an application of $\vee$-elimination. All other elimination rules (when applied as the final step of Π) involve only one immediate non-minor subargument. The latter's final step will therefore be the sole penultimate step in Π. Note that we count as canonical the degenerate case of

$$\frac{\neg A \qquad A}{\perp}$$

which has no penultimate 'step', unless one wishes to regard assuming A as 'making a step'. In order to cover this case, we could perhaps reformulate the definition of 'canonical' so that a canonical disproof is a disproof whose final step is an elimination, and all of whose penultimate steps are assumptions or eliminations.

[9]A logical argument is one that uses no rules from a basis. That is, it uses only the rule of trivial proof and the logical rules of introduction and elimination. The latter rules are, of course, the lax ones of a standard system of natural deduction; not the more carefully restricted ones that we favour in our definition above of proof and of disproof.

is the logical product of the old normalization theorem for proofs (due to Prawitz)[10] and the further normalization theorem for disproofs given above. By definition, complex arguments in normal form (as just defined) are irreducible; while complex arguments not in normal form are reducible. Reducing a complex argument consists precisely in turning it into the kind of normal form required (which, in the case of disproofs, remember, is slightly more demanding).

We shall assume that it is clear what is meant by a strict immediate sub-argument of a given argument—it is a sub-argument exposed by deleting the last step of the given argument. Another syntactic notion of some importance is that of a closed (substitution) instance of an argument. One obtains a closed (substitution) instance of an argument by appending, to each undischarged assumption occurrence therein, a closed proof that has as its conclusion the sentence whose occurrence as an assumption in the original argument is in question. Note that a closed substitution instance of an argument need not itself count as an argument. This is because it might violate the requirement of normality that is built into arguments by our very definition of proof and of disproof. Nevertheless, we shall require that any closed substitution instance of an argument will at least reduce to an argument, that is, a correctly formed proof or disproof.[11] A warrant is a very special kind of argument—namely, one that is closed and in normal form; and—if it is a proof with a logically complex conclusion—in canonical form also. Note that a warrant can have undischarged atomic assumptions.

We are concerned to define the notion of valid argument relative to a basis B. For brevity let us speak of B-validity.

DEFINITION of Valid Argument (Proof)

I. A *closed* argument is B-valid

    iff

it reduces to one that is either

    1. in B, or

    2. in canonical form with B-valid strict immediate sub-arguments.

---

[10] Cf. *Natural Deduction: A Proof-Theoretical Study*, Almqvist & Wiksell, Stockholm, 1965.

[11] This much is guaranteed for *IR* by the normalization and extraction theorems.

II. An *open* argument is $\mathcal{B}$-valid

> iff

for every extension $\mathcal{B}^+$ of $\mathcal{B}$:

every closed substitution instance of the argument obtained by appending normal closed $\mathcal{B}^+$-valid arguments for its undischarged assumptions is $\mathcal{B}^+$-valid (that is, appending $\mathcal{B}^+$-warrants for the assumptions yields a closed $\mathcal{B}^+$-valid argument for the conclusion).

This is the very same form of definition as that given in $AR\mathcal{E}L^{12}$ except for the fact that we now allow a closed argument to have undischarged atomic assumptions. The definition still accords differential priority to introduction rules (and to proofs). This is because the only closed and non-atomic canonical arguments are proofs of complex conclusions, which must end with introductions. Is there any way of defining validity so that priority is accorded to the elimination rules, via an essential definitional dependence on canonical disproofs?

12.6 Validity of *reductio*

Let us call an argument that establishes inconsistency (i.e. an argument with $\perp$ as conclusion) a *reductio*.[13] We can now specify what the $\mathcal{B}$-validity of a *reductio* consists in. The definition is as follows:

---

[12] At p. 136. The original recursive definition of validity in a basis was due to Prawitz, 'On the Idea of a General Proof Theory', *Synthese*, 27, 1974, pp. 63–77. An unsatisfactory aspect of the original definition, and of its version presented in $AR\mathcal{E}L$, is that it does not allow for a single application of an inconsistency rule in a basis to count as valid via clause (I). Such an argument had to be construed as an open argument, and its validity conferred (by default) by clause (II). We say 'by default' because *a fortiori* there could be no closed substitution instances of the kind mentioned in clause (II), since the old treatment required bases to be consistent. The old treatment also validated the Lewis argument

$$\frac{\neg A \qquad A}{B}$$

It is a virtue of the new treatment that the Lewis argument is not validated.

[13] The plural will be '*reductios*' rather than '*reductiones*'.

DEFINITION of Valid *Reductio*

I. A *closed reductio* is $\mathcal{B}$-valid

iff

it reduces to one that is in $\mathcal{B}$

II. An *open reductio* Σ is $\mathcal{B}$-valid

iff

either

(i) Σ has a complex undischarged assumption other than a negation or a conditional, and $\underline{\Sigma \text{ reduces to a}}$ $\underline{reductio \text{ that is in canonical form}}$ with $\mathcal{B}$-valid strict immediate sub*reductios*,

or

(ii) each complex undischarged assumption of Σ is a negation or a conditional, and $\underline{\Sigma \text{ reduces to a } reductio}$ $\underline{\Sigma^* \text{ that is in one or other of the canonical forms}}$ satisfying (a) or (b) below:

$$
\text{(a)} \quad \frac{\neg P \quad \overset{\textstyle\Pi}{P}}{\bot}
$$

where for any extension $\mathcal{B}^+$ of $\mathcal{B}$, for any $\mathcal{B}^+$-valid *reductio* Θ of P modulo other atomic assumptions,

$$
\frac{\overset{\textstyle\Pi}{\underset{\textstyle\Theta}{(P)}}}{\bot}
$$

is a $\mathcal{B}^+$-valid *reductio*;

$$
\text{(b)} \qquad \quad
\begin{array}{ccc}
& & \overset{\displaystyle \frac{}{Q}{}^{-(i)}}{\underset{}{}} \\[2pt]
& \Pi & \Xi \\
P \supset Q & P & \bot {}_{(i)} \\
\hline
& \bot &
\end{array}
$$

where for any extension $\mathcal{B}^{+}$ of $\mathcal{B}$, **for any $\mathcal{B}^{+}$-valid argument Θ for the conclusion** Q from the assumption P and possibly other atomic assumptions,

$$
\begin{array}{c}
\Pi \\
(P) \\
\Theta \\
(Q) \\
\Xi \\
\bot
\end{array}
$$

is a $\mathcal{B}^{+}$-valid *reductio*.

Clause II (in the case of *reductios*) is made possible by our normal form theorem for disproofs. Note that the part of clause (II.ii.b) in boldface appears to presuppose that we already have in hand the notion of validity of proofs of (possibly complex) conclusions. But this is of minor consequence; for the latter notion has already been supplied, and the mentioned premiss P and conclusion Q of the proof Θ have lower combined complexity than the target premiss $P \supset Q$ for the *reductio* Σ^{*} whose validity depends on the validity of the proof Θ. It is fair to maintain that this last definition, overall, focuses on elimination rules and on disproofs, by virtue of the underlined reductions to canonical forms of disproof. The 'presupposition' that we have highlighted in boldface does not induce any circular interdependence between introduction and elimination rules (or between proofs and disproofs), because of the recursion involved. Moreover, to the blunter objection that disproofs are, anyway, special forms of *proof*, there is a sharper response: which is to say that this is only an artefact of our present conventions of definition. It is possible to do away with the absurdity symbol $\bot$ and to define two classes of construction—proof and disproof—in a recursively interdependent way, so that the latter is no longer a special case of the former.[14] If this approach is

---

[14]For details of such a treatment, see my 'Negation, Absurdity and Contrariety', in D. Gabbay and H. Wansing (eds.), *Negation*, Kluwer Academic Press, forthcoming.

followed, then it becomes absolutely clear that there is no conceptual priority of proof over disproof.

What we have here, then, is the foreshadowed account of constructive falsifiability, which can be put to philosophical use by the empirically minded anti-realist. When our discourse is that of empirical science, our logical interest is in the inconsistency of a set of assumptions. (Such a set, as we have seen, will usually contain scientific hypotheses, boundary condition statements, and observation statements; and usually also some mathematical statements.)

12.7   The anti-realist construal of empirical claims that cannot be proved

The anti-realist content of the unprovable empirical generalization that all F's are G's is really this: *Nature will not confound the assertion that all F's are G's.* That is, Nature will not yield a case of an F that is not a G. In general, the anti-realist content of any empirical assertion P of which, by virtue of its general or hypothetical nature, we can say *a priori* that it cannot admit of proof, is: *Nature will not refute P.*[15] For such a belief will only ever be entertained as an explanatory hypothesis, and as a generator of predictions; and, as such, is subject only to refutation, not proof. Refutation, however, would always be modulo some set of assumptions that were firmer than the belief P in question. The Poincaré–Duhem–Quine problem is simply that of how we focus on the particular P that we might take to have been refuted, once we have a disproof of a set of assumptions containing it. But that is a problem for applications. All that our deductive logic can be expected to provide is the various disproofs of these sets of assumptions as the intellectual opportunity or need arises. Now to this end, the construal of any (unprovable) empirical assertion P as being to the effect that Nature will not refute P makes the system $I\!R$ of intuitionistic relevant logic proposed above perfectly adequate for empirical science, with its deductive testing of explanatory and predictive hypotheses against the evidence. If we

---

[15]The classicist is committed to this immediately by maintaining that 'All F's are G's' is logically equivalent (in particular, entailed by) 'It is not the case that some F is not a G'. Popper, for example, urges that one use the latter *in place of* the former when regimenting our scientific theories. For the anti-realist, for whom 'It is not the case that some F is not a G' does not in general entail 'All F's are G's', greater discrimination is called for. Thus when the latter form of words is used for the formulation of a scientific hypothesis, our proposed reading secures the logical licence that is generally withheld.

agree that we may turn any claim of the form $\forall x(Fx \supset Gx)$ into the corresponding form $\neg\exists x(Fx \land \neg Gx)$, then we can supply in IR all the disproofs needed for empirical science. For, in the language based on $\neg$, $\land$, $\lor$, $\supset$, and $\exists$, we have the metatheorem:

If Δ can be disproved in classical logic, then Δ can be disproved in IR.

That is all very well, says the objector; but what about the case where one is drawing out a logical consequence in the form of a prediction which has not yet been refuted? How does the anti-realist using only IR match that? The answer is that if one has derived the prediction P from the assumptions Δ using classical logic, then in IR one can at least derive $\neg\neg P$ from Δ. $\neg\neg P$ is the regimentation of 'Nature will not refute P'. And this is the appropriate propositional attitude to have, according to the anti-realist, towards the prediction P, which cannot, on the basis of the present evidence, admit of proof. The 'proof' by means of which we make the prediction P will of course involve as undischarged assumptions the higher-level hypotheses of our explanatory empirical theory; and since these assumptions cannot admit of proof, nothing that depends on them for 'proof' is really proved. The only genuine proof one could ever have for a prediction P would be based on various atomic axioms that will only be available in the future, once events have run their course. Our theories can enjoy no proof in the present, but at best withstand the test of time. If and when the countervailing evidence comes in the form of $\neg P$, however, then there is nothing to choose between the following two logical passages:

$$
\begin{array}{ccc}
\Delta & & \Delta \\
\vdots \;\text{via classical logic} & \text{via } IR\; \vdots & \\
\underline{\neg P \qquad P} & & \underline{\neg\neg P \qquad \neg P} \\
\bot & & \bot
\end{array}
$$

Another objection worth disposing of here is the following allegation of circularity: 'You say that the content of an empirical assertion P of which, by virtue of its general or hypothetical nature, we can say *a priori* that it cannot admit of proof, is: *Nature will not refute P*. But to understand the latter, we need first to understand P itself.' This objection implies that our account is unable to provide the content P independently, so that it can later be embedded in the context 'Nature will not refute ...'.

But this is to misunderstand the overall division of conceptual labour that we have provided. The content of P is already available via composition out of the meanings of its constituent expressions. The latter, in turn, have had their meanings conferred on them by the inferential liaisons that they enjoy within the empirical theory (if they are empirical terms) or by the rules of inference that govern them (if they are logico-mathematical terms). That yields us the *sentential content P*. Now, when we advance to consider an *assertion of P*, we are free to append a further analysans to P, in order to capture the special illocutionary force involved.

All's well that ends well.

It remains to address one last possible objection. We are holding a strong falsificationist view of logical reasoning in empirical discourse. We are saying that it is all a matter of disproof. We are taking the above definition of the validity of *reductios* to confer priority on the elimination rules as meaning-consituting (within empirical discourse) and to reveal the introduction rules as sense-explicating. Very well then, says the objector: call the logical operators of empirical discourse thus characterized $\neg^e$, $\wedge^e$, $\vee^e$, $\supset^e$, $\exists^e$, and $\forall^e$. Note that these are prima facie different from the logical operators for logico-mathematical discourse, say $\neg^i$, $\wedge^i$, $\vee^i$, $\supset^i$, $\exists^i$, and $\forall^i$. The latter have been characterized by the earlier definition of validity of proof, in which it was the introduction rules that were sense-constituting, and the elimination rules that were sense-explicating. The potential objection now takes the form: with what assurance do we take ourselves to be dealing, respectively, with the same logical operators? That is, how can we be assured that the logical operators that we use for mathematics are precisely the same operators that we use for empirical science? How do we know that λ^e is λ^i?

The answer to this potential objection lies in the principle of harmony. We are assured that they are the same logical operators because the introduction rules are in harmony with the elimination rules. Each set of rules simply provides a different entrée into the world of logical meaning. If we are concerned with apodeictic demonstration, as in mathematics, then the introduction rules are to the fore. But if we are concerned with refutation, as in empirical science, then the elimination rules are to the fore. In each case, what is backgrounded is what is foregrounded in the other case. And foreground and background bring the same operators into semantic focus because they are in harmonious balance. This is the answer to the age-old question of why it is that logic and mathematics are applicable to reality. The rules toggle as we traverse the gap between the abstract and the necessary, on the one hand, and the concrete and the contingent, on the other.

Chapter 13

Summary and Conclusion

Moderate anti-realism—the philosophical position that insists on the determinacy of epistemically constrained, substantial truth-conditions but the possible indeterminacy of truth-value—is well-motivated, internally coherent and methodologically adequate. We located this brand of anti-realism within a spectrum of philosophical positions that were surveyed and characterized by means of certain platitudes and key theses. Anti-realism makes substantive claims about sentence meanings: they are determinate; they are given by truth-conditions; they are compositional; they are communicable; and grasp of them is fully manifestable in observable behaviour.

To avoid being confined to a pale projectivist rehash of this position, we took on the threat of content irrealism, or scepticism about meaning. We revealed defects in an attempted quick transcendental *reductio* of content irrealism. Thus we were obliged to pass on to the more detailed work of showing exactly how implausibly lunatic is the claim, from Kripke's meaning sceptic, that one can reinterpret central terms of our language in a deviant or 'bent' way.

Moderate anti-realism takes as its point of departure from the prevailing realist tradition an insistence on the public character of meaning. Grasp of meaning is fully manifestable in observable behaviour; and meaning (*pace* Quine and Kripkenstein) is reasonably determinate. Manifestation of grasp is via the exercise of recognitional capacities: crucially, capacities brought to bear on would-be truth-makers for assertions. A natural corollary is that all truths are knowable in principle.

We have been at some pains to explain what is meant here by '...-able in principle'; and have defended moderate anti-realism against two strong attacks that focus, respectively, on the two underlying principles that grasp of meaning is manifestable, and that all truths are knowable.

The first attack, from the strict finitist, was directed primarily at the Manifestation Requirement. It sought to set anti-realism on a slide to strict finitism, by arguing that only the *feasibly* manifestable could be countenanced by the philosophical behaviourism underlying the anti-realist's position. We warded off this attack by developing an account of *aspectual appraisal* of would-be truth-makers. This gave us a 'factorizable' way of understanding the demands of the Manifestation Requirement. This new understanding is liberal enough to ward off standard misconceptions of manifestationism as overly exigent, but still of no avail to the realist who wishes to justify the Principle of Bivalence. Factorizable competence preserves the conceptual homogeneity needed on this side of the '...-able in principle' divide, and thus averts the threatened slide to strict finitism.

We showed that the Manifestation Argument as presented by Dummett against the principle of bivalence was flawed. But we were able to apply the Manifestation Requirement in the case of undecidable discourses to show, via a new argument, how the anti-realist has principled reason to give up the Principle of Bivalence. We surveyed the possible positions on the relationships between the decidable, the knowable, the true and the complete, and levelled principled objections against all the main possible rival positions: naïve verificationism, orthodox realism, Gödelian optimism, and M-realism.

We turned then to the second of the attacks mentioned above on a foundational principle of anti-realism. This time the assault was from the realist, and directed at the Principle of Knowability. The realist wielded the well-known Fitchian *reductio* argument to the effect that if all truths are knowable then all truths are known. We warded off this attack by motivating a principled restriction on the Principle of Knowability, limiting it to what we called 'Cartesian' propositions. Among the latter would be all the propositions of mathematics and natural science. The restriction to Cartesian propositions prevents the Fitchian argument from gaining any purchase, and thus permits the Principle of Knowability still to mark a major disagreement with the realist.

Moderate anti-realism has reason to rehabilitate the analytic-synthetic distinction, since one of its central consequences is that logic is to be justified by appeal to meanings alone. We undertook a survey of the controversies over how one might classify various claims as analytic or synthetic, and as *a priori* or *a posteriori*. We proposed a radical departure from past tradition, by maintaining that certain analytic truths could well carry ontological commitment to *necessary* existents.

We addressed the question of which logic, by the anti-realist's lights, is the right logic. We proposed, in addition to the intuitionist's epistemic constraint on truth, a new epistemic constraint on logical consequence, or deducibility. The Principle of Non-Forfeiture of Epistemic Gain tells us that a stronger logical result is always to be preferred to a weaker one, and that it should therefore be possible always to substitute a proof of a stronger result for a proof of a weaker one. Larger proofs within which such substitutions are effected should still be proofs—indeed, as a result of those substitutions, they will be proofs of possibly even stronger results than before. Obedience to this new epistemic constraint on consequence entails a form of *relevance* that turned out to be exactly codifiable within both a natural deduction system and a sequent system. Epistemic constraint on *truth* constructivizes; epistemic constraint on *deducibility* relevantizes. The result of the two epistemic constraints is the system *IR* of intuitionistic relevant logic.

Anti-realism, following Dummett, has usually been confined, in its underpinnings and its upshot, to the realm of mathematical discourse, where one can make apodeictic assertions on the basis of proof. The last major contribution undertaken in this work has been to provide a moderate anti-realist account of the nature and workings of defeasible, empirical discourse. We turned to the problem of a criterion of cognitive significance, and elaborated a new criterion that appears to overcome all the various kinds of difficulties that have plagued such criteria in the past. We presented the criterion in reasonably classical logical terms, so as not to allow our proposed logical reforms to deprive the criterion of the independent interest it should hold even for the classically-minded reader. The criterion can, however, be developed entirely within the ambit of *IR*; and therefore affords an anti-realist account of the meaningfulness of theoretical terms and sentences that are indirectly but systematically related to 'basic sensory experience'. In this way empirical sense is shown to be logically rooted in human sensibility.

Finally, we developed an account of constructive falsifiability that complements Prawitz's proof-theoretic account of constructive truth and validity. This allows one to account fully for the single logic behind both mathematics and empirical science, while using only the constructive proof-theoretic resources traditionally favoured by the anti-realist.

Bibliography

Ayer, A. J., 1946. *Language, Truth and Logic*, Gollancz, London, 2nd edn..

Barker, S., 1957. *Induction and Hypothesis*, Cornell University Press, Ithaca.

Berlin, I., 1938–9. 'Verification', *Proceedings of the Aristotelian Society*, 39, pp. 225–48.

Blackburn, S., 1984, *Spreading the Word*, Oxford University Press.

———, 1984. 'The Individual Strikes Back', *Synthese*, 58, pp. 281–301.

Boghossian, P., 1990. 'The Status of Content', *The Philosophical Review*, 99, pp. 157–84.

———, 1990. 'The Status of Content Revisited', *Pacific Philosophical Quarterly*, 71, pp. 264–78.

———, 1995. 'Analyticity', forthcoming in C. Wright and R. Hale (eds.), *A Companion to the Philosophy of Language*, Oxford, Blackwell.

Brouwer, L. E. J., 1912. *Intuitionisme en Formalisme*, Amsterdam. English translation in *Bulletin of the American Mathematical Society*, 20, 1913, pp. 81–96.

Brueckner, A., 1992. 'The Anti-Realist's Master Argument', *Midwest Studies in Philosophy*, 17, pp. 214–23.

Carnap, R., 1921. *Der Raum, Kantstudien Ergänzungsheft*.

———, 1934. *Logische Syntax der Sprache*, Springer, Vienna; translated by A. Smeaton as *The Logical Syntax of Language*, Kegan Paul, Trench & Trubner, London, 1937.

———, 1950. 'Empiricism, Semantics and Ontology', *Revue Internationale de Philosophie*, 4, pp. 20–40.

———, 1956. 'The Methodological Character of Theoretical Concepts', in H. Feigl and M. Scriven (eds.), *The Foundations of Science and the Concepts of Psychology and Psychoanalysis*, Minnesota Studies in the Philosophy of Science, Vol. I, University of Minnesota Press, pp. 38–76.

Carnap, R., 1963. 'Carl G. Hempel on Scientific Theories', in P.A. Schilpp (ed.), *The Philosophy of Rudolf Carnap*, Library of Living Philosophers, Vol. XI, Open Court, La Salle, pp. 958–66.

Church, A., 1936. 'A note on the Entscheidungsproblem', *Journal of Symbolic Logic*, 1, pp. 40–1; *Correction, ibid.*, pp. 101–2.

_____, 1949. 'Review of Ayer's Language, Truth and Logic, 2nd Edition.', *Journal of Symbolic Logic*, 14, pp. 52–3.

Churchland, Paul, 1981. 'Eliminative Materialism and the Propositional Attitudes', *Journal of Philosophy*, 78, pp. 67–90.

Cohen, P. J., 1963. 'The independence of the continuum hypothesis', *Proc. Nat. Acad. Sci. U. S. A.*, 50, pp. 1143–8.

Creath, R., 1976. 'On Kaplan on Carnap on significance', *Philosophical Studies*, 30, pp. 393–400.

Davidson, D., 1970. 'Mental Events', in L. Foster and J.W. Swanson (eds.), *Experience and Theory*, University of Massachusetts Press, Amherst, pp.79–101.

Dennett, D., 1971. 'Intentional Systems', *Journal of Philosophy*, 68, pp. 87–106.

Devitt, M., 1990. 'Transcendentalism about Content', *Pacific Philosophical Quarterly*, 71, pp. 247–63.

Dummett, M. A. E., 1973. *Frege: Philosophy of Language*, Duckworth.

_____, 1976. 'What is a Theory of Meaning? (II)', in G. Evans and J. McDowell (eds.), *Truth and Meaning*, Clarendon Press, Oxford, pp. 67–137.

_____, 1978. *Truth and Other Enigmas*, Duckworth, pp. 215–47.

_____, 1981. *The Interpretation of Frege's Philosophy*, Duckworth.

_____, 1991. *The Logical Basis of Metaphysics*, Harvard University Press.

_____, 1993. *The Seas of Language*, Oxford University Press.

Edgington, D., 1985. 'The Paradox of Knowability', *Mind*, 94, pp. 557–68.

Feldman, W., 1976. 'An Intuitionistic Completeness Theorem for Intuitionistic Predicate Logic', *Journal of Symbolic Logic*, 41, pp. 159–66.

Field, H., 1980. *Science without Numbers*, Blackwell, Oxford.

_____, 1989. *Realism, Mathematics and Modality*, Blackwell, Oxford.

_____, 1993. 'The Conceptual Contingency of Mathematical Objects', *Mind*, 102, pp. 285–99.

Fitch, F. B., 1963. 'A Logical Analysis of Some Value Concepts', *Journal of Symbolic Logic*, 28, pp. 135–42.

Fodor, J., 1987. *Psychosemantics*, MIT Press, Cambridge, Mass.

Foster, J., 1985. *A. J. Ayer*, Routledge and Kegan Paul, pp. 19–20.

Fraassen, B.C. van, 1980. *The Scientific Image*, Clarendon Press, Oxford.

Frege, G., 1884. *Grundlagen der Arithmetik*, Koebner, Bresnau; translated by J. L. Austin as *Foundations of Arithmetic*, Blackwell, Oxford, 1950.

———, 1918. 'Der Gedanke', *Beiträge zur Philosophie des deutschen Idealismus*; translated by A. M. and Marcelle Quinton as 'The Thought: a Logical Inquiry', in *Mind*, 65, 1956, pp. 289–311; also by P. T. Geach and R. H. Stoothoff as 'Thoughts' in *Logical Investigations*, ed. by P. T. Geach, Blackwell, Oxford, 1977, pp. 1–30.

Friedman, H., 1996. 'Finite Functions and the Necessary Use of Large Cardinals', unpublished, 132 pp.

Gödel, K., 1930. 'Die Vollständigkeit der Axiome des logischen Funktionenkalküls', *Monatshefte für Mathematik und Physik*, 37, pp. 349–60.

———, 1931. 'Uber formal unentscheidbare Sätze der Principia Mathematica und verwandter Systeme I.', *Monatshefte für Mathematik und Physik*, 37, pp. 173–98.

———, 1940. *The consistency of the axiom of choice and of the generalized continuum-hypothesis with the axioms of set theory*, Annals of Mathematics studies, no. 3, Princeton University Press.

Goldfarb, W., 1985. 'Kripke on Wittgenstein on Rules', *Journal of Philosophy*, 82, pp. 471–88.

Goodman, N., 1973. *Fact, Fiction, and Forecast*, 3rd edn., Bobbs-Merrill, Indianapolis.

Haldane, J. and C. J. G. Wright, 1993. 'Editorial Introduction', in *Reality, Representation and Projection*, Oxford University Press, pp. 3–12.

Hart, W. D., 1979. 'Access and Inference', *Proceedings of the Aristotelian Society*, Supp. Vol. 53, pp. 153–65.

Hart, W. D., and C. McGinn, 1976. 'Knowledge and Necessity', *Journal of Philosophical Logic*, 5, pp. 205–8.

Hempel, C. G., 1950. 'Problems and Changes in the Empiricist Criterion of Meaning', *Revue Internationale de Philosophie*, 4, pp. 41–63.

———, 1963. 'Implications of Carnap's work for the philosophy of science', in P. A. Schilpp (ed.), *The Philosophy of Rudolf Carnap*, Library of Living Philosophers, Vol. XI, Open Court, La Salle, pp. 685–709.

———, 1965. 'Empiricist Criteria of Cognitive Significance: Problems and Changes', *Aspects of Scientific Explanation and Other Essays in the Philosophy of Science*, Macmillan, New York.

Herzberger, H., 1982. 'Notes on Naive Semantics', *Journal of Philosophical Logic*, 11, pp. 61–102.

Hintikka, K. J. J., 1962. *Knowledge and Belief: An Introduction to the Logic of the Two Notions*, Cornell University Press.

———, 1973. *Logic, Language Games and Information*, Oxford University Press.

Horwich, P., 1984. 'Critical Notice: Saul Kripke: *Wittgenstein on Rules and Private Language*', *Philosophy of Science*, 51, pp. 163–71.

Hume, D., 1739. *A Treatise of Human Nature*.

Isaacson, D., 1987. 'Some considerations on arithmetical truth and the ω-rule', in *Logic Colloquium '85*, ed. by The Paris Logic Group, Elsevier Science Publishers B.V. (North-Holland), pp. 147–69.

Jackson, F., 1982. 'Epiphenomenal Qualia', *Philosophical Quarterly*, 32, pp. 127–36.

Johnston, M., 1992. 'Objectivity Refigured: Pragmatism without Verificationism', in J. Haldane and C. Wright (eds.), *Reality: Representation and Projection*, New York, Oxford University Press, pp. 85–130.

Kalmár, L., 1934–5. 'Über die Axiomatisierbarkeit des Aussagenkalküls', *Acta Sci. Math.* (Szeged) 7, pp. 222–43.

Kant, I., 1781. *Kritik der Reinen Vernunft*, Königsberg; 2nd edn., 1787; translated by N. Kemp Smith as *Critique of Pure Reason*, Macmillan, London, 2nd edn., 1929.

Kaplan, D., 1975. 'Significance and Analyticity: A Comment on Some Recent Proposals of Carnap', in J. Hintikka (ed.), *Rudolf Carnap, Logical Empiricist: Materials and Perspectives*, Reidel, Dordrecht, pp. 87–94.

Kraut, R., 1993. 'Robust Deflationism', *The Philosophical Review*, 102, pp. 247–63.

Kripke, S., 1980. *Naming and Necessity*, Harvard University Press, Cambridge, Mass.

———, 1982. *Wittgenstein on Rules and Private Language*, Harvard University Press, Cambridge, Mass.

Lewis, D., 1988. 'Statements Partly About Observation', *Philosophical Papers*, pp. 1–31.

Lipton, P., 1991. *Inference to the Best Explanation*, Routledge, London.

McDowell, J., 1976. 'Truth Conditions, Bivalence and Verificationism', in G. Evans and J. McDowell (eds.), *Truth and Meaning*, Oxford University Press, pp. 42–66.

Mackie, J. L., 1977. *Ethics — Inventing Right and Wrong*, Penguin, Harmondsworth.

Martin-Löf, P., 1994. 'Analytic and synthetic judgements in type theory', in P. Parrini (ed.), *Kant and Contemporary Epistemology*, Kluwer, pp. 87–99.

Milne, P., 1994. 'Intuitionistic Relevant Logic and Perfect Validity', *Analysis*, 54, pp. 140–42.

Mundici, D., 1980. 'Natural Limitations of Algorithmic Procedures in Logic', *Atti dell'Accademia Nazionale dei Lincei. Classe di Scienze Fisiche Mathematiche e Naturali*. Rendiconti (Series 8) 69 (3–4), pp. 101–5.

Neumann, J. v., 1956. 'Probabilistic logic and the synthesis of reliable organisms from unreliable components', in C.E. Shannon and J. McCarthy (eds.), *Automata Studies*, Annals of Mathematics Studies, 34, Princeton University Press, pp. 43–98.

O'Neill, O., 1976. 'Space and Objects', *Journal of Philosophy*, 73, pp. 29–45.

Paris, J., and L.Harrington, 1977. 'A Mathematical Incompleteness in Peano Arithmetic', in J. Barwise (ed.), *Handbook of Mathematical Logic*, Amsterdam, North-Holland, pp. 1133–42.

Peacocke, C., 1979. *Holistic Explanation: Action, Space and Interpretation*, Clarendon Press, Oxford.

———, 1986. *Thoughts*, Blackwell, Oxford.

Prawitz, D., 1965. *Natural Deduction: A Proof-Theoretical Study*, Almqvist & Wiksell, Stockholm.

———, 1974. 'On the Idea of a General Proof Theory', *Synthese*, 27, pp. 63–77.

Presburger, M., 1930. 'Über die Vollständigkeit eines gewissen Systems der Arithmetik ganzer Zahlen, in welchem die Addition als einzige Operation hervortritt', *Comptes-rendus du I Congrès des Mathématiciens des Pays Slaves*, Warsaw, pp. 92–101, 395.

Priest, G., 1979. 'Two Dogmas of Quineanism', *Philosophical Quarterly*, 29, pp. 289–301.

Putnam, H., 1967. 'Psychological Predicates', in W. H. Capitan and D. D. Merrill (eds.), *Art, Mind and Religion*, University of Pittsburgh Press, pp. 37–48.

———, 1983. '"Two Dogmas" Revisited', in *Realism and Reason, Philosophical Papers Vol. 3*, Cambridge University Press, pp. 87–97.

———, 1990. *Realism with a Human Face*, Harvard University Press.

_____, 1994. 'The Dewey Lectures', *Journal of Philosophy*, 91, pp. 445–517.

Quine, W. V. O., 1960. *Word and Object*, Cambridge, Mass.

_____, 1990. *The Pursuit of Truth*, Harvard University Press.

_____, 1994. 'Comment', in W. Salmon and G. Wolters (eds.), *Logic, Language, and the Structure of Scientific Theories*, University of Pittsburgh Press, pp. 345–51.

Rabin, M., 1963. 'Probabilistic automata', *Information and Control*, 6, pp. 230–45.

Rosenberg, J., 1974. *Linguistic Representation*, Reidel, Dordrecht.

Russell, B., 1940. *An Inquiry into Meaning and Truth*, Allen & Unwin, London.

Salmon, W., 1974. 'Barker's Theory of the Absolute', *Philosophical Studies*, 10, pp. 50–3.

Schlesinger, G., 1964. 'The formalization of empirical significance', *Philosophy of Science*, 31, pp. 65–7.

Schlick, M., 1918. *Allgemeine Erkenntnislehre*, Springer, Berlin; revised edn. of 1925 translated (by A. E. Blumberg) as *General Theory of Knowledge*, Open Court, La Salle, 1985.

Searle, J., 1987. 'Indeterminacy, Empiricism and the First Person', *Journal of Philosophy*, 84, pp. 123–46.

Shapiro, S., 1985. 'Epistemic and Intuitionistic Arithmetic', in S. Shapiro (ed.), *Intensional Mathematics*, North-Holland, pp. 11–46.

Shapiro, S., 1991. *Foundations without Foundationalism: A Case for Second-order Logic*, Clarendon Press, Oxford.

_____, 1993. 'Anti-Realism and Modality', in J. Czermak (ed.), *Philosophy of Mathematics*, Proceedings of the 15th International Wittgenstein-Symposium, Part 1, Hölder-Pichler-Tempsky, Vienna, pp. 269–87.

_____, 1994. 'Reasoning, Logic and Computation', *Philosophia Mathematica*, 3, pp. 31–51.

Skolem, T., 1930. 'Über einige Satzfunktionen in der Arithmetik, *Skrifter utgitt av Det Norske Videnskaps-Akademi i Oslo, I. Matematisk-naturvidenskapelig klass 1930*, no. 7, 28 pp.

Smart, J. J. C., 1986. 'Wittgenstein, Following a Rule and Scientific Psychology', Lecture given at the Van Leer Jerusalem Foundation, Israel.

Soames, S., 1995. 'Skepticism about Meaning: Indeterminacy, Normativity and the Rule-Following Paradox', Chapel Hill Philosophy Colloquium.

de Swart, H., 1976. 'Another Intuitionistic Completeness Proof', *Journal of Symbolic Logic*, 41, pp. 644–62.

de Swart, H., 1977. 'An Intuitionistically Plausible Interpretation of Intuitionistic Logic', *Journal of Symbolic Logic*, 42, pp. 564–78.

Tarski, A., 1956. 'The Concept of Truth in Formalized Languages', in *Logic, Semantics, Metamathematics*, Clarendon Press, Oxford, pp. 152–278.

_____, A. Mostowski, and A. Robinson, 1968. *Undecidable Theories*, North-Holland, Amsterdam.

Tennant, N., 1978. *Natural Logic*, Edinburgh University Press; 2nd, revised, edn. 1990.

_____, 1979. 'Entailment and Proofs', *Proceedings of the Aristotelian Society*, 79, pp. 167–89.

_____, 1980. 'A Proof-theoretic approach to entailment', *Journal of Philosophical Logic*, 9, pp. 185–209.

_____, 1982. 'Proof and Paradox', *Dialectica*, 36, pp. 265–96.

_____, 1984. 'How is Meaning Possible?', *Philosophical Books*, 26, pp. 65–82.

_____, 1984. 'Perfect validity, entailment and paraconsistency', *Studia Logica*, 43, pp. 179–98.

_____, 1984.'Intentionality, Syntactic Structure and the Evolution of Language', in C. Hookway (ed.), *Minds, Machines and Evolution*, Cambridge University Press, pp. 73–103.

Tennant, N., 1985. 'Minimal logic is adequate for Popperian science', *British Journal for Philosophy of Science*, 36, pp. 325–29.

_____, 1987. 'Natural Deduction and Sequent Calculus for Intuitionistic Relevant Logic', *Journal of Symbolic Logic*, 52, pp. 665–90.

_____, 1992. *Autologic*, Edinburgh University Press.

_____, 1992. 'Manifestationism without Verificationism?', paper to the Ockham Society in Oxford to honour Michael Dummett on the occasion of his retirement from the Wykeham Chair of Logic; forthcoming in a collection to be ed. by M. Lievers.

_____, 1994. 'Automated Deduction and Artificial Intelligence', in R. Casati, B. Smith, and G. White (eds.), *Philosophy and the Cognitive Sciences: Proceedings of the 16th International Wittgenstein Colloquium*, Hölder-Pichler-Tempsky, Vienna, pp. 273–86.

_____, 1994. 'Carnap and Quine', in W. Salmon and G. Wolters (eds.), *Logic, Language, and the Structure of Scientific Theories*, University of Pittsburgh Press, pp. 305–44.

_____, 1994. 'Changing the Theory of Theory Change: Towards a Computational Approach', in *British Journal for Philosophy of Science*, pp. 865–97.

_____, 1994. 'Intuitionistic Mathematics Does Not Need *Ex Falso Quodlibet*', *Topoi*, in a special issue on Intuitionistic Truth, pp. 127–33.

_____, 1994. 'On Maintaining Concentration', *Analysis*, pp. 143–52.

_____, 1994. 'Transmission of Truth and Transitivity of Proof', in D. Gabbay (ed.), *What is a Logical System?*, Studies in Logic and Computation Series, Vol. 4, Oxford University Press, pp. 161–77.

_____, 1995. 'On Paradox without Self-Reference', *Analysis*, 55, pp. 199–207.

_____, 1995. 'On negation, truth and warranted assertibility', *Analysis*, 55, pp. 98–104.

_____, 1996. 'Delicate Proof Theory', in J. Copeland (ed.), *Logic and Reality: Essays on the Legacy of Arthur Prior*, Oxford University Press, pp. 351–85.

_____, forthcoming. 'On the Necessary Existence of Numbers', *Noûs*.

_____, forthcoming. 'The Law of Excluded Middle is Synthetic *A Priori*, if Valid', *Philosophical Topics*.

Tennant, N., 'Negation, Absurdity and Contrariety', in D. Gabbay and H. Wansing (eds.), *Negation*, Kluwer Academic Press.

_____, unpublished. 'Natural Foundations for Projective Geometry', typescript.

Ullian, J., 1965. 'A Note on Scheffler on Nidditch', *Journal of Philosophy*, 62, pp. 274–5.

Vollmer, G., 1975. *Evolutionäre Erkenntnistheorie*, Hirzel, Stuttgart.

Watkins, J. W. N., 1953. 'Ideal Types and Historical Explanations', in H. Feigl and M. Brodbeck (eds.), *Readings in the Philosophy of Science*, New York, pp. 723–43.

Williamson, T., 1982. 'Intuitionism Disproved?', *Analysis*, 42, pp. 203–7.

_____, 1987. 'On the Paradox of Knowability', *Mind*, 96, pp. 256–61.

_____, 1988. 'Knowability and Constructivism', *Philosophical Quarterly*, 38, pp. 422–32.

Wright, C. J. G., 1982. 'Strict Finitism', Synthese 51, pp. 203–82.

_____, 1983. *Frege's Conception of Numbers as Objects*, Aberdeen University Press.

_____, 1984. 'Kripke's Account of the Argument against Private Language', *Journal of Philosophy*, 81, pp. 759–78.

_____, 1987. 'On Making Up One's Mind: Wittgenstein on Intention', in *Proceedings of the 11th International Wittgenstein Symposium, 1986, Kirchberg*, Hölder-Pichler-Tempsky, Vienna, pp. 391–404.

_____, 1986. 'Scientific Realism, Observation and the Verification Principle', in G. Macdonald and C. Wright (eds.), *Fact, Science and Morality*, Blackwell, Oxford, pp. 247–74.

_____, 1988. 'Realism, Antirealism, Irrealism, Quasi-Realism', *Midwest Studies in Philosophy, Vol. XII: Realism and Antirealism*, pp. 25–49.

_____, 1989. 'The Verification Principle: Another Puncture — Another Patch', *Mind*, 98, pp. 611–22.

_____, 1992. *Truth and Objectivity*, Harvard University Press.

_____, 1993. 'Realism: The Contemporary Debate — W(h)ither Now?', in J. Haldane and C. Wright (eds.), *Reality, Representation and Projection*, Oxford University Press, pp. 63–84.

_____, 1993. *Realism, Meaning and Truth*, 2nd edn., Blackwell.

Veldman, W., 1976. 'An intuitionistic completeness theorem for intuitionistic predicate logic', *Journal of Symbolic Logic*, 41, pp. 159-66.

Index